For the Love of SAT Chemistry

by

Chris Reddick

Michael Cerro

Published by Private Prep
Printed by Kindle Direct Publishing, an Amazon.com company
Original cover art by Owen Hill - owen.hill@privateprep.com
Version 2019-2020

ACKNOWLEDGMENTS

We would like to both acknowledge a few individuals that helped make this journey possible:

To Brooke Rothberg, our editor. Your insight was invaluable.

To Thomas Stillwell, our original third author. Thank you for starting this journey with us and best wishes on yours.

To Owen Hill. Always pushing the team.

From Chris:

To my students, I am in a wonderful position to constantly be challenged on a daily basis by those I am supposed to teach. I am sure I learn just as much, if not more, from you all :)

To my science teachers through the years, Ms. Wijesinghe, Mr. Singh, Mr. Fransowie, Ms. Dizengoff, Ms. Martin, Ms. Lesmes, and Ms. O'Brien. This long list that spans 13 years worth of education is an incredible reflection of how lucky I have been. Thank you all so much!

From Michael:

To my coauthor Chris. Rise and grind.

To Emily Lubejko and Kyla Haggerty. Grinders never sleep.

And finally, I would like to acknowledge anyone who stumbles on this page and doubts they are capable of extraordinary things. You are capable. One my favorite quotes is from Audrey Hepburn who brilliantly stated, "Nothing is impossible, the word itself says 'I'm possible'!"

A few years ago Chris and I joked at the Private Prep Long Island office that we should write a SAT Chemistry book. Well, here we are. Nothing is impossible. But, also, it is important to remember that nothing will be perfect. Go for the impossible, be aggressive, make mistakes. If you make enough aggressive mistakes eventually you stumble on excellence. You'll never reach perfection, but you'll come darn close. This book is not perfect, but it's darn close. We hope you enjoy the journey working through it - for science!

Contents

How to use our book by Chris

Hi folks! We know that prepping for the SAT Chemistry exam might seem a bit daunting, but we are here to help! While we hope that everyone gets exactly what they need from this book, we do recognize that not everyone who picks up this book will be in the same situation. Below I have outlined a general structure that you can use to help fit your situation depending on the amount of time you have to prepare for the exam.

The below flow chart is designed to take about 2 weeks. Feel free to work through faster if that seems to work better for you. Also, feel free to cycle through this up to 4 times.

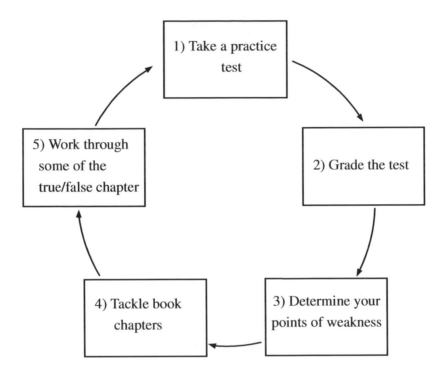

1) Take a practice test

- Be sure to give yourself an hour to take the test.
- Be sure to do what you can to ensure you are in a relatively quite and undisturbed place during that time.

2) Grade the test

- Use the instructions and scale that Mike put together for you to help you grade it properly.

3) Determine your points of weakness

- Take look through the questions that you got wrong and make a brief list of every chapter that popped up.
- Order the list from most frequently occurring chapter to least.

4) Tackle book chapters

- Read and answer the questions from each chapter starting at the top of the list.
- Do not skip around. Once you start a chapter be sure to finish it. The chapters are designed to help you build on the concepts presented.

5) Work through some of the true/false chapter

- Do at least 25 of the 101 questions in chapter 14.

How to score above a 700 by Michael

So you want to score above a 700? A 750? The content that Chris and I wrote in this book will surely help. The purpose of why you are reading this page is to help optimize your score on our practice tests at the end of our book. Not only do you need to apply the knowledge you learn in the chapters and have good test-taking accuracy, but you also need to know when to **omit** a question and when to **guess**. First, you need to understand the timing and scoring.

- 60 minutes for the entire exam (90 minutes if you have time and a half)

- +1 point gained for a correct answer

- 0 points for an omitted question

- $-1/4$ points removed for an incorrect answer

Since you lose $1/4$ of a point for answering a question incorrectly, there is an easy rule to follow:
If you can eliminate AT LEAST 2 answer choices (and have 3 remaining), then you should GUESS. If you CANNOT eliminate at least 2 answer choices, then OMIT.

If your goal is a 700, check out the generic SAT Chemistry Chemistry curve on the next page. You will see that you need to finish with a raw score of at least a 60. For example, if you answer 62 questions correctly, answer 8 questions incorrectly, and omit 15 questions, you will have a raw score of a 60 and a scaled score of a 700. $(62 - \frac{1}{4} \times 8 = 60)$

For the True/False Part B section, if you know that one of the columns is false then you must GUESS the second column. This will gain you more points in the long run. If you know one of the columns is true but are unsure about the second column, then you should OMIT.

If you feel yourself struggling with the True/False Part B portion of the exam, then consider doing that part last after going through Part A and Part C. Some students have found this useful for their pacing.

And most importantly, never give up! If you feel the test is not going your way, don't worry, other students feel the same way. Just remember the following phrase while taking the exam:

"Just keep grabbing points"

If you finish the work through this book and analyze your mistakes on our practice exams, you will be ready.

Good luck!

See a typical SAT Chemistry Chemistry curve below:

Raw Score	Scaled Score	Raw Score	Scaled Score	Raw Score	Scaled Score
85	800	45	620	5	410
84	800	44	620	4	400
83	800	43	610	3	400
82	800	42	610	2	390
81	800	41	600	1	390
80	800	40	600	0	390
79	790	39	590	−1	380
78	790	38	590	−2	380
77	780	37	580	−3	370
76	780	36	570	−4	370
75	770	35	570	−5	360
74	770	34	560	−6	360
73	760	33	550	−7	360
72	760	32	550	−8	350
71	750	31	550	−9	350
70	750	30	540	−10	340
69	740	29	540	−11	340
68	740	28	530	−12	330
67	730	27	530	−13	330
66	730	26	520	−14	330
65	720	25	510	−15	320
64	720	24	510	−16	320
63	710	23	500	−17	310
62	710	22	500	−18	310
61	700	21	490	−19	300
60	700	20	490	−20	300
59	690	19	480	−21	290
58	690	18	480		
57	680	17	470		
56	680	16	460		
55	670	15	460		
54	670	14	450		
53	660	13	450		
52	660	12	440		
51	650	11	440		
50	650	10	430		
49	640	9	430		
48	640	8	420		
47	630	7	420		
46	630	6	410		

CHAPTER +1

ELEMENT BEHAVIOR

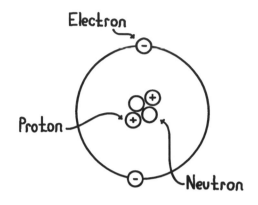

Protons → positive charge & 1 atomic mass unit (amu)

Neutrons → neutral charge & 1 amu

Electrons → negative charge & negligible mass

The number of protons in the element (atomic number)

2
He
4.0026

The mass of the element (atomic mass)

← Periods are horizontal rows across →

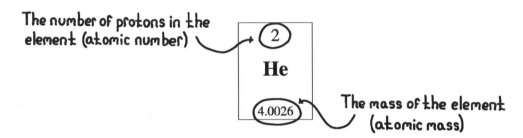

Families/groups are vertical columns

Transition metals

													2 He 4
3 Li 7	4 Be 9									8 O 16	9 F 19	10 Ne 20
11 Na 23	12 Mg 24									16 S 32	17 Cl 35	18 Ar 40
19 K 39	20 Ca 40	21 Sc 45	22 Ti 48	...	29 Cu 64	30 Zn 65	... ...	34 Se 79	35 Br 80	36 Kr 85
37 Rb 85	38 Sr 88	39 Y 89	40 Zr 91	...	47 Ag 108	48 Cd 112	... ...	52 Te 128	53 I 127	54 Xe 131
55 Cs 133	56 Ba 137	57 *La 139	72 Hf 178	...	79 Au 197	80 Hg 201	... ...	84 Po 209	85 At 210	86 Rn 222

Alkaline earth metals

Alkali metals

Halogens

Noble gases

1. How many protons does a grounded atom of lithium have in its nucleus?

    (A) 3
    (B) 4
    (C) 5
    (D) 6
    (E) 7

2. Which of the following is closest to the total mass, in amu, of all electrons contained in a florine atom?

    (A) 0
    (B) 9
    (C) 10
    (D) 19
    (E) 20

3. Which of the following elements is considered an alkaline earth metal?

    (A) Li
    (B) Be
    (C) Na
    (D) K
    (E) Cl

4. How many protons does the alkali metal in period 3 have in its nucleus?

    (A) 1
    (B) 3
    (C) 11
    (D) 19
    (E) 37

5. Which of the following elements is considered a noble gas?

    (A) F
    (B) Cl
    (C) Ne
    (D) Br
    (E) Zn

6. Which of the following is closest to the total mass, in amu, of all protons contained in a copper atom?

    (A) 19
    (B) 29
    (C) 35
    (D) 40
    (E) 64

7. Which of the following halogens is located in period 2?

    (A) F
    (B) Cl
    (C) Br
    (D) I
    (E) At

8. Which of the following elements is considered a transition metal?

    (A) Na
    (B) Mg
    (C) Sc
    (D) Cl
    (E) Ar

Nuclear chemistry is the study of the result of the change of the nucleus of an atom: also known as *transmutation*. These symbols might seem intimidating at first, but they are actually quite simple.

Decay Chart

Decay type	Emission	Example	Summary
Alpha decay	^4_2He or $^4_2\alpha$	$^{222}_{88}Ra \rightarrow {^4_2He} + {^{218}_{86}Rn}$	• Helium nucleus/alpha particle is emitted. • Atom drops by 2 protons and 2 neutrons.
Beta decay	$^0_{-1}e$ or $^0_{-1}\beta$	$^{14}_6C \rightarrow {^{14}_7N} + {^0_{-1}\beta}$	• A negatively charged beta particle/electron is emitted • Mass does not change. Atomic number goes up by 1.
Positron emission	$^0_{+1}e$ or $^0_{+1}\beta$	$^{50}_{25}Mn \rightarrow {^{50}_{24}Na} + {^0_{+1}e}$	• A positively charged beta particle/positron is emitted. • Mass does not change. Atomic number goes down by 1.
Gamma emission	$^0_0\gamma$	$^{40}_{18}Ar \rightarrow {^{40}_{18}Ar} + {^0_0\gamma}$	• Gamma radiation is emitted. • Atom does not change.

An *isotope* is two or more forms of the same element that contain a different amount of neutrons. For example, C-14 is known as "carbon 14", having 6 protons and 8 neutrons, while C-12, or, "carbon 12", has 6 protons and 6 neutrons.

Fusion and Fission

Nuclear Fusion—The process of lighter elements combining to produce heavier elements.

e.g. Stars are large fusion reactions.

$$^2_1H + {^2_1H} \rightarrow {^4_2He}$$

Nuclear Fission—The process of heavier elements being broken up into lighter elements.

e.g. Nuclear power plants.

$$^{235}_{92}U + {^1_0n} \rightarrow {^{141}_{56}Ba} + {^{92}_{36}Kr} + 3{^1_0n}$$

$$? \rightarrow {}^{210}_{82}\text{Pb} + {}^{4}_{2}\text{He}$$

1. The missing reactant in the equation above is

   (A) ${}^{214}_{82}\text{Pb}$

   (B) ${}^{210}_{82}\text{Pb}$

   (C) ${}^{214}_{80}\text{Pb}$

   (D) ${}^{210}_{84}\text{Po}$

   (E) ${}^{214}_{84}\text{Po}$

$$^{14}_{6}\text{C} \rightarrow {}^{14}_{7}\text{N} + ?$$

2. The missing product in the equation above is

   (A) ${}^{4}_{2}\text{He}$

   (B) ${}^{0}_{-1}\text{e}$

   (C) ${}^{0}_{+1}\text{e}$

   (D) ${}^{0}_{0}\gamma$

   (E) ${}^{1}_{0}\text{n}$

$$? \rightarrow {}^{61}_{28}\text{Ni} + {}^{0}_{0}\gamma$$

3. The missing reactant in the equation above is

   (A) ${}^{60}_{28}\text{Ni}$

   (B) ${}^{61}_{28}\text{Ni}$

   (C) ${}^{62}_{28}\text{Ni}$

   (D) ${}^{60}_{29}\text{Cu}$

   (E) ${}^{61}_{29}\text{Cu}$

4. Which of the following nuclear reactions represents nuclear fusion?

   (A) ${}^{2}_{1}\text{H} + {}^{2}_{1}\text{H} \rightarrow {}^{4}_{2}\text{He}$

   (B) ${}^{4}_{2}\text{He} \rightarrow {}^{2}_{1}\text{H} + {}^{2}_{1}\text{H}$

   (C) ${}^{239}_{92}\text{U} \rightarrow {}^{238}_{92}\text{U} + {}^{1}_{0}\text{n}$

   (D) ${}^{242}_{96}\text{Cm} + {}^{1}_{0}\text{n} \rightarrow {}^{239}_{94}\text{Pu} + {}^{4}_{2}\text{He}$

   (E) ${}^{226}_{88}\text{Ra} \rightarrow {}^{4}_{2}\text{He} + {}^{222}_{86}\text{Rn}$

$$^{14}_{8}\text{O} \rightarrow ? + {}^{14}_{7}\text{N}$$

5. The missing product in the equation above is

   (A) ${}^{4}_{2}\text{He}$

   (B) ${}^{0}_{-1}\text{e}$

   (C) ${}^{0}_{+1}\text{e}$

   (D) ${}^{0}_{0}\gamma$

   (E) ${}^{1}_{0}\text{n}$

$$^{32}_{17}\text{Cl} \rightarrow ? + {}^{32}_{16}\text{S}$$

6. The missing product in the equation above is

   (A) ${}^{4}_{2}\text{He}$

   (B) ${}^{0}_{-1}\text{e}$

   (C) ${}^{0}_{+1}\text{e}$

   (D) ${}^{0}_{0}\gamma$

   (E) ${}^{1}_{0}\text{n}$

$$^{68}_{31}\text{Ga} + {}^{0}_{-1}\text{e} \rightarrow ?$$

7. The missing product in the equation above is

   (A) ${}^{67}_{31}\text{Ga}$

   (B) ${}^{68}_{31}\text{Ga}$

   (C) ${}^{69}_{31}\text{Ga}$

   (D) ${}^{67}_{30}\text{Zn}$

   (E) ${}^{68}_{30}\text{Zn}$

8. Which of the following nuclear reactions represents nuclear fission?

   (A) ${}^{239}_{92}\text{U} \rightarrow {}^{234}_{90}\text{Th} + {}^{4}_{2}\text{He}$

   (B) ${}^{226}_{88}\text{Cm} \rightarrow {}^{222}_{86}\text{Rn} + {}^{4}_{2}\text{He}$

   (C) ${}^{2}_{1}\text{H} + {}^{2}_{1}\text{H} \rightarrow {}^{4}_{2}\text{He}$

   (D) ${}^{4}_{2}\text{He} \rightarrow {}^{2}_{1}\text{H} + {}^{2}_{1}\text{H}$

   (E) ${}^{35}_{16}\text{S} \rightarrow {}^{0}_{-1}\text{e} + {}^{35}_{17}\text{Cl}$

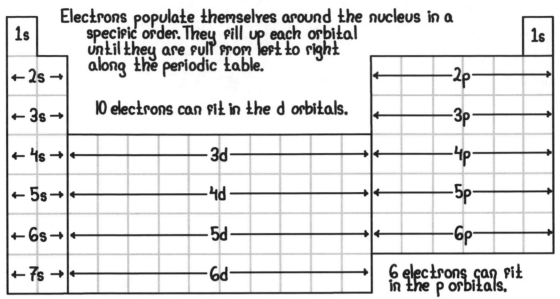

Electrons populate themselves around the nucleus in a specific order. They fill up each orbital until they are full from left to right along the periodic table.

10 electrons can fit in the d orbitals.

6 electrons can fit in the p orbitals.

2 electrons can fit in the s orbitals.

*The f orbital begins to fill following the $6s$ orbital. A more detailed periodic table can be found in Chapter 13.

What is the electron configuration of sulfur?

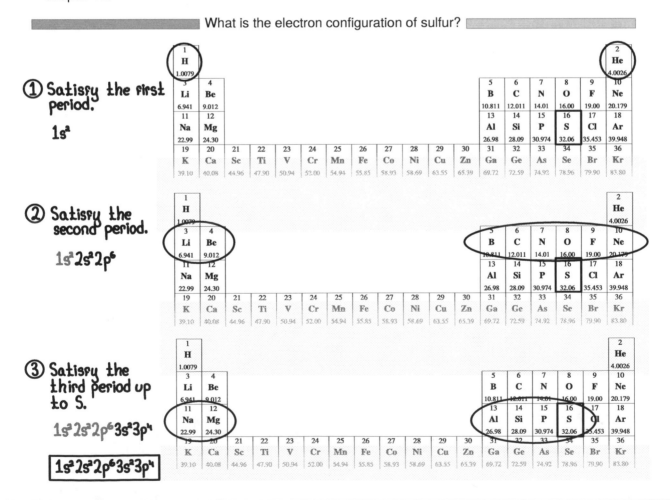

① Satisfy the first period.

$1s^2$

② Satisfy the second period.

$1s^2 2s^2 2p^6$

③ Satisfy the third period up to S.

$1s^2 2s^2 2p^6 3s^2 3p^4$

$1s^2 2s^2 2p^6 3s^2 3p^4$

1. Which of the following is the correct electron configuration for Cl?

    (A) $1s^22s^22p^5$
    (B) $1s^22s^22p^6$
    (C) $1s^22s^22p^63s^23p^4$
    (D) $1s^22s^22p^63s^23p^5$
    (E) $1s^22s^22p^63s^23p^6$

2. Which of the following is the correct electron configuration for Cl⁻?

    (A) $1s^22s^22p^5$
    (B) $1s^22s^22p^6$
    (C) $1s^22s^22p^63s^23p^4$
    (D) $1s^22s^22p^63s^23p^5$
    (E) $1s^22s^22p^63s^23p^6$

3. Which of the following is the correct electron configuration for Na?

    (A) $1s^22s^1$
    (B) $1s^22s^22p^6$
    (C) $1s^22s^22p^63s^1$
    (D) $1s^22s^22p^63s^2$
    (E) $1s^22s^22p^63s^23p^64s^1$

4. Which of the following is the correct electron configuration for Na⁺?

    (A) $1s^22s^1$
    (B) $1s^22s^22p^6$
    (C) $1s^22s^22p^63s^1$
    (D) $1s^22s^22p^63s^2$
    (E) $1s^22s^22p^63s^23p^64s^1$

5. Which of the following is the correct electron configuration for Sr?

    (A) $1s^22s^22p^63s^23p^64s^1$
    (B) $1s^22s^22p^63s^23p^64s^2$
    (C) $1s^22s^22p^63s^23p^64s^23d^{10}4p^6$
    (D) $1s^22s^22p^63s^23p^64s^13d^{10}4p^65s^1$
    (E) $1s^22s^22p^63s^23p^64s^23d^{10}4p^65s^2$

6. Which of the following is the correct electron configuration for Se²⁻?

    (A) $1s^22s^22p^63s^23p^64s^1$
    (B) $1s^22s^22p^63s^23p^64s^2$
    (C) $1s^22s^22p^63s^23p^64s^23d^{10}4p^6$
    (D) $1s^22s^22p^63s^23p^64s^13d^{10}4p^65s^1$
    (E) $1s^22s^22p^63s^23p^64s^13d^{10}4p^65s^2$

7. Which of the following is the correct electron configuration for H?

    (A) 1
    (B) $1s^0$
    (C) $1s^1$
    (D) $1s^2$
    (E) $1p^1$

8. Which of the following electron configurations represents an excited state?

    (A) $1s^22s^1$
    (B) $1s^22s^22p^53s^1$
    (C) $1s^22s^22p^63s^1$
    (D) $1s^22s^22p^63s^2$
    (E) $1s^22s^22p^63s^23p^64s^1$

9. Which of the following is the correct electron configuration for Pr?

    (A) $[\text{Kr}]5s^24f^3$
    (B) $[\text{Kr}]5s^25p^66s^24f^3$
    (C) $[\text{Kr}]5s^26s^24f^3$
    (D) $[\text{Xc}]6s^24f^1$
    (E) $[\text{Xc}]6s^24f^3$

10. Which of the following is the correct electron configuration for U?

    (A) $[\text{Xe}]6s^24f^{14}$
    (B) $[\text{Xe}]6s^24f^{14}7s^25f^3$
    (C) $[\text{Rn}]7s^25f^3$
    (D) $[\text{Rn}]7s^26d^15f^3$
    (E) $[\text{Rn}]7s^26d^25f^3$

Although electrons typically spend the majority of their time in a given orbital, they can be excited into higher energy states by absorbing energy.

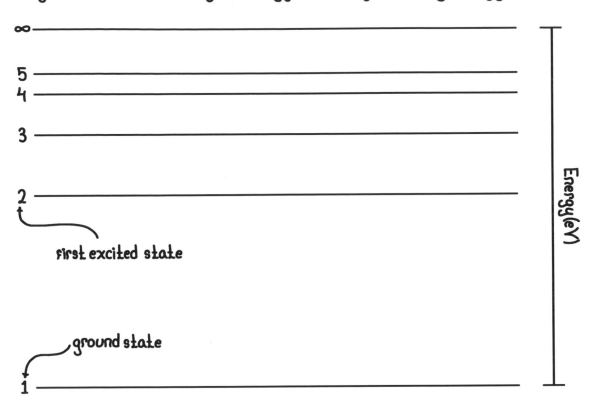

∞ ──────────────────────────────

5 ──────────────────────────────
4 ──────────────────────────────

3 ──────────────────────────────

2 ──────────────────────────────

first excited state

ground state

1 ──────────────────────────────

Energy(eV)

-The IONIZATION ENERGY is the energy required to eject an electron from an atom.

-The jump from a lower state to a higher state indicates the absorption of energy.

-The jump from a higher state to a lower state indicates the release of energy.

Increasing Ionization Energy →

Increasing Ionization Energy ↑

1 H 1.0079																	2 He 4.0026
3 Li 6.941	4 Be 9.012											5 B 10.811	6 C 12.011	7 N 14.01	8 O 16.00	9 F 19.00	10 Ne 20.179
11 Na 22.99	12 Mg 24.30											13 Al 26.98	14 Si 28.09	15 P 30.974	16 S 32.06	17 Cl 35.453	18 Ar 39.948
19 K 39.10	20 Ca 40.08	21 Sc 44.96	22 Ti 47.90	23 V 50.94	24 Cr 52.00	25 Mn 54.94	26 Fe 55.85	27 Co 58.93	28 Ni 58.69	29 Cu 63.55	30 Zn 65.39	31 Ga 69.72	32 Ge 72.59	33 As 74.92	34 Se 78.96	35 Br 79.90	36 Kr 83.80
37 Rb 85.47	38 Sr 87.62	39 Y 88.91	40 Zr 91.22	41 Nb 92.91	42 Mo 95.94	43 Tc (98)	44 Ru 101.1	45 Rh 102.91	46 Pd 106.42	47 Ag 107.87	48 Cd 112.41	49 In 114.82	50 Sn 118.71	51 Sb 121.75	52 Te 127.60	53 I 126.91	54 Xe 131.29
55 Cs 132.91	56 Ba 137.33	57 *La 138.91	72 Hf 178.49	73 Ta 180.95	74 W 183.85	75 Re 186.21	76 Os 190.2	77 Ir 192.2	78 Pt 195.08	79 Au 196.97	80 Hg 200.59	81 Tl 204.38	82 Pb 207.2	83 Bi 208.98	84 Po (209)	85 At (210)	86 Rn (222)
87 Fr (223)	88 Ra 226.02	89 †Ac 227.03	104 Rf (261)	105 Db (262)	106 Sg (266)	107 Bh (264)	108 Hs (277)	109 Mt (268)	110 Ds (271)	111 Rg (272)	112 § (277)	§ Not yet named					

Questions 1-5 refer to the following quantum energy diagram.

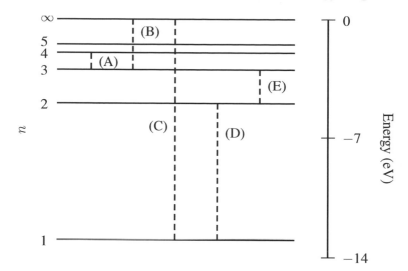

The diagram above is a plot of the quantum principle numbers, n, and energy levels, in eV, for the electron in H. The vertical dashed lines represent transitions that can occur in the atom.

1. The transition that represents the ionization energy of H

2. The transition that could release the LEAST amount of light energy

3. The transition from the ground state to the first excited state of H

4. The transition from approximately -4 eV to -5.5 eV

5. The transition that represents a total energy change of approximately -3 eV

Increasing Electronegativity →

← Increasing Atomic Radius (left, vertical, downward)
Increasing Electronegativity → (right, vertical, upward)

1	2	3	4	5	6	7	8	9	10	11	12	13	14	15	16	17	18
1 **H** 1.0079																	2 **He** 4.0026
3 **Li** 6.941	4 **Be** 9.012											5 **B** 10.811	6 **C** 12.011	7 **N** 14.01	8 **O** 16.00	9 **F** 19.00	10 **Ne** 20.179
11 **Na** 22.99	12 **Mg** 24.30											13 **Al** 26.98	14 **Si** 28.09	15 **P** 30.974	16 **S** 32.06	17 **Cl** 35.453	18 **Ar** 39.948
19 **K** 39.10	20 **Ca** 40.08	21 **Sc** 44.96	22 **Ti** 47.90	23 **V** 50.94	24 **Cr** 52.00	25 **Mn** 54.94	26 **Fe** 55.85	27 **Co** 58.93	28 **Ni** 58.69	29 **Cu** 63.55	30 **Zn** 65.39	31 **Ga** 69.72	32 **Ge** 72.59	33 **As** 74.92	34 **Se** 78.96	35 **Br** 79.90	36 **Kr** 83.80
37 **Rb** 85.47	38 **Sr** 87.62	39 **Y** 88.91	40 **Zr** 91.22	41 **Nb** 92.91	42 **Mo** 95.94	43 **Tc** (98)	44 **Ru** 101.1	45 **Rh** 102.91	46 **Pd** 106.42	47 **Ag** 107.87	48 **Cd** 112.41	49 **In** 114.82	50 **Sn** 118.71	51 **Sb** 121.75	52 **Te** 127.60	53 **I** 126.91	54 **Xe** 131.29
55 **Cs** 132.91	56 **Ba** 137.33	57 ***La** 138.91	72 **Hf** 178.49	73 **Ta** 180.95	74 **W** 183.85	75 **Re** 186.21	76 **Os** 190.2	77 **Ir** 192.2	78 **Pt** 195.08	79 **Au** 196.97	80 **Hg** 200.59	81 **Tl** 204.38	82 **Pb** 207.2	83 **Bi** 208.98	84 **Po** (209)	85 **At** (210)	86 **Rn** (222)
87 **Fr** (223)	88 **Ra** 226.02	89 **†Ac** 227.03	104 **Rf** (261)	105 **Db** (262)	106 **Sg** (266)	107 **Bh** (264)	108 **Hs** (277)	109 **Mt** (268)	110 **Ds** (271)	111 **Rg** (272)	112 **§** (277)						

§ Not yet named

← Increasing Atomic Radius

Increasing Nonmetallic Character →

← Increasing Metallic Character (left, vertical, downward)
Increasing Nonmetallic Character → (right, vertical, upward)

1	2	3	4	5	6	7	8	9	10	11	12	13	14	15	16	17	18
1 **H** 1.0079																	2 **He** 4.0026
3 **Li** 6.941	4 **Be** 9.012											5 **B** 10.811	6 **C** 12.011	7 **N** 14.01	8 **O** 16.00	9 **F** 19.00	10 **Ne** 20.179
11 **Na** 22.99	12 **Mg** 24.30											13 **Al** 26.98	14 **Si** 28.09	15 **P** 30.974	16 **S** 32.06	17 **Cl** 35.453	18 **Ar** 39.948
19 **K** 39.10	20 **Ca** 40.08	21 **Sc** 44.96	22 **Ti** 47.90	23 **V** 50.94	24 **Cr** 52.00	25 **Mn** 54.94	26 **Fe** 55.85	27 **Co** 58.93	28 **Ni** 58.69	29 **Cu** 63.55	30 **Zn** 65.39	31 **Ga** 69.72	32 **Ge** 72.59	33 **As** 74.92	34 **Se** 78.96	35 **Br** 79.90	36 **Kr** 83.80
37 **Rb** 85.47	38 **Sr** 87.62	39 **Y** 88.91	40 **Zr** 91.22	41 **Nb** 92.91	42 **Mo** 95.94	43 **Tc** (98)	44 **Ru** 101.1	45 **Rh** 102.91	46 **Pd** 106.42	47 **Ag** 107.87	48 **Cd** 112.41	49 **In** 114.82	50 **Sn** 118.71	51 **Sb** 121.75	52 **Te** 127.60	53 **I** 126.91	54 **Xe** 131.29
55 **Cs** 132.91	56 **Ba** 137.33	57 ***La** 138.91	72 **Hf** 178.49	73 **Ta** 180.95	74 **W** 183.85	75 **Re** 186.21	76 **Os** 190.2	77 **Ir** 192.2	78 **Pt** 195.08	79 **Au** 196.97	80 **Hg** 200.59	81 **Tl** 204.38	82 **Pb** 207.2	83 **Bi** 208.98	84 **Po** (209)	85 **At** (210)	86 **Rn** (222)
87 **Fr** (223)	88 **Ra** 226.02	89 **†Ac** 227.03	104 **Rf** (261)	105 **Db** (262)	106 **Sg** (266)	107 **Bh** (264)	108 **Hs** (277)	109 **Mt** (268)	110 **Ds** (271)	111 **Rg** (272)	112 **§** (277)						

§ Not yet named

← Increasing Metallic Character

1. Which of the following elements has the most metallic character?

   (A) Na
   (B) K
   (C) Rb
   (D) Cs
   (E) Fr

2. Which of the following elements has the least metallic character?

   (A) Li
   (B) Be
   (C) B
   (D) C
   (E) N

3. Which of the following elements has the highest electronegativity?

   (A) F
   (B) Ar
   (C) Br
   (D) Xe
   (E) At

4. Which of the following elements has the lowest electronegativity?

   (A) B
   (B) Al
   (C) Ga
   (D) Sn
   (E) Pb

5. Which of the following elements has the highest electronegativity?

   (A) Fe
   (B) Co
   (C) Pd
   (D) Ag
   (E) Zn

6. Which of the following elements has the largest atomic radius?

   (A) Si
   (B) P
   (C) S
   (D) Cl
   (E) Ar

7. Which of the following elements has the largest atomic radius?

   (A) H
   (B) Be
   (C) Mg
   (D) Na
   (E) Li

8. Which of the following elements has the smallest atomic radius?

   (A) F
   (B) Ne
   (C) Ar
   (D) Cl
   (E) Kr

9. Which of the following elements has the most metallic character?

   (A) Mn
   (B) Fe
   (C) Co
   (D) Ni
   (E) Cu

10. Which of the following elements has the highest electronegativity of all elements?

   (A) N
   (B) O
   (C) F
   (D) S
   (E) Cl

Questions 1-5 refer to the following terms.

    (A) Halogen
    (B) Noble gas
    (C) Alkali metal
    (D) Transition metal
    (E) Alkaline earth metal

1. Ag

2. K

3. He

4. Sr

5. Br

Questions 6-10 refer to the following terms.

    (A) Alpha decay
    (B) Beta decay
    (C) Positron emission
    (D) Gamma emission
    (E) Neutron

6. $_{0}^{0}\gamma$

7. $_{2}^{4}\text{He}$

8. $_{0}^{1}\text{n}$

9. $_{-1}^{0}\beta$

10. $_{+1}^{0}\beta$

---

101. The atomic mass of C is 12.011   BECAUSE   atomic mass of an element is calculated by the weighted average of all naturally occurring isotopes.

102. A radioactive isotope loses protons during beta decay   BECAUSE   when a radioactive isotope undergoes beta decay, the isotope emits a $_{-1}^{0}\beta$.

103. All types of decay cause a radioactive isotope to transmutate into a different element   BECAUSE   radioactive isotopes are generally unstable.

104. An atom with the electron configuration of $1s^2 2s^1$ has a larger quantity of electrons than a grounded He atom   BECAUSE   He in its ground state has 4 electrons.

105. The ionization energy for an atom is the amount of energy required to completely remove an electron   BECAUSE   when electrons drop to lower energy states they release energy in the form of light.

106. The d subshell can hold a maximum of 10 electrons   BECAUSE   Cu is a transition metal.

$$_{1}^{2}\text{H} + _{1}^{2}\text{H} \rightarrow _{2}^{4}\text{He}$$

107. The nuclear reaction shown above is considered a nuclear fission reaction   BECAUSE   nuclear fission occurs when two smaller isotopes collide to form one larger isotope.

11. How many neutrons does an atom of C-14 contain in its nucleus?

    (A) 6
    (B) 7
    (C) 8
    (D) 12
    (E) 14

12. Which of the following elements is considered an alkaline earth metal?

    (A) Na
    (B) Mg
    (C) Cu
    (D) Ag
    (E) Cl

$$? \rightarrow {}^{61}_{28}\text{Ni} + {}^{4}_{2}\text{He}$$

13. The missing reactant in the equation above is

    (A) ${}^{64}_{28}\text{Ni}$

    (B) ${}^{65}_{28}\text{Ni}$

    (C) ${}^{64}_{30}\text{Zn}$

    (D) ${}^{65}_{30}\text{Zn}$

    (E) ${}^{66}_{30}\text{Zn}$

$${}^{32}_{17}\text{Cl} \rightarrow ? + {}^{32}_{18}\text{Ar}$$

14. The missing product in the equation above is

    (A) ${}^{4}_{2}\text{He}$

    (B) ${}^{0}_{-1}\text{e}$

    (C) ${}^{0}_{+1}\text{e}$

    (D) ${}^{0}_{0}\gamma$

    (E) ${}^{1}_{0}\text{n}$

15. Which of the following is the correct electron configuration for Li^+?

    (A) $1s^1$

    (B) $1s^2$

    (C) $1s^1 2s^1$

    (D) $1s^2 2s^1$

    (E) $1s^2 2s^2$

16. Which of the following electron configurations represents an excited state?

    (A) $1s^2 2s^1$
    (B) $1s^2 2s^2 2p^4$
    (C) $1s^2 2s^1 2p^6 3s^1$
    (D) $1s^2 2s^2 2p^6 3s^2$
    (E) $1s^2 2s^2 2p^6 3s^2 3p^6 4s^1$

Questions 17-19 are based on the table below.
Energy values represent the change in electronvolts, eV, between two unknown principal quantum numbers.

Transition	Energy, eV
1	3.91
2	5.23
3	−6.72
4	−13.2
5	0

17. Which of the following transitions represents an increase in principal quantum number?

    (A) Transition 1 only
    (B) Transition 4 only
    (C) Transition 5 only
    (D) Transitions 1 and 2
    (E) Transitions 3 and 4

18. Which of the following transitions would result in a release of light energy?

    (A) Transition 1 only
    (B) Transition 2 only
    (C) Transitions 1 and 2
    (D) Transitions 3 and 4
    (E) Transitions 3, 4, and 5

19. Suppose a grounded Li atom reacts to form Li^+. Which transition would represent the energy change of the $1s^1$ electron?

    (A) Transition 1
    (B) Transition 2
    (C) Transition 3
    (D) Transition 4
    (E) Transition 5

CHAPTER

+2

BONDING AND INTERMOLECULAR FORCES

Lewis dot structures are a way of drawing elements to determine how their valence electrons will interact and pair up to form bonds. Elements tend to be most stable when they have 8 valence electrons.

═══════════════ Valence Lewis dot structures ═══════════════

1							8
·H	2		3	4	5	6	7	He:
·Li	·Be·	...	·Ḃ	·Ċ·	·Ṅ·	:Ö·	:Ḟ·	:Ṅe:
·Na	·Mg·	...	·Äl	·Ṡi·	·Ṗ·	:Ṡ·	:Ċl·	:Är:
·K	·Ca·	...	·Ġa	·Ge·	·Äs·	:Ṡe·	:Ḃr·	:Ḱr:
·Rb	·Sr·	...	·Ịn	·Sn·	·Ṡb·	:Ṫe·	:Ị·	:Ẋe:

Note that each element has 8 electrons in its valence once it pairs up. This is known as the OCTET RULE.

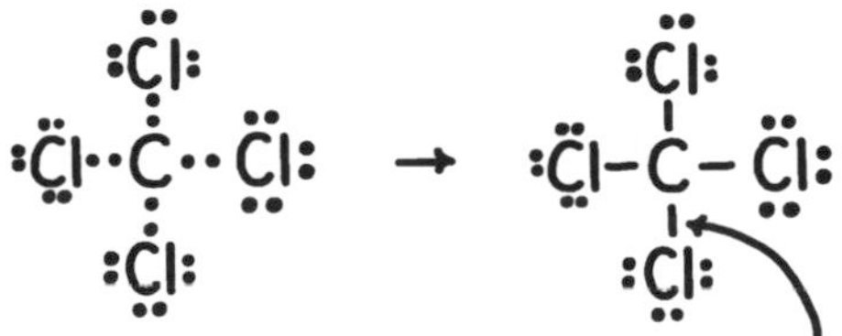

:Cl:
:Cl··C··Cl: →   :Cl–C–Cl:
:Cl: :Cl:

Each line represents the sharing of a pair of electrons. This is a COVALENT BOND.

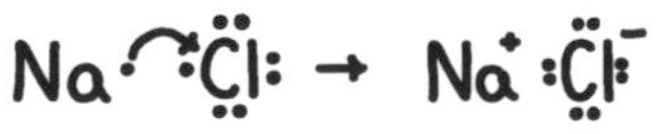

Na⌢:Cl: → Na⁺ :Cl:⁻

Na has a far easier time achieving its octet by completely losing its one valence electron and adopting the electron configuration of [Ne]. This complete transfer of an electron produces an IONIC BOND.

An ionic bond is formed between an *anion*, a negatively charged particle, and a *cation*, a positively charged particle.

1. Which of the following is a cation?

   (A) Hg
   (B) Ca^{2+}
   (C) Cl^-
   (D) F_2
   (E) NaF

2. In which of the following molecules are valence electrons transferred from one atom to another?

   (A) CO_2
   (B) CsCl
   (C) CH_4
   (D) N_2
   (E) NH_3

3. Which of the following molecules contains only covalent bonds?

   (A) H_2SO_4
   (B) NO_3
   (C) Na_2CO_3
   (D) $BaCl_2$
   (E) KI

4. All of the following are true of covalent bonds EXCEPT

   (A) They involve sharing of valence electrons between bonding atoms.
   (B) They arise from an electronegativity difference of less than 2.0.
   (C) They each have a characteristic vibrational frequency.
   (D) The atoms sharing the bond are called "ions".
   (E) They can have equal or unequal sharing of electrons.

5. A molecule with exactly three covalent bonds is

   (A) NH_3
   (B) Na_3PO_4
   (C) O_3
   (D) $AlCl_3$
   (E) SO_3

6. An atom of which of the following elements has the greatest number of valence electrons?

   (A) Oxygen
   (B) Carbon
   (C) Xenon
   (D) Barium
   (E) Arsenic

101. In the molecule CH_4, the carbon atom single bonds to four hydrogens — BECAUSE — most nonmetals will bond to have a full octet of valence electrons.

102. BF_3 has a lone pair of electrons on the central Boron atom — BECAUSE — all atoms bond to have a full octet of electrons.

103. CH_4 loses an H to form a carbocation — BECAUSE — positively charged ions are referred to as cations.

104. Ar has 18 valence electrons — BECAUSE — valence electrons are the number of electrons in the atom of an element.

105. An ionic bond is present in a KCl molecule — BECAUSE — K is an alkali metal.

$$:\ddot{O}\cdots\dot{C}\cdots\ddot{O}: \;\rightarrow\; \ddot{O}=C=\ddot{O}$$

A DOUBLE BOND occurs to satisfy the octet around each element in a molecule of CO_2 (carbon dioxide).

$$:\dot{N}\cdot\;\cdot\dot{N}: \;\rightarrow\; :N\equiv N:$$

A TRIPLE BOND occurs to satisfy the octet around each element in a molecule of N_2.

When double and triple bonds occur the electrons must form a path that keeps out of the way of the electrons that form the single, sigma (σ), bond. To do this, a pi (π) bond is formed.

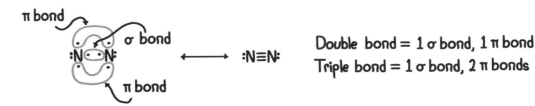

π bond

σ bond

π bond

$$\longleftrightarrow\; :N\equiv N:$$

Double bond = 1 σ bond, 1 π bond
Triple bond = 1 σ bond, 2 π bonds

Resonance

Resonance structures occur when there seems to be more than one bonding configuration that are equally suitable. A resonance structure allows for the indication of electrons that are *delocalized* (electrons that are not necessarily associated with a single atom or bond).

$$:\ddot{O}=\overset{\ddot{O}}{\dots}-\ddot{O}: \;\longleftrightarrow\; :\ddot{O}-\overset{\ddot{O}}{\dots}=\ddot{O}:$$

A RESONANCE STRUCTURE is used to indicate the proper bond configuration of O_3 (ozone).

Coordinate Covalent Bond

Coordinate covalent bonds occur when one element has to donate an entire lone pair of electrons to help satisfy the octet fore very element.

$$\cdot\dot{C}\cdots\dot{O}\cdot \;\rightarrow\; :C=\ddot{O}$$

Yikes! Carbon doesn't have enough electrons! To fix this, oxygen donates two electrons. Oxygen isn't super thrilled about this, but she'll lend a hand to make things work.

$$\cdot\dot{C}\cdots\dot{O}\cdot \;\rightarrow\; :C\overset{\frown}{=}\ddot{O} \;\rightarrow\; :C\equiv O:$$

$$\cdot\dot{C}\cdots\dot{O}\cdot \;\rightarrow\; :C\equiv O:$$

A COORDINATE COVALENT BOND occurs to satisfy the octet around each element in a molecule of CO (carbon monoxide).

Single, Double, and Triple Bonds—*Practice*

1. Which of the following molecules accepts an H^+ ion in a coordinate covalent bond?

   (A) NaCl
   (B) H_2SO_4
   (C) CH_4
   (D) Hg_2
   (E) NH_3

2. Each of the following hydrocarbons contains a multiple bond, EXCEPT

   (A) C_2H_2
   (B) C_3H_6
   (C) C_6H_6
   (D) C_4H_{10}
   (E) CH_2CH_2

3. In a double bond there are

   (A) two sigma bonds and one pi bond
   (B) one sigma and two pi bonds
   (C) one sigma and one pi bond
   (D) three pi bonds
   (E) no sigma bonds

4. All of the following are true about the bonds between the atoms in a N_2 molecule, EXCEPT

   (A) It is a triple bond
   (B) It is a covalent bond
   (C) The electrons spend more time in motion near one atom
   (D) The atoms will not dissociate when the molecule is placed in water
   (E) It is a bond order of three

5. Which of the following bond types is strongest?

   (A) Single
   (B) Double
   (C) Triple
   (D) Hydrogen
   (E) Metallic

6. Which of the following diatomic molecules has the shortest bond length?

   (A) N_2
   (B) O_2
   (C) F_2
   (D) Cl_2
   (E) I_2

7. All of the following substances are stabilized through resonance, EXCEPT

   (A) benzene
   (B) sulfur trioxide
   (C) nitrogen dioxide
   (D) ozone
   (E) methane

8. In a triple bond there are

   (A) two sigma bonds and one pi bond
   (B) one sigma and two pi bonds
   (C) three sigma bonds
   (D) three pi bonds
   (E) no sigma bonds

9. Which type of bond is present in a molecule of O_2?

   (A) Resonant
   (B) Single
   (C) Double
   (D) Triple
   (E) Gaseous

10. All of the following have single covalent bonds EXCEPT

   (A) NH_3
   (B) H_2
   (C) O_2
   (D) Br_2
   (E) K_3PO_4

Type of bond	Example	Electronegativity Difference (ΔEN)
Nonpolar Covalent	F–F	ΔEN < 0.5
Polar Covalent	$S^{\delta^+}\!-\!O^{\delta^-}$	0.5 < ΔEN < 1.5
Ionic	$\overset{+}{Na}\overset{-}{Cl}$	2.0 < ΔEN

Note: δ indicates the dipole moment. δ^+ indicates a slight positive charge and δ^- indicates a slight negative charge.

Electronegativity Periodic Table

Note: Notice hydrogen, H, in the above periodic table. Hydrogen has an electronegativity more like a nonmetal than a metal. Hence, any binary compound containing hydrogen is most likely a molecular compound and NOT an ionic compound. For example, HCl is molecular whereas NaCl is ionic.

Polar & Nonpolar Bonds—*Practice*

1. Which of the following molecules is nonpolar despite having polar bonds?

    (A) NaCl
    (B) H_2SO_4
    (C) CO_2
    (D) Hg
    (E) NH_3

2. The difference in electronegativity between the atoms sharing a polar covalent bond could be

    (A) 0
    (B) 0.2
    (C) 1.5
    (D) 2.5
    (E) 4.0

3. All of the following are true about the bond between hydrogen and chlorine, EXCEPT

    (A) It is a single bond
    (B) It is an ionic bond
    (C) The electrons spend more time in motion near the chlorine atom
    (D) The atoms will dissociate when the molecule is placed in water
    (E) The hydrogen atom is the positive pole

4. NH_3 donates its electron pair to form a bond with BF_3. This bond is categorized as

    (A) ionic
    (B) polar covalent
    (C) nonpolar covalent
    (D) coordinate covalent
    (E) metallic

5. Which type of bonding is present in a molecule of SiO_2?

    (A) Ionic
    (B) Nonpolar Covalent
    (C) Polar Covalent
    (D) Coordinate Covalent
    (E) Metallic

6. A molecule with the general formula X_2 must have

    (A) a high boiling point
    (B) nonpolar covalent bonding
    (C) ionic bonding
    (D) a triple bond
    (E) no lone pairs of electrons

7. In which of the following molecules are valence electrons unevenly shared?

    (A) NaCl
    (B) O_2
    (C) O_3
    (D) HCl
    (E) LiF

101. H_2O is a polar molecule   BECAUSE   an asymmetrical distribution of bond polarity contributes to molecule polarity.

102. CCl_4 is nonpolar   BECAUSE   it is a planar molecule.

103. Na_3PO_4 has both ionic and covalent bonds   BECAUSE   sodium is extremely electropositive, while phosphorus and oxygen are electronegative.

104. The electronegativity difference in CO_2 is greater than the electronegativity difference in NaCl   BECAUSE   polar covalent compounds have the greatest difference in electronegativity of the bonding atoms.

105. Electrons can be expected to spend the same amount of time around both atoms in I_2 BECAUSE   electrons are unequally shared in polar covalent compounds.

Orbital hybridization occurs when electrons in differing energy level configurations (s,p,d) are required to help bond with other atoms.

<u>Hybrid Orbital</u> – An orbital formed through the mixing of s,p, and d orbitals to produce an orbital with an intermediate energy level.

<u>Region of Electron Density</u> – Single bond, double bond, triple bond, lone pair.

<u>Hybrid Orbital</u>	<u>Orbital Mixture</u>	<u>Regions of Electron Density</u>
sp	1s and 1p orbital	2
sp^2	1s and 2p orbitals	3
sp^3	1s and 3p orbitals	4
dsp^3	1d, 1s, and 3p orbitals	5
d^2sp^3	2d, 1s, and 3p orbitals	6

Orbital hybridization Sample Questions

1. What is the orbital hybridization of oxygen in H_2O?

   (A) sp
   (B) sp^2
   (C) sp^3
   (D) dsp^3
   (E) d^2sp^3

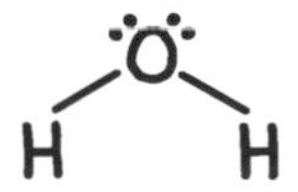

   2 lone pairs + 2 single bonds = 4 regions of electron density

   $$\downarrow$$

   sp^3

2. What is the orbital hybridization of oxygen in CO_2?

   (A) sp
   (B) sp^2
   (C) sp^3
   (D) dsp^3
   (E) d^2sp^3

   $:O=C=O:$

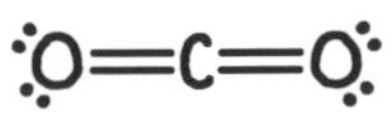

   1 double bond + 2 lone pairs = 3 regions of electron density

   $$\downarrow$$

   sp^2

Orbital Hybridization—*Practice*

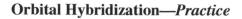

Questions 3-22 refer to the following central atom orbital hybridizations, unless otherwise specified

(A) sp
(B) sp^2
(C) sp^3
(D) dsp^3
(E) d^2sp^3

3. BeF_2
4. H_2O
5. CO_2
6. NH_3
7. CH_4
8. BF_3
9. CCl_4
10. H_2S
11. SF_6
12. BH_3
13. SO_2
14. SO_3
15. NO_2^-
16. ICl_4^-
17. PF_5
18. SCl_6
19. SeH_2
20. XeF_4
21. NH_4^+
22. Each carbon in C_2H_4

Intermolecular forces are the forces that dictate the way molecules interact with one another. Regions of a molecule with low electron density will be positively charged compared to regions with a high electron density.

IMF Strength Chart

Intermolecular force	Match up	Example	Strength
Ion-dipole	Ion vs polar molecule	$Na^+ \cdots O \begin{smallmatrix} H \\ H \end{smallmatrix}$	
Hydrogen bond	Molecules that have covalent bonds between H and N, O, or F		
Dipole-dipole	Polar molecule vs polar molecule	$H-Cl \cdots H-Cl$	
Ion-induced dipole	Ion vs nonpolar molecule	$Fe^{2+} \cdots O_2$	
Dipole-induced dipole	Polar molecule vs nonpolar molecule	$H-Cl \cdots Cl_2$	
London dispersion	Nonpolar molecule vs nonpolar molecule	$F_2 \cdots F_2$	

How does electronegativity affect IMF?

Differences in electronegativity between elements that are covalently bound will produce regions of relatively high and low electron density. This, in effect, turns molecules into small magnet like objects of varying strengths that interact with one another accordingly.

Higher EN difference = Stronger IMF

Questions 1-5 refer to the following intermolecular forces.

   (A) Hydrogen bonds
   (B) Dipole-dipole
   (C) Ion-induced dipole
   (D) Dipole-induced dipole
   (E) London dispersion forces

1. Greatest electronegativity difference

2. Intermolecular forces between iron(III) oxide molecules

3. Typically present in nonpolar substances

4. The intermolecular H-N bond in NH_3

5. The forces experienced between CH_4 molecules

101. Of all intermolecular forces, the weakest bond type are London dispersion forces   BECAUSE   the dissociation energy, on average, of London dispersion forces is lower than other intermolecular forces.

102. Of all intermolecular forces, the strongest bond type are ion-dipole forces   BECAUSE   ion-dipole forces have relatively large electronegativity differences.

6. Consider a 1 L reaction chamber containing $SO_2(g)$ and $F_2(g)$. The intermolecular forces experienced between a molecule of $SO_2(g)$ and a molecule of $F_2(g)$ are best known as

   (A) dipole-dipole forces
   (B) ion-induced dipole forces
   (C) dipole-induced dipole forces
   (D) London dispersion forces
   (E) hydrogen bonds

7. Which of the following explains why the boiling point of $H_2O(l)$ is much greater than that of $H_2S(l)$?

   (A) Liquid water and hydrogen disulfide are the same phase
   (B) Liquid water and hydrogen disulfide are different phases
   (C) Liquid water experiences hydrogen bonding, whereas hydrogen disulfide does not
   (D) Hydrogen disulfide experiences hydrogen bonding, whereas liquid water does not
   (E) Liquid water contains more hydrogen atoms per molecule than hydrogen disulfide

Questions 1-4 refer to the following.

    (A) CCl_4
    (B) H_2
    (C) CO_2
    (D) NH_3
    (E) MgO

1. Is a polar covalent molecule

2. Is a linear nonpolar covalent molecule with polar bonds

3. Has at least one multiple covalent bond

4. Has an electronegativity difference between bonding atoms that is greater than 2.0

Questions 5-8 refer to the following.

    (A) London Dispersion
    (B) Dipole-Dipole
    (C) Ion-Dipole
    (D) Hydrogen Bonding
    (E) Ion-Induced Dipole

5. Attractive force that explains the solubility of CH_3CH_2OH in water

6. Attractive force observed when sodium sulfate is added to water

7. Attractive force that explains the relatively high boiling point of NH_3

8. Attractive force between molecules of $CH_4(l)$

Questions 9-13 refer to the following.

    (A) Double Bond
    (B) Triple Bond
    (C) Coordinate Covalent Bond
    (D) Anion
    (E) Cation

9. Describes the shortest multiple covalent bond

10. Describes the sodium ion when bonded with chloride

11. Describes the intramolecular force using two electrons from the same atom

12. Describes NO_3^-

13. Describes the intramolecular force involving four shared electrons

Questions 14-15 refer to the following.

    (A) Electronegativity
    (B) Resonance
    (C) Conjugation
    (D) Sigma
    (E) Pi

14. Can be used to predict the polarity of a heteroatomic molecule

15. Can be used to predict the relative stability of a compound from its Lewis structure

101. H_2O has a higher boiling point than H_2S	BECAUSE	London Dispersion forces are stronger than Hydrogen Bonding intermolecular forces.
102. NH_4^+ contains two different kinds of covalent bonds	BECAUSE	a nonpolar covalent bond involves equal sharing of electrons donated from both atoms, while a coordinate covalent bond involves a pair of electrons donated from only one atom.
103. SO_3 is an ionic molecule	BECAUSE	the electronegativity difference between Sulfur and Oxygen is greater than 2.0.
104. $CsCl(s)$ is soluble in water	BECAUSE	H_2O has a bent structure and polar bonds.

16. Which of the following contains both covalent and ionic bonds?

    (A) CO_2
    (B) CH_3OH
    (C) CH_4
    (D) NH_4Cl
    (E) LiH

17. Which of the following is NOT present in a sample of $CO_2(g)$?

    (A) Double Bonds
    (B) Polar Covalent Bonds
    (C) 16 valence electrons per molecule
    (D) London Dispersion Forces
    (E) Hydrogen Bonding

18. Which of the following contains the greatest number of valence electrons?

    (A) Fluorine
    (B) Oxygen
    (C) Potassium
    (D) Sulfur
    (E) Carbon

19. A hydrocarbon with the general formula C_nH_{2n+2} must have

    (A) only single bonds
    (B) only double bonds
    (C) only triple bonds
    (D) a mix of single and double bonds
    (E) a mix of double and triple bonds

20. Which of the following molecules is polar?

    (A) C_2H_6
    (B) CBr_4
    (C) Cl_2
    (D) $PO_4{}^{3-}$
    (E) PCl_3

21. The stability of Benzene can be attributed to its

    (A) Nonpolar Covalent Bonds
    (B) Hydrogen Bonding
    (C) Resonance Contributors
    (D) Coordinate Covalent Bonds
    (E) Ratio of Carbon to Hydrogen Atoms

22. Each of the following species has the same number of electrons, EXCEPT

    (A) S^{2-}
    (B) Cl^-
    (C) K^+
    (D) Ar
    (E) Ne

23. All of the following are soluble in water, EXCEPT

    (A) NH_3
    (B) $NaCl$
    (C) PCl_3
    (D) H_2
    (E) $KClO_3$

24. CF_2Cl_2 is a polar molecule. This can be partially attributed to each of the following, EXCEPT

    (A) The electronegativity difference between carbon and chlorine
    (B) The electronegativity difference between carbon and fluorine
    (C) The electronegativity difference between fluorine and chlorine
    (D) The tetrahedral structure
    (E) Multiple resonance structures

Mol

STOICHIOMETRY

Avogadro's number → 6.022×10^{23} = 1 mole

6.022×10^{23} elephants = 1 mole of elephants
6.022×10^{23} sunflowers = 1 mole of sunflowers
6.022×10^{23} particles = 1 mole of particles
6.022×10^{23} atoms = 1 mole of atoms

This tells us that, on average, 1 mole of carbon has a mass of 12.011 grams.

On average, 1 mole of oxygen has a mass of 16.00 grams.

One mole of any gas under standard temperature and pressure (STP) will occupy 22.4L.

1 mole of H_2 gas under STP = 22.4L of gas
1 mole of O_2 gas under STP = 22.4L of gas
1 mole of He gas under STP = 22.4L of gas

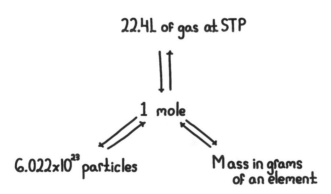

22.4L of gas at STP

1 mole

6.022×10^{23} particles

Mass in grams of an element

1. 15.0 g of which of the following gases at STP has the greatest volume?

(A) $H_2(g)$
(B) $He(g)$
(C) $O_2(g)$
(D) $Cl_2(g)$
(E) $Xe(g)$

Notice these are getting heavier.

- Convert answers to moles by setting up a proportion and solving.
- The greatest number of moles will occupy the most space.

(A) $\dfrac{moles}{grams} \rightarrow \dfrac{1\ mole}{2\ grams} = \dfrac{x\ moles}{15\ grams}$

$\dfrac{2x}{2} = \dfrac{15}{2} \quad x = 7.5\ moles$

The heavier we go the fewer moles there will be in 15 grams of gas, so we can stop here.

2. The mass of 2.0 moles of carbon dioxide is

(A) 12.0 g
(B) 28.0 g
(C) 44.0 g
(D) 56.0 g
(E) 88.0 g

CO_2

Mass of C	Mass of O_2
$\dfrac{1\ mole}{12\ grams} = \dfrac{2\ moles}{x\ grams}$	$\dfrac{1\ mole}{32\ grams} = \dfrac{2\ moles}{x\ grams}$
$x = 24\ grams$	$x = 64\ grams$

$24 + 64 = \boxed{88\ grams}$

3. A certain hydrocarbon has 84 percent carbon and 16 percent hydrogen by mass. The empirical formula of this compound is represented by

(A) CH_4
(B) C_2H_6
(C) C_6H_9
(D) C_7H_{16}
(E) $C_{84}H_{16}$

① Let's assume we have 100 grams of the substance. Then we can say that we have 84g of carbon & 16g of hydrogen.

② Convert to moles.

Moles of C	Moles of H
$\dfrac{1\ mole}{12\ grams} = \dfrac{x\ moles}{84\ grams}$	$\dfrac{1\ mole}{1\ gram} = \dfrac{x\ moles}{16\ grams}$
$\dfrac{84}{12} = \dfrac{12x}{12}$	$x = 16\ moles$
$x = 7\ moles$	

$C_7 H_{16}$

Stoichiometry—*Practice*

4. The mass of 1 mole of $NaHCO_3$, is

    (A) 12 g
    (B) 23 g
    (C) 48 g
    (D) 64 g
    (E) 84 g

8. The mass of 2 moles of HNO_2, is

    (A) 47 g
    (B) 50 g
    (C) 61 g
    (D) 88 g
    (E) 94 g

5. How many moles of $H_2(g)$ occupy 44.8 L of space?

    (A) 0.5 mol
    (B) 1 mol
    (C) 2 moles
    (D) 4 moles
    (E) 5 moles

9. How many molecules of $He(g)$ are present in a 22.4 L container at 1 atm and 273 K?

    (A) 1 molecule
    (B) 6.02 molecules
    (C) 3.01×10^{23} molecules
    (D) 6.02×10^{23} molecules
    (E) 1.20×10^{24} molecules

6. How many moles of $Cl_2(g)$ occupy 11.2 L of space?

    (A) 0.5 mol
    (B) 1 mol
    (C) 2 moles
    (D) 4 moles
    (E) 5 moles

10. The mass of 1 mole of $NaClO_4$, is

    (A) 100 g
    (B) 120 g
    (C) 122 g
    (D) 130 g
    (E) 132 g

11. The mass of 0.10 mole of $KClO_2$, is

    (A) 11 g
    (B) 54 g
    (C) 107 g
    (D) 200 g
    (E) 214 g

7. The mass of 0.5 mole of HPO_4 is

    (A) 48 g
    (B) 96 g
    (C) 106 g
    (D) 142 g
    (E) 284 g

12. The mass of 0.10 mole of H_2SO_3, is

   (A)   8.2 g
   (B)   41 g
   (C)   55 g
   (D)   82 g
   (E)   164 g

16. 9 g of which of the following gases at 1 atm and 273 K has the greatest volume?

   (A) $F_2(g)$
   (B) $Cl_2(g)$
   (C) $He(g)$
   (D) $Ne(g)$
   (E) $Ar(g)$

13. How many molecules of $F_2(g)$ are present in a 44.8 L container at 1 atm and 273 K?

   (A) 1 molecule
   (B) 6.02 molecules
   (C) 3.01×10^{23} molecules
   (D) 6.02×10^{23} molecules
   (E) 1.20×10^{24} molecules

17. How many atoms of helium are present in a 22.4 L container of $He(g)$ at 1 atm and 273 K?

   (A) 1 molecule
   (B) 6.02 molecules
   (C) 3.01×10^{23} molecules
   (D) 6.02×10^{23} molecules
   (E) 1.20×10^{24} molecules

14. How many atoms of chlorine are present in a 22.4 L container of $Cl_2(g)$ at 1 atm and 273 K?

   (A) 1 molecule
   (B) 6.02 molecules
   (C) 3.01×10^{23} molecules
   (D) 6.02×10^{23} molecules
   (E) 1.20×10^{24} molecules

18. How many atoms of hydrogen are present in a 22.4 L container of $H_2(g)$ at 1 atm and 273 K?

   (A) 1 molecule
   (B) 6.02 molecules
   (C) 3.01×10^{23} molecules
   (D) 6.02×10^{23} molecules
   (E) 1.20×10^{24} molecules

15. 22.4 g of which of the following gases at STP has the smallest volume?

   (A) $H_2(g)$
   (B) $N_2(g)$
   (C) $O_2(g)$
   (D) $F_2(g)$
   (E) $Cl_2(g)$

19. The mass of 1 mole of NH_4MnO_4, is

   (A) 101 g
   (B) 134 g
   (C) 137 g
   (D) 164 g
   (E) 196 g

How do we balance a reaction?

$$C_2H_{10} + O_2 \rightarrow CO_2 + H_2O$$

	reactant total	product total
C	2	1
H	10	2
O	2	3

① Save any element that's by itself for last (O in this case). We will start with C; we can clearly see that the moles of CO_2 will always need to be double that of C_2H_{10}.

$$C_2H_{10} + O_2 \rightarrow 2CO_2 + H_2O$$

C	2	2 ✓
H	10	2
O	2	5

② Now we can move to H.

$$C_2H_{10} + O_2 \rightarrow 2CO_2 + 5H_2O$$

C	2	2 ✓
H	10	10 ✓
O	2	9

③ The O is troubling because 2 does not go into 9. We will need to double the coefficent in front of every species that contains an already balanced element.

$$2C_2H_{10} + O_2 \rightarrow 4CO_2 + 10H_2O$$

C	4	4 ✓
H	20	20 ✓
O	2	18

④ 2 does go into 18 so now we can balance O.

$$2C_2H_{10} + 9O_2 \rightarrow 4CO_2 + 10H_2O$$

C	4	4 ✓
H	20	20 ✓
O	18	18 ✓

$$\boxed{2C_2H_{10} + 9O_2 \rightarrow 4CO_2 + 10H_2O}$$

Balancing reactions—*Practice*

$$\ldots \text{Fe}(s) + \ldots \text{O}_2(g) \rightarrow \ldots \text{Fe}_2\text{O}_3(s)$$

1. When the equation for the reaction represented above is balanced and the coefficients are reduced to the lowest integer values, the coefficient for $\text{Fe}_2\text{O}_3(s)$ is

   (A) 1
   (B) 2
   (C) 3
   (D) 4
   (E) 5

$$\ldots \text{Al}(s) + \ldots \text{O}_2(g) \rightarrow \ldots \text{Al}_2\text{O}_3(s)$$

2. When the equation for the reaction represented above is balanced and the coefficients are reduced to the lowest integer values, the coefficient for $\text{Al}_2\text{O}_3(s)$ is

   (A) 1
   (B) 2
   (C) 3
   (D) 4
   (E) 5

$$\ldots \text{CH}_4(g) + \ldots \text{O}_2(g) \rightarrow \ldots \text{CO}_2(g) + \ldots \text{H}_2\text{O}(l)$$

3. When the equation for the reaction represented above is balanced and the coefficients are reduced to the lowest integer values, the coefficient for $\text{O}_2(g)$ is

   (A) 1
   (B) 2
   (C) 3
   (D) 4
   (E) 5

$$\ldots KOH(aq) + \ldots H_3PO_4(aq) \rightarrow \ldots K_3PO_4(aq) + \ldots H_2O(l)$$

4. When the equation for the reaction represented above is balanced and the coefficients are reduced to the lowest integer values, the coefficient for $K_3PO_4(aq)$ is

   (A) 1
   (B) 2
   (C) 3
   (D) 4
   (E) 5

$$\ldots C_4H_6O_3(l) + \ldots H_2O(l) \rightarrow \ldots C_2H_4O_2(l)$$

5. When the equation for the reaction represented above is balanced and the coefficients are reduced to the lowest integer values, the coefficient for $C_2H_4O_2(l)$ is

   (A) 1
   (B) 2
   (C) 3
   (D) 4
   (E) 5

$$\ldots Ca_3(PO_4)_2(aq) + \ldots H_2SO_4(aq) \rightarrow \ldots CaSO_4(aq) + \ldots Ca(H_2PO_4)_2(aq)$$

6. When the equation for the reaction represented above is balanced and the coefficients are reduced to the lowest integer values, the coefficient for $Ca(H_2PO_4)_2(aq)$ is

   (A) 1
   (B) 2
   (C) 3
   (D) 4
   (E) 5

$$\ldots P_4O_{10}(s) + \ldots H_2O(g) \rightarrow \ldots H_3PO_4(s)$$

7. When the equation for the reaction represented above is balanced and the coefficients are reduced to the lowest integer values, the coefficient for $H_3PO_4(s)$ is

    (A) 1
    (B) 2
    (C) 3
    (D) 4
    (E) 5

$$\ldots NH_3(g) + \ldots CuO(s) \rightarrow \ldots Cu(s) + \ldots N_2(g) + \ldots H_2O(l)$$

8. When the equation for the reaction represented above is balanced and the coefficients are reduced to the lowest integer values, the coefficient for $CuO(s)$ is

    (A) 1
    (B) 2
    (C) 3
    (D) 4
    (E) 5

$$\ldots Cu(s) + \ldots HNO_3(aq) \rightarrow \ldots Cu(NO_3)_2(aq) + \ldots NO(g) + \ldots H_2O(l)$$

9. When the equation for the reaction represented above is balanced and the coefficients are reduced to the lowest integer values, the coefficient for $NO(g)$ is

    (A) 1
    (B) 2
    (C) 3
    (D) 4
    (E) 5

Questions 1-4 refer to the following.

    (A) H_2
    (B) O_2
    (C) CH_4
    (D) CO_2
    (E) NH_3

1. Has a molecular mass of 2 g/mol

2. Has a molecular mass of 16 g/mol

3. The least volume at STP with a mass of 10 g

4. The greatest volume at STP with a mass of 20 g

Questions 5-8 refer to the following.

    (A) 1 mole
    (B) 2 moles
    (C) 3 moles
    (D) 4 moles
    (E) 5 moles

5. 44. grams of CO_2

6. 2. grams of hydrogen gas, H_2

7. 32. grams of methane, CH_4

8. 64. grams of oxygen gas, O_2

101. 20 grams of xenon gas, Xe, has a larger volume than 20 grams of helium gas, He, at standard temperature and pressure   BECAUSE   heavier gas molecules hold more volume at standard temperature and pressure.

102. Ethane, C_2H_6 has an empirical formula of CH_3 BECAUSE   an empirical formula is derived by reducing all elements in a compound to their lowest whole-number quantities.

103. 2 moles of oxygen gas, O_2, under standard temperature and pressure have a volume of 89.6 L.   BECAUSE   1 mole of any gas at standard temperature and pressure has a volume of 22.4 L.

9. The mass of 5. moles of ammonia, NH_3, is

    (A) 8.5 g
    (B) 17.0 g
    (C) 34.0 g
    (D) 51.0 g
    (E) 85.0 g

10. A certain hydrocarbon has 75 percent carbon and 25 percent hydrogen by mass. The molecular formula of this compound is represented by

    (A) CH_4
    (B) C_2H_6
    (C) C_3H_8
    (D) C_4H_{10}
    (E) $C_{75}H_{25}$

11. The mass of 2 moles of KCl, is

    (A)   4 g
    (B)   35 g
    (C)   39 g
    (D)   74 g
    (E)   149 g

15. The mass of 1 mole of H_2SO_4, is

    (A)   22 g
    (B)   32 g
    (C)   64 g
    (D)   98 g
    (E)   196 g

12. The mass of 3 moles of $CaCl_2$, is

    (A)   40 g
    (B)   75 g
    (C)   110 g
    (D)   333 g
    (E)   440 g

16. The mass of 1 mole of Li_3PO_4, is

    (A)   116 g
    (B)   121 g
    (C)   131 g
    (D)   148 g
    (E)   200 g

13. 1 g of which of the following gases at STP has the greatest volume?

    (A) $F_2(g)$
    (B) $Cl_2(g)$
    (C) $Ne(g)$
    (D) $Ar(g)$
    (E) $Kr(g)$

17. The mass of 2 moles of AlI_3, is

    (A) 127 g
    (B) 408 g
    (C) 816 g
    (D) 952 g
    (E) 512 g

14. A certain compound has 42 percent carbon and 58 percent oxygen by mass. The empirical formula of this compound is represented by

    (A) CO
    (B) CO_2
    (C) C_2O
    (D) CO_3
    (E) C_2O_3

18. A certain compound has 4 percent hydrogen and 96 percent oxygen by mass. The empirical formula of this compound is represented by

    (A) HO
    (B) H_2O
    (C) HO_2
    (D) H_2O_3
    (E) H_3O_2

$$\ldots S(s) \;+\; \ldots HNO_3(aq) \;\rightarrow\; \ldots H_2SO_4(aq) \;+\; \ldots NO_2(g) \;+\; \ldots H_2O(l)$$

19. When the equation for the reaction represented above is balanced and the coefficients are reduced to the lowest integer values, the coefficient for $S(s)$ is

    (A) 1
    (B) 2
    (C) 3
    (D) 4
    (E) 5

## CHAPTER 4

PVnRt

GAS PROPERTIES AND LAWS

Properties of ideal gases:

- The volume occupied by a single particle of gas is ignored.

- Gas particles move in random straight line motion.

- Collisions that ideal gas particles have result in no loss of energy and are considered to be elastic collisions.

- Intermolecular forces are ignored.

NOTE: Gases act ideally under standard temperature and pressure (STP).

Standard temperature: 0°C / 273.15 K / 32°F
  - Gases will behave more ideally at higher temperatures.

Standard pressure: 1 atm / 101.3 kPa / 760 mmHg / 760 torr
  - Gases will behave more ideally at lower pressures.

Sample Question

---

1. Helium gas exhibits most ideal behavior under which of the following conditions?

   (A) 100 K and 10 atm
   (B) 273 K and 1 atm
   (C) 300 K and 760 mmHg
   (D) 400 K and 7600 mmHg
   (E) 400 K and 760 torr

   (E) has the highest temperature and lowest pressure

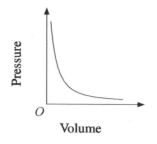

Boyle's Law

$$P \propto \frac{1}{V} \quad \text{or} \quad PV = \text{constant} \qquad P_1 V_1 = P_2 V_2 \qquad \text{Inverse}$$

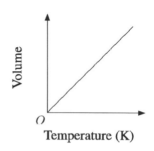

Charles's Law

$$V \propto T \quad \text{or} \quad \frac{V}{T} = \text{constant} \qquad \frac{V_1}{T_1} = \frac{V_2}{T_2} \qquad \text{Direct}$$

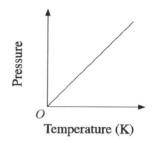

Gay-Lussac's Law

$$P \propto T \quad \text{or} \quad \frac{P}{T} = \text{constant} \qquad \frac{P_1}{T_1} = \frac{P_2}{T_2} \qquad \text{Direct}$$

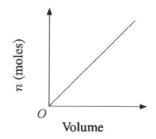

Avogadro's Principle

$$V \propto n \quad \text{or} \quad \frac{n}{V} = \text{constant} \qquad \frac{n_1}{V_1} = \frac{n_2}{V_2} \qquad \text{Direct}$$

Combine gas law!

$$PV = nRT \quad \text{or} \quad \frac{PV}{nT} = R \qquad \frac{P_1 V_1}{n_1 T_1} = \frac{P_2 V_2}{n_2 T_2}$$

constant!

2. A sample of $H_2(g)$ is stored in a 1.00 L closed vessel at 500.0 torr and 250. K. The gas is heated in the container to a temperature of 500. K. Which of the following statements about the gas is true?

    (A) The number of moles of gas increases
    (B) The number of moles of gas decreases
    (C) The volume of the gas increases to 2.00 L
    (D) The temperature of the air surrounding the container decreases
    (E) The pressure of the gas increases to 1000.0 torr

-The container is closed, and we aren't adding gas. A, B, and C are wrong.

-We are looking for a PRESSURE given a TEMPERATURE change. Let's use Gay-Lussac's Law.

$$\frac{500 \text{ torr}}{250 \text{ k}} = \frac{x \text{ torr}}{500 \text{ K}} \longrightarrow \boxed{1000 \text{ torr}}$$

3. The pressure of 3 L of a gas at 25°C is 800 mm Hg. What is the volume of this gas at standard temperature and pressure?

    (A) $V = 3 \times \dfrac{0}{25} \times \dfrac{800}{760}$

    (B) $V = 3 \times \dfrac{25}{0} \times \dfrac{800}{760}$

    (C) $V = 3 \times \dfrac{273}{298} \times \dfrac{760}{800}$

    (D) $V = 3 \times \dfrac{298}{273} \times \dfrac{760}{800}$

    (E) $V = 3 \times \dfrac{273}{298} \times \dfrac{800}{760}$

-We are given VOLUME TEMPERATURE and PRESSURE.

$$\frac{P_1 V_1}{T_1} = \frac{P_2 V_2}{T_2}$$

"n" doesn't change, so we can exclude it from the combined gas law.

$$\frac{(3L)(800 \text{mmHg})}{(298K)} = \frac{(xL)(760 \text{mmHg})}{(273K)}$$

always convert celsius to kelvin

$$\boxed{xL = (3L) \cdot \frac{(273K)}{(298K)} \cdot \frac{(800 \text{mmHg})}{(760 \text{mmHg})}}$$

4. A 2.0 L container of Xenon gas has a pressure of 1.78 atm at 300K. Which of the following expressions could be used to find the mass of the Xenon gas?

    (A) $131.29 \times \dfrac{(1.78)(2.0)}{(0.0821)(300)}$

    (B) $131.29 \times \dfrac{(0.0821)(300)}{(1.78)(2.0)}$

    (C) $131.29 \times \dfrac{(2.0)}{(1.78)(300)}$

    (D) $2.0 \times \dfrac{1.78}{1.0} \times \dfrac{273}{300}$

    (E) $1.78 \times \dfrac{2.0}{22.4} \times \dfrac{300}{273}$

① Solve for n, the number of moles.

$$n = \frac{PV}{RT} \xrightarrow{\text{plug in!}} n = \frac{(1.78 \text{atm})(2L)}{(0.0821)(300K)}$$

② Convert to mass by multiplying by the molar mass of Xe.

$$\boxed{(131.29) \cdot \frac{(1.78 \text{atm})(2L)}{(0.0821)(300K)}}$$

5. Nitrogen gas, N_2, exhibits *least* ideal behavior under which of the following conditions?

   (A) 273 K and 2 atm
   (B) 273 K and 10 atm
   (C) 300 K and 1 atm
   (D) 400 K and 1 atm
   (E) 400 K and 2 atm

6. A sample of $O_2(g)$ is stored in a 2 L closed vessel at 760 torr and 200 K. The gas is heated in the container to a temperature of 400 K at a constant pressure. Which of the following statements about the gas is true?

   (A) The number of moles of gas increases
   (B) The number of moles of gas decreases
   (C) The volume of the gas increases to 4 L
   (D) The temperature of the air surrounding the container decreases
   (E) The pressure of the gas increases to 1,520 torr

7. A 2 L container of $Cl_2(g)$ has 0.478 atm of pressure at 298 K. Which of the following is used to find the mass of $Cl_2(g)$?

   (A) $2.0 \times \dfrac{0.478}{1.0} \times \dfrac{273}{298}$

   (B) $1.78 \times \dfrac{2.0}{22.4} \times \dfrac{298}{273}$

   (C) $71 \times \dfrac{(2.0)}{(0.478)(298)}$

   (D) $71 \times \dfrac{(0.478)(2.0)}{(0.0821)(298)}$

   (E) $71 \times \dfrac{(0.0821)(298)}{(0.478)(2.0)}$

8. The pressure of 3 L of a gas at 25°C is 800 mm Hg. What is the volume of this gas at standard temperature and pressure?

   (A) $V = 3 \times \dfrac{0}{25} \times \dfrac{800}{760}$

   (B) $V = 3 \times \dfrac{25}{0} \times \dfrac{800}{760}$

   (C) $V = 3 \times \dfrac{273}{298} \times \dfrac{760}{800}$

   (D) $V = 3 \times \dfrac{298}{273} \times \dfrac{760}{800}$

   (E) $V = 3 \times \dfrac{273}{298} \times \dfrac{800}{760}$

9. The pressure of V L of a gas at T K is P. What is the final volume, V_f, of this gas at standard temperature, T_o, and pressure, P_o?

   (A) $V_f = V \times \dfrac{T}{T_o} \times \dfrac{P}{P_o}$

   (B) $V_f = V \times \dfrac{T_o}{T} \times \dfrac{P}{P_o}$

   (C) $V_f = V \times \dfrac{T_o}{T} \times \dfrac{P_o}{P}$

   (D) $V_f = V \times \dfrac{T}{T_o} \times \dfrac{P_o}{P}$

   (E) $V_f = V \times T_o \times P_o$

When gases are mixed together the sum of their individual partial pressures equals the total pressure of the system.

Dalton's Law of Partial Pressures

$$P_{total} = P_1 + P_2 + P_3 + \ldots + P_n$$

$$\frac{P_1}{P_{total}} = \frac{n_1}{n_{total}} \quad , \quad \frac{P_2}{P_{total}} = \frac{n_2}{n_{total}}$$

1. When 4.0 g of $H_2(g)$ and 32.0 g of $O_2(g)$ are combined in a closed vessel at a pressure of 6.0 atm, the partial pressure of hydrogen gas is

   (A) 6.0 atm
   (B) 5.0 atm
   (C) 4.0 atm
   (D) 3.0 atm
   (E) 1.0 atm

① Calculate the number of moles of each gas to determine the total moles of gas.

$$\underline{H_2}$$

$$\frac{2g}{1mol} = \frac{4g}{n_1 mol} \rightarrow n_1 = 2\,mol$$

$$\underline{O_2}$$

$$\frac{32g}{1mol} = \frac{32g}{n_2 mol} \quad n_2 = 1\,mol$$

$$n_{total} = n_1 + n_2 \rightarrow n_{total} = 2 + 1 = 3$$

② $$\frac{H_2}{total} = \frac{P_1}{6atm} = \frac{2mol}{3mol} \rightarrow \boxed{P_1 = 4atm}$$

Effusion and Diffusion

EFFUSION is when a gas moves through a pinhole into a vacuum.

DIFFUSION is when a gas moves from one container into another container that is already occupied by some amount of gas.

Graham's Law of Effusion/Diffusion

$$Rate \propto \frac{1}{\sqrt{molar\ mass(M)}} \quad or \quad \frac{Rate_1}{Rate_2} = \sqrt{\frac{M_2}{M_1}}$$

2. At the same temperature and pressure, which of the following gases has the lowest rate of effusion through a pinhole?

   (A) H_2
   (B) Cl_2
   (C) H_2O
   (D) N_2O
   (E) Xe

   Xe has the highest mass thus the lowest rate.

3. When 1 mol of $H_2(g)$ and 1 mol of $F_2(g)$ are combined in a closed vessel at a pressure of 3.0 atm, the partial pressure of $F_2(g)$ is

   (A) 3.0 atm
   (B) 2.5 atm
   (C) 2.0 atm
   (D) 1.5 atm
   (E) 1.0 atm

4. When 2.0 g of $H_2(g)$ and 16.0 g of $O_2(g)$ are combined in a closed vessel at a pressure of 3.0 atm, the partial pressure of $H_2(g)$ is

   (A) 5.0 atm
   (B) 4.0 atm
   (C) 3.0 atm
   (D) 2.0 atm
   (E) 1.0 atm

5. When 1.0 g of $H_2(g)$ and 14.0 g of $N_2(g)$ are combined in a closed vessel at a pressure of 4.0 atm, the partial pressure of $H_2(g)$ is

   (A) 5.0 atm
   (B) 4.0 atm
   (C) 3.0 atm
   (D) 2.0 atm
   (E) 1.0 atm

6. When 20.0 g of $Ne(g)$ and 88.0 g of $CO_2(g)$ are combined in a closed vessel at a pressure of 6 atm, the partial pressure of $CO_2(g)$ is

   (A) 5.0 atm
   (B) 4.0 atm
   (C) 3.0 atm
   (D) 2.0 atm
   (E) 1.0 atm

7. At standard temperature and pressure, which of the following gases has the lowest rate of effusion through a pinhole?

   (A) He
   (B) Ne
   (C) Ar
   (D) Kr
   (E) Xe

8. At standard temperature and pressure, which of the following gases has the lowest rate of effusion through a pinhole?

   (A) H_2
   (B) F_2
   (C) N_2O
   (D) CO_2
   (E) Kr

9. At standard temperature and pressure, which of the following gases has the highest rate of effusion through a pinhole?

   (A) H_2
   (B) F_2
   (C) N_2O
   (D) CO_2
   (E) Kr

10. Gas A with a molecular mass of 44 g/mol moves through a pinhole alongside gas B, which has a molecular mass of 40 g/mol. Which of the following statements is true concerning the rate of effusion of gases A and B? The gas which has the higher rate of effusion is

   (A) gas A, because it has a higher molecular mass than gas B.
   (B) gas A, because it has a lower molecular mass than gas B.
   (C) gas B, because it has a higher molecular mass than gas A.
   (D) gas B, because it has a lower molecular mass than gas A.
   (E) unable to be determined because the amount of moles of each gas are unknown.

Questions 1-4 refer to the following.

(A) 2 atm
(B) 3 atm
(C) 4 atm
(D) 5 atm
(E) 6 atm

1. The partial pressure of 40% $O_2(g)$ by volume in a 5 atm gas mixture

2. The partial pressure of $H_2(g)$ in a 10 atm mixture containing 2 mol $H_2(g)$ and 8 mol $O_2(g)$

3. The partial pressure of $Cl_2(g)$ in a 6 atm mixture containing 70 g $Cl_2(g)$ and 80 g $Ar(g)$

4. The partial pressure of $Ne(g)$ in a 9 atm mixture containing 14 g $N_2(g)$ and 20 g $Ne(g)$

Questions 5-8 refer to the following.

(A) 1 atm and 273 K
(B) 1 atm and 298 K
(C) 1 atm and 303 K
(D) 2 atm and 273 K
(E) 2 atm and 298 K

5. Standard pressure and room temperature

6. The temperature and pressure at which 1 mole of gas occupies 22.4 L

7. Of the above, the temperature and pressure at which gases exhibit the most ideal behavior

8. Of the above, the temperature and pressure at which gases exhibit the least ideal behavior

101. In a 2 L container at 1 atm holding 1 L of oxygen gas, $O_2(g)$, and 1 L of nitrogen gas, $N_2(g)$, the partial pressure of $O_2(g)$ is 0.5 atm	BECAUSE	Dalton's Law of partial pressures states that the total pressure of a mixture of gases is equal to the sum of the pressures of each gas.
102. He gas has a lower rate of effusion than Ne gas	BECAUSE	according to Graham's Law, the molecular mass of a gas and the rate of effusion are directly proportional.
103. At constant temperature, as the volume of a gas increases the pressure decreases	BECAUSE	according to Boyle's Law, the ratio of the pressure and volume of a gas is constant.
104. At constant volume, as the temperature of a gas decreases the pressure decreases	BECAUSE	according to Gay-Lussac's Law, the product of pressure and temperature is constant.
105. At constant pressure, as the temperature of a gas increases the volume decreases	BECAUSE	according to Charles's Law, the ratio of the volume and temperature of a gas is constant.

9. When 2 mol of $O_2(g)$ and 2 mol of $F_2(g)$ are combined in a closed vessel at a pressure of 3.0 atm, the partial pressure of $O_2(g)$ is

    (A) 3.0 atm
    (B) 2.5 atm
    (C) 2.0 atm
    (D) 1.5 atm
    (E) 1.0 atm

10. At standard temperature and pressure, which of the following gases has the highest rate of effusion through a pinhole?

    (A) He
    (B) Ne
    (C) Ar
    (D) Kr
    (E) Xe

11. Helium gas, He, exhibits *most* ideal behavior under which of the following conditions?

    (A) 273 K and 2 atm
    (B) 273 K and 10 atm
    (C) 300 K and 1 atm
    (D) 400 K and 1 atm
    (E) 400 K and 2 atm

12. The pressure of 1.5 L of a gas at 25°C is 2 atm. What is the volume of this gas at standard temperature and pressure?

    (A) $V = 1.5 \times \dfrac{0}{25} \times \dfrac{2}{1}$

    (B) $V = 1.5 \times \dfrac{25}{0} \times \dfrac{2}{1}$

    (C) $V = 1.5 \times \dfrac{273}{298} \times \dfrac{1}{2}$

    (D) $V = 1.5 \times \dfrac{298}{273} \times \dfrac{1}{2}$

    (E) $V = 1.5 \times \dfrac{273}{298} \times \dfrac{2}{1}$

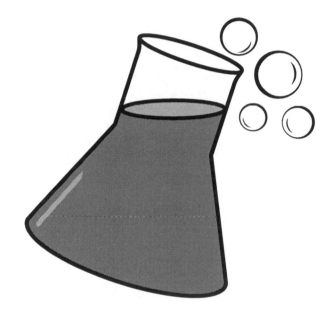

CHAPTER

+5

P

PHASES

As the strength of the intermolecular forces in a system goes up, the amount of order increases, which means a decrease in entropy.

ENTROPY (S) is the degree of disorder in a system.

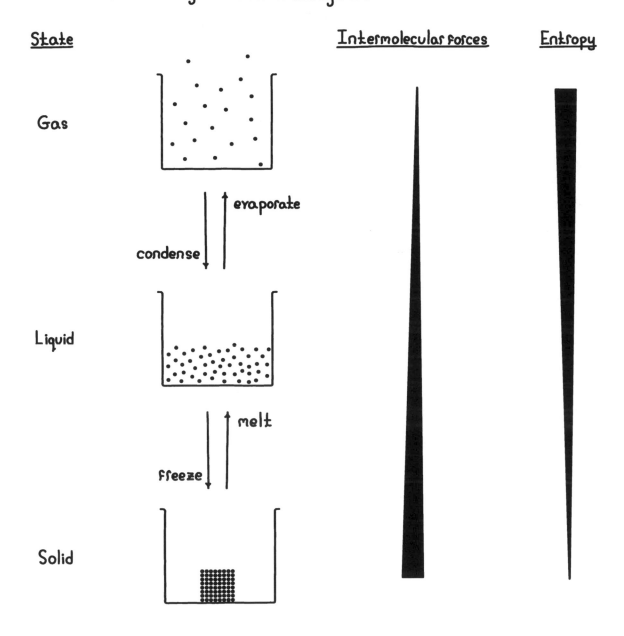

As energy is added to a system, the average kinetic energy (temperature) goes up. At the temperature where a system undergoes freezing and boiling the temperature does not change, however; this accounts for the flat lines where vaporization/condensation and melting/freezing occur.

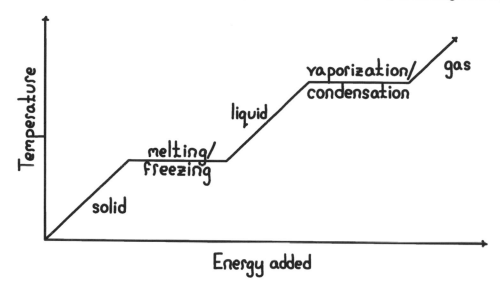

Specific heat

Different substance require differing amounts of energy to change in temperature. Specific heat capacity is used to quantify necessary energy inputs to see certain changes in temperature of various substances.

<u>Specific Heat</u> - The amount of heat, given in calories or joules, required to raise the temperature of 1 gram of a substance 1 degree (Kelvin or celcius).

$$Q = cm\Delta T$$

heat added → Q = cmΔT ← change in temperature

mass

specific heat

For $H_2O(l)$, specific heat capacity, c, equals 1 calorie g^{-1} K^{-1}

Questions 1-5 are based on the following heating curve for a pure substance. The substance begins as a solid and ends as a gas; each segment represents a different process.

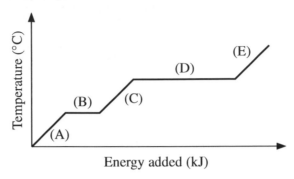

1. Boiling

2. Melting

3. A gas is heated.

4. A liquid is heated.

5. A solid is heated.

Questions 6-10 are based on the following cooling curve for a pure substance. The substance begins as a gas and ends as a solid; each segment represents a different process.

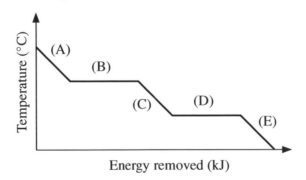

6. Condensing

7. Freezing

8. A solid is cooling.

9. A liquid is cooling.

10. A gas is cooling.

11. Which of the following compounds has the greatest strength in intermolecular forces of attraction?

    (A) $H_2O(g)$
    (B) $N_2(g)$
    (C) $H_2O(l)$
    (D) $Br(l)$
    (E) $H_2O(s)$

12. Which of the following compounds has the lowest strength in intermolecular forces of attraction?

    (A) $H_2O(g)$
    (B) $N_2(g)$
    (C) $H_2O(l)$
    (D) $Br(l)$
    (E) $H_2O(s)$

13. Consider a 2 g sample of $H_2O(l)$ at 25°C. How much energy is needed to raise the temperature to 35°C? (The specific heat of $H_2O(l)$ is 1 calorie $g^{-1}\,°C^{-1}$)

    (A) 20 calories
    (B) 30 calories
    (C) 40 calories
    (D) 50 calories
    (E) 60 calories

14. Which of the following does NOT increase the entropy of a system?

    (A) Evaporating $H_2O(l)$
    (B) Melting $Cu(s)$
    (C) Decomposing $H_2CO_3(aq)$
    (D) Dissolving $C_4H_9OH(l)$ in $H_2O(l)$
    (E) Condensing $H_2O(g)$

15. Which of the following does increase the entropy of a system?

    (A) Evaporating $H_2O(l)$
    (B) Freezing $Cu(s)$
    (C) Formation of $PbI_2(s)$
    (D) Purification of $H_2O(l)$
    (E) Condensing $Cl_2(g)$

16. Consider a 5 g sample of $H_2O(l)$ at 2°C. How much energy is needed to raise the temperature to 42°C? (The specific heat of $H_2O(l)$ is 1 calorie $g^{-1}\,°C^{-1}$)

    (A) 100 calories
    (B) 140 calories
    (C) 180 calories
    (D) 200 calories
    (E) 420 calories

<u>Vapor Pressure</u> -The pressure of the vapor escaping from a liquid.

<u>Boiling Point</u> -An equilibrium point where the vapor pressure is equal to the atmospheric pressure.

	<u>Standard Atmospheric Pressure</u>		<u>Vapor Pressure</u>	<u>Boiling?</u>
Liquid H$_2$O 20°C	760 mmHg	>	17.5 mmHg	Nope
Liquid H$_2$O 50°C	760 mmHg	>	92.5 mmHg	Nope
Liquid H$_2$O 100°C	760 mmHg	=	760 mmHg	YES!

1. Suppose 1 L of $H_2O(l)$ was boiling at standard pressure. If the atmospheric pressure is increased, will the $H_2O(l)$ sample continue to boil?

   (A) Yes, because the atmospheric pressure is now greater than the vapor pressure of the $H_2O(l)$ sample
   (B) No, because the atmospheric pressure is now greater than the vapor pressure of the $H_2O(l)$ sample
   (C) Yes, because the atmospheric pressure is now less than the vapor pressure of the $H_2O(l)$ sample
   (D) No, because the atmospheric pressure is now less than the vapor pressure of the $H_2O(l)$ sample
   (E) The atmospheric pressure does not affect the boiling properties of $H_2O(l)$

2. Suppose 1 L of $H_2O(l)$ was boiling at standard pressure. If the vapor pressure of the $H_2O(l)$ sample were increased by increasing the ambient temperature, will the $H_2O(l)$ sample continue to boil?

   (A) Yes, because the atmospheric pressure is now greater than the vapor pressure of the $H_2O(l)$ sample
   (B) No, because the atmospheric pressure is now greater than the vapor pressure of the $H_2O(l)$ sample
   (C) Yes, because the atmospheric pressure is now less than the vapor pressure of the $H_2O(l)$ sample
   (D) No, because the atmospheric pressure is now less than the vapor pressure of the $H_2O(l)$ sample
   (E) The vapor pressure does not affect the boiling properties of $H_2O(l)$

3. Consider a 2 L container of $H_2O(l)$ at 25°C and 760 mm Hg. If the vapor pressure of the $H_2O(l)$ sample is 23.8 mm Hg, which of the following statements is true? If left untouched, the $H_2O(l)$ sample will

   (A) solidify and form $H_2O(s)$
   (B) boil to $H_2O(g)$
   (C) increase in temperature to a maximum of 90°C
   (D) decrease in temperature to a minimum of 10°C
   (E) not show any chemical or physical change

4. Suppose 1 L of $H_2O(l)$ was boiling at standard pressure. If the atmospheric pressure is decreased, will the $H_2O(l)$ sample continue to boil?

   (A) Yes, because the atmospheric pressure is now greater than the vapor pressure of the $H_2O(l)$ sample
   (B) No, because the atmospheric pressure is now greater than the vapor pressure of the $H_2O(l)$ sample
   (C) Yes, because the atmospheric pressure is now less than the vapor pressure of the $H_2O(l)$ sample
   (D) No, because the atmospheric pressure is now less than the vapor pressure of the $H_2O(l)$ sample
   (E) The atmospheric pressure does not affect the boiling properties of $H_2O(l)$

5. Suppose 1 L of $H_2O(l)$ was boiling at standard pressure. If the vapor pressure of the $H_2O(l)$ sample were decreased by decreasing the ambient temperature, will the $H_2O(l)$ sample continue to boil?

   (A) Yes, because the atmospheric pressure is now greater than the vapor pressure of the $H_2O(l)$ sample
   (B) No, because the atmospheric pressure is now greater than the vapor pressure of the $H_2O(l)$ sample
   (C) Yes, because the atmospheric pressure is now less than the vapor pressure of the $H_2O(l)$ sample
   (D) No, because the atmospheric pressure is now less than the vapor pressure of the $H_2O(l)$ sample
   (E) The vapor pressure does not affect the boiling properties of $H_2O(l)$

6. Consider a 2 L container of $H_2O(l)$ at 100°C and 760 mm Hg. If the vapor pressure of the $H_2O(l)$ sample is 760 mm Hg, which of the following statements is true? If left untouched, the $H_2O(l)$ sample will

   (A) solidify and form $H_2O(s)$
   (B) boil to $H_2O(g)$
   (C) increase in temperature to a maximum of 150°C
   (D) decrease in temperature to a minimum of 50°C
   (E) not show any chemical or physical change

Ionic Solids- When ionic bonds hold a network of ions together.

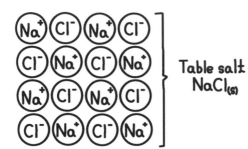

Table salt
NaCl$_{(s)}$

Note: Ionic solids have very high melting and boiling points.

Molecular Solids – When London dispersion forces of hydrogen bonds hold a network of molecules together.

Ice
H$_2$O$_{(s)}$

Note: Most substances are more dense in their solid state; HOWEVER, water must spread out to accommodate every molecules hydrogen bond; therefore ice is less dense than liquid water.

Covalent Network Solids- When covalent bonds hold a network of atoms together.

Diamond
C(diamond)$_{(s)}$

Note: Extremely high temperatures and pressures are required to form these substances.

Metallic Bonds- The transition metals have a very free relationship with their valence electrons. This allows for a sea of delocalized electrons to hold the atoms together like a glue.

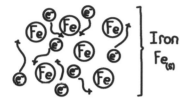

Iron
$Fe_{(s)}$

Note: The freedom of movement the electrons have is what makes metallic solids so good at conducting electricity.

Amorphous Solids –These solids lack an organized pattern. Glass plastic and gels are common examples.

Types of Solids Practice

1. An example of an ionic solid is

    (A) dry ice, CO_2
    (B) zinc sulphide, ZnS
    (C) baking soda, $NaHCO_3$
    (D) bleach (solid), $NaBO_3$
    (E) diamond, C

2. Which of the following elements does NOT exhibit metallic bonding?

    (A) cobalt, Co
    (B) gold, Au
    (C) silver, Ag
    (D) copper, Cu
    (E) phosphorous, P

3. ReB_2, rhenium diboride, has a high melting point because its solid state structure is

    (A) ionic
    (B) metallic
    (C) hydrogen bonded
    (D) nonpolar covalent molecular
    (E) covalent network

4. An example of a molecular solid is

    (A) dry ice, CO_2
    (B) zinc sulphide, ZnS
    (C) baking soda, $NaHCO_3$
    (D) potassium bromide, KBr
    (E) diamond, C

5. An example of a network solid is

    (A) bleach (solid), $NaBO_3$
    (B) dry ice, CO_2
    (C) baking soda, $NaHCO_3$
    (D) hydrogen bromide, HBr
    (E) diamond, C

6. CO_2, carbon dioxide, has a low melting point because its structure is

    (A) ionic
    (B) metallic
    (C) hydrogen bonded
    (D) nonpolar covalent molecular
    (E) covalent network

Questions 1-4 refer to the following.

  (A) Boiling
  (B) Condensation
  (C) Enthalpy
  (D) Freezing
  (E) Entropy

1. The process where $H_2O(l)$ is changed to $H_2O(s)$

2. The process where $H_2O(l)$ is changed to $H_2O(g)$

3. The measure of disorder of a system

4. An example of an increase in potential energy and disorder during a phase change

Questions 5-9 refer to the following terms.

  (A) Ionic substance
  (B) Metallic substance
  (C) Polar covalent molecule
  (D) Nonpolar covalent molecule
  (E) Network solid

5. caesium, Cs

6. sulfur trioxide, SO_3

7. diamond, C

8. baking soda, $NaHCO_3$

9. gold, Au

101. As the temperature of a system increases, the entropy, S, of the system also increases   BECAUSE   the amount of disorder of a system is directly proportional to the average kinetic energy of the particles.

102. As the temperature of a system increases, the strength of the intermolecular forces between molecules increases   BECAUSE   the strength of intermolecular forces is directly proportional to the average kinetic energy of the particles.

103. If the atmospheric pressure is greater than the vapor pressure of the liquid, the liquid will boil   BECAUSE   the molecules of a liquid overcome forces of attractions between one another to enter the vapor phase.

104. Network solids are formed when London dispersion forces hold a network together   BECAUSE   London dispersion forces are necessary for bonds between molecules of solid substances.

10. An example of a network solid is

  (A) dry ice, CO_2
  (B) iodine, I_2
  (C) baking soda, $NaHCO_3$
  (D) bleach (solid), $NaBO_3$
  (E) diamond, C

11. Which of the following compounds has the greatest strength in intermolecular forces of attraction?

  (A) $H_2O(g)$
  (B) $H_2O(s)$
  (C) $O_2(g)$
  (D) $Hg(l)$
  (E) $Br(l)$

12. Which of the following does NOT increase the entropy of a system?

    (A) Melting $Ag(s)$
    (B) Decomposing $H_2CO_3(aq)$
    (C) Condensing $H_2O(g)$
    (D) Dissolving $NH_3(g)$ in $H_2O(l)$
    (E) Evaporating $Br_2(l)$

13. Consider a 1 L container of $H_2O(l)$ at 98°C and 760 mm Hg. If the vapor pressure of the $H_2O(l)$ sample is 760 mm Hg, which of the following statements is true? If left untouched, the $H_2O(l)$ sample will

    (A) solidify and form $H_2O(s)$
    (B) boil to $H_2O(g)$
    (C) increase in temperature to a maximum of 150°C
    (D) decrease in temperature to a minimum of 50°C
    (E) not show any chemical or physical change

14. Which of the following statements about a liquid, such as ethanol, that readily evaporates at 25°C is correct?

    (A) The liquid has a low vapor pressure.
    (B) The liquid should be stored in a clear container.
    (C) The liquid is considered to be nonvolatile.
    (D) The liquid would make a container feel cold to the touch.
    (E) The liquid has weak intermolecular forces.

15. Consider a 1 L sample of N_2, initially at standard temperature and pressure. A rise in temperature would cause an increase in all of the following EXCEPT the

    (A) mass of the N_2 in the sample
    (B) average kinetic energy of the N_2 molecules in the sample
    (C) average velocity of the N_2 molecules in the sample
    (D) vapor pressure of the N_2 in the sample
    (E) volume of the N_2 sample

Chapter +6

(aq)

Solutions

Solvent: A substance (usually a liquid) that allows for the uniform suspension of a solute to form a solution.

$+$

Solute: A substance that is uniformly suspended in a solvent to form a solution.

Solution: The uniform suspension of a solute in a solvent

Note: When dissolving solutes into solvents, they must have similar polarity characteristics: polar dissolves polar; nonpolar dissolves nonpolar.

Some descriptive terms for solutions-

Concentrated: When there is a relatively large amount of solute to solvent.

Dilute: When there is a relatively small amount of solute to solvent.

Some quantitative terms for solutions-

Unsaturated: When a given amount of solution can dissolve more solute.

Saturated: When a given amount of solution has dissolved exactly as much solute as it can accommodate: a solution at equilibrium.

Supersaturated: When a solution is tricked into holding additional solute passed its typical point of saturation. This can be done by heating a saturated solution, adding additional solute, then bringing the temperature back down.

How to measure concentration

Molarity(M): $\dfrac{\text{moles solute}}{\text{volume of solvent(L)}}$

Molality(m): $\dfrac{\text{moles solute}}{\text{mass of solvent(Kg)}}$

1. An aqueous solution containing 30% by mass sodium chloride, NaCl, is stored in a 1 L beaker. Which substance, NaCl or H_2O, if either, in the solution is considered the solvent?

    (A) NaCl, because the sodium chloride is dissolved in H_2O
    (B) NaCl, because H_2O dissolves in sodium chloride
    (C) H_2O, because the sodium chloride is dissolved in H_2O
    (D) H_2O, because H_2O dissolves in sodium chloride
    (E) Neither substance can be considered a solvent

2. An aqueous solution containing 10% by mass sodium chloride, KCl, is stored in a 1 L beaker. Which substance, KCl or H_2O, if either, in the solution is considered the solute?

    (A) KCl, because the potassium chloride is dissolved in H_2O
    (B) KCl, because H_2O dissolves in potassium chloride
    (C) H_2O, because the potassium chloride is dissolved in H_2O
    (D) H_2O, because H_2O dissolves in potassium chloride
    (E) Neither substance can be considered a solvent

3. 5 g of magnesium sulfate, $MgSO_4$, is added to a beaker containing 2 L of benzene, C_6H_6, a non-polar substance. Which of the following is most likely to occur?

    (A) The C_6H_6 will evaporate off
    (B) The $MgSO_4$ will react violently with C_6H_6
    (C) All of the $MgSO_4$ will dissolve into solution with C_6H_6
    (D) Most of the $MgSO_4$ will dissolve into solution with C_6H_6
    (E) None of the $MgSO_4$ will dissolve into solution with C_6H_6

4. At 50°C, 50 g of ammonium chloride, NH_4Cl, in 100 g of H_2O forms a saturated solution. Which of the following quantities of NH_4Cl, when dissolved in 100 g of H_2O at 50°C, would form a supersaturated solution?

    (A) 20 g
    (B) 30 g
    (C) 40 g
    (D) 50 g
    (E) 60 g

5. At 50°C, 80 g of potassium nitrate, KNO_3, in 100 g of H_2O forms a saturated solution. Which of the following quantities of KNO_3, when dissolved in 100 g of H_2O at 50°C, would form a unsaturated solution?

    (A) 70 g
    (B) 80 g
    (C) 90 g
    (D) 100 g
    (E) 110 g

6. At 80°C, 50 g of potassium chloride, KCl, in 100 g of H_2O forms a saturated solution. Which of the following quantities of KCl, when dissolved in 200 g of H_2O at 80°C, would form a saturated solution?

    (A) 60 g
    (B) 80 g
    (C) 100 g
    (D) 120 g
    (E) 140 g

7. A 2 L aqueous saturated solution at 25°C and 1 atm of NH_4Cl is present in a beaker. Which of the following procedures can result in a supersaturated solution?

    (A) Raising the temperature of the solution to 30°C, adding additional NH_4Cl, then cooling back to 25°C
    (B) Raising the temperature of the solution to 30°C, then cooling back to 25°C
    (C) Raising the pressure of the solution to 1.2 atm, then lowering back to 1 atm
    (D) Lowering the pressure of the solution to 0.7 atm, then raising back to 1 atm
    (E) Adding additional NH_4Cl to the aqueous solution

As temperature increases the solubility of most substances increases.

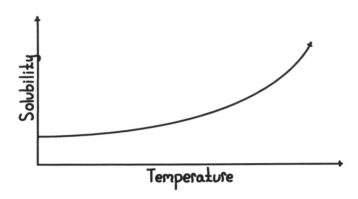

*However, gases dissolve more readily into liquids under high pressures and **low temperatures**

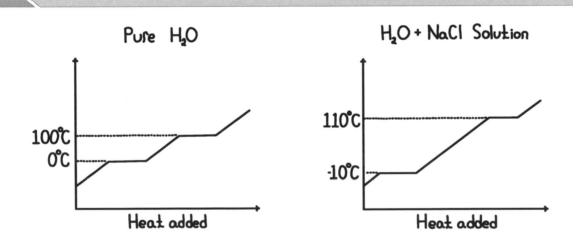

The addition of NaCl to the liquid H_2O increases the boiling point and reduces the freezing point.

To determine the exact freezing point depression or boiling point elevation the following equations can be used.

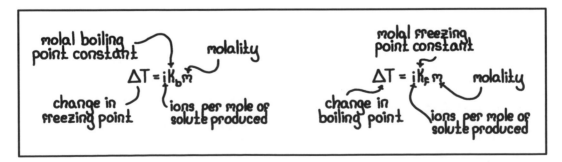

1. As the temperature of a solution increases, the quantity of solute that can be dissolved typically

   (A) increases only
   (B) decreases only
   (C) increases, then decreases
   (D) decreases, then increases
   (E) remains relatively constant

2. As the temperature of a solution decreases, the quantity of solute that can be dissolved typically

   (A) increases only
   (B) decreases only
   (C) increases, then decreases
   (D) decreases, then increases
   (E) remains relatively constant

3. As the pressure of a solution increases, the quantity of solute that can be dissolved typically

   (A) increases only
   (B) decreases only
   (C) increases, then decreases
   (D) decreases, then increases
   (E) remains relatively constant

4. Which of the following could be performed to an aqueous solution of magnesium nitrate, $Mg(NO_3)_2$, to increase its boiling point?

   (A) Removing some of the magnesium nitrate solute
   (B) Adding additional magnesium nitrate solute
   (C) Increasing the ambient temperature
   (D) Decreasing the ambient temperature
   (E) Increasing the ambient pressure

5. A beaker contains 3 L of H_2O at standard pressure. If 10 g of NaCl is added to the beaker, which of the following could be a result?

   (A) The NaCl will sink to the bottom of the beaker
   (B) The pressure of the solution will increase
   (C) The boiling point of the solution will be higher than 100°C
   (D) The boiling point of the solution will be lower than 100°C
   (E) The freezing point of the solution will be higher than 0°C

6. A beaker contains 10 L of H_2O at standard pressure. If 2 g of KCl is added to the beaker, which of the following could be a result?

   (A) The KCl will react with the H_2O to form a gas
   (B) The pressure of the solution will decrease
   (C) The boiling point of the solution will be lower than 100°C
   (D) The freezing point of the solution will be lower than 0°C
   (E) The freezing point of the solution will be higher than 0°C

7. Consider a flask containing 1,000 g of pure water at 25°C. How would the boiling point of the water change if 1 mole of CH_3OH were added to the flask? (The K_b value for H_2O is 0.5 °C m^{-1}) The boiling point of the water would:

   (A) increase by 0.5°C
   (B) increase by 1°C
   (C) increase by 2°C
   (D) decrease by 1°C
   (E) decrease by 2°C

8. Consider a flask containing 1,000 g of pure water at 25°C. How would the freezing point of the water change if 1 mole of NaF were added to the flask? (The K_f value for H_2O is 1.86 °C m^{-1}) The freezing point of the water would:

   (A) increase by 1.86°C
   (B) increase by 3.72°C
   (C) increase by 5.58°C
   (D) decrease by 1.86°C
   (E) decrease by 3.72°C

9. Consider a flask containing 1,000 g of pure water at 25°C. How would the boiling point of the water change if 1 mole of HCl were added to the flask? (The K_b value for H_2O is 0.5 °C m^{-1}) The boiling point of the water would:

   (A) increase by 0.5°C
   (B) increase by 1°C
   (C) increase by 2°C
   (D) decrease by 1°C
   (E) decrease by 2°C

Questions 1-5 refer to the following terms.

(A) Dilute
(B) Concentrated
(C) Unsaturated
(D) Saturated
(E) Supersaturated

1. A chemical solution containing the maximum concentration of a solute dissolved in solvent

2. A chemical solution containing more than the maximum concentration of a solute dissolved in solvent

3. A chemical solution containing less than the maximum concentration of a solute dissolved in solvent

4. A relative high quantity of solute compared to solvent

5. A relative low quantity of solute compared to solvent

Questions 6-8 refer to the following terms.

(A) Boiling point
(B) Freezing point
(C) Solubility
(D) Molarity
(E) Molality

6. Directly related to the concentration of solute in an aqueous solution

7. Inversely related to the concentration of solute in an aqueous solution

8. The ability for a given substance or solute to dissolve in a another given substance or solvent

101. Adding additional solvent to a saturated solution will result in a dilute solution | BECAUSE | the ratio of solute to solvent determines saturation.

102. A concentrated solution is also typically considered to be supersaturated | BECAUSE | the ratio of solute to solvent is relativity high in concentrated solutions.

103. The freezing point of a dilute solution of salt in water is higher than the freezing point of pure water | BECAUSE | the freezing point of pure sugar is lower than the freezing point of pure water.

104. The boiling point of liquid water, $H_2O(l)$, is lower than that of a 0.2 M solution of potassium sulfate, K_2SO_4, | BECAUSE | the boiling point of water increases proportionally to the number of dissolved ions.

9. Of the following solutions, which has the highest freezing point?

    (A) 2 *m* fructose, $C_6H_{12}O_6$
    (B) 2 *m* sodium chloride, NaCl
    (C) 2 *m* magnesium chloride, $MgCl_2$
    (D) 2 *m* boron floride, BF_3
    (E) 2 *m* acetic acid, $HC_2H_3O_2$

10. Of the following solutions, which has the highest boiling point?

    (A) 2 *M* fructose, $C_6H_{12}O_6$
    (B) 2 *M* sodium chloride, NaCl
    (C) 2 *M* magnesium chloride, $MgCl_2$
    (D) 2 *M* boron floride, BF_3
    (E) 2 *M* acetic acid, $HC_2H_3O_2$

11. Which of the following aqueous solutions has the highest boiling point?

    (A) 0.10 *M* KCl
    (B) 0.10 *M* $CaCl_2$
    (C) 0.20 *M* NaBr
    (D) 0.20 *M* K_2SO_4
    (E) 0.20 *M* $HC_2H_3O_2$

12. Which of the following aqueous solutions has the highest freezing point?

    (A) 0.10 *m* KCl
    (B) 0.10 *m* $CaCl_2$
    (C) 0.20 *m* NaBr
    (D) 0.20 *m* K_2SO_4
    (E) 0.20 *m* $HC_2H_3O_2$

13. Suppose 1 mol of NaCl is dissolved in 1,000 g of H_2O at standard temperature and pressure. The resulting boiling point increase would be identical if 1 mol of which other substance was added instead of NaCl?

    (A) $HC_2H_3O_2$
    (B) $CaCl_2$
    (C) C_2H_5OH
    (D) $Mg(NO_3)_2$
    (E) Na_2SO_4

14. Suppose 1 mol of NaCl is dissolved in 1,000 g of H_2O at standard temperature and pressure. The resulting boiling point increase is greater than if 1 mol of which other substance was added instead of NaCl?

    (A) KCl
    (B) $CaCl_2$
    (C) C_2H_5OH
    (D) $NaNO_3$
    (E) Na_2SO_4

15. Suppose 1 mol of $C_6H_{12}O_6$ is dissolved in 1,000 g of H_2O at standard temperature and pressure. The resulting boiling point increase would be exactly three times as great if 1 mol of which other substance was added instead of $C_6H_{12}O_6$?

    (A) KCl
    (B) $CaCl_2$
    (C) C_2H_5OH
    (D) $NaNO_3$
    (E) Na_2SO_4

16. Consider a flask containing 1,000 g of pure water at 25°C. How would the freezing point of the water change if 1 mole of KCl were added to the flask? (The K_f value for H_2O is 1.86 °C m^{-1}) The freezing point of the water would:

    (A) increase by 1.86°C
    (B) increase by 3.72°C
    (C) increase by 5.58°C
    (D) decrease by 1.86°C
    (E) decrease by 3.72°C

17. Consider a flask containing 1,000 g of pure water at 25°C. How would the boiling point of the water change if 1 mole of KCl were added to the flask? (The K_b value for H_2O is 0.5 °C m^{-1}) The boiling point of the water would:

    (A) increase by 0.5°C
    (B) increase by 1°C
    (C) increase by 2°C
    (D) decrease by 1°C
    (E) decrease by 2°C

CHAPTER +7

k[A]

REACTION RATES

<u>Factors that affect the rate at which a reaction occurs:</u>

1) <u>Bond Type</u>-The nature of the bonds that must be broken/formed for the reaction to occur.

2) <u>Surface Area</u>-Increasing surface area will speed up a reaction.

-Chewing food makes it easier for stomach acid to break the food down, because it increase the surface area of the food.

 <u>break apart</u>

3) <u>Concentratration</u>- Higher concentrations of reactants will result in reactions occuring more quickly.

 <u>double concentration</u>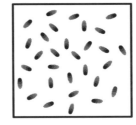

4) <u>Temperature</u>- Higher temperature tends to increase the reaction rate. Higher Kinetic energy increases molecule collision rate which increases reaction rate.

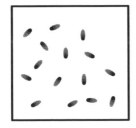 <u>raise temperature</u>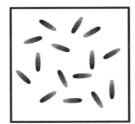

5) <u>Catalysts</u>- Catalysts are substances that create a more expedient pathway for reactions to occur, increasing reaction rate. Catalysts are not used up in the reaction.

For catalysts, see the next section for a more visual explanation

1. As the temperature surrounding a reaction increases, the rate of reaction

   (A) increases only
   (B) decreases only
   (C) increases, then decreases
   (D) decreases, then increases
   (E) remains relatively constant

2. As the surface area of the reactants increase, the rate of reaction

   (A) increases only
   (B) decreases only
   (C) increases, then decreases
   (D) decreases, then increases
   (E) remains relatively constant

3. As the concentration of the reactants decrease, the rate of reaction

   (A) increases only
   (B) decreases only
   (C) increases, then decreases
   (D) decreases, then increases
   (E) remains relatively constant

4. As the pressure surrounding a non-gaseous reaction decreases, the rate of reaction

   (A) increases only
   (B) decreases only
   (C) increases, then decreases
   (D) decreases, then increases
   (E) remains relatively constant

5. Vanadium oxide is a catalyst used for the oxidation of sulfur dioxide, SO_2, to sulfur trioxide, SO_3. Which of the following statements is most likely true of this oxidation process?

   (A) Vanadium oxide is chemically altered into a different substance
   (B) Sulfur dioxide loses oxygen atoms
   (C) Vanadium oxide is not chemically altered
   (D) The oxidation occurs slower due to the presence of vanadium oxide
   (E) The temperature of the container increases during oxidation

6. The Haber process is a synthesis reaction that products ammonia, NH_3, by reacting hydrogen gas, H_2, and N_2. Which of the following procedural steps would decrease the rate of production of NH_3?

   (A) Adding 50% more H_2 to the reaction chamber
   (B) Adding 50% more N_2 to the reaction chamber
   (C) Introducing an inert catalyst to the system
   (D) Increasing the temperature of the reaction chamber by $10°C$
   (E) Decreasing the temperature of the reaction chamber by $10°C$

<u>Activation Energy</u>- The energy required to cause a reaction to proceed forward.

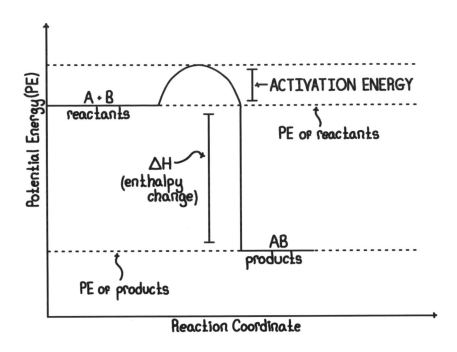

What happens when we add a catalyst?

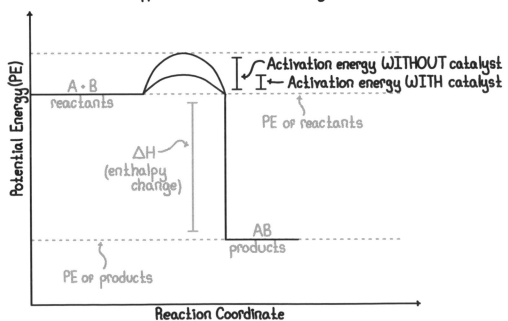

Activation Energy and Catalysts—*Practice*

Questions 1-5 refer to the following energy diagram.

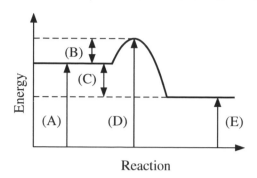

1. Energy of the reactants

2. Energy of the products

3. Heat of formation of the reaction

4. Activation energy of the forward reaction

5. Energy of the activated complex

How do we actually quantify the rate of a rate of a reaction, though?

-The rate of a reaction is proportional to the product of the concentration of the reactants and can typically be generalized in the following way.

$$2A + B \rightarrow 3D + 2C$$

proportionality
constant

coefficients in front
of A&B

$$Rate = K[A]^2[B]^1$$

concentrations of
A & B

Determining rate law with data

The rate law that is assumed using the coefficients in front of the reactions can be checked against experimental data in the following way.

Trial	[A]	[B]	Rate(M/s)
1	1.0	1.0	2.0×10^{-7}
2	1.0	2.0	2.1×10^{-7}
3	2.0	1.0	8.0×10^{-7}

① Nothing happens from trial 1 to 2 when [B] is doubled, so our rate law should reflect that [B] has no effect on the reaction rate.

$$Rate = K[A]^2[B]^0$$

② When [A] is doubled from trial 1 to 3 the rate gets multiplied by 4, so the rate law should reflect that the rate changes by a factor equal to the square of the change in [A].

$$Rate = K[A]^2[B]^0$$
$$rate\ law = K[A]^2[B]^0$$
$$reaction\ order = 2 + 0 = 2$$

This is a second order reaction.

$$A + 3B \rightarrow 2C$$

1. Consider the theoretical chemical reaction above. Which of the following expressions represents the reaction rate?

   (A) $k[C]^2$
   (B) $k[A][C]^2$
   (C) $k[A]^2[B]$
   (D) $k[A][B]^3$
   (E) $k[A]^2[B]^2$

$$3H_2 + N_2 \rightarrow 2NH_3$$

2. The chemical reaction shown above is called the Haber process. Which of the following expressions represents the reaction rate law for the Haber process?

   (A) $k[NH_3]^2$
   (B) $k[H_2][NH_3]^2$
   (C) $k[H_2]^2[N_2]$
   (D) $k[H_2]^3[N_2]$
   (E) $k[H_2]^3[N_2]^2$

$$CO_2 + 4H_2 \rightarrow CH_4 + 2H_2O$$

3. The chemical reaction shown above is called the Sabatier process. Which of the following expressions represents the reaction rate law for the Sabatier process?

   (A) $k[CO_2][H_2]^4$
   (B) $k[CH_4][H_2O]^2$
   (C) $k[CO_2]^2[H_2]^4$
   (D) $k[CH_4]^4[H_2O]^2$
   (E) $k[CO_2][H_2O]^2$

4. Consider a chemical reaction with $NO(g)$ and $H_2(g)$ reactants. Data for this reaction is shown below:

Trial	[NO]	[H₂]	Rate (M/s)
1	0.1	0.1	1.0×10^{-2}
2	0.2	0.1	1.0×10^{-2}
3	0.2	0.2	2.0×10^{-2}

What order is the reaction based on the data?

   (A) Zeroth-order reaction
   (B) First-order reaction
   (C) Second-order reaction
   (D) Third-order reaction
   (E) Fourth-order reaction

5. Consider a chemical reaction with $H_2(g)$ and $CO_2(g)$ reactants. Data for this reaction is shown below:

Trial	[CO₂]	[H₂]	Rate (M/s)
1	0.1	0.1	1.0×10^{-2}
2	0.2	0.1	4.0×10^{-2}
3	0.2	0.2	1.6×10^{-1}

What order is the reaction based on the data?

   (A) Zeroth-order reaction
   (B) First-order reaction
   (C) Second-order reaction
   (D) Third-order reaction
   (E) Fourth-order reaction

6. Consider a chemical reaction with $HCl(aq)$ and $NaOH(aq)$ reactants. Data for this reaction is shown below:

Trial	[HCl]	[NaOH]	Rate (M/s)
1	0.1	0.1	1.0×10^{-3}
2	0.2	0.1	2.0×10^{-3}
3	0.2	0.2	4.0×10^{-3}

What order is the reaction based on the data?

   (A) Zeroth-order reaction
   (B) First-order reaction
   (C) Second-order reaction
   (D) Third-order reaction
   (E) Fourth-order reaction

Questions 1-5 refer to the following terms.

    (A) Surface area
    (B) Catalyst
    (C) Potential energy
    (D) Activation energy
    (E) Reaction rate

1. Often expressed in amount per unit volume per time

2. Inert substance which increases reaction rate

3. The space where effective collisions can occur between reactants

4. Stored energy in chemical bonds within a substance

5. The quantity of energy needed to begin a reaction from its starting energy

Questions 6-10 refer to the following energy diagram.

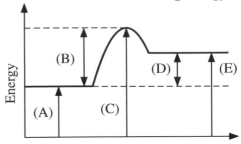

6. Energy of the reactants

7. Energy of the products

8. Heat of formation of the reaction

9. Activation energy of the forward reaction

10. Energy of the activated complex

---

101. Decreasing the surface area of the reactants will increase the rate of reaction   BECAUSE   surface area is measured in spacial units cubed.

102. Introducing a catalyst to a reaction will result in a faster production of products   BECAUSE   catalysts are inert substances that are not chemically altered.

103. The activation energy of a reaction is the difference between the energy of the activated complex and the energy of the products   BECAUSE   the potential energy of a compound is the sum of all bond energies contained within the compound.

104. The potential energy of the products equals the potential energy of the reactants plus the activation energy   BECAUSE   in an exothermic reaction energy is released and overall energy is conserved.

105. Increasing the temperature of a reaction chamber will increase the rate of reaction   BECAUSE   molecules will move faster and increase the quantity of effective collisions per unit time.

106. In a reaction of hydrochloric acid, $HCl(aq)$, with magnesium solid, $Mg(s)$, crushed magnesium solid will react faster than blocks of magnesium solid   BECAUSE   crushed $Mg(s)$ has a larger surface area than blocks of $Mg(s)$, which allows for more locations for reaction collisions.

Questions 11-14 are based on the Sabatier reaction.
The Sabatier reaction occurs at elevated temperatures of 300-400°C in the presence of a Ni catalyst.

$$CO_2 + H_2 \rightarrow CH_4 + 2H_2O$$

11. Which of the following procedural steps would NOT increase the rate of production of CH_4?

    (A) Introducing an inert catalyst to the system
    (B) Adding 50% more CO_2 to the reaction chamber
    (C) Adding 50% more H_2 to the reaction chamber
    (D) Increasing the temperature of the reaction chamber by 10°C
    (E) Decreasing the temperature of the reaction chamber by 10°C

12. Which of the following is most likely to happen to the Ni catalyst as a result of the experiment? The Ni will

    (A) dissolve into the water product
    (B) be oxidized to form NiO
    (C) react with CH_4 and ignite
    (D) melt in the presence of H_2
    (E) not be chemically altered

13. A student is conducting an experiment and chooses the Sabatier process. Which of the following temperatures within the optimal range will yield the slowest reaction rate?

    (A) 300°C
    (B) 320°C
    (C) 340°C
    (D) 350°C
    (E) 370°C

14. The ΔH of the Sabatier process is −165.0 kJ/mol. Based on this value, which of the following statements is true? The energy of the

    (A) reactants is greater than the energy of the products
    (B) reactants is less than the energy of the products
    (C) reactants is greater than the activation energy
    (D) activated complex is less than the energy of the products
    (E) products is less than the activation energy

15. The activation energy of a reaction is best described by which of the following?

    (A) The initial amount of energy held within the reactants
    (B) The highest energy total throughout a reaction
    (C) The additional amount of energy needed to start a reaction
    (D) The difference in energy between the energy of the products and the energy of the reactions
    (E) The difference between the total amount of energy needed to start a reaction with, and without, a catalyst

16. Which of the following about catalysts is true? Catalysts

    (A) decrease the value of equilibrium
    (B) decrease the concentration of the reactants
    (C) are permanently altered during the chemical reaction
    (D) decrease the amount of product present at equilibrium
    (E) reduce the activation energy of the chemical reaction

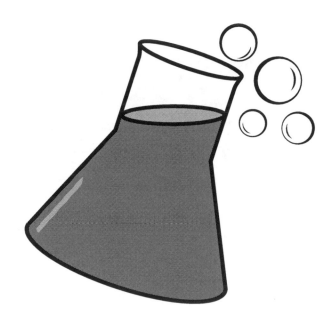

CHAPTER +8

Keq

EQUILIBRIUM

When reactions occur, they happen in both the forward and reverse direction.

$$AB \rightleftharpoons A \cdot B$$

$$\left.\begin{array}{l} AB \rightarrow A \cdot B \\ A \cdot B \rightarrow AB \end{array}\right\}$$ Both occur. Depending on the conditions one reaction may occur more quickly giving the appearance of only one occuring

Saturation is a form of DYNAMIC EQUILIBRIUM. Dynamic equilibrium is the point at which the rate of the forward reaction is the same as the reverse.

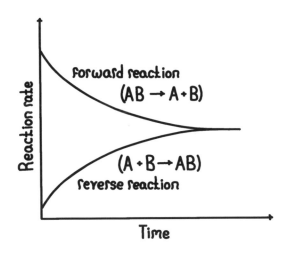

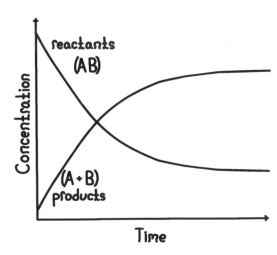

<u>Equilibrium Constant</u>: The equilibrium constant (K_c) is the number that expresses the relative concentrations of products and reactants at equilibrium.

$$\text{reactants} \rightleftharpoons \text{products}$$

$$K_c = \frac{\text{products}}{\text{reactants}}$$

$$2A + B \rightleftharpoons C + 2D$$

$$K_c = \frac{[C][D]^2}{[A]^2[B]}$$

$[A]^2$ represents the concentration of A. It is taken to the second power because there is a coefficient of 2 in front of A in the balanced reaction.

<u>Solubility Product</u>: The solubility product (K_{sp}) is the equilibrium constant for a solid dissolving into an aqueous solution.

$$AB_{(s)} \rightleftharpoons A_{(aq)} + B_{(aq)}$$

$$K_{sp} = [A][B]$$

<u>Note</u>- The concentration of AB is absent in the expression. Pure solids and pure liquids are excluded from equilibrium constants.

$$A(aq) + B(aq) \rightleftarrows C(aq) + D(aq)$$

1. Which of the following is the correct expression for the equilibrium constant, K_c, for the reaction represented above?

   (A) $[C][D]$

   (B) $\dfrac{[C][D]}{[A][B]}$

   (C) $\dfrac{[A][B]}{[C][D]}$

   (D) $\dfrac{[C]+[D]}{[A][B]}$

   (E) $\dfrac{[A]+[B]}{[C][D]}$

$$A_2(aq) + B(aq) \rightleftarrows C(aq) + D_3(aq)$$

2. Which of the following is the correct expression for the equilibrium constant, K_c, for the reaction represented above?

   (A) $[C][D]^3$

   (B) $\dfrac{[C][D_3]}{[A_2][B]}$

   (C) $\dfrac{[A_2][B]}{[C][D_3]}$

   (D) $\dfrac{[C][D]^3}{[A]^2[B]}$

   (E) $\dfrac{[A]^2[B]}{[C][D]^3}$

$$2\,A(aq) + B(aq) \rightleftarrows C(aq) + 3\,D(aq)$$

3. Which of the following is the correct expression for the equilibrium constant, K_{eq}, for the reaction represented above?

   (A) $[C][D]^3$

   (B) $\dfrac{[C][D]}{[A][B]}$

   (C) $\dfrac{[A][B]}{[C][D]}$

   (D) $\dfrac{[C][D]^3}{[A]^2[B]}$

   (E) $\dfrac{[A]^2[B]}{[C][D]^3}$

$$2\,A(s) + B_3(l) \rightleftarrows 4\,C(aq) + 3\,D(aq)$$

4. Which of the following is the correct expression for the equilibrium constant, K_{eq}, for the reaction represented above?

   (A) $[C]^4[D]^3$

   (B) $\dfrac{[C][D]}{[A]^2[B]}$

   (C) $\dfrac{[A][B]}{[C][D]}$

   (D) $\dfrac{[C]^4[D]^3}{[A]^2[B]^3}$

   (E) $\dfrac{[A]^2[B]^3}{[C]^4[D]^3}$

$$N_2(g) + 3\,H_2(g) \rightleftarrows 2\,NH_3(g)$$

5. Which of the following is the correct expression for the equilibrium constant, K_p, for the reaction represented above?

(A) $[NH_3]^2$

(B) $\dfrac{[NH_3]^2}{[N_2]\,[H_2]^3}$

(C) $\dfrac{[NH_3]^2}{[N_2]\,[H_2]}$

(D) $\dfrac{[NH_3]}{[N_2]\,[H_2]^3}$

(E) $\dfrac{[NH_3]}{[N_2]\,[H_2]}$

$$2\,SO_3(g) \rightleftarrows 2\,SO_2(g) + O_2(g)$$

7. Which of the following is the correct expression for the equilibrium constant, K_p, for the reaction represented above?

(A) $[SO_2]^2\,[O_2]$

(B) $\dfrac{[SO_2]\,[O_2]}{[SO_3]}$

(C) $\dfrac{[SO_2]^2\,[O_2]}{[SO_3]}$

(D) $\dfrac{[SO_2]^2\,[O_2]}{[SO_3]^2}$

(E) $\dfrac{[SO_2]\,[O_2]}{[SO_3]^2}$

6. Suppose the molar concentration of Na^+ ions in a 1 L saturated water solution of sodium chloride at 298 K was measured to be 1.0×10^{-1}. What is the value of K_{sp} for sodium chloride?

(A) 1.0×10^{-1}
(B) 1.0×10^{-2}
(C) 1.0×10^{-3}
(D) 2.0×10^{-1}
(E) 2.0×10^{-2}

8. Suppose the molar concentration of Mg^{2+} ions in a 1 L saturated water solution of magnesium chloride at 298 K was measured to be 1.0×10^{-1}. What is the value of K_{sp} for magnesium chloride?

(A) 1.0×10^{-1}
(B) 2.0×10^{-2}
(C) 4.0×10^{-3}
(D) 1.0×10^{-4}
(E) 2.0×10^{-4}

Le Châtelier's Principle: This principle states that when a system in equilibrium has a change applied to it, it will respond by restoring equilibrium.

What happens when concentration is changed?

1) $A + B \rightleftharpoons C + D$

1) At equilibrium.

2)

2) Add C to the system.

$A + B \rightleftharpoons C + D$

3) $A + B \rightleftharpoons C + D$

3) The rate of the reverse reaction will temporarily increase to restore the necessary relative concentrations.

4) $A + B \rightleftharpoons C + D$

4) Equilibrium restored.

---

1) $A + B \rightleftharpoons C + D$

1) At equilibrium.

2)

2) Add B to the system.

$A + B \rightleftharpoons C + D$

3) $A + B \rightleftharpoons C + D$

3) The rate of the forward reaction will temporarily increase to restore the necessary relative concentrations.

4) $A + B \rightleftharpoons C + D$

4) Equilibrium restored.

What happens when heat is added?

Exothermic

1) $A + B \rightleftharpoons C + Heat$

2) $A + B \rightleftharpoons C + Heat$

3) $A + B \rightleftharpoons C + Heat$

4) $A + B \rightleftharpoons C + Heat$

1) At equilibrium.

2) Add heat to the system.

3) The rate of the reverse reaction will temporarily increase to restore the necessary relative concentrations.

4) Equilibrium restored.

Endothermic

1) $Heat + B \rightleftharpoons C + D$

2) $Heat + B \rightleftharpoons C + D$

3) $Heat + B \rightleftharpoons C + D$

4) $Heat + B \rightleftharpoons C + D$

1) At equilibrium.

2) Add heat to the system.

3) The rate of the forward reaction will temporarily increase to restore the necessary relative concentrations.

4) Equilibrium restored.

What happens when volume is changed in a gaseous system?

1)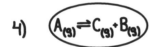

1) At equilibrium

2)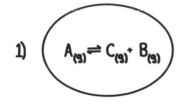

2) Decrease volume.

3)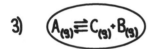

3) The system gets crowded, so the rate of the reverse reaction will increase and push the concentration toward the side with fewer moles of gas.

4)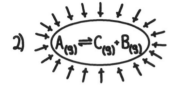

4) Equilibrium restored.

---

1)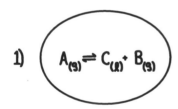

1) At equilibrium

2)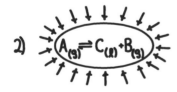

2) Decrease volume.

3)

3) Nothing happens because there are equal moles of gas on each side.

$$A(aq) + B(aq) \leftrightharpoons C(aq) + D(aq)$$

1. Suppose the chemical equation above is at equilibrium. If additional $A(aq)$ is added to the system, the equilibrium will shift to the

    (A) right, because the rate of the forward reaction will temporarily increase
    (B) right, because the rate of the forward reaction will temporarily decrease
    (C) left, because the rate of the reverse reaction will temporarily increase
    (D) left, because the rate of the reverse reaction will temporarily decrease
    (E) left, temporarily increasing the concentration of $B(aq)$

$$A(aq) + B(aq) \leftrightharpoons C(aq) + D(aq)$$

2. Suppose the chemical equation above is at equilibrium. If $A(aq)$ is removed from the system, the equilibrium will shift to the

    (A) right, because the rate of the forward reaction will temporarily increase
    (B) right, because the rate of the forward reaction will temporarily decrease
    (C) left, because the rate of the forward reaction will temporarily increase
    (D) left, because the rate of the forward reaction will temporarily decrease
    (E) left, temporarily increasing the concentration of $C(aq)$

$$A(aq) + B(aq) \leftrightharpoons C(aq) + D(aq)$$

3. Suppose the chemical equation above is at equilibrium. If $C(aq)$ is removed from the system, the equilibrium will shift to the

    (A) right, because the rate of the reverse reaction will temporarily increase
    (B) right, because the rate of the reverse reaction will temporarily decrease
    (C) left, because the rate of the reverse reaction will temporarily increase
    (D) left, because the rate of the reverse reaction will temporarily decrease
    (E) right, temporarily increasing the concentration of $B(aq)$

$$A(aq) + B(aq) \leftrightharpoons C(aq) + heat$$

4. Suppose the chemical equation above is at equilibrium. If the temperature of the system is increased, the equilibrium will shift to the

    (A) right, because the rate of the forward reaction will temporarily increase
    (B) right, because the rate of the forward reaction will temporarily decrease
    (C) left, because the rate of the reverse reaction will temporarily increase
    (D) left, because the rate of the reverse reaction will temporarily decrease
    (E) left, temporarily increasing the concentration of $C(aq)$

$$A(aq) + B(aq) \leftrightharpoons C(aq) + heat$$

5. Suppose the chemical equation above is at equilibrium. If the temperature of the system is decreased, the equilibrium will shift to the

    (A) right, because the rate of the reverse reaction will temporarily increase
    (B) right, because the rate of the reverse reaction will temporarily decrease
    (C) left, because the rate of the reverse reaction will temporarily increase
    (D) left, because the rate of the reverse reaction will temporarily decrease
    (E) left, temporarily increasing the concentration of $B(aq)$

$$A(aq) + B(aq) \leftrightharpoons C(aq) + heat$$

6. Suppose the chemical equation above is at equilibrium. If $C(aq)$ is removed from the system, the equilibrium will shift to the

    (A) right, because the rate of the reverse reaction will temporarily increase
    (B) right, because the rate of the reverse reaction will temporarily decrease
    (C) left, because the rate of the reverse reaction will temporarily increase
    (D) left, because the rate of the reverse reaction will temporarily decrease
    (E) left, temporarily increasing the concentration of $B(aq)$

Questions 1-5 refer to the following terms.

(A) Equilibrium constant
(B) Solubility product constant
(C) Reaction rate
(D) Endothermic
(E) Exothermic

1. A process requiring the release of heat

2. Normally measured in mol L^{-1} s^{-1}

3. A value which indicates the degree at which solids dissolve in water

4. A process requiring the absorption of heat

5. The ratio of the concentration of the products to the concentration of the reactants

Questions 6-9 refer to the following terms.

(A) LeChatlier's principle
(B) Completion
(C) Pressure
(D) Volume
(E) Experiment duration

6. If increased, will shift the equilbrium of a gas only reaction towards the side with more moles of gas

7. If increased, will shift the equilbrium of a gas only reaction towards the side with less moles of gas

8. A nonreversible reaction that typically leads to the formation of a different phase

9. States that when a system experiences a disturbance, it will compensate to reach a new equilibrium state

---

101. If the forward reaction of an equilibrium is exothermic, adding heat to the system favors the forward reaction | BECAUSE | adding heat causes a disturbance on the system, which responds by restoring a new equilibrium state.

102. If the forward reaction of an equilibrium is endothermic, adding heat to the system favors the forward reaction | BECAUSE | adding heat causes a disturbance on the system, which responds by restoring a new equilibrium state.

103. In a gas only reaction, increasing the pressure of the system favors the side with more moles of gas | BECAUSE | an increase in pressure leads to a decrease in volume for gases.

104. Solids and pure liquids are not accounted for in equilibrium constant ratios | BECAUSE | the gaseous phase particles contain high kinetic energy.

105. As the temperature of a system increases, the rate of reaction also increases | BECAUSE | due to an increased average kinetic energy of the particles, more effective collisions can occur per unit of time.

106. The solubility product constant is directly related to the degree of dissociation of the solute | BECAUSE | the stronger the dissociation the more ions that dissolve into solution.

---

10. Suppose the molar concentration of K^+ ions in a 1 L saturated water solution of potassium chloride at 298 K was measured to be 2.0×10^{-2}. What is the value of K_{sp} for potassium chloride?

    (A) 1.0×10^{-2}
    (B) 2.0×10^{-2}
    (C) 4.0×10^{-2}
    (D) 2.0×10^{-4}
    (E) 4.0×10^{-4}

11. Suppose the molar concentration of Ca^{2+} ions in a 1 L saturated water solution of calcium sulfate at 298 K was measured to be 2.0×10^{-2}. What is the value of K_{sp} for calcium sulfate?

    (A) 4.0×10^{-2}
    (B) 2.0×10^{-4}
    (C) 4.0×10^{-4}
    (D) 4.0×10^{-6}
    (E) 8.0×10^{-6}

$$H_2(g) + I_2(g) \rightleftharpoons 2HI(g)$$

12. Which of the following is the correct expression for the equilibrium constant, K_p, for the reaction represented above?

    (A) $\dfrac{[H_2][I_2]}{[HI_2]}$

    (B) $\dfrac{[H_2][I_2]}{[HI]^2}$

    (C) $\dfrac{[HI]^2}{[H_2][I_2]}$

    (D) $\dfrac{[HI]^2}{[H_2][I]^2}$

    (E) $\dfrac{[HI_2]}{[H_2][I]^2}$

$$CaCO_3(s) \rightleftharpoons CaO(s) + CO_2(g)$$

13. Which of the following is the correct expression for the equilibrium constant, K_c, for the reaction represented above?

    (A) $[CO_2]$

    (B) $\dfrac{[CO_2][CaO]}{[CaCO_3]}$

    (C) $\dfrac{[CO_2] + [CaO]}{[CaCO_3]}$

    (D) $\dfrac{[CaCO_3]}{[CO_2][CaO]}$

    (E) $\dfrac{[CaCO_3]}{[CO_2] + [CaO]}$

$$X(aq) + 2\,Y(aq) \rightleftharpoons 3\,Z(aq)$$

14. Which of the following is most likely to have the greatest effect on the equilibrium constant, K, in the chemical reaction represented above?

    (A) Adding a catalyst to the system
    (B) Decreasing the temperature of the system by 1 K
    (C) Adding 1 mol of $X(aq)$ to the system
    (D) Adding 1 mol of $Y(aq)$ to the system
    (E) Removing 1 mol of $Z(aq)$ from the system

$$2\,NO_2(g) \rightleftharpoons N_2O_4(g)$$

15. For the system represented above, which of the following actions will shift the position of equilibrium to the right?

    (A) Increasing the pressure of the reaction container
    (B) Increasing the volume of the reaction container
    (C) Adding additional $N_2O_4(g)$ to the reaction container
    (D) Removing some $NO_2(g)$ from the reaction container
    (E) Using a more malleable reaction container material

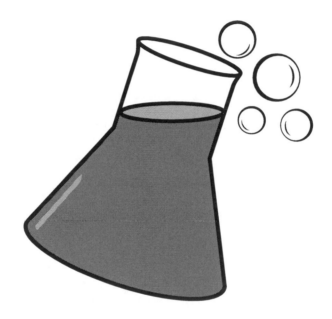

CHAPTER +9

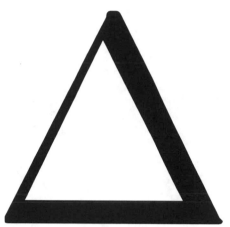

TYPES OF REACTIONS

ΔH is the symbol used to express the enthalpy (heat) change of a system.

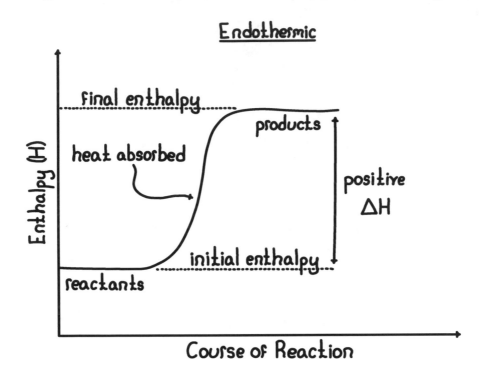

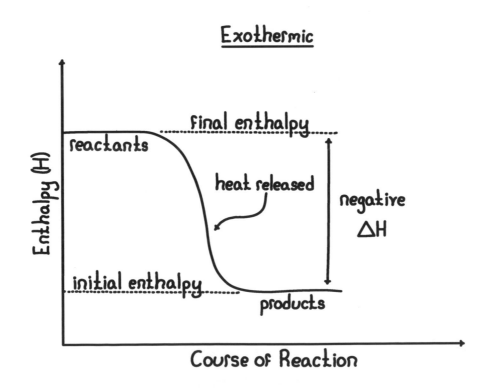

Enthalpy - endothermic and exothermic—*Practice*

1. Consider a reaction where the sum of the energy of the reactants is 4 kJ and the sum of the energy of the products is 3.5 kJ. This reaction is considered

   (A) exothermic, because ΔH for this reaction is negative
   (B) exothermic, because ΔH for this reaction is positive
   (C) endothermic, because ΔH for this reaction is negative
   (D) endothermic, because ΔH for this reaction is positive
   (E) isothermic, because ΔH for this reaction is zero

$$A(g) + B(g) \rightarrow C(g)$$

2. Consider the gaseous chemical equation above, where the energies of $A(g)$, $B(g)$, and $C(g)$ are 10 kJ, 15 kJ, and 20 kJ, respectively. Which of the following statements is most likely true?

   (A) The heat of formation, ΔH, of the reaction is negative, and thus the reaction is considered exothermic
   (B) The heat of formation, ΔH, of the reaction is positive, and thus the reaction is considered exothermic
   (C) The heat of formation, ΔH, of the reaction is negative, and thus the reaction is considered endothermic
   (D) The heat of formation, ΔH, of the reaction is positive, and thus the reaction is considered endothermic
   (E) The heat of formation, ΔH, cannot be determined from the given information

3. Consider a reaction where the sum of the energy of the reactants is 10 kJ and the sum of the energy of the products is 11 kJ. This reaction is considered

   (A) exothermic, because ΔH for this reaction is negative
   (B) exothermic, because ΔH for this reaction is positive
   (C) endothermic, because ΔH for this reaction is negative
   (D) endothermic, because ΔH for this reaction is positive
   (E) isothermic, because ΔH for this reaction is zero

$$A(g) \rightarrow B(g) + C(g)$$

4. Consider the gaseous chemical equation above, where the energies of $A(g)$, $B(g)$, and $C(g)$ are 10 kJ, 15 kJ, and 20 kJ, respectively. Which of the following statements is most likely true?

   (A) The heat of formation, ΔH, of the reaction is negative, and thus the reaction is considered exothermic
   (B) The heat of formation, ΔH, of the reaction is positive, and thus the reaction is considered exothermic
   (C) The heat of formation, ΔH, of the reaction is negative, and thus the reaction is considered endothermic
   (D) The heat of formation, ΔH, of the reaction is positive, and thus the reaction is considered endothermic
   (E) The heat of formation, ΔH, cannot be determined from the given information

To calculate the heat of a reaction (ΔH), the following equation is used.

ΔH of products − ΔH of reactants

Hess's Law: When given the steps of a reaction, the ΔH values of the intermediate steps can be summed to calculate the ΔH for the entire reaction.

$$A \rightarrow C \quad \Delta H = ?$$
$$A \rightarrow B \quad \Delta H = -234 \text{ kJ}$$
$$C \rightarrow B \quad \Delta H = -315 \text{ kJ}$$

We can go from $A \rightarrow B \rightarrow C$, but we will have to flip $C \rightarrow B$ to $B \rightarrow C$.

$$A \rightarrow \cancel{B} \quad \Delta H = -234 \text{ kJ}$$
$$\cancel{B} \rightarrow C \quad \Delta H = +315 \text{ kJ} \quad ^+$$
$$\overline{A \rightarrow C \quad \Delta H = +81 \text{ kJ}}$$

Hess' Law Sample Question

$$C \text{ (graphite)} + O_2(g) \rightarrow CO_2(g) \qquad \Delta H = \quad 400 \text{ kJ}$$
$$CO + 0.5\, O_2(g) \rightarrow CO_2(g) \qquad \Delta H = -280 \text{ kJ}$$

1. On the basis of the information above, what is the change in enthalpy, ΔH, for the following reaction?

$$C \text{ (graphite)} + \tfrac{1}{2} O_2(g) \rightarrow CO(g)$$

(A) −680 kJ
(B) −120 kJ
(C) −2 kJ
(D) +120 kJ
(E) +680 kJ

$$^+ \quad C \cdot O_2 \rightarrow \cancel{CO_2} \quad \Delta H = -400 \text{ kJ}$$
$$\cancel{CO_2} \rightarrow CO + \tfrac{1}{2}O_2 \quad \Delta H = +280 \text{ kJ}$$
$$\overline{C + \tfrac{1}{2}O_2 \rightarrow CO \quad \boxed{\Delta H = -120 \text{ kJ}}}$$

this reaction needs to flip

$$2\,S(s) + 2\,O_2(g) \rightarrow 2\,SO_2(g) \qquad \Delta H = -600\,\text{kJ}$$
$$2\,SO_2(g) + O_2(g) \rightarrow 2\,SO_3(g) \qquad \Delta H = -200\,\text{kJ}$$

2. On the basis of the information above, what is the change in enthalpy, ΔH, for the following reaction?

$$2\,S(s) + 3\,O_2(g) \rightarrow 2\,SO_3(g)$$

(A) −800 kJ
(B) −400 kJ
(C)   −3 kJ
(D) +400 kJ
(E) +800 kJ

$$2\,Rh(s) + O_2(g) \rightarrow 2\,RhO(s) \qquad \Delta H = -800\,\text{kJ}$$
$$2\,RhO(s) + O_2(g) \rightarrow 2\,RhO_2(s) \qquad \Delta H = -300\,\text{kJ}$$

3. On the basis of the information above, what is the change in enthalpy, ΔH, for the following reaction?

$$Rh(s) + O_2(g) \rightarrow RhO_2(s)$$

(A) −1,100 kJ
(B)   −550 kJ
(C)   −500 kJ
(D)   +500 kJ
(E) +1,100 kJ

$$2\,Al(s) + Fe_2O_3(s) \rightarrow 2\,Fe(l) + Al_2O_3(s) \quad \Delta H = -730\,\text{kJ}$$
$$2\,Fe(l) \rightarrow 2\,Fe(1{,}758°C)(s) \qquad \Delta H = -30\,\text{kJ}$$
$$Fe(1{,}758°C)(s) \rightarrow Fe(25°C)(s) \qquad \Delta H = -45\,\text{kJ}$$

4. On the basis of the information above, what is the change in enthalpy, ΔH, for the following reaction at 25°C?

$$2\,Al(s) + Fe_2O_3(s) \rightarrow Al_2O_3(s) + 2\,Fe(s)$$

(A) −850 kJ
(B) −700 kJ
(C) −500 kJ
(D) +700 kJ
(E) +850 kJ

<u>Combination/Synthesis:</u> When a reaction results in products that are the direct union of the reactants.

$$A \cdot B \rightarrow AB$$

E.g. $2Na_{(s)} + Cl_{2(g)} \longrightarrow 2NaCl_{(s)}$

$SO_{2(g)} + H_2O_{(l)} \longrightarrow H_2SO_{3(aq)}$

How do we know when a synthesis reaction is likely to spontaneously occur?

Heat of Formation (ΔH_f)	Spontaneous?
negative	yes
positive	no

<u>Decomposition/Analysis:</u> When a reaction results in products that are the components that made up the reactant.

$$AB \rightarrow A \cdot B$$

E.g. $2H_2O_{(l)} \longrightarrow 2H_{2(g)} + O_{2(g)}$

$2H_2O_{2(l)} \longrightarrow O_{2(g)} + 2H_2O_{(l)}$

How do we know when a decomposition reaction is likely to spontaneously occur?

Heat of Formation (ΔH_f)	Spontaneous?
negative	no
positive	yes

Synthesis and Decomposition—*Practice*

$$X_2(g) + Y_2(g) \rightarrow Z(g)$$

1. Consider the chemical reaction above. If the heat of formation, ΔH_f, of this reaction is -82 kJ/mol, which of the following statements is most likely true?

   (A) The above reaction is a synthesis reaction, which will occur spontaneously
   (B) The above reaction is a decomposition reaction, which will occur spontaneously
   (C) The above reaction is a synthesis reaction, which will NOT occur spontaneously
   (D) The above reaction is a decomposition reaction, which will NOT occur spontaneously
   (E) The above reaction is neither a synthesis nor decomposition reaction

$$X_2(g) + Y_2(g) \rightarrow Z(g)$$

2. Consider the chemical reaction above. If the heat of formation, ΔH_f, of this reaction is 106 kJ/mol, which of the following statements is most likely true?

   (A) The above reaction is a synthesis reaction, which will occur spontaneously
   (B) The above reaction is a decomposition reaction, which will occur spontaneously
   (C) The above reaction is a synthesis reaction, which will NOT occur spontaneously
   (D) The above reaction is a decomposition reaction, which will NOT occur spontaneously
   (E) The above reaction is neither a synthesis nor decomposition reaction

$$X_2(g) \rightarrow Y_2(g) + Z(g)$$

3. Consider the chemical reaction above. If the heat of formation, ΔH_f, of this reaction is 106 kJ/mol, which of the following statements is most likely true?

   (A) The above reaction is a synthesis reaction, which will occur spontaneously
   (B) The above reaction is a decomposition reaction, which will occur spontaneously
   (C) The above reaction is a synthesis reaction, which will NOT occur spontaneously
   (D) The above reaction is a decomposition reaction, which will NOT occur spontaneously
   (E) The above reaction is neither a synthesis nor decomposition reaction

$$X_2(g) \rightarrow Y_2(g) + Z(g)$$

4. Consider the chemical reaction above. If the heat of formation, ΔH_f, of this reaction is -82 kJ/mol, which of the following statements is most likely true?

   (A) The above reaction is a synthesis reaction, which will occur spontaneously
   (B) The above reaction is a decomposition reaction, which will occur spontaneously
   (C) The above reaction is a synthesis reaction, which will NOT occur spontaneously
   (D) The above reaction is a decomposition reaction, which will NOT occur spontaneously
   (E) The above reaction is neither a synthesis nor decomposition reaction

$$W(g) + X_2(g) \rightarrow Y_2(g) + Z(g)$$

5. Consider the chemical reaction above. If the heat of formation, ΔH_f, of this reaction is -82 kJ/mol, which of the following statements is most likely true?

   (A) The above reaction is a synthesis reaction, which will occur spontaneously
   (B) The above reaction is a decomposition reaction, which will occur spontaneously
   (C) The above reaction is a synthesis reaction, which will NOT occur spontaneously
   (D) The above reaction is a decomposition reaction, which will NOT occur spontaneously
   (E) The above reaction is neither a synthesis nor decomposition reaction

$$8\,Fe(s) + S_8(s) \rightarrow 8\,FeS(s)$$

6. Consider the chemical reaction above. If the heat of formation, ΔH_f, of this reaction is 2,512 kJ/mol, which of the following statements is most likely true?

   (A) The above reaction is a synthesis reaction, which will occur spontaneously
   (B) The above reaction is a decomposition reaction, which will occur spontaneously
   (C) The above reaction is a synthesis reaction, which will NOT occur spontaneously
   (D) The above reaction is a decomposition reaction, which will NOT occur spontaneously
   (E) The above reaction is neither a synthesis nor decomposition reaction

<u>Single replacement</u>: When one element replaces another element in a compound.

$$A + BC \longrightarrow AB + C$$

E.g. $Cu_{(s)} + 2AgNO_{3(aq)} \longrightarrow Cu(NO_3)_{2\,(aq)} + 2Ag_{(s)}$

   $Cl_{2(g)} + 2NaI_{(aq)} \longrightarrow 2NaCl_{(aq)} + I_{2(s)}$

ΔH_f of products − ΔH_f of reactants	Will the single replacement occur?
negative	yes
positive	no

More reactive elements will replace less reactive ones in a single replacement reaction. Refer to the activity list in Chapter 13.

<u>Double replacement</u>: When there is an exchange of partners between compounds.

$$AB + CD \longrightarrow AD + CB$$

E.g. $AgNO_{3(aq)} + NaCl_{(aq)} \longrightarrow AgCl_{(s)} + NaNO_{3(aq)}$

Will the reaction go to completion? One of the following 3 needs to be true.

1) An insoluble precipitate is formed.
   (carbonates, phosphates, sulfides, hydroxides)

2) A substance that is nonionizing is formed.
   $HCl + NaOH \longrightarrow H_2O + Na^+ + Cl^-$
   water is a nonionizing product

3) Gas is evolved.

A more comprehensive table of insoluble substances can be found in Chapter 13.

$Cl_2(g) + 2 NaI(aq) \rightarrow 2 NaCl(aq) + I_2(s)$

1. Consider the chemical reaction above. If the heat of formation, ΔH_f, of this reaction is -59 kJ/mol, which of the following statements is most likely true?

   (A) The above reaction is single replacement, which will occur spontaneously
   (B) The above reaction is double replacement, which will occur spontaneously
   (C) The above reaction is single replacement, which will NOT occur spontaneously
   (D) The above reaction is double replacement, which will NOT occur spontaneously
   (E) The above reaction is neither a single nor double replacement

$H_2(g) + MgCl_2(aq) \rightarrow 2 HCl(aq) + Mg(s)$

4. Consider the chemical reaction above. If the heat of formation, ΔH_f, of this reaction is 526 kJ/mol, which of the following statements is most likely true?

   (A) The above reaction is single replacement, which will occur spontaneously
   (B) The above reaction is double replacement, which will occur spontaneously
   (C) The above reaction is single replacement, which will NOT occur spontaneously
   (D) The above reaction is double replacement, which will NOT occur spontaneously
   (E) The above reaction is neither a single nor double replacement

$NaCl(aq) + AgNO_3(aq) \rightarrow NaNO_3(aq) + AgCl(s)$

2. Consider the chemical reaction above. Will this reaction go to completion?

   (A) Yes, because the insoluble precipitate, $NaNO_3(aq)$, is formed
   (B) Yes, because the insoluble precipitate, $AgCl(s)$, is formed
   (C) No, because the insoluble precipitate, $NaNO_3(aq)$, is formed
   (D) No, because the insoluble precipitate, $AgCl(s)$, is formed
   (E) No, because all substances are aqueous

$Cu(s) + 2 AgNO_3(aq) \rightarrow 2 Ag(s) + Cu(NO_3)_2(aq)$

5. Consider the chemical reaction above. If it can be determined, is this reaction spontaneous?

   (A) Yes, because $Ag(s)$ is more active than $Cu(s)$
   (B) Yes, because $Ag(s)$ is less active than $Cu(s)$
   (C) No, because $Ag(s)$ is more active than $Cu(s)$
   (D) No, because $Ag(s)$ is less active than $Cu(s)$
   (E) Cannot be determined because ΔH is not given

$Ca(OH)_2(aq) + HCl(aq) \rightarrow CaCl_2(aq) + H_2O(aq)$

3. Consider the chemical reaction above. Will this reaction go to completion?

   (A) Yes, because the insoluble precipitate, $CaCl_2(aq)$, is formed
   (B) Yes, because the insoluble precipitate, $H_2O(aq)$, is formed
   (C) No, because the insoluble precipitate, $CaCl_2(aq)$, is formed
   (D) No, because the insoluble precipitate, $H_2O(aq)$, is formed
   (E) No, because all substances are aqueous

$Cl_2(g) + 2 NaBr(aq) \rightarrow 2 NaCl(aq) + Br_2(l)$

6. Consider the chemical reaction above. If it can be determined, is this reaction spontaneous?

   (A) Yes, because $Cl_2(g)$ is more active than $Br_2(l)$
   (B) Yes, because $Cl_2(g)$ is less active than $Br_2(l)$
   (C) No, because $Cl_2(g)$ is more active than $Br_2(l)$
   (D) No, because $Cl_2(g)$ is less active than $Br_2(l)$
   (E) Cannot be determined because ΔH is not given

Gibbs free energy(G) is used to quantify and evaluate whether a reaction will be spontaneous by combining entropy(S) and enthalpy(H).

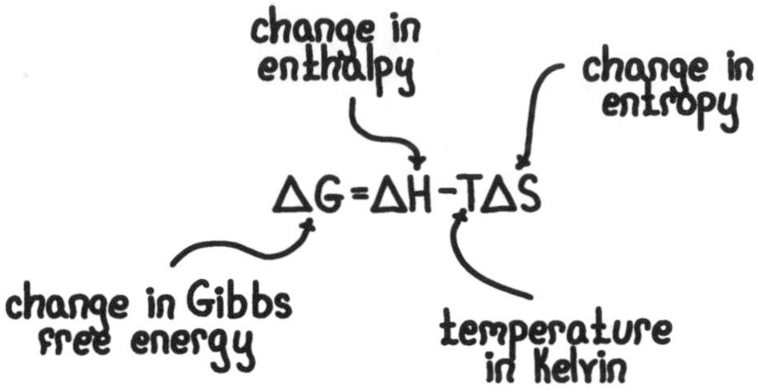

change in enthalpy

change in entropy

$$\Delta G = \Delta H - T\Delta S$$

change in Gibbs free energy

temperature in Kelvin

ΔG	spontaneous?
negative	yes
positive	no

Consider how changes in sign and magnitude of ΔH & ΔS affect spontaneity.

Gibbs Free Energy Sample Question

1. Consider a reaction where $\Delta H = -200$ kJ and $\Delta S = +100$ kJ. These parameters indicate a

   (A) spontaneous reaction, because ΔG is negative.
   (B) spontaneous reaction, because ΔG is positive.
   (C) non-spontaneous reaction, because ΔG is negative.
   (D) non-spontaneous reaction, because ΔG is positive.
   (E) equilibrium reaction, because ΔG is neither positive nor negative.

$$\Delta G = \Delta H - T\Delta S$$
$$\Delta G = -200 - T(100)$$

-Typically a temperature is necessary, but we just need the sign of ΔG.

$\Delta H < 0$
$\Delta S > 0$ } ΔG is always negative under these conditions.

Questions 2-3 pertain to the data below, which shows enthalpy and entropy values for a certain chemical reaction at 27°C.

Parameter	Value (kJ)
ΔH	−70
ΔS	−100

2. The change in Gibbs free energy, ΔG, for the parameters listed above is closest to which of the following?

    (A) −29,930 kJ
    (B) −2,630 kJ
    (C) 2,630 kJ
    (D) 6,700 kJ
    (E) 29,930 kJ

3. Do the parameters listed above indicate a spontaneous or non-spontaneous reaction? The reaction is

    (A) spontaneous, because ΔG is negative.
    (B) spontaneous, because ΔG is positive.
    (C) non-spontaneous, because ΔG is negative.
    (D) non-spontaneous, because ΔG is positive.
    (E) at equilibrium, because ΔG is neither positive nor negative.

Questions 4-5 pertain to the data below, which shows enthalpy and entropy values for a certain chemical reaction at 27°C.

Parameter	Value (kJ)
ΔH	−100
ΔS	+100

4. The change in Gibbs free energy, ΔG, for the parameters listed above is closest to which of the following?

    (A) −30,100 kJ
    (B) −10,300 kJ
    (C) −2,800 kJ
    (D) 2,800 kJ
    (E) 30,100 kJ

5. Do the parameters listed above indicate a spontaneous or non-spontaneous reaction? The reaction is

    (A) spontaneous, because ΔG is negative.
    (B) spontaneous, because ΔG is positive.
    (C) non-spontaneous, because ΔG is negative.
    (D) non-spontaneous, because ΔG is positive.
    (E) at equilibrium, because ΔG is neither positive nor negative.

Questions 6-7 pertain to the data below, which shows enthalpy and entropy values for a certain chemical reaction at 27°C.

Parameter	Value (kJ)
ΔH	−1,500
ΔS	−5

6. The change in Gibbs free energy, ΔG, for the parameters listed above is closest to which of the following?

    (A) −7,200 kJ
    (B) −1,365 kJ
    (C) 0 kJ
    (D) 1,365 kJ
    (E) 7,200 kJ

7. Do the parameters listed above indicate a spontaneous or non-spontaneous reaction? The reaction is

    (A) spontaneous, because ΔG is negative.
    (B) spontaneous, because ΔG is positive.
    (C) non-spontaneous, because ΔG is negative.
    (D) non-spontaneous, because ΔG is positive.
    (E) at equilibrium, because ΔG is neither positive nor negative.

Questions 1-5 refer to the following terms.

    (A) Endothermic
    (B) Exothermic
    (C) Single replacement
    (D) Double replacement
    (E) Precipitate

1. $\Delta H < 0$

2. $\Delta H > 0$

3. A solid product that comes out of solution

4. A type of reaction where the energy of the products are less than the energy of the reactants

5. When an isolated element replaces another element within a compound

Questions 6-10 refer to the following compounds.

    (A) $NaCl(aq)$
    (B) $H_2(g)$
    (C) $I_2(s)$
    (D) $Fe(OH)_3(aq)$
    (E) $H_2O(l)$

6. Formed in a synthesis reaction of $Na(s)$ and $Cl_2(g)$

7. A product of a double replacement reaction between $NaOH(aq)$ and $Fe(NO_3)_3(aq)$

8. A product from a single replacement reaction between $Br_2(l)$ and $KI(aq)$

9. A product from a double replacement reaction between $H_2SO_4(aq)$ and $NaOH(aq)$

10. A product from a single replacement reaction between $Zn(s)$ and $HCl(aq)$

101. The production of an insoluble precipitate indicates the reaction has gone to completion   BECAUSE   the reaction is considered irreversible.

102. In a single replacement reaction, a negative value for ΔH indicates a spontaneous reaction   BECAUSE   the energy of the products is less than the energy of the reactants in an exothermic reaction.

103. The total enthalpy, ΔH, change for a reaction is the sum of all enthalpy changes   BECAUSE   according to Hess' Law, enthalpy is considered a state function.

104. A single replacement reaction will occur if the isolated element is more active than the element in the compound being replaced   BECAUSE   single replacement reactions only occur if ΔH is less than zero.

105. The reaction between copper (II) sulfate and sodium hydroxide goes to completion   BECAUSE   a non-ionizing product is formed.

$Pb(NO_3)_2(aq) + KI(aq) \rightarrow PbI_2(s) + KNO_3(aq)$

11. Consider the chemical reaction of $Pb(NO_3)_2$ and KI above. This reaction can be classified as which of the following?

    I. Synthesis
    II. Single-replacement
    III. Double-replacement

    (A) II only
    (B) III only
    (C) I and III
    (D) II and III
    (E) I, II, and III

$Fe(s) + Cu(NO_3)(aq) \rightarrow Fe(NO_3)_2(aq) + Cu(s)$

12. Consider the chemical reaction of Fe and $Cu(NO_3)_2$ above. This reaction can be classified as which of the following?

    I. Synthesis
    II. Single-replacement
    III. Double-replacement

    (A) II only
    (B) III only
    (C) I and III
    (D) II and III
    (E) I, II, and III

13. The heat of formation of carbon dioxide, CO_2, is $\Delta H = -393.5$kJ/mol. The fact that the heat of formation of CO_2 is negative indicates that

    (A) heat is absorbed when CO_2 is produced
    (B) the decomposition of CO_2 is non-spontaneous
    (C) 393.5 kJ must be added to reduce one mole of C
    (D) CO_2 is formed from C (graphite) and O_2 by an endothermic reaction
    (E) the reaction of C (graphite) and O_2 to form CO_2 occurs only at standard temperature and pressure

14. The heat of formation of magnesium oxide, MgO, is $\Delta H = 601.6$ kJ/mol. The fact that the heat of formation of MgO is positive indicates that

    (A) 601.6 kJ must be added to reduce one mole of Mg
    (B) the reaction of Mg and O_2 to form MgO occurs rapidly at standard temperature and pressure
    (C) heat is liberated when O_2 is oxidized
    (D) O_3 is formed from Mg and O_2 by an endothermic reaction
    (E) the synthesis of MgO is non-spontaneous

$$2\,CH_4(g) + 3\,O_2(g) \rightarrow 2\,CO(g) + 4\,H_2O(l) \qquad \Delta H = -1,200 \text{ kJ}$$
$$H_2O(g) \rightarrow H_2O(l) \qquad \Delta H = -50 \text{ kJ}$$

15. On the basis of the information above, what is the change in enthalpy, ΔH, for the following reaction?

$$2\,CO(g) + 4\,H_2O(g) \rightarrow 2\,CH_4(g) + 3\,O_2(g)$$

    (A) $-1,250$ kJ
    (B) $-1,150$ kJ
    (C) $-1,000$ kJ
    (D) $+1,000$ kJ
    (E) $+1,150$ kJ

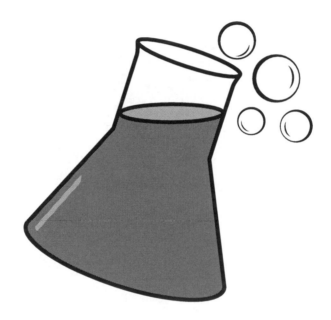

pH

ACIDS AND BASES

Arrhenius Acid: Any substance that increases the concentration of H^+ ions in a solution.

$$HCl_{(g)} + H_2O \longrightarrow H^+_{(aq)} + Cl^-_{(aq)}$$

Arrhenius Base: Any substance that increases the concentration of OH^- ions in a solution.

$$KOH_{(s)} + H_2O \longrightarrow K^+_{(aq)} + OH^-_{(aq)}$$

Brønsted-Lowry Acid: Any substance that donates a proton.

$$HCl + H_2O \longrightarrow H^+_{(aq)} + Cl^-_{(aq)}$$

Brønsted-Lowry acid
because it gives up a proton.

Brønsted-Lowry Base: Any substance that accepts a proton.

$$H_2O + NH_3 \longrightarrow OH^- + NH_4^+$$

Brønsted-Lowry base
because it accepts a proton.

Lewis Acid: A compound that accepts an electron.

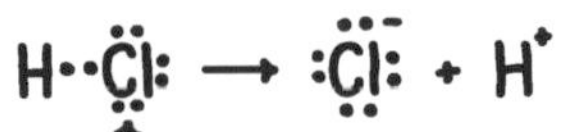

$$H\cdot\cdot\ddot{\underset{\cdot\cdot}{Cl}} \longrightarrow \colon\ddot{\underset{\cdot\cdot}{Cl}} \colon + H^+$$

Lewis acid because
it takes the electron away
from the hydrogen

Lewis Base: A compound that donates an electron

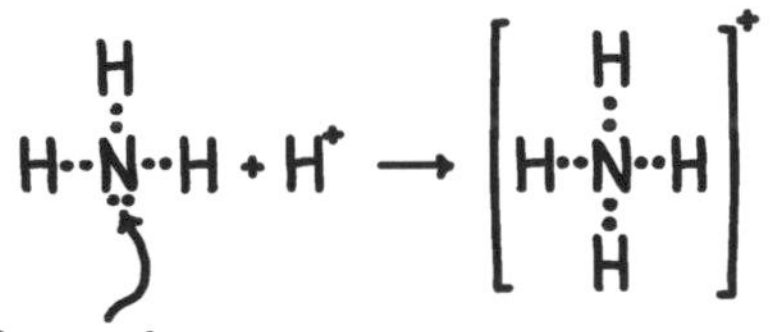

$$H\cdot\cdot\overset{\cdot\cdot}{\underset{\cdot\cdot}{N}}\cdot\cdot H + H^+ \longrightarrow \left[H\cdot\cdot\overset{\cdot\cdot}{\underset{\cdot\cdot}{N}}\cdot\cdot H \right]^+$$

Lewis base because
it donates an electron
to the hydrogen.

Acids & Bases Definitions—*Practice*

1. Which of the following compounds is considered an Arrhenius Acid?

(A) NaCl
(B) $MgSO_4$
(C) HNO_3
(D) $CaCl_2$
(E) LiCl

2. Which of the following compounds is considered an Arrhenius Base?

(A) NaOH
(B) CH_3OH
(C) HCl
(D) NaCl
(E) MgO

3. Which of the following compounds is considered an Arrhenius Base?

(A) CaO
(B) $Ca(OH)_2$
(C) Na_2O
(D) K_2O
(E) C_2H_5OH

$$NH_3 + H_2O \rightarrow NH_4^+ + OH^-$$

4. In the chemical reaction shown above, which of the following compounds is considered the Bronsted-Lowry acid?

(A) NH_3
(B) H_2O
(C) NH_4^+
(D) H_3O^+
(E) OH^-

$$NH_3 + H_2O \rightarrow NH_4^+ + OH^-$$

5. In the chemical reaction shown above, which of the following compounds is considered the Bronsted-Lowry base?

(A) NH_3
(B) H_2O
(C) NH_4^+
(D) H_3O^+
(E) OH^-

$$HCl + H_2O \leftrightarrows H_3O^+ + Cl^-$$

6. In the reverse reaction of the chemical equilibrium shown above, which of the following compounds is considered the Bronsted-Lowry acid?

(A) HCl
(B) H_2O_2
(C) H_2O
(D) H_3O^+
(E) Cl^-

$$HCl + H_2O \leftrightarrows H_3O^+ + Cl^-$$

7. In the reverse reaction of the chemical equilibrium shown above, which of the following compounds is considered the Bronsted-Lowry base?

(A) HCl
(B) H_2O_2
(C) H_2O
(D) H_3O^+
(E) Cl^-

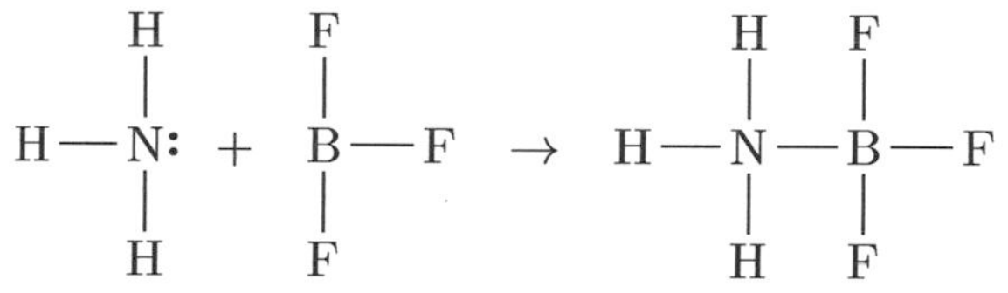

8. Which substance in the chemical equation above is considered a Lewis acid?

(A) NH_3
(B) $NH4^+$
(C) BF_3
(D) BF_3^-
(E) NH_3BF_3

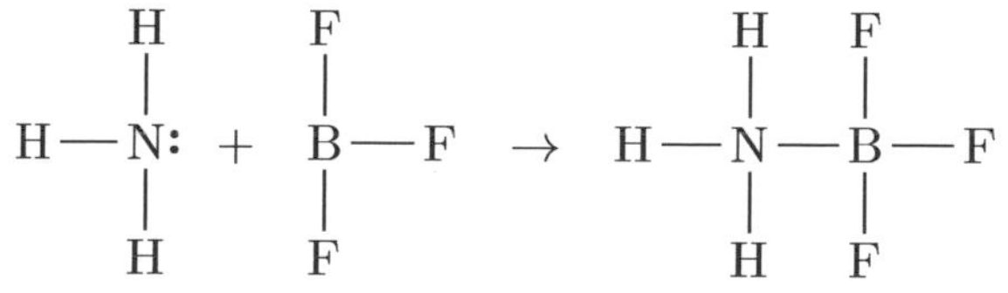

9. Which substance in the chemical equation above is considered a Lewis base?

(A) NH_3
(B) $NH4^+$
(C) BF_3
(D) BF_3^-
(E) NH_3BF_3

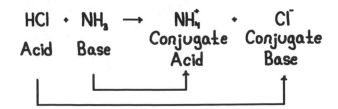

HCl · NH₃ → NH₄⁺ · Cl⁻

$$HCl \cdot NH_3 \rightarrow NH_4^+ \cdot Cl^-$$

Acid   Base   Conjugate Acid   Conjugate Base

$HCl \rightarrow Cl^-$
Acid   Base

Note: HCl turns into Cl⁻ which is a base because if it were to react with an acid it would accept a proton/donate an electron.

$NH_3 \rightarrow NH_4^+$
Base   Acid

Note: NH₃ turns into NH₄⁺ which is an acid beause if it were to react with a base it would donate a proton/accept an electron.

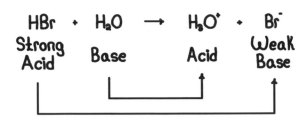

$$HBr \cdot H_2O \rightarrow H_3O^+ \cdot Br^-$$

HBr   H₂O   H₃O⁺   Br⁻
Strong Acid   Base   Acid   Weak Base

Note: Strong acids produce weak conjugate bases, and strong bases produce weak conjugate acids.

--- Metallic and nonmetallic oxides ---

1 H 1.0079																	2 He 4.0026
3 Li 6.941	4 Be 9.012											5 B 10.811	6 C 12.011	7 N 14.01	8 O 16.00	9 F 19.00	10 Ne 20.179
11 Na 22.99	12 Mg 24.30											13 Al 26.98	14 Si 28.09	15 P 30.974	16 S 32.06	17 Cl 35.453	18 Ar 39.948
19 K 39.10	20 Ca 40.08	21 Sc 44.96	22 Ti 47.90	23 V 50.94	24 Cr 52.00	25 Mn 54.94	26 Fe 55.85	27 Co 58.93	28 Ni 58.69	29 Cu 63.55	30 Zn 65.39	31 Ga 69.72	32 Ge 72.59	33 As 74.92	34 Se 78.96	35 Br 79.90	36 Kr 83.80
37 Rb 85.47	38 Sr 87.62	39 Y 88.91	40 Zr 91.22	41 Nb 92.91	42 Mo 95.94	43 Tc (98)	44 Ru 101.1	45 Rh 102.91	46 Pd 106.42	47 Ag 107.87	48 Cd 112.41	49 In 114.82	50 Sn 118.71	51 Sb 121.75	52 Te 127.60	53 I 126.91	54 Xe 131.29
55 Cs 132.91	56 Ba 137.33	57 *La 138.91	72 Hf 178.49	73 Ta 180.95	74 W 183.85	75 Re 186.21	76 Os 190.2	77 Ir 192.2	78 Pt 195.08	79 Au 196.97	80 Hg 200.59	81 Tl 204.38	82 Pb 207.2	83 Bi 208.98	84 Po (209)	85 At (210)	86 Rn (222)
87 Fr (223)	88 Ra 226.02	89 †Ac 227.03	104 Rf (261)	105 Db (262)	106 Sg (266)	107 Bh (264)	108 Hs (277)	109 Mt (268)	110 Ds (271)	111 Rg (272)	112 § (277)						

Metallic oxides produce basic solutions in water: MgO, Na₂O₂.

Nonmetallic oxides produce acidic solutions in water: CO₂, SO₂.

Questions 1-4 refer to the chemical equation below.

$$H_2PO_4^- + H_2O \rightleftarrows H_3O^+ + HPO_4^{2-}$$

1. Which of the following pairs of compounds correctly lists a base and its conjugate acid, respectively, for the *forward* reaction?

   (A) $H_2PO_4^-$ and H_2O
   (B) $H_2PO_4^-$ and H_3O^+
   (C) H_2O and H_3O^+
   (D) $H_2PO_4^-$ and HPO_4^{2-}
   (E) H_3O^+ and HPO_4^{2-}

2. Which of the following pairs of compounds correctly lists an acid and its conjugate base, respectively, for the *forward* reaction?

   (A) $H_2PO_4^-$ and H_2O
   (B) $H_2PO_4^-$ and H_3O^+
   (C) H_2O and H_3O^+
   (D) $H_2PO_4^-$ and HPO_4^{2-}
   (E) H_3O^+ and HPO_4^{2-}

3. Which of the following pairs of compounds correctly lists a base and its conjugate acid, respectively, for the *reverse* reaction?

   (A) H_2O and $H_2PO_4^-$
   (B) H_3O^+ and $H_2PO_4^-$
   (C) H_3O^+ and H_2O
   (D) HPO_4^{2-} and $H_2PO_4^-$
   (E) HPO_4^{2-} and H_3O^+

4. Which of the following pairs of compounds correctly lists an acid and its conjugate base, respectively, for the *reverse* reaction?

   (A) H_2O and $H_2PO_4^-$
   (B) H_3O^+ and $H_2PO_4^-$
   (C) H_3O^+ and H_2O
   (D) HPO_4^{2-} and $H_2PO_4^-$
   (E) HPO_4^{2-} and H_3O^+

Questions 5-8 refer to the chemical equation below.

$$CH_3COOH + H_2O \rightleftarrows H_3O^+ + CH_3COO^-$$

5. Which of the following pairs of compounds correctly lists a base and its conjugate acid, respectively, for the *forward* reaction?

   (A) CH_3COOH and H_2O
   (B) CH_3COOH and H_3O^+
   (C) CH_3COOH and CH_3COO^-
   (D) H_2O and H_3O^+
   (E) H_2O and CH_3COO^-

6. Which of the following pairs of compounds correctly lists an acid and its conjugate base, respectively, for the *forward* reaction?

   (A) CH_3COOH and H_2O
   (B) CH_3COOH and H_3O^+
   (C) CH_3COOH and CH_3COO^-
   (D) H_2O and H_3O^+
   (E) H_2O and CH_3COO^-

7. Which of the following pairs of compounds correctly lists a base and its conjugate acid, respectively, for the *reverse* reaction?

   (A) H_3O^+ and CH_3COOH
   (B) H_3O^+ and H_2O
   (C) H_3O^+ and H_3O^+
   (D) CH_3COO^- and CH_3COOH
   (E) CH_3COO^- and H_3O^+

8. Which of the following pairs of compounds correctly lists an acid and its conjugate base, respectively, for the *reverse* reaction?

   (A) H_3O^+ and CH_3COOH
   (B) H_3O^+ and H_2O
   (C) H_3O^+ and H_3O^+
   (D) CH_3COO^- and CH_3COOH
   (E) CH_3COO^- and H_3O^+

Acidity is measured and expressed in terms of the H⁺ ion concentration in a solution.

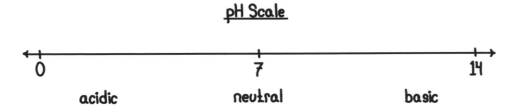

$-\log$ $\overbrace{pH}$ $[H^+]= H^+$ ion concentration

$-\log[H^+]$

pH Scale

```
+----+------+------+
0          7          14
acidic   neutral    basic
```

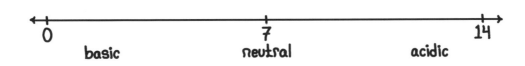

$-\log$ $\overbrace{pOH}$ $[OH^-]= OH^-$ ion concentration

$-\log[OH^-]$

pOH Scale

```
+----+------+------+
0          7          14
basic    neutral    acidic
```

$$[H^+][OH^-]=10^{-14} \longleftrightarrow pH + pOH = 14$$

================ How Logarithms work for pH ================

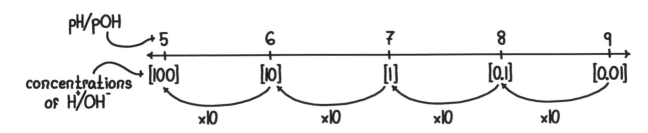

pH/pOH → 5   6   7   8   9

concentrations
of H⁺/OH⁻ → [100]   [10]   [1]   [0.1]   [0.01]

         ×10   ×10   ×10   ×10

<u>Note</u>: As pH/pOH goes up or down by 1 the H⁺/OH⁻
ion concentration decreases/increases by a factor of 10.

1. What is the pH value of a solution with
   $[H^+]=1.0 \times 10^{-9}$

   (A) −9
   (B) −5
   (C) 0
   (D) 5
   (E) 9

   $[H^+] = 1.0 \times 10^{-9}$ Given that the number in the front is 1.0, the pH is simply the absolute value of the exponent.

   $pH = |-9|$

   $pH = 9$

2. If a solution has a pOH of 10, the pH of the solution is

   (A) 2
   (B) 4
   (C) 10
   (D) 12
   (E) 13

   $pH + pOH = 14$
   $\quad -pOH \quad -pOH$
   _____
   $pH = 14 - pOH$

   $pH = 14 - 10$

   $pH = 4$

3. What is the pH value of a solution with
   $[OH^-] = 1.0 \times 10^{-9}$

   (A) −9
   (B) −5
   (C) 0
   (D) 5
   (E) 9

   ① Solve for pOH.

   $[OH^-] = 1.0 \times 10^{-9}$ Given that the number in the front is 1.0, the pOH is simply the absolute value of the exponent.

   $pOH = |-9|$

   $pOH = 9$

   ② Solve for pH.

   $pH + pOH = 14$
   $\quad -pOH \quad -pOH$
   _____
   $pH = 14 - pOH$

   $pH = 14 - 9$

   $pH = 5$

4. Which of the following pH values is that of an acid?

   (A) 6.5
   (B) 7
   (C) 7.5
   (D) 8.5
   (E) 9

8. What is the pH value of a solution with $[H^+]=1.0 \times 10^{-5}$

   (A) −9
   (B) −5
   (C) 0
   (D) 5
   (E) 9

5. Which of the following pH values is that of a base?

   (A) 1
   (B) 4
   (C) 5
   (D) 7
   (E) 11

9. What is the pH value of a solution with $[H^+]=1.0 \times 10^{-6}$

   (A) −9
   (B) −8
   (C) 6
   (D) 7
   (E) 8

6. If a solution has a pH of 10, the pOH of the solution is

   (A) 2
   (B) 4
   (C) 10
   (D) 12
   (E) 13

10. What is the pH value of a solution with $[OH^-]=1.0 \times 10^{-6}$

   (A) −9
   (B) −8
   (C) 6
   (D) 7
   (E) 8

7. If a solution has a pOH of 12, the pH of the solution is

   (A) 2
   (B) 7
   (C) 10
   (D) 12
   (E) 14

11. What is the pH value of a solution with $[OH^-]=1.0 \times 10^{-5}$

   (A) −9
   (B) −5
   (C) 0
   (D) 5
   (E) 9

12. If the [H$^+$] of a solution equals 1.0×10^{-7}, the [OH$^-$] of that same solution equals

    (A) 1.0×10^{-6}
    (B) 1.0×10^{-7}
    (C) 1.0×10^{-8}
    (D) 2.0×10^{-6}
    (E) 2.0×10^{-8}

13. If the [H$^+$] of a solution equals 1.0×10^{-6}, the [OH$^-$] of that same solution equals

    (A) 1.0×10^{-6}
    (B) 1.0×10^{-7}
    (C) 1.0×10^{-8}
    (D) 2.0×10^{-6}
    (E) 2.0×10^{-8}

14. If the [H$^+$] of a solution equals 1.0×10^{-2}, the [OH$^-$] of that same solution equals

    (A) 1.0×10^{-2}
    (B) 1.0×10^{-7}
    (C) 1.0×10^{-9}
    (D) 1.0×10^{-10}
    (E) 1.0×10^{-12}

Questions 15-21 refer to the following pH ranges.

    (A) Less than 3
    (B) Between 3 and 7
    (C) Equal to 7
    (D) Between 7 and 11
    (E) Greater than 11

15. A solution with a H$^+$ concentration of 1.0×10^{-12}

16. A solution with a OH$^-$ concentration of 6.7×10^{-12}

17. A solution with a H$^+$ concentration of 2.3×10^{-4}

18. A solution with a OH$^-$ concentration of 1×10^{-7}

19. A solution with a H$^+$ concentration of 5.5×10^{-6}

20. 1 L of a 0.1 M HCl solution

21. 5 L of a 0.1 M H$_2$SO$_4$ solution

K_a is just an equilibrium constant. It is the specific equilibrium constant for an acid. It tells us the degree to which an acid dissociates and releases protons into a solution.

$$HA_{(aq)} + H_2O_{(l)} \rightleftharpoons H_3O^+ + A^-_{(aq)}$$

Acid   Base   Conjugate   Conjugate
                Acid   Base

$$K_a = \frac{[H_3O^+][A^-]}{[HA]} = \frac{[H^+][A^-]}{[HA]}$$

$$pK_a = -\log K_a$$

Note: Large K_a values indicate a strong acid. Small K_a values indicate a weak acid. Large pK_a values indicate a weak acid. Small pK_a values indicate a strong acid.

───── K_a Practice Questions ─────

$$HCl(aq) + H_2O(l) \rightleftharpoons H_3O^+(aq) + Cl^-(aq)$$

1. Consider the equilibrium equation above. Which of the following correctly lists the equation for the K_a of the forward reaction?

(A) $[H^+][Cl^-]$

(B) $\dfrac{[H^+][Cl^-]}{[HCl][H_2O]}$

(C) $\dfrac{[HCl][H_2O]}{[H^+][Cl^-]}$

(D) $\dfrac{[H^+][Cl^-]}{[HCl]}$

(E) $\dfrac{[HCl]}{[H^+][Cl^-]}$

$$HNO_3(aq) + H_2O(l) \rightleftharpoons H_3O^+(aq) + NO_3^-(aq)$$

2. Consider the equilibrium equation above. Which of the following correctly lists the equation for the K_a of the forward reaction?

(A) $[H^+][NO_3^-]$

(B) $\dfrac{[H^+][NO_3]}{[HNO_3][H_2O]}$

(C) $\dfrac{[HNO_3][H_2O]}{[H^+][NO_3^-]}$

(D) $\dfrac{[H^+][NO_3^-]}{[HNO_3]}$

(E) $\dfrac{[HNO_3]}{[H^+][NO_3^-]}$

Questions 3-4 refer to the following K_a values.

Acid	K_a
H_3O^+	1.0×10^0
H_2SO_3	1.5×10^{-2}
$HClO_2$	1.1×10^{-2}
HF	7.2×10^{-4}
HCOOH	1.8×10^{-4}

3. Of the above acids listed, which of the following is the weakest acid?

    (A) H_3O^+
    (B) H_2SO_3
    (C) $HClO_2$
    (D) HF
    (E) HCOOH

4. Of the above acids listed, which of the following is the strongest acid?

    (A) H_3O^+
    (B) H_2SO_3
    (C) $HClO_2$
    (D) HF
    (E) HCOOH

5. Which of the following statements is most likely true concerning hydrobromic acid, HBr?

    (A) Hydrobromic acid is insoluble in water
    (B) Hydrobromic acid is soluble in water, with slight dissociation
    (C) Hydrobromic acid is soluble in water, with complete dissociation
    (D) The K_a value of hydrobromic acid is less than 1.0×10^{-5}
    (E) The pK_a value of hydrobromic acid is greater than 5

6. Hydrosulfuric acid, H_2S, has a K_a value of 1.0×10^{-7}, whereas carbonic acid, H_2CO_3 has a K_a value of 4.3×10^{-7}. Which compound has a greater acid strength?

    (A) Hydrosulfuric acid, because its pK_a value is lower
    (B) Hydrosulfuric acid, because its pK_a value is higher
    (C) Carbonic acid, because its pK_a value is lower
    (D) Carbonic acid, because its pK_a value is higher
    (E) Hydrosulfuric acid and carbonic acid have equal hydronium ion dissociation

Questions 1-5 refer to the following terms.

   (A) Acid
   (B) Base
   (C) K_a
   (D) K_b
   (E) Buffer

1. A pH value less than 7

2. A measure of acid strength through hydronium ion dissociation

3. Substances which are resilient to changes in pH

4. NaOH

5. H_2SO_4

Questions 6-10 refer to the following terms.

   (A) Arrenhius base
   (B) Brownsted-Lowry acid
   (C) Lewis acid
   (D) Conjugate acid
   (E) Analyte

6. An acid of unknown identity or concentration

7. Any substance that donates a proton

8. The proton accepted partner of a base

9. Any substance that increases the hydroxide ion, OH^-, concentration in a solution

10. A compound that accepts an electron

101. The conjugate base of sulfuric acid, H_2SO_4, is HSO_4^- BECAUSE H_2SO_4 completely dissociates when in solution.

102. A buffer is a solution that resists a change in pH when an acid or base is added   BECAUSE   buffers contains salts which produce conjugate acids or bases to help mitigate large deviations in $[H^+]$ and $[OH^-]$.

103. An acid with a larger pKa value is a stronger acid   BECAUSE   stronger acids have greater hydronium ion dissociation.

104. If an acid is added to a solution the pH of that solution will increase   BECAUSE   more acidic character equates to a greater value of $[H^+]$.

105. Hydrochloric acid, HCl, will have a weak base as its conjugate   BECAUSE   strong acids such as HCl behave as proton donors.

106. The numbers on the pH scale equal the $[H^+]$ of a solution   BECAUSE   the pOH scale numbers equal the $[OH^-]$ of a solution.

11. Which of the following best describes the resulting solution when $KClO(s)$ is dissolved in $H_2O(l)$? The dissociation of $KClO(s)$ forms a

    (A) strong base and weak acid
    (B) strong base and strong acid
    (C) weak base and weak acid
    (D) weak base and strong acid
    (E) a salt and water

12. Which of the following best describes the resulting solution when $NH_4I(s)$ is dissolved in $H_2O(l)$? The dissociation of $NH_4I(s)$ forms a

    (A) strong base and weak acid
    (B) strong base and strong acid
    (C) weak base and weak acid
    (D) weak base and strong acid
    (E) a salt and water

13. Which of the following best describes the resulting solution when $Ca(NO^{-3})_3(s)$ is dissolved in $H_2O(l)$? The dissociation of $Ca(NO^{-3})_3(s)$ forms a

    (A) strong base and weak acid
    (B) strong base and strong acid
    (C) weak base and weak acid
    (D) weak base and strong acid
    (E) a salt and water

$$H_2SO_4 + H_2O \rightleftharpoons HSO_4^- + H_3O^+$$

14. Consider the chemical reaction above showing the dissociation of sulfuric acid, H_2SO_4, in H_2O. Which of the following compounds is the conjugate of sulfuric acid?

    (A) H_2SO_4
    (B) H_2O
    (C) HSO_4^-
    (D) H_3O^+
    (E) SO_4^{2-}

Questions 15-17 refer to the chemical equation below.

$$NH_3 + H_2O \rightleftharpoons NH_4^+ + OH^-$$

15. Which of the following conjugate pairs is correctly listed as base and conjugate acid, respectively, for the *forward* reaction?

    (A) NH_3 and H_2O
    (B) NH_3 and NH_4^+
    (C) NH_3 and OH^-
    (D) H_2O and NH_4^+
    (E) H_2O and OH^-

16. The K_a value for the ammonium ion, NH_4^+, is 5.6×10^{-10}. Which of the following statements is most likely true? NH_4^+

    (A) has a smaller K_a value than NH_3, because NH_3 is reacting with H_2O
    (B) is considered a weak acid, but the strongest acid in the above reaction
    (C) reacts with OH^- because NH_4^+ has a lower K_a value than H_2O
    (D) completely dissociates into NH_3 when reacting with OH^-
    (E) is a solid at 25°C and 1 atm

17. Which of the following correctly lists the equation for the K_a of the forward reaction?

    (A) $[NH_4^+] [OH^-]$

    (B) $\dfrac{[NH_4^+] [OH^-]}{[NH_3] [H_2O]}$

    (C) $\dfrac{[NH_4^+] [OH^-]}{[NH_3]}$

    (D) $\dfrac{[NH_3] [H_2O]}{[NH_4^+] [OH^-]}$

    (E) $\dfrac{[NH_3]}{[NH_4^+] [OH^-]}$

CHAPTER +11

mV

REDOX

What is the oxidation number of S in SO_3?

① Assign oxidation numbers to the elements that can be depended on.

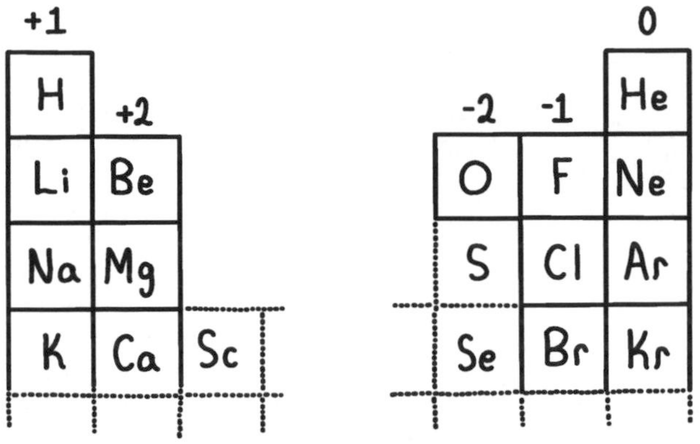

+1

H	+2
Li	Be
Na	Mg
K	Ca	Sc

0

		He
O	F	Ne
S	Cl	Ar
Se	Br	Kr

-2 -1

We can depend on O having an oxidation number of -2.

$(-2)3$
SO_3

② Assign oxidation numbers to the remaining elements such that the sum of all of the oxidation numbers is the charge of the molecule.

$$O_3 + S = SO_3$$
$$(-2)3 + S = 0$$
$$-6 + S = 0$$
$$+6 \qquad +6$$
$$\boxed{S = +6}$$

Note: Oxygen typically has an oxidation number of −2, however, an important exception is in peroxides where oxygen has an oxidation number of −1.

━━━━━━━ Oxidation Sample Questions ━━━━━━━

1. The oxidation number of N in HNO_2^- is

   (A) +2
   (B) +3
   (C) +4
   (D) +5
   (E) +6

① $+1 \quad (-2)2$
HNO_2^-

② $H + N + O_2 = -1$
$+1 + N + (-4) = -1$
$\boxed{N = +2}$

Finding oxidation numbers—*Practice*

2. The oxidation number of N in NO_2^- is

(A) −1
(B) +1
(C) +2
(D) +3
(E) +4

3. The oxidation number of H in $NaHCO_3$ is

(A) −2
(B) −1
(C) +1
(D) +2
(E) +3

4. The oxidation number of S in H_2SO_4 is

(A) −6
(B) −2
(C) +2
(D) +4
(E) +6

5. The oxidation number of Cl in ClO_4^- is

(A) +2
(B) +4
(C) +6
(D) +7
(E) +8

6. The oxidation number of F in H_2F^+ is

(A) −2
(B) −1
(C) +1
(D) +2
(E) +3

7. The oxidation number of H in H_3O^+ is

(A) −2
(B) −1
(C) +1
(D) +2
(E) +3

8. The oxidation number of S in SO_2 is

(A) +1
(B) +2
(C) +3
(D) +4
(E) +6

9. The oxidation number of H is +1 in all of the following, except

(A) H_2SO_4
(B) HCl
(C) HNa_2PO_4
(D) LiH
(E) H_2O_2

10. The oxidation number of O is −2 in all of the following, except

(A) NaOH
(B) MgO
(C) CO_2
(D) H_2SO_4
(E) H_2O_2

11. Cu has an oxidation state of +2 in which of the following compounds?

(A) $CuCl_3$
(B) Cu_2O
(C) $Cu(OH)_2$
(D) Cu_2S
(E) CuH

12. Fe has an oxidation state of +3 in which of the following compounds?

(A) $FeCO_3$
(B) $Fe(NO_3)_2$
(C) $Fe(NO_2)_2$
(D) $Fe_2(CO_3)_3$
(E) $Fe_3(PO_4)_2$

For the vast majority of the reactions we have seen thus far, oxidation numbers of elements on either side of a reaction have remained constant. <u>Redox</u> reactions are when the <u>oxidation numbers change.</u>

NOT a redox reaction, because all of the elements keep the same oxidation number on both sides.

$$\overset{-2 \,+1}{NaOH} + \overset{+1}{HCl} \rightarrow \overset{+1}{NaCl} + \overset{(+1)2}{H_2O}$$
$$\underset{+1 \ +1 \ \ -1}{} \quad \underset{-1}{} \quad \underset{-2}{}$$

A redox reaction because zinc goes from 0 to +2 and copper goes from +2 to 0.

$$\overset{0}{Zn_{(s)}} + \overset{+2}{Cu^{2+}_{(aq)}} \rightarrow \overset{}{Zn^{2+}_{(aq)}} + Cu_{(s)}$$
$$\underset{+2}{} \qquad \underset{0}{}$$

loses 2 electrons

$$Zn_{(s)} + Cu^{2+}_{(aq)} \rightarrow Zn^{2+}_{(aq)} + Cu_{(s)}$$

gains 2 electrons

Zn is being oxidized because it's oxidation number is becoming more positive.

Zn is the reducing agent because it gives electrons to Cu^{2+}.

Cu^{2+} is being reduced because it's oxidation number is becoming more negative.

Cu^{2+} is the oxidizing agent because it takes electrons from Zn.

━━━━━━━ The Voltaic Cell ━━━━━━━

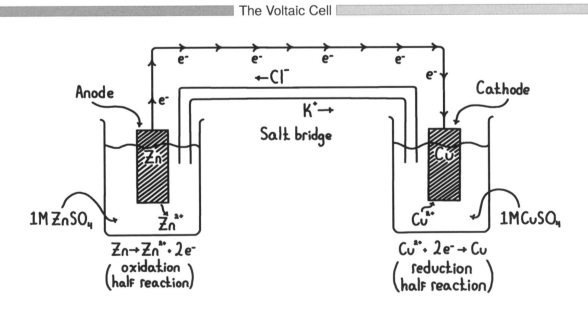

$$4\,Al(s) + 3\,O_2(g) \rightarrow 2\,Al_2O_3(s)$$

1. Which of the following is true of the reaction above?

   (A) $Al(s)$ is reduced and gains electrons
   (B) $Al(s)$ is the oxidizing agent and is oxidized
   (C) $O_2(g)$ is the oxidizing agent and gains electrons
   (D) $Al_2O_3(s)$ is a metallic compound
   (E) This is a disproportionation reaction

2. Which of the following is always true of a reducing agent?

   (A) It forms a metallic bond
   (B) It can be oxidized
   (C) It is in gaseous form at room temperature
   (D) It is present in the salt bridge of a voltaic cell
   (E) It can be reduced

3. All of the following can be classified as oxidation-reduction reactions, EXCEPT

   (A) $Cl_2 + 2\,NaBr \rightarrow 2\,NaCl + Br_2$
   (B) $2H_2 + O_2 \rightarrow 2H_2O$
   (C) $CO_3^{2-} + 2H^+ \rightarrow CO_2 + H_2O$
   (D) $H_2 + Cl_2 \rightarrow 2HCl$
   (E) $4\,Fe(s) + 3\,O_2(g) \rightarrow 2\,Fe_2O_3(s)$

4. Which of the following is always true of an oxidizing agent?

   (A) It is metallic
   (B) It can be reduced
   (C) It forms nonpolar covalent bonds
   (D) It is in gaseous form at room temperature
   (E) It is present in the salt bridge of a voltaic cell

5. Oxygen is oxidized in all of the following, EXCEPT

   (A) $2\,SO_2(g) + O_2(g) \rightarrow 2\,SO_3(g) + heat$
   (B) $2H_2O_2 \rightarrow 2H_2O + O_2$
   (C) $2\,KClO_3(g) \rightarrow 2\,KCl(s) + O_2(g)$
   (D) $2\,H_2O(l) \rightarrow 2\,H_2(g) + O_2(g)$
   (E) $CO_2(g) \rightarrow C(s) + O_2(g)$

6. Which of the following is true of a working voltaic cell?

   (A) Oxidation occurs at the cathode
   (B) Oxidation occurs at the salt bridge
   (C) Polyatomic ions are not able to migrate freely
   (D) Electrons flow from the cathode to the anode
   (E) An oxidation-reduction reaction occurs spontaneously

7. What is the purpose of the salt bridge in a working voltaic cell?

   (A) It allows ions to migrate freely
   (B) It generates electricity
   (C) It is soluble in water
   (D) It allows combustion to occur at the cathode
   (E) A salt bridge is not necessary in a voltaic cell

8. In which direction do electrons flow in a working voltaic cell?

   (A) From the oxidizing agent to the reducing agent
   (B) From the anode to the cathode
   (C) From the salt bridge to the battery
   (D) From the battery to the galvanic cell
   (E) From the protons to the neutrons

Half-reaction	E° (V)
$Li^+(aq) + e^- \rightarrow Li(s)$	−3.04
$K^+(aq) + e^- \rightarrow K(s)$	−2.90
$Ca^{2+}(aq) + 2e^- \rightarrow Ca(s)$	−2.76
$Zn^{2+}(aq) + 2e^- \rightarrow Zn(s)$	−0.76
$Cu^{2+}(aq) + 2e^- \rightarrow Cu(s)$	0.34
$Ag+(aq) + e^- \rightarrow Ag(s)$	0.80
$F_2(g) + 2e^- \rightarrow 2 F-(aq)$	2.87

Each half reaction has a reduction potential associated with it.

In a redox reaction, the half reaction with the more positive reduction potential will be reduced.

Cell Potential Sample Questions

$$Fe \mid Fe^{2+} \parallel Cu^{2+} \mid Cu$$

1. What is the net cell potential of the electrochemical cell above?

$$Fe^{2+}(aq) + 2e^- \rightarrow Fe(s) \qquad -0.45 \text{ V}$$
$$Cu^{2+}(aq) + 2e^- \rightarrow Cu(s) \qquad +0.34 \text{ V}$$

(A) +1.58 V
(B) +0.79 V
(C) +0.11 V
(D) −0.11 V
(E) −0.79 V

① $Fe^{2+} + 2e^- \rightarrow Fe_{(s)}$ $\quad -0.45V$

This reaction needs to flip because

$$-0.45V < +0.34$$

② $Fe_{(s)} \rightarrow Fe^{2+} + 2e^- \qquad +0.45V$
+
$Cu^{2+} + 2e^- \rightarrow Cu \qquad +0.34V$

$Fe_{(s)} + Cu^{2+} \rightarrow Cu + Fe^{2+}$ $\boxed{+0.79V}$

$$Cr \mid Cr^{3+} \parallel Pb^{2+} \mid Pb$$

2. Which substance is the electrode that gains mass during operation of this electrochemical cell?

$$Cr^{3+}(aq) + 3e^- \rightarrow Cr(s) \qquad -0.74 \text{ V}$$
$$Pb^{2+}(aq) + 2e^- \rightarrow Pb(s) \qquad -0.13 \text{ V}$$

(A) The anode
(B) The salt bridge
(C) Cr(s)
(D) Pb(s)
(E) Cr³⁺(aq)

→ The cathode gains mass.
→ The cathode is the site of reduction.

$$-0.74V < -0.13V$$

$\boxed{Pb_{(s)} \text{ gains mass}}$

Cell potential—*Practice*

Questions 3-5 refer to the cell potential half-reaction table on the previous page.

3. What is the net cell potential of the electrochemical reaction shown below?

$$Li(s) + Ag^{+}(aq) \rightarrow Ag(s) + Li^{+}(aq)$$

(A) −3.84 V
(B) −2.24 V
(C) −0.40 V
(D) +2.24 V
(E) +3.84 V

4. What is the net cell potential of the electrochemical reaction shown below?

$$2\,K(s) + Cu^{2+}(aq) \rightarrow Cu(s) + 2\,K^{+}(aq)$$

(A) −6.10 V
(B) −3.24 V
(C) −2.58 V
(D) +3.24 V
(E) +6.10 V

5. What is the net cell potential of the electrochemical reaction shown below?

$$Zn(s) + Cu^{2+}(aq) \rightarrow Cu(s) + Zn^{2+}(aq)$$

(A) −2.10 V
(B) −1.10 V
(C) −0.42 V
(D) +0.42 V
(E) +1.10 V

Questions 1-5 refer to the following oxidation values.

    (A) -2
    (B) -1
    (C) 1
    (D) 4
    (E) 5

1. The oxidation number of carbon in H_2CO_3

2. The oxidation number of phosphorous in Na_3PO_4

3. The oxidation number of phosphorous in $NaHPO_4^{2-}$

4. The oxidation number of oxygen in $H_2PO_4^-$

5. The oxidation number of potassium in $KClO_4$

Questions 6-10 refer to the following terms.

    (A) Anode
    (B) Cathode
    (C) Salt bridge
    (D) Oxidation
    (E) Reduction

6. A tube providing an electrical path between two solutions

7. The positively charged electrode by which electrons leave

8. A decrease in oxidation state by a molecule, atom, or ion

9. The negatively charged electrode by which electrons flow towards

10. An increase in oxidation state by a molecule, atom, or ion

101. In a voltaic cell, electrons flow from the cathode to the anode   BECAUSE   electrons flow towards the positively charged electrode.

102. A change in oxidation number of any element in a chemical reaction indicates that the reaction is a reduction-oxidation reaction   BECAUSE   in reduction-oxidation reactions there is a transfer of electrons.

103. Noble gases typically have an oxidation number of 0   BECAUSE   noble gases begin with a perfect octet and do not want to gain or lose electrons.

104. A voltaic cell requires a power source to begin an electrochemical reaction   BECAUSE   the flow of electrons in a volatic cell start at the anode and end at the cathode.

105. Alkaline earth metals typically have an oxidation number of +1   BECAUSE   Group 1 metals have 1 valence electron.

106. The metallic slab at the positive electrode, over time, loses mass in a voltaic cell   BECAUSE   the positive electrode undergoes oxidation and converts a solid metal to an ion and electrons.

11. The oxidation number of N in NO_3^- is

    (A) -6
    (B) 0
    (C) $+3$
    (D) $+5$
    (E) $+7$

12. The oxidation number of Al in $Al_2(SO_4)_3$ is

    (A) -2
    (B) -1
    (C) $+1$
    (D) $+2$
    (E) $+3$

13. The oxidation number of C in $Ca(HCO_3)_2$ is

    (A) -1
    (B) $+1$
    (C) $+2$
    (D) $+3$
    (E) $+4$

14. All of the following are always true of an anode in a voltaic cell, EXCEPT

    (A) It is the electrode that undergoes reduction
    (B) Electrons originate from the anode
    (C) Metallic ions are produced
    (D) The mass of the metallic slab decreases over time
    (E) It receives negative ions from the salt bridge

15. All of the following can be classified as oxidation-reduction reactions, EXCEPT

    (A) $CO_2(g) + H_2(g) \rightarrow 2\,CO(g) + H_2O(g)$
    (B) $Zn(s) + 2\,H^+(aq) \rightarrow Zn^+(aq) + H_2(g)$
    (C) $2NH_3 + OCl^- \rightleftharpoons N_2H_4 + H_2O + Cl$
    (D) $CH_4(g) + 2\,O_2(g) \rightarrow CO_2(g) + 2\,H_2O(g)$
    (E) $H_2(g) + F_2(g) \rightarrow 2\,HF(g)$

16. The oxidation number of Fe in $K_3Fe(CN)_6$ is

    (A) -2
    (B) -1
    (C) $+1$
    (D) $+2$
    (E) $+3$

17. The oxidation number of H in $(NH_4)_2O$ is

    (A) -2
    (B) -1
    (C) $+1$
    (D) $+2$
    (E) $+3$

18. The oxidation number of Cr in $H_2Cr_2O_7$ is

    (A) $+1$
    (B) $+2$
    (C) $+3$
    (D) $+6$
    (E) $+7$

$$Zn(s) + 2\,H^+(aq) \rightarrow Zn^+(aq) + H_2(g)$$

19. Which of the following is true of the reaction above?

    (A) $H_2(g)$ is a precipitate
    (B) This is a single-replacement reaction
    (C) $Zn(s)$ is oxidized and loses electrons
    (D) $H^+(aq)$ is the reducing agent and is oxidized
    (E) $H^+(aq)$ is the reducing agent and gains electrons

20. Which of the following reactions can be classified as an oxidation-reduction reaction?

    (A) $CO_2(g) + H_2(g) \rightarrow 2\,CO(g) + H_2O(g)$
    (B) $HCl + NaOH \rightarrow NaCl + H_2O$
    (C) $Na_2SO_4 + KCl \rightarrow K_2SO_4 + NaCl$
    (D) $Mg(NO_3)_2 + CaF_2 \rightarrow MgF_2 + Ca(NO_3)_2$
    (E) $NH_4NO_3 + NaOH \rightarrow NaNO_3 + NH_4OH$

Chapter +12

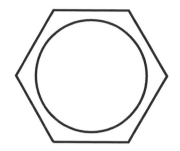

Organic Chemistry

Organic chemistry just means chemistry involving carbon based compounds, that have C-H bonds.

Why does carbon get its own branch of chemistry?

-Carbon has 4 valence electrons, which means that it can form long complex chains of elements

Benzene, drawn in two ways here, is an example of an organic molecule.

-Carbon can also form double and triple bonds with other carbon.

$$C=C \qquad -C\equiv C-$$

These flexible properties of carbon and the fact that it is the fourth most abundant element in the universe make it a great backbone for life.

Note-
• Organic compounds are typically nonpolar.
• Organic compounds are typically flammable.

What are combustion reactions?

Combustion reactions involve an organic compound and $O_2(g)$ as reactants, and $CO_2(g)$ and $H_2O(l)$ as the *only* products. For example:

$$CH_4(g) + 2\,O_2(g) \rightarrow CO_2(g) + 2\,H_2O(l)$$

1. Which of the following is an organic compound?

   (A) Ethanol, C_2H_5OH
   (B) Carbon dioxide, CO_2
   (C) Carbon monoxide, CO
   (D) Hydrogen cyanide, HCN
   (E) Sodium carbonate, Na_2CO_3

2. Every organic compound contains which of the following?

   I. $C—H$
   II. $C{=}H$
   III. $C{=}O$

   (A) I only
   (B) II only
   (C) III only
   (D) I and II only
   (E) I, II, and III

3. Which of the following is an organic compound?

   (A) $C{=}O$

   (B) $O{=}C{=}C{=}C{=}O$

   (C)
   $$C—\underset{\underset{C}{|}}{\overset{\overset{C}{|}}{C}}—\underset{\underset{C}{|}}{\overset{\overset{C}{|}}{C}}—\underset{\underset{C}{|}}{\overset{\overset{C}{|}}{C}}—C$$

   (D)
   $$Cl—\underset{\underset{H}{|}}{\overset{\overset{H}{|}}{C}}—C{\overset{O}{\underset{Br}{<}}}$$

   (E)
   $$H—\underset{\underset{H}{|}}{\overset{\overset{H}{|}}{N}}—N{\overset{O}{\underset{OH}{<}}}$$

4. Which of the following is an organic compound?

   (A) Diamond, C
   (B) Benzene, C_6H_6
   (C) Carbon suboxide, C_3O_2
   (D) Chromium carbide, Cr_3C_2
   (E) Aluminum carbide, Al_4C_3

5. Which of the following statements is always true concerning chemical organic compounds? Organic compounds

   (A) hold large quantities of energy, making them useful in combustion reactions
   (B) are very soluble in polar solvents, such as $H_2O(l)$
   (C) have strong bonds between elements of group 14
   (D) react violently with hydrogen gas, $H_2(g)$
   (E) always contain a $C—C$ bond

6. All of the following chemical structures are organic, EXCEPT

   (A) $O{=}C{=}O$

   (B)
   $$H—\underset{\underset{H}{|}}{\overset{\overset{H}{|}}{C}}—H$$

   (C)
   $$H—\underset{\underset{H}{|}}{\overset{\overset{H}{|}}{C}}—C{\overset{O}{\underset{H}{<}}}$$

   (D)
   $$H—\underset{\underset{H}{|}}{\overset{\overset{H}{|}}{C}}—C{\overset{O}{\underset{OH}{<}}}$$

   (E)
   $$H—\underset{\underset{H}{|}}{\overset{\overset{H}{|}}{C}}—\overset{\overset{O}{||}}{C}—\underset{\underset{H}{|}}{\overset{\overset{H}{|}}{C}}—H$$

Hydrocarbons are chains of carbon and hydrogen.

<u>Alkanes:</u> Hydrocarbons that only consist of single bonds.

$$H-\underset{\underset{H}{|}}{\overset{\overset{H}{|}}{C}}-H \qquad CH_4 \text{ methane}$$

$$H-\underset{\underset{H}{|}}{\overset{\overset{H}{|}}{C}}-\underset{\underset{H}{|}}{\overset{\overset{H}{|}}{C}}-\underset{\underset{H}{|}}{\overset{\overset{H}{|}}{C}}-\underset{\underset{H}{|}}{\overset{\overset{H}{|}}{C}}-H \qquad C_4H_{10} \text{ butane}$$

<u>Alkenes:</u> Hydrocarbons that have atleast 1 double bond.

$$\underset{H}{\overset{H}{>}}C=C\underset{H}{\overset{H}{<}} \qquad C_2H_4 \text{ ethylene}$$

$$\underset{H}{\overset{H}{>}}C=\underset{}{C}-\underset{\underset{H}{|}}{\overset{\overset{H}{|}}{C}}-\underset{\underset{H}{|}}{\overset{\overset{H}{|}}{C}}-H \qquad C_4H_8 \text{ butene}$$

<u>Alkynes:</u> Hydrocarbons that have at least 1 triple bond.

$$H-C\equiv C-H \qquad C_2H_2 \text{ ethyne/acetylene}$$

$$H-C\equiv C-\underset{\underset{H}{|}}{\overset{\overset{H}{|}}{C}}-H \qquad C_3H_4 \text{ propyne}$$

<u>Isomers:</u> Compounds that are composed of the same atoms but with different structural organization.

$$\underset{H}{\overset{H}{>}}C=\underset{}{C}-\underset{\underset{H}{|}}{\overset{\overset{H}{|}}{C}}-\underset{\underset{H}{|}}{\overset{\overset{H}{|}}{C}}-H \qquad 1-\text{butene } C_4H_8$$

$$H-\underset{\underset{H}{|}}{\overset{\overset{H}{|}}{C}}-\underset{}{C}=\underset{}{C}-\underset{\underset{H}{|}}{\overset{\overset{H}{|}}{C}}-H \qquad 2-\text{butene } C_4H_8$$

Class	General Formula	Examples	
Alcohol	R—OH	ethanol	
Alkyl halides	R—X (X = F, Cl, Br, or I)	methyl chloride	
Ether	R—O—R′	methoxy methane	
Aldehyde	R—C(=O)H	formaldehyde	
Ketone	R—C(=O)—R′	acetone	
Carboxylic acid	R—C(=O)OH	acetic acid	
Ester	R—C(=O)—O—R′	metyl ethynoate	
Amine	R—N(H)(H)	methyl amine	

*The C═O double bond between a carbon atom and an oxygen atom is called a *carbonyl group*.

*The OH group attached to organic compounds is known as the *hydroxyl* group.

Questions 1-8 refer to the 5 organic structures below.

(A)   HC≡CH

(B)
$$\underset{H}{\overset{H}{\diagdown}}C=C\underset{H}{\overset{H}{\diagup}}$$

(C)
$$H-\underset{\overset{\displaystyle |}{H}}{\overset{\overset{\displaystyle H}{|}}{C}}-\underset{\overset{\displaystyle |}{H}}{\overset{\overset{\displaystyle H}{|}}{C}}-H$$

(D)
$$H-\underset{\overset{\displaystyle |}{H}}{\overset{\overset{\displaystyle H}{|}}{C}}-C\underset{\diagdown H}{\overset{\diagup O}{}}$$

(E)
$$H-\underset{\overset{\displaystyle |}{H}}{\overset{\overset{\displaystyle H}{|}}{C}}-\overset{\overset{\displaystyle O}{\|}}{C}-\underset{\overset{\displaystyle |}{H}}{\overset{\overset{\displaystyle H}{|}}{C}}-H$$

1. Ketone

2. Alkane

3. Alkene

4. Acetylene

5. Aldehyde

6. Ethane

7. Proponone

8. Alkyne

9. Which of the following best describes a alcohol?

(A) A group of atoms bonded to a group 17 ion
(B) A group of atoms bonded to an oxygen atom, which is bonded to a hydrogen
(C) A group of atoms bonded to a carbonyl group, which is bonded to a hydroxy group
(D) A group of atoms bonded to a carbonyl group, which is bonded to a different group of atoms
(E) A group of atoms bonded to a carbonyl group, which is bonded to an oxygen atom, which is bonded to a different group of atoms

10. Which of the following best describes an alkyl halide?

(A) A group of atoms bonded to a group 17 ion
(B) A group of atoms bonded to an oxygen atom, which is bonded to a hydrogen
(C) A group of atoms bonded to a carbonyl group, which is bonded to a hydroxy group
(D) A group of atoms bonded to a carbonyl group, which is bonded to a different group of atoms
(E) A group of atoms bonded to a carbonyl group, which is bonded to an oxygen atom, which is bonded to a different group of atoms

11. Which of the following best describes an ester?

(A) A group of atoms bonded to a group 17 ion
(B) A group of atoms bonded to an oxygen atom, which is bonded to a hydrogen
(C) A group of atoms bonded to a carbonyl group, which is bonded to a hydroxy group
(D) A group of atoms bonded to a carbonyl group, which is bonded to a different group of atoms
(E) A group of atoms bonded to a carbonyl group, which is bonded to an oxygen atom, which is bonded to a different group of atoms

12. Which of the following best describes a ketone?

    (A) A group of atoms bonded to an oxygen atom, which is bonded to a hydrogen
    (B) A group of atoms bonded to an oxygen atom, which is bonded to a different group of atoms
    (C) A group of atoms bonded to a carbonyl group, which is bonded to a hydroxy group
    (D) A group of atoms bonded to a carbonyl group, which is bonded to a hydrogen atom
    (E) A group of atoms bonded to a carbonyl group, which is bonded to a different group of atoms

13. Which of the following best describes an aldehyde?

    (A) A group of atoms bonded to an oxygen atom, which is bonded to a hydrogen
    (B) A group of atoms bonded to an oxygen atom, which is bonded to a different group of atoms
    (C) A group of atoms bonded to a carbonyl group, which is bonded to a hydroxy group
    (D) A group of atoms bonded to a carbonyl group, which is bonded to a hydrogen atom
    (E) A group of atoms bonded to a carbonyl group, which is bonded to a different group of atoms

14. Which of the following best describes an ether?

    (A) A group of atoms bonded to an oxygen atom, which is bonded to a hydrogen
    (B) A group of atoms bonded to an oxygen atom, which is bonded to a different group of atoms
    (C) A group of atoms bonded to a carbonyl group, which is bonded to a hydroxy group
    (D) A group of atoms bonded to a carbonyl group, which is bonded to a hydrogen atom
    (E) A group of atoms bonded to a carbonyl group, which is bonded to a different group of atoms

Questions 15-22 refer to the 5 chemical structures below.

(A) $H-\overset{\overset{\displaystyle H}{|}}{\underset{\underset{\displaystyle H}{|}}{C}}-H$

(B) $O=C=O$

(C)   structure showing $C=C-C$ chain with hydrogens

(D)   structure showing $H-C-C-C-C$ chain ending in a carbonyl and OH group

(E) $H-\overset{\overset{\displaystyle H}{|}}{\underset{\underset{\displaystyle H}{||}}{C}}-N\overset{H}{\underset{H}{<}}$

15. Alkene

16. An inorganic gas

17. Methane

18. Alkane

19. Butanoic acid

20. Carboxylic acid

21. Methylamine

22. Propene

Questions 1-5 refer to the following oxidation values.

(A) Alkane
(B) Alkene
(C) Alkyne
(D) Isomer
(E) Hydrocarbon

1. Chains of carbon and hydrogens

2. Methane

3. An organic compound that consists at least one triple bond

4. Same atoms but different structural organization

5. Butyne

Questions 6-10 refer to the following terms.

(A) Ester
(B) Ether
(C) Ketone
(D) Aldehyde
(E) Carboxylic acid

6. Acetone

7. Ethanal

8. Proponone

9. Methoxy methane

10. Pentanoic acid

101. All organic compounds are insoluble in H_2O BECAUSE   organic compounds generally have low dissociation character.

102. Hydrocarbons contain at least one non-single bond in their chemical structure   BECAUSE   hydrocarbons are groups of bonded carbon and hydrogen.

103. The carbon atom, within an organic compound, bonds up to 4 times with surrounding elements   BECAUSE   carbon contains 4 valence electrons.

104. One mole of an alcohol in its liquid phase contains hydrogen bonding   BECAUSE   hydrogen bonding occurs when H^+ is bonded to an oxygen, fluorine, or nitrogen atom from an adjacent molecule.

105. Carboxylic acids, when dissolved in solution, lowers the pH of the solution   BECAUSE   carboxylic acid contains hydroxide ions, OH^-, which add to the overall $[OH^-]$ of the solution.

106. $C_6H_{12}O_6$, glucose, is an organic compound   BECAUSE   an organic compound contains carbon, hydrogen, and oxygen atoms.

11. Which of the following is an organic compound?

(A) Cementite, Fe_3C
(B) Carbon monoxide, CO
(C) Sodium cyanide, NaCN
(D) Pentane, C_5H_{12}
(E) Calcium carbonate, $CaCO_3$

12. Which of the following best describes a carboxylic acid? A group of atoms which are bonded to a(n)

(A) oxygen atom, which is bonded to a hydrogen
(B) oxygen atom, which is bonded to a different group of atoms
(C) carbonyl group, which is bonded to a hydroxy group
(D) carbonyl group, which is bonded to a hydrogen atom
(E) carbonyl group, which is bonded to a different group of atoms

13. All of the following chemical structures are organic, EXCEPT

(A) H—C—H (with H above and below C)

(B) H—C—C—H (with H above and below each C)

(C) H—C—C with =O above and H below (aldehyde structure, H and H on first carbon)

(D) H—C—C with =O above and OH, and H's on first carbon

(E) C—C—C—C—C with C above and below the middle three carbons

14. All of the following statements are true concerning organic compounds, EXCEPT

(A) organic compounds contain at least one carbon-hydrogen bond
(B) molecules containing the amine functional group do not contain any carbon atoms
(C) organic compounds typically have low boiling points
(D) nonpolar solvents are more useful for creating organic solutions than polar solvents
(E) different compounds that contain similar functional groups share similar reaction characteristics

15. Which of the following best describes an amine? A group of atoms which are bonded to a(n)

(A) nitrogen atom, which is bonded to hydrogen atoms
(B) nitrogen group, which is bonded to a hydroxy group
(C) nitrogen atom, which is bonded to a different group of atoms
(D) carbonyl group, which is bonded to hydrogen atoms
(E) carbonyl group, which is bonded to a hydroxy group

16. Dimethyl ether contains which of the following bonds?

I. C—H
II. C—O
III. C=O

(A) I only
(B) II only
(C) III only
(D) I and II only
(E) I, II, and III

CHAPTER +13

?

RANDOM FACTS

This chapter is a slightly deeper dive into the various topics covered throughout the book. You need not master these topics to perform well on your SAT Chemistry exam. Feel free to read through this chapter to feel more comfortable with extra terms and chemistry ideas!

Below is a list of some advanced terms so you feel more comfortable reading through the SAT Chemistry exam. Also, we added random facts that are infrequently tested, but still tested!

Term	Definition
Mixture	When two or more substances are combined, but not chemically combined.
Hydrolysis	The chemical breakdown of a compound when reacting with water. For example: $CH_3COOCH_3 + H_2O \rightarrow CH_3COOH + CH_3OH$
Viscosity	The magnitude of internal friction, measured in force per area. More viscous liquids move slower than less viscous liquids.
Miscible liquids	Two liquids that form a mixed solution without any discernible difference. For example, water and apple juice.
Immiscible liquids	Two liquids that form a mixed solution with distinct layers. For example, water and oil.
Sublimation	A phase change from solid to gas, skipping the liquid phase entirely. A common example is carbon dioxide, $CO_2(s) \rightarrow CO_2(g)$
Deposition	A phase change from gas to solid, skipping the liquid phase entirely.
C (graphite)	You may see carbon expressed this way on the exam. This simply means the graphite form of carbon. This typically presents itself in questions involving Hess' Law. You need not worry about molecular mass or the like. Simply balancing the quantity of graphite carbons on both sides of an equation is enough.
C (diamond)	See above for C(graphite). Similarly for carbon in the diamond form, you may also see other notations such as C(fullerite) and C(70).
Analyte	In titration, a solution of known quantity and unknown concentration that receives a solution of known concentration (titrant).
Titrant	In titration, a solution of known concentration that is delivered via a buret to a solution of known quantity but unknown concetration (analyte).
Alloys	Combination of two separate metals. For example: brass, bronze, and steel.
Amphoteric	A substance that can behave as an acid or a base. For example, HSO_4^- can act as an acid and become SO_4^{2-}, or, act as a base and become H_2SO_4.
Haber process	The synthesis of ammonia from hydrogen gas and nitrogen gas. $H_2(g) + N_2(g) \rightleftarrows NH_3(g)$
Mass spectrometer	An apparatus that analyzes a substance based on the mass of its components.
Volatile	A substance that easily evaporates at standard temperature and pressure. An example is acetone, or nail polish remover.
Chemical/Physical Change	Examples of a chemical change are combustion, oxidation, and decomposition. Examples of a physical change are evaporation. condensation, and freezing/melting.

Here are some random facts about select elements.

Element	Random fact
Sulfur, S	Compounds containing sulfur, S, could lead to the production of acid rain. $SO_3(g) + H_2O(l) \rightarrow H_2SO_4(aq)$ Also tends to have a rotten egg odor.
Iron, Fe	Compounds tend to have a reddish-brown color.
Hydrogen, H_2	Burns with a blue flame. Highly explosive.
Fluorine, F_2	Pale yellow gas at 25°C.
Chlorine, Cl_2	Green gas at 25°C.
Bromine, Br_2	Dark-red liquid at 25°C.
Iodine, I_2	Purple-black solid at 25°C.
Sodium, Na	Burns yellow.
Potassium, K	Burns violet.
Lithium, Li	Burns crimson.
Calcium, Ca	Burns orange-red.
Barium, Ba	Burns green.
Strontium, Sr	Burns bright red.

Here are some common names for compounds that have appeared on the SAT Chemistry.

Name	Compound	What to know
Baking soda	$NaHCO_3$	Baking soda is typically used a cleaning product or antacid because it is basic.
Dry ice	$CO_2(s)$	Dry ice simply stands for solid carbon dioxide. It will readily sublime in standard conditions.
Ozone	$O_3(g)$	You probably know ozone protects us from ultraviolet radiation from the sun. Its chemical formula is O_3.
Vinegar	$HC_2H_3O_2$	Acetic acid is commonly known as vinegar.
Saturated hydrocarbon	C_nH_{2n+2}	An alkane with the generic formula C_nH_{2n+2}

Ions That Form Soluble Compounds	Exceptions
Group 1 ions (Li^+, Na^+, etc.)	
ammonium (NH_4^+)	
nitrate (NO_3^-)	
acetate ($C_2H_3O_2^-$ or CH_3OO^-)	
hydrogen carbonate (HCO_3^-)	
chlorate (ClO_3^-)	
perchlorate (ClO_4^-)	
halides (Cl^-, Br^-, I^-)	when combined with Ag^+, Pb^{2+}, and Hg_2^{2+}
sulfates (SO_4^-)	when combined with Ag^+, Ca^{2+}, Sr^{2+}, Ba^{2+}, and Pb^{2+}

Ions That Form Insoluble Compounds	Exceptions
carbonate (CO_3^{2-})	when combined with Group 1 ions or ammonium (NH_4^+)
chromate (CrO_4^{2-})	when combine with Group 1 ions, Ca^{2+}, Mg^{2+}, or ammonium (NH_4^+)
phosphate (PO_4^{3-})	when combined with Group 1 ions or ammonium (NH_4^+)
sulfide (S_2^-)	when combined with Group 1 ions or ammonium (NH_4^+)
hydroxide (OH^-)	when combined with Group 1 ions, Ca^{2+}, Ba^{2+}, Sr^{2+}, or ammonium (NH_4^+)

The valence shell electron pair repulsion (VSEPR) theory shows how different bond angles form different shapes of molecules depending on the quantity of bonds and lone pair electrons.

Bonds	Lone pairs	Shape	Bond angle	Example	Structure
2	0	Linear	180°	CO_2	$O\!=\!C\!=\!O$
2	1	Bent	120°	SO_2	
2	2	Bent	109.5°	H_2O	
3	0	Trigonal planar	120°	BF_3	
3	1	Trigonal pyramidal	107°	NH_3	
4	0	Tetrahedral	109.5°	CH_4	

What are bond lengths?

For the SAT Chemistry test, you should know that single bonds have the *longest* bond length, then double bonds, then triple bonds. The shorter the bond length the stronger the bond strength. This makes sense since triple bonds are the strongest, yet they are the shortest!

Below you will see an expanded version of the periodic table. The f orbitals have been shaded in dark gray to show where they would theoretically go if one were to expand the periodic table typically used.

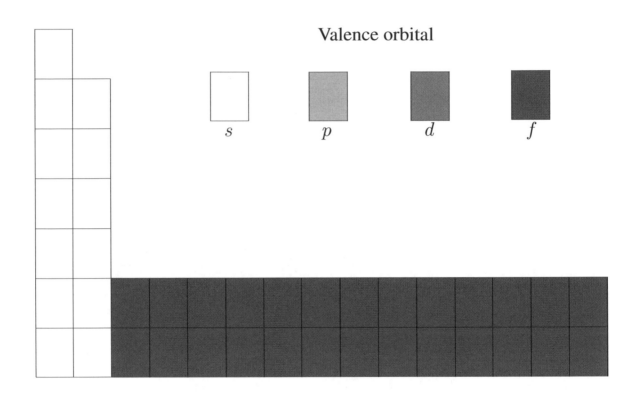

How can I remember this on the SAT Chemistry exam?

On the periodic table that you are given during the exam, the *Lanthanide Series and the †Actinide Series are labeled for you. These two series represent the elements that have valence f orbitals.

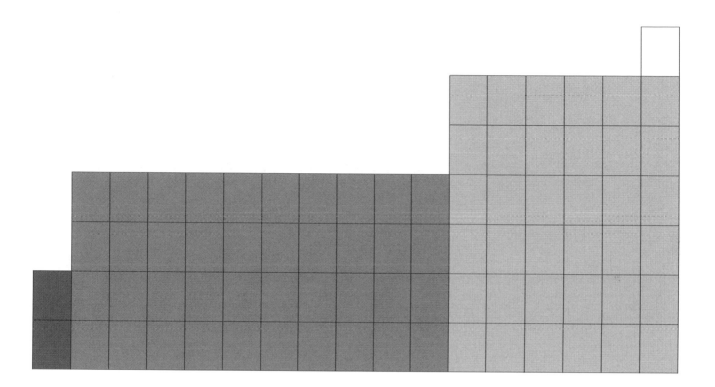

Quantum number	Name	Label	Possible values	Notes
n	principle	electron energy level	1, 2, 3, ...	
l	angular momentum	orbital type (s, p, d, f)	0, 1, 2, ..., $(n-1)$	$0 = s$ orbital $1 = p$ orbital $2 = d$ orbital $3 = f$ orbital
m_l	magnetic	orbital sub-type	$-l$ and $+l$	Each orbital shell sub-type can only fit 2 electrons.
m_s	spin	electron spin	$\pm 1/2$	

Where have I seen them?

You have seen quantum numbers within electron configurations. Below you will notice that not all of the quantum numbers are being represented. The magnetic and spin quantum numbers are not typically written when we write out electron configurations. This is because the behavior of the electrons on that level is not explored in a typical high school chemistry class.

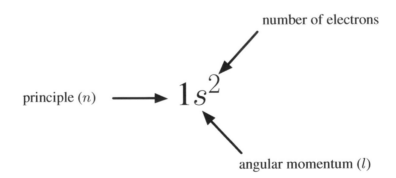

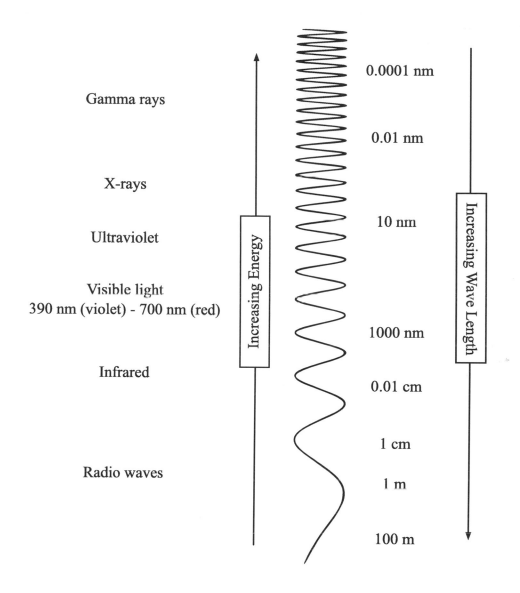

Gamma rays — 0.0001 nm

— 0.01 nm

X-rays

— 10 nm

Ultraviolet

Visible light
390 nm (violet) - 700 nm (red)

— 1000 nm

Increasing Energy

Increasing Wave Length

Infrared

— 0.01 cm

— 1 cm

Radio waves

— 1 m

— 100 m

What can the SAT Chemistry exam ask me?

Remember that a shorter wavelength means more energy, and a longer wavelength means less energy. You will also want to know that the range for visible light is between 390 nm (violet/purple) and 700 nm (red).

Welcome to a little bit of science history! This page talks about how the structure of the atom came to be and which scientists were involved in the progression. Don't turn the page so fast - we made it easy to follow. Enjoy a trip back in time with 4 important scientists and their discoveries!

J. J. Thomson names the electron

In 1987, J. J. Thomson discovered the first subatomic particle (the electron). Thomson suggested that one of the fundamental units was more than 1,000 times smaller than the atom (Today we know that electrons basically have no mass). He found that particles in cathode rays traveled much further through air than expected, which meant they must have been much lighter than atoms. He concluded the rays were made up of tiny, negatively charged, particles. Thomson called these particles *corpuscles*, but later scientists named the particle the *electron*.

Ernest Rutherford discovers the nucleus

In 1899, Ernest Rutherford conducted his famous gold foil experiment. He used thin sheets of metal foil and bombarded the space with alpha particles, $_2^4\text{He}$. Because most of the alpha particles went through without changing direction, Rutherford concluded that the atoms of the metals used must be made up of mostly empty space. A small quantity of alpha particles did change direction, and so Rutherford stated that all of the positive charge and all essentially all the mass of an atom is concentrated in an infinitesimally small space and negliglbe volume of the total volume of the atom. He called this space the *nucleus*.

Niels Bohr proposes a structure for the atom

In 1913, Niels Bohr showed the atom to be a small positively charged nucleus surrounded by electrons that traveled in orbits around the center. This model is very similar to our solar system. We know now that electrons DO NOT travel in circular orbits, but rather, are contained in probability spaces known as orbitals. The quantum energy levels, n, described in Chapter 1 are a modern depiction of the Bohr model.

Werner Heisenberg unknowingly discovers orbitals

In 1927, Werner Heisenberg proposed his uncertainty principle, which states that the position and velocity of an object cannot be measured exactly at the same time. This occurs in chemistry when trying to pinpoint the speed and position of electrons. We cannot know precisely where electrons are, so, instead, we use orbitals to showcase the probability clouds of where electrons *probably are*.

13.9- ADVANCED NUCLEAR CHEMISTRY

There are a few additional facts that could be helpful on the SAT Chemistry exam with respect to nuclear chemistry.

Half-life

The half-life of a radioisotope is defined as the duration of time for the amount of the isotope to fall to half its original value. For example, let's say you have 100 g of C-14 (carbon with a mass of 14). The known half-life of C-14 is 5.3 years. So, this means that after 5.3 years you will now have 50 g of C-14. After an additional 5.3 years, or 10.6 years in total, you will now have 25 g of C-14, and so on and so forth.

The half-life durations of essentially all radioisotopes are known and can be found in most chemistry reference tables.

What can the SAT Chemistry exam ask me?

The SAT Chemistry exam will likely give you a radioisotope mass and its half-life, then ask you to determine the remaining mass after a duration of time.

What is a Geiger counter?

I am glad you asked. So a Geiger counter is an instrument you can use to detect radiation. It will detect alpha particles, beta particles, and gamma rays.

What can the SAT Chemistry exam ask me?

So, if you ever come across a Geiger counter (named after Hans Geiger, who actually had Ernest Rutherford as his adviser), think radioisotopes, half-life, and radiation detection.

This is a distillation apparatus. We can use this to separate many miscible liquids based on their different *boiling points*. Substances with lower boiling points will distill before substances with higher boiling points as the flask heats up. They will then cool and be collected in the beaker.

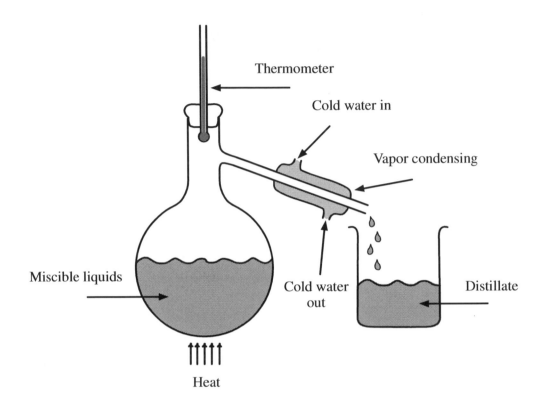

What can the SAT Chemistry exam ask me?

We anticipate that the exam could ask anything about separating miscible liquids by boiling points and having the answer be distillation. You can also see an apparatus such as the one above and be asked about the different parts.

To read a meniscus properly, read the bottom center level of the liquid and NOT where the liquid touches the graduated cylinder. This dip is due to the surface tension between the graduated cylinder and the liquid.

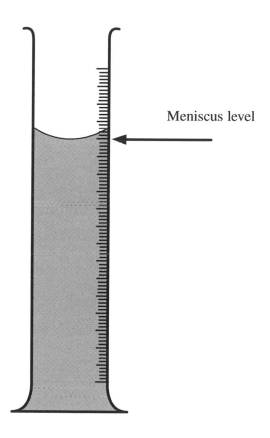

Meniscus level

What can the SAT Chemistry exam ask me?

You can have the above figure in front of you and a question can ask what is the volume of the liquid in the graduated cylinder. In which case, you will need to be sure to read the meniscus level.

13.12- ADVANCED ACIDS AND BASES, BUFFERS, AND INDICATORS

Here are two tables showcasing some common acids and bases that you should know. Most are strong acids and bases with complete dissocation. Being familiar with their names is very helpful on most acids/bases questions.

Common acids	
Formula	Name
$HCl(aq)$	hydrochloric acid [δ]
$HNO_3(aq)$	nitric acid [δ]
$H_2SO_4(aq)$	sulfuric acid [δ]
$H_3PO_4(aq)$	phosphoric acid [δ]
$H_2CO_3(aq)$	carbonic acid
$HC_2H_3O_2(aq)$	acetic acid

[δ] Strong acid

Common bases	
Formula	Name
$NaOH(aq)$	sodium hydroxide
$KOH(aq)$	potassium hydroxide
$Ca(OH)_2(aq)$	calcium hydroxide
$NH_3(aq)$	aqueous ammonia

Buffers

A buffer is a solution that resists changes in pH when acids or bases are added to it. Substances inside of buffers that help it resist pH change are salts and conjugate acids and bases.

The most common example of a buffer on the SAT Chemistry exam is human blood. It has a pH of around 7.3 and has a significant resistance to pH change.

Acid/base indicators

Below is a table of 5 acid/base indicators, their pH transition range, and their color range as pH increases. Common indicators are litmus and phenolphthalein.

Indicator	pH transition range	Color change
methyl orange	3-4.5	red to yellow
bromcresol green	3.8-5.4	yellow to blue
litmus	4.5-8.3	red to blue
bromthymol blue	6.0-7.6	yellow to blue
phenolphthalein	8-9	colorless to pink

Titration is the process through which a known concentration of an acid or base (*titrant* - contained in the buret) is added to a known quantity, but unknown concentration, of a different acid or base (*analyte*).

The titrant is added to the analyte until the pH indicator changes color. At which point, the volume of titrant used to produce the color change is utilized to calculate the concentration of the analyte.

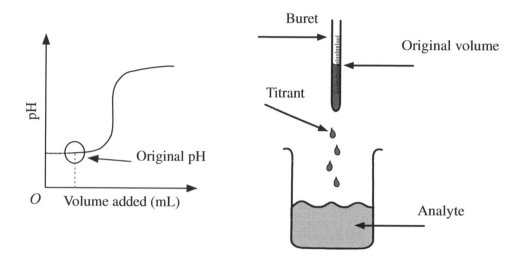

The top-right diagram illustrates the titrant is beginning to be added to the analyte. The top-left diagram shows the pH of the solution is slowly starting to increase.

The bottom-right diagram illustrates the color change of the solution, at which point titration is halted. The bottom-left diagram shows the *equivalent point* (the moles of the titrant equal the moles of the analyte).

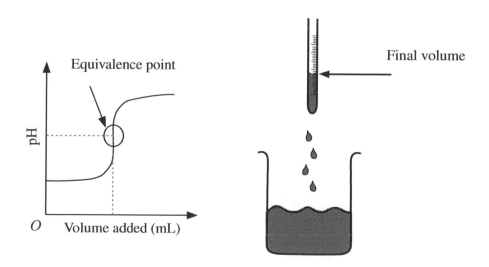

13.14- ACTIVITY LIST

More active metals and nonmetals are on top, least active metals and nonmetals are on bottom

Most active ↑ / Least active ↓

Metals	Nonmetals
Li	F_2
Rb	Cl_2
K	Br_2
Cs	I_2
Ba	
Sr	
Ca	
Na	
Mg	
Al	
Ti	
Mn	
Zn	
Cr	
Fe	
Co	
Ni	
Sn	
Pb	
H_2*	
Cu	
Ag	
Au	

What can the SAT Chemistry exam ask me?

Questions will typically compare metals less active than H_2 and ones more active than H_2. If you remember copper, silver, and gold are below H_2 in descending order, then by default any other metal is more active!

Paper chromatography is a way of separating chemical substances that are dissolved in solution. Substances have a choice: stay in the solution or adsorb into the paper. Substances that have a higher affinity to stay in solution will travel farther up the paper, while substances that have a higher affinity to adsorb into the paper will show a spot more towards the bottom of the page.

A sample of the apparatus is shown below

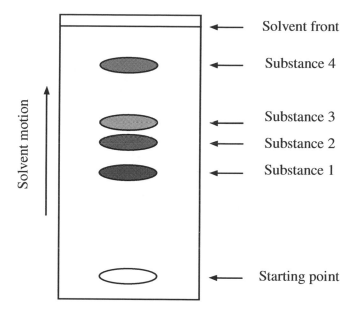

What can the SAT Chemistry exam ask me?

When you see the word *chromatography*, think *separating substances*. Paper chromatography is just one way of separating substances.

A manometer can be used to measure the vapor pressure of a solution or gas in a flask. It measures the pressure difference between the solution or gas and the atmosphere.

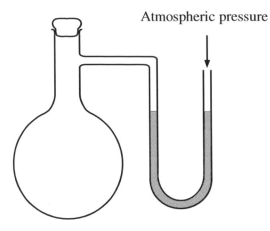

If the levels on both sides of the manometer are equal, the pressure of the solution or gas is equivalent to the atmospheric pressure.

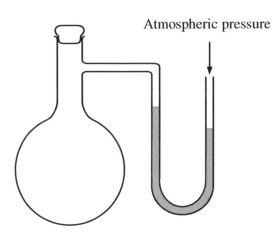

If the level closest to the flask is higher, then the solution or gas has a lower pressure than atmospheric pressure.

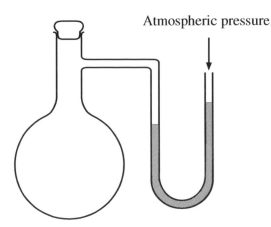

If the level closest to the flask is lower, then the solution or gas has a greater pressure than atmospheric pressure.

The triple point curve shows the 3 phases of a certain substance at varying pressures and temperatures.

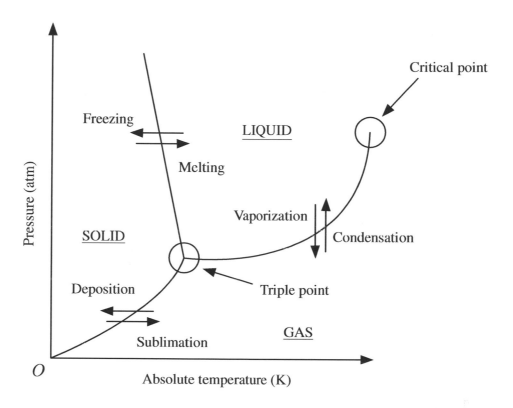

Triple point is the pressure and temperature at which all 3 phases are present at the same time.
Critical point is the pressure and temperature above which the liquid and gas phase are indistinguishable.

What can the SAT Chemistry exam ask me?

You should be able to identify where the gas, liquid, and solid phases are by looking at a blank triple point curve.

13.18- The 3 Laws of Thermodynamics

Welcome to the 3 laws of thermodynamics. You may be asking yourself, "Chris and Mike, what does thermodynamics mean?" Glad you asked! Thermodynamics is the understanding of how heat and other forms of energy (such as energy in chemical bonds) relate to one another. If we break a bond between two nitrogen atoms, what happens? Thermodynamics helps us to understand the result.

There are 3 laws of thermodynamics that we must follow when analyzing energy. We have listed them in a friendly manner below:

1. The first law, also known as the Law of Conversation of Energy, states that energy can neither be created nor destroyed. Ever see someone throw a fireball in a movie? Yeah, that can't happen. Unless the person created the fireball from energy within their body. The energy must come from somewhere! If you rub sandpaper back and forth against a rough surface, that surface will feel hot if you try to touch it. That heat came from the friction you created with the sandpaper and the surface. Energy comes in many forms and is always changing, but never created out of nothing and never destroyed into nothing!

2. The second law states that entropy always increases. As you know since you read the entire book and remember everything, the change in entropy is ΔS and is more commonly known as the change in disorder of a system. Disorder...well let's think. If you don't do anything, what will happen to your room? It will probably get messy. You need to put energy into your room to clean it up. This is why ΔS for systems is naturally positive, because disorder naturally goes up. Boom, the second law!

3. The third law states that entropy of a system approaches a constant value as temperature approaches absolutely zero (0 Kelvin). This law is not too useful when taking the SAT Chemistry exam. However, it is good to know that at absolute zero the entropy of a system is typically zero. Molecules essentially stop vibrating all together. How cold is absolute zero you ask? Only $-273°C$ or $-460°F$. That's cold.

Those are the 3 laws. We hope you have a better understanding as to how energy moves and changes about a system!

Prefixes

Nano	Micro	Milli	Centi	Deci	Unit	Kilo	Mega	Giga
n	μ	m	c	d		k	M	G
10^{-9}	10^{-6}	10^{-3}	10^{-2}	10^{-1}	10^{0}	10^{3}	10^{6}	10^{9}
nm	μm	mm	cm	dm	m	km	Mm	Gm

Significant Figures

Significant figures are the digits of a measured result that are accurate based on the precision of the apparatus used. You do not really need to know the theory, but you should know how to tell how many significant figures are present within a number. The rules are as follows:

1. If the number has a decimal place, start with the left-most nonzero digit and count the number of digits scanning to the right.

2. If the number does not have a decimal place, start with the right-most nonzero digit and count the number of digits scanning to the left.

For example, 4200 has 2 significant figures, while 4200.1 has 5 significant figures.

If you multiply or divide two or more numbers together, take the lowest quantity of significant figures as the result. If you add or subtract two or more numbers together, take the lowest quantity of decimal places as the result.

## CHAPTER 14

CE

101 TRUE FALSE QUESTIONS

PLEASE USE THE SECTION AT THE LOWER LEFT-HAND CORNER
OF THE ANSWER SHEET AND ANSWER QUESTIONS 101-115
ACCORDING TO THE DIRECTIONS DESCRIBED BELOW.

Part B

Directions: Each question below consists of two statements, I in the left-hand column and II in the right-hand column. For each question, determine whether statement I is true or false <u>and</u> whether statement II is true or false and fill in the corresponding T or F circles on your answer sheet. Fill in circle CE only if statement II is a correct explanation of the true statement I.

EXAMPLES:		
I		**II**
EX 1. $Ca(OH)_2$ is a strong acid	BECAUSE	$Ca(OH)_2$ contains calcium.
EX 2. In a chemical reaction mass is conserved	BECAUSE	matter is neither created nor destroyed.

SAMPLE ANSWERS

	I		II		CE*
EX 1	⊤	●	●	Ⓕ	○
EX 2	●	Ⓕ	●	Ⓕ	●

I		**II**
101. As a radioactive isotope undergoes alpha decay, the isotope loses 4 neutrons and 2 protons	BECAUSE	alpha decays involves the release of a helium nucleus, ^4_2He
102. In a molecule of methane, CH_4, there are 4 nonpolar C-H bonds	BECAUSE	CH_4 is nonpolar.
103. Ozone, O_3, exhibits resonance and is represented by the superposition of two chemical structures	BECAUSE	O_3 contains a single bond and a double bond.
104. HCl is an ionic compound	BECAUSE	hydrogen is a metal and chlorine is a nonmetal, a transfer of electrons occurs.
105. Cl_2 experiences no intermolecular forces of attraction between molecules	BECAUSE	nonpolar substances with symmetrical structures experience no dipole moments.
106. NH_4F contains two different types of bonds, ionic and covalent,	BECAUSE	NH_4^+ exhibits sharing of electrons between nitrogen and hydrogen, while NH_4^+ and F^- experience a transfer of electrons.
107. 44.8 L of $H_2O(l)$ is equivalent to 2 moles	BECAUSE	at standard temperature and pressure, 22.4 L of any substance is equivalent to 6.022×10^{23} molecules.
108. Methane, CH_4 has an empirical formula of CH_4	BECAUSE	an empirical formula is equivalent to the molecular formula for organic compounds.

109. Collisons that ideal gas particles experience result in no loss of energy and are completely elastic — BECAUSE — ideal behavior is most favorable at high temperatures and low pressures.

110. According to Boyle's Law, as the volume of a gas increases, the pressure of the gas decreases — BECAUSE — Boyle's Law states that the product of pressure and volume of a particular gas is constant.

111. Krypton, Kr, has a larger rate of effusion than helium, He, — BECAUSE — the mass of a gas and the rate of effusion are directly related.

112. In a 1 L container at 5 atm holding 0.25 L of oxygen gas, $O_2(g)$, and 0.75 L of nitrogen gas, $N_2(g)$, the partial pressure of $O_2(g)$ is 1.25 atm — BECAUSE — the sum of the partial pressures of each gas in a mixture equal the total pressure of the mixture.

113. The reaction $H_2(g) + O_2(g) \rightarrow H_2O(l)$ shows a decrease in entropy, ΔS — BECAUSE — entropy decreases as substances go from a gas state to a liquid state.

114. The melting of $H_2O(s)$ to $H_2O(l)$ is the result of an increase in the average kinetic energy of the particles — BECAUSE — ideal gas particles are in constant nonlinear motion.

115. A 3 L container of $H_2O(l)$ at standard pressure with a vapor pressure of 100 mm Hg will not experience boiling — BECAUSE — $H_2O(l)$ always experiences boiling at $100°C$.

116. All solid substances are more dense than their respective liquid phase — BECAUSE — density is measured in mass per unit volume.

117. A concentrated solution is also considered supersaturated — BECAUSE — a supersaturated state can be obtained by isothermically adding additional solute to a saturated solution.

118. $H_2O(l)$ has a higher boiling point than $H_2O(aq)$ — BECAUSE — pure substances contain stronger bonds than aqueous solutions.

119. Chemical reactions that reach equilibrium eventually stop reacting and yield constant concentrations — BECAUSE — the equilibrium constant is the ratio of concentrations of products to concentrations of reactants.

120. The solubility product of $NaCl(s)$ is represented by the product of $[Na^+]$ and $[Cl^-]$ — BECAUSE — $NaCl(s)$ is an ionic substance, which dissociates into ions when placed in $H_2O(l)$.

121. An endothermic reaction at $25°C$ will favor the production of more products when the temperature of the reaction chamber is raised to $30°C$ — BECAUSE — in an endothermic reaction heat behaves as a reactant.

122. As the temperature of a reaction chamber decreases, the rate of reaction also decreases — BECAUSE — a decrease in the average kinetic energy of particles results in a loss of effective collisions.

$$\text{Li}(s) + \text{FeNO}_3(aq) \rightarrow \text{Fe}(s) + \text{LiNO}_3(aq)$$

123. In the reaction above, if the pressure of the reaction chamber increases the rate of production of $\text{Fe}(s)$ increases BECAUSE the NO_3^- anion bonded to any cation is soluble in $\text{H}_2\text{O}(l)$.

124. Endothermic reactions have ΔH values greater than 0 BECAUSE in an endothermic reaction, the enthalpy of the products is greater than the enthalpy of the reactants.

125. During a synthesis reaction if $\Delta H_f > 0$ then the reaction can spontaneously occur BECAUSE a synthesis reaction involves one, relatively larger molecule, forming two or more smaller molecules.

126. A double replacement reaction cannot occur if an insoluble precipitate is to be formed BECAUSE a solid product indicates a nonspontaneous reaction.

127. A reaction between copper (III) sulfate and sodium carbonate goes to completion BECAUSE $\text{CuCO}_3(s)$ is produced.

128. The enthalpy change of multiple subreactions can be summed to calculate the total enthalpy change of a reaction BECAUSE enthalpy is a state function.

129. $\text{HCl}(aq)$ is considered to be an Arrhenius acid BECAUSE an Arrhenius acid is defined by a substance that donates a proton.

130. Lewis bases are electron acceptors BECAUSE an increase in oxidation state defines a Lewis base.

131. When $\text{HCl}(aq)$ reacts with $\text{NH}_3(g)$, a weak conjugate base, $\text{Cl}^-(aq)$, is formed BECAUSE strong acids produce weak conjugate bases.

132. A solution with a pH of 3 has a higher concentration of hydrogen ions, $[\text{H}]^+$, than a solution with a pH of 2 BECAUSE the pH scale equals the negative log of $[\text{H}]^+$

133. A larger K_a value indicates a stronger acid BECAUSE K_a measures the quantity of dissociation of an acid.

134. The K_a values of strong acids are essentially greater than 1 BECAUSE strong acids, such as $\text{HBr}(aq)$, have complete dissociation when put into solution.

135. Human blood resists large changes in pH BECAUSE human blood holds salts that produce conjugate bases and/or acids to counteract pH change.

136. The conjugate acid of $\text{H}_2\text{O}(l)$ is $\text{H}_3\text{O}^+(aq)$ BECAUSE according to Bronsted-Lowry definitions, conjugate acids are the proton-accepted form of bases.

137. The breaking of a single bond happens at a faster rate than the breaking of a double bond BECAUSE the total potential energy of a molecule is equal to the sum of all bond energies.

138. The minimum activation energy of a reaction is lowered when introduced to a catalyst   BECAUSE   a catalyst is chemically altered when used during a chemical reaction.

139. If the potential energy of the reactants and products for a particular reaction is 50 kJ and 70 kJ, respectively, the reaction is considered to be endothermic   BECAUSE   energy is absorbed during an endothermic reaction.

140. If $\Delta H < 0$, the reaction occurs spontaneously   BECAUSE   lower energy states are more stable and desirable.

141. As the concentration of the reactants increases, the rate of reaction also increases   BECAUSE   the rate of a reaction is proportional to the product of the concentration of the reactants.

142. In a reaction of hydrobromic acid, $HBr(aq)$, with calcium solid, $Ca(s)$, crushed $Ca(s)$ will react slower than blocks of $Ca(s)$ BECAUSE   crushed $Ca(s)$ has a larger surface area than blocks of $Ca(s)$, which allows for more effective collisions.

143. ΔH for the Haber process is approximately -92 kJ, which indicates a non-spontaneous reaction   BECAUSE   the Haber process is a synthesis reaction.

144. The oxidation number of N in HNO_3 is $+3$ BECAUSE   nitrogen is a halogen.

145. Cu is a transition metal   BECAUSE $Cu(s)$ has two oxidation states, $+2$ and $+3$.

146. The anode of a voltaic cell is the site of oxidation   BECAUSE   cations are formed at the anode.

147. Electron flow can be in either direction in a voltaic cell   BECAUSE   the charge of the anode and/or the cathode can be positive or negative.

148. A voltaic cell requires an energy source and is non-spontaneous   BECAUSE   in a voltaic cell, electrons are required to flow from the negatively charged electrode to the positively charged electrode.

$$NaOH(aq) + HCl(aq) \rightarrow NaCl(aq) + H_2O(l)$$

149. The reaction shown above is considered a oxidation-reduction reaction   BECAUSE   in an oxidation-reduction reaction, the oxidation state of at least two elements must change.

150. Alkali metals typically have an oxidation number of +1   BECAUSE   alkali metals react violently with $H_2O(l)$.

151. The oxidation states of H, P, and O, in $H_2PO_4^-$ sum to -1 BECAUSE   dihydrogen phosphate is considered a weak acid.

152. An organic compound contains at least 1 C-C bond   BECAUSE   carbon has 4 valence electrons.

153. Ethene, C_2H_4, contains one double bond   BECAUSE C_2H_4 belongs to the alkene homologous series.

154. Butene produces more energy during a combustion reaction than methane | BECAUSE | C_4H_{10} contains more total bond energy than CH_4.

155. CH_3OH and CH_4O are isomers | BECAUSE | isomer compounds have identical chemical structures, but different reaction properties.

156. Dimethyl ether has the chemical formula CH_3OCH_3 | BECAUSE | ethers are organic compounds that contain at least one oxygen atom.

157. In its ground state, a potassium atom has more electrons in its outer shell than a sodium atom | BECAUSE | the total number of electrons in a potassium atom is greater than the total number of electrons in a sodium atom.

158. To prepare a 1 M solution of Cl^- from NaCl (molar mass 58 g/mol), 58 g of NaCl should be dissolved in 2 L of solution | BECAUSE | each mole of NaCl dissolves to produce 1 mol of Cl^-.

159. H_2SO_4 is a stronger acid than HCl | BECAUSE | H_2SO_4 contains 2 mol of H^+ per mol of molecule, whereas HCl contains 1 mol of H^+ per mol of molecule.

160. An ideal gas cooled from 80°C to 50°C at constant pressure will contract in volume | BECAUSE | as temperature decreases volume decreases for an ideal gas.

161. At 1 atm, the boiling point of 2 L of $H_2O(l)$ is greater than the boiling point of 2 L of a 0.5 M NaCl(aq) solution | BECAUSE | $H_2O(l)$ is a polar solvent.

162. Gases approach ideal behavior at low pressures and high temperatures | BECAUSE | at low pressures and high temperatures the attractive forces between gas molecules and the actual volume of gas molecules becomes negligible.

163. $^{12}_{6}C$ and $^{14}_{6}C$ are isotopes | BECAUSE | isotopes are atoms of the same element with a different quantity of neutrons.

164. The oxidation state of oxygen can be −1 | BECAUSE | oxygen has a −1 oxidation state when in peroxides.

165. SO_3 exhibits resonance | BECAUSE | the structure of SO_3 has multiple locations for its double bond.

166. Alkynes have the general formula C_nH_{2n} | BECAUSE | alkynes contain at least one triple bond.

167. At 25°C, 2 L of $Cl_2(g)$ contains more molecules than 2 L of $F_2(g)$ | BECAUSE | $Cl_2(g)$ has a larger molecular mass than $F_2(g)$.

168. For Ca, the second ionization energy is less than the first ionization energy | BECAUSE | the valence shell of Ca holds 2 electrons.

169. Sulfur compounds can potentially lead to the production of acid rain | BECAUSE | H_2SO_4 is a strong acid.

170. A reaction between $H_2(g)$ and $CuSO_4(aq)$ will go to completion — BECAUSE — $Cu(s)$, as a product, is an insoluble precipitate.

171. The pH of a 1.0×10^{-6} M solution of $NaOH(aq)$ is 8 — BECAUSE — the pOH of a solution is calculated by $-\log[OH^-]$

172. After equilibrium is reached, the concentration of the reactants and products does not change — BECAUSE — the rate of forward and reverse reactions go to 0.

173. The empirical formula of $C_6H_{12}O_6$ is CH_2O — BECAUSE — glucose is an organic compound that is insoluble in $H_2O(l)$.

174. An element that has a ground-state electron configuration of $1s^2 2s^2 2p^5$ is a halogen — BECAUSE — grounded halogens have 7 electrons in their valence shell.

175. Cl^- ions and Ar molecules have equal electronegativity values — BECAUSE — Cl^- ions and Ar molecules have an equal amount of valence electrons.

176. A solution with a pH of 10 has 2 times the concentration of $[H^+]$ ions than a solution with a pH of 5 — BECAUSE — the pH of a solution depends on the quantity of $[H^+]$ ions.

$$3\,H_2(g) \;+\; N_2(g) \;\rightleftarrows\; 2\,NH_3(g)$$

177. In the above equilibrium reaction, an increase in the pressure of the reaction chamber at a constant temperature results in a decrease in $N_2(g)$ concentration — BECAUSE — $N_2(g)$ has a larger molecular mass than $NH_3(g)$.

178. As electrons move to higher principal quantum energy levels, energy is released in the form of light — BECAUSE — electrons are more stable at higher energy levels.

179. The first ionization energy of an alkali metal is typically less than the second ionization energy — BECAUSE — ionization energy is the amount of energy needed to complete remove an electron from the atom.

180. Methane is nonpolar — BECAUSE — the C-H bond is a nonpolar bond.

181. The central carbon atom in a molecule of CO_2 contains 2 σ bonds and 2 π bonds — BECAUSE — a double bond is composed of 1 σ bond and 1 π bond.

182. At STP, 0.5 mol of chlorine gas, Cl_2, occupies 22.4 L of volume — BECAUSE — each molecule of Cl_2 contains two chlorine atoms.

183. At STP, a 10 g sample of Ne occupies a larger volume than a 10 g sample of O_2 — BECAUSE — Ne has a larger molecular mass than O_2.

184. At constant temperature, as the volume of a gas increases the pressure of the gas increases   BECAUSE   the volume and pressure of a gas are directly related.

185. In a 1 L container at 1 atm holding 5 L $N_2(g)$ and 15 L $O_2(g)$, the partial pressure of $N_2(g)$ is 0.15 atm   BECAUSE   the total pressure of a mixture of gases is equal to the sum of the partial pressure of each gas.

$$CO_2(s) \rightleftarrows CO_2(g)$$

186. In the theoretical equilibrium reaction above, $\Delta S > 0$ for the forward reaction   BECAUSE   gas particles contain more disorder and greater quantities of kinetic energy than solid particles.

187. H_2S boils at a lower temperature than H_2O BECAUSE H_2S has a lower molecular mass than H_2O.

188. At STP, a 2 L container of $H_2O(l)$ has a higher boiling point than a 1 L container of $NaCl(aq)$ BECAUSE   the boiling point of a sample is an intensive property.

189. A supersaturated solution is obtained by heating a saturated solution to a higher solubility, adding solute, and then returning to the original temperature   BECAUSE   supersaturated solutions hold more solute past the point of saturation.

$$N_2(g) + 2 O_2(g) \rightleftarrows 2 NO_2(g)$$

190. If the pressure of the reaction chamber containing the reaction above increased, the reaction equilibrium would shift to the right   BECAUSE   an increase in pressure shifts the production to the side of a gaseous equilibrium reaction with less moles of gas.

191. The K_{sp} of a 2 L $NaCl(aq)$ solution with $[Na]^+$ of 1×10^{-2} is 1×10^{-4} BECAUSE   the solubility product constant is calculated by the product of the concentration of dissociated ions.

$$H_2(g) + MgCl_2(aq) \rightarrow$$

192. The reaction above has a positive value for ΔH BECAUSE H^+ is a less active cation than Mg^{2+}.

193. Double replacement reactions are always equilibrium reactions   BECAUSE   insoluble precipitates can never form during double replacement reactions.

194. MgO, when dissolved in solution, yields a solution with a pH greater than 7   BECAUSE   metallic oxides form basic solutions.

195. A weak acid can yield a strong conjugate base   BECAUSE NH_4^+ and NH_3 are both soluble in $H_2O(l)$.

$$CO_2(g) + H_2(g) + Ni(s) \rightarrow CH_4(g) + 2\,H_2O(l) + Ni(s)$$

196. The chemical reaction above contains a catalyst

BECAUSE a catalyst lowers the activation energy of a reaction.

197. If the total energy of the reactants and total energy of the products of a chemical reaction are 50 kJ and 60 kJ, respectively, the reaction is considered to be endothermic

BECAUSE endothermic reactions require additional energy to reach activation, whereas exothermic reactions do not.

198. A substance with a pH value of 4 has a pOH value of 10

BECAUSE $[H^+][OH^-] = 1.0 \times 10^{-7}$ for all substances.

199. The metallic slab at the negative electrode in a voltaic cell, over time, loses mass

BECAUSE the negative electrode undergoes reduction and synthesizes metallic ions and electrons to form a metallic solid.

200. Every carbon atom in an organic compound contains 4 σ bonds

BECAUSE carbon has 4 valence electrons.

201. C_2H_5OH and CH_3CH_2OH are isomers

BECAUSE isomers have the same quantity of elements but different chemical structures.

PERIODIC TABLE OF ELEMENTS

1 H 1.0079																	2 He 4.0026
3 Li 6.941	4 Be 9.012											5 B 10.811	6 C 12.011	7 N 14.01	8 O 16.00	9 F 19.00	10 Ne 20.179
11 Na 22.99	12 Mg 24.30											13 Al 26.98	14 Si 28.09	15 P 30.974	16 S 32.06	17 Cl 35.453	18 Ar 39.948
19 K 39.10	20 Ca 40.08	21 Sc 44.96	22 Ti 47.90	23 V 50.94	24 Cr 52.00	25 Mn 54.94	26 Fe 55.85	27 Co 58.93	28 Ni 58.69	29 Cu 63.55	30 Zn 65.39	31 Ga 69.72	32 Ge 72.59	33 As 74.92	34 Se 78.96	35 Br 79.90	36 Kr 83.80
37 Rb 85.47	38 Sr 87.62	39 Y 88.91	40 Zr 91.22	41 Nb 92.91	42 Mo 95.94	43 Tc (98)	44 Ru 101.1	45 Rh 102.91	46 Pd 106.42	47 Ag 107.87	48 Cd 112.41	49 In 114.82	50 Sn 118.71	51 Sb 121.75	52 Te 127.60	53 I 126.91	54 Xe 131.29
55 Cs 132.91	56 Ba 137.33	57 *La 138.91	72 Hf 178.49	73 Ta 180.95	74 W 183.85	75 Re 186.21	76 Os 190.2	77 Ir 192.2	78 Pt 195.08	79 Au 196.97	80 Hg 200.59	81 Tl 204.38	82 Pb 207.2	83 Bi 208.98	84 Po (209)	85 At (210)	86 Rn (222)
87 Fr (223)	88 Ra 226.02	89 †Ac 227.03	104 Rf (261)	105 Db (262)	106 Sg (266)	107 Bh (264)	108 Hs (277)	109 Mt (268)	110 Ds (271)	111 Rg (272)	112 § (277)						

§ Not yet named

*Lanthanide Series

58 Ce 140.12	59 Pr 140.91	60 Nd 144.24	61 Pm (145)	62 Sm 150.4	63 Eu 151.97	64 Gd 157.25	65 Tb 158.93	66 Dy 162.50	67 Ho 164.93	68 Er 167.26	69 Tm 168.93	70 Yb 173.04	71 Lu 174.97

†Actinide Series

90 Th 232.04	91 Pa 231.04	92 U 238.03	93 Np 237.05	94 Pu (244)	95 Am (243)	96 Cm (247)	97 Bk (247)	98 Cf (251)	99 Es (252)	100 Fm (257)	101 Md (258)	102 No (259)	103 Lr (262)

CHAPTER

+15

PT1

PRACTICE TEST 1

PRACTICE TEST 1

Note: For all solution questions, the solvent used is water unless noted differently.

Throughout the exam the units below have the listed definitions specified unless noted differently.

H = enthalpy	atm = atmosphere(s)
M = molar	g = gram(s)
n = number of moles	J = joule(s)
P = pressure	kJ = kilojoule(s)
R = molar gas constant	L = liter(s)
S = entropy	mL = milliliter(s)
T = temperature	mm = millimeter(s)
V = volume	mol = mole(s)
	V = volt(s)
	Sw = Stillwell(s)

Part A

Directions: Each set of answer choices below pertains to the numbered statements or questions immediately following it. Select the answer choice that best fits each statement. A choice may be used once, more than once, or not at all in each set.

Questions 1-4 refer to the following terms.

    (A) Density
    (B) Mole
    (C) Atomic mass
    (D) Molarity
    (E) Molality

1. A concentration measure that is expressed in moles of solute per liter of solution

2. The mass to volume ratio of a substance

3. The weighted average of all naturally occurring isotopes of an element or the isotopic distribution sum of elements in a compound

4. The amount of a chemical substance that contains as many particles as there are atoms in 12 grams of Carbon-12

Questions 5-8 refer to the following substances at STP.

    (A) NO_2
    (B) CO_2
    (C) H_2O
    (D) SiO_2
    (E) O_2

5. Is a liquid with a bent molecular structure

6. Is a solid which is toxic when finely divided and inhaled

7. Is a gas with a nonpolar structure and polar bonds

8. Is a gas with a nonpolar structure and nonpolar bonds

Questions 9-14 refer to the following electron configurations.

(A) $1s^2\,2s^2$
(B) $1s^2\,2s^2\,2p^1$
(C) $1s^2\,2s^2\,2p^2$
(D) $1s^2\,2s^2\,2p^5$
(E) $1s^2\,2s^2\,2p^2\,3p^1$

9. An excited state configuration

10. N^{2-}

11. Represents the element with an oxidation number of -1

12. Represents the element with the lowest first-ionization energy

13. Represents the element required for all organic compounds

Questions 14-17 refer to the following terms.

(A) Reduction
(B) Oxidation
(C) Decomposition
(D) Synthesis
(E) Combustion

Which of the above terms best describes the reaction represented by each of the following?

14. $2\,C_2H_6(g)\ +7\,O_2(g)\ \rightarrow 4\,CO_2(g)\ +6\,H_2O(l)$

15. $Zn(s)\ \rightarrow\ Zn^{2+}(aq)\ +2e^-$

16. $3\,H_2(g)\ +\ N_2(g)\ \rightarrow 2\,NH_3(g)$

17. $2\,MgO(s)\ \rightarrow 2\,Mg(s)\ +\ O_2(g)$

Questions 18-21 refer to the following.

(A) Hydrogen bonding
(B) Dipole-dipole attractions
(C) London dispersion forces
(D) Metallic bonding
(E) Network covalent bonding

18. Responsible for the high boiling point of water compared to other group 16 hydrides

19. A weak intermolecular force typically found in nonpolar structures

20. Formed by electrostatic attractive forces between delocalized electrons and positively charged metal ions

21. Responsible for the high melting point, hardness, and insolubility of large molecules

Questions 22-25 refer to following compounds

(A) O_3
(B) CCl_3F
(C) CH_4
(D) SO_2
(E) H_2O_2

22. Forms the solar radiation protection layer in the atmosphere

23. Can lead to the formation of acid ran

24. Harmful against the solar radiation protection layer in the atmosphere

25. The main constituent of natural gases

**PLEASE USE THE SECTION AT THE LOWER LEFT-HAND CORNER
OF THE ANSWER SHEET AND ANSWER QUESTIONS 101-115
ACCORDING TO THE DIRECTIONS DESCRIBED BELOW.**

Part B

Directions: Each question below consists of two statements, I in the left-hand column and II in the right-hand column. For each question, determine whether statement I is true or false <u>and</u> whether statement II is true or false and fill in the corresponding T or F circles on your answer sheet. Fill in circle CE only if statement II is a correct explanation of the true statement I.

<table>
<tr><td colspan="3">EXAMPLES:</td></tr>
<tr><td>I</td><td></td><td>II</td></tr>
<tr><td>EX 1. Ca(OH)$_2$ is a strong acid</td><td>BECAUSE</td><td>Ca(OH)$_2$ contains calcium.</td></tr>
<tr><td>EX 2. In a chemical reaction mass is conserved</td><td>BECAUSE</td><td>matter is neither created nor destroyed.</td></tr>
</table>

SAMPLE ANSWERS

	I		II		CE*
EX 1	T	●	●	F	○
EX 2	●	F	●	F	●

I		II
101. Water at STP is a polar substance	BECAUSE	only at standard temperature and pressure does water exhibit an asymmetrical molecular structure.
102. $C_8H_{18}(l)$ is flammable, whereas HF(*aq*) is not	BECAUSE	the mass percent of hydrogen is greater in HF than it is in C_8H_{18}.
103. To prepare a 1 *M* solution of fluoride ions from MgF$_2$ (molar mass 62 g/mol), 62 g of MgF$_2$ should be dissolved in 1 L of solution	BECAUSE	each mole of MgF$_2$ dissolves to produce 2 mol of fluoride ions.
104. In its ground state, a sodium atom has more electrons in its outer shell than does a calcium atom	BECAUSE	the total number of electrons in a calcium atom is greater than the total number of electrons in a sodium atom.
105. An ideal gas heated from 25°C to 30°C at constant pressure will expand in volume	BECAUSE	temperature and volume vary directly at constant pressure.
106. At 25°C, the value of K_w for the chemical reaction represented by the equation $2\,H_2O(l) \rightleftarrows H_3O^+(aq) + OH^-(aq)$ is 10^{-14}	BECAUSE	at 25°C, the concentrations of $H_3O^+(aq)$ and $OH^-(aq)$ in pure water are each 10^{-7} mole per liter.
107. Hydrofluoric acid, HF, is a stronger acid than chloric acid, HClO$_3$,	BECAUSE	hydrofluoric acid has fewer atoms than chloric acid.

I		II
108. 100 calories of heat will increase the temperature of 1 gram of water from 0°C to 100°C	BECAUSE	the specific heat capacity of water is 1 calorie per gram of water per degree Celsius.
109. Nonmetallic oxides react with water to form acidic solutions	BECAUSE	nonmetals bond with hydronium ions to form acids.
110. A non-spontaneous reaction typically has a negative value for its heat of reaction	BECAUSE	a non-spontaneous reaction needs to absorb energy to activate.

$$C_3H_8(g) + 5\,O_2(g) \rightarrow 3\,CO_2(g) + 4\,H_2O(l)$$

I		II
111. For the combustion reaction represented above, the entropy decreases as the products form	BECAUSE	in the combustion reaction represented above, the reactants consist of only gaseous substances while the products contain at least one non-gaseous substance.
112. Rutherford's gold foil experiment led to the discovery of the electron	BECAUSE	the majority of alpha particles emitted were not deflected.
113. The freezing point of a dilute solution of sugar in water is higher than the freezing point of pure water	BECAUSE	the freezing point of $C_6H_{12}O_6(s)$ is lower than the freezing point of $H_2O(l)$.
114. After an equilibrium reaction has reached equilibrium, the addition of one of the reactants will lead to less product formed	BECAUSE	more reactant particles will lead to less successful collisions, thus decreasing the concentration of the products.
115. The energy per mole required to activate $K(g) \rightarrow K^+(g) + e^-$ is less than the energy per mole required to activate $K^+(g) \rightarrow K^{2+}(g) + e^-$	BECAUSE	the amount of electrons contained within the K atom is less than the amount of electrons contained within the K^+ ion.

PRACTICE TEST 1

Part C

Directions: Each of the questions below is followed by five answer choices or completions. Select the one that is best in each case and then bubble in the corresponding circle on the answer sheet.

26. All of the following involve a chemical change EXCEPT

    (A) the evaporation of acetone at STP
    (B) the formation of $MgCl_2$ from Mg and Cl
    (C) the oxidation of Fe
    (D) the production of NH_3 when NH_4Cl is used with basic powders
    (E) the burning of hydrocarbons to form carbon dioxide and water

27. A ground-state atom of which of the following elements has the most valence electrons?

    (A) Beryllium
    (B) Flourine
    (C) Bromine
    (D) Neon
    (E) Potassium

28. How many moles of carbon dioxide would be produced if 8.0 g of methane (molar mass 16 g/mol) were burned completely to produce carbon dioxide and water?

    (A) 0.5 mol
    (B) 1.0 mol
    (C) 2.0 mol
    (D) 4.0 mol
    (E) 5.0 mol

    $$\ldots NH_3(g) + \ldots F_2(g) \rightarrow \ldots N_2(g) + \ldots HF$$

29. When the equation for the reaction represented above is balanced with all the coefficients reduced to the lowest whole-number terms, the coefficient for $N_2(g)$ is

    (A) 1
    (B) 2
    (C) 3
    (D) 4
    (E) 6

30. What is the maximum number of electrons that can be held in a single f orbital?

    (A) 2
    (B) 6
    (C) 10
    (D) 14
    (E) 18

31. The activation energy of a reaction is best described by which of the following?

    (A) The minimum amount of energy needed to start a reaction
    (B) The total amount of energy needed to start a reaction
    (C) The difference in energy between the energy of the products and the energy of the reactions
    (D) The difference between the total amount of energy needed to start a reaction with, and without, a catalyst
    (E) The initial amount of energy held within the reactants

32. Aromatic hydrocarbons are represented by which of the following chemical structures?

    I. H—C—H (with H above, H below)

    II. HC≡CH

    III. (benzene ring structure with CH, HC, CH, HC, CH, CH)

    (A) I only
    (B) III only
    (C) I and II only
    (D) II and III only
    (E) I, II, and III

33. Which of the following methods is best for separating and recovering components of a solution of ethyl alcohol, water, and vinegar?

    (A) Paper chromatography
    (B) Filtration
    (C) Distillation
    (D) Gel Electrophoresis
    (E) Centrifugation

34. Which of the following best describes the products of a reaction between acetic acid and sodium hydroxide? The products which form will contain

    (A) at least one precipitate
    (B) a weak acid and water
    (C) a weak base and water
    (D) a weak base and a salt
    (E) a strong base and water

35. Consider radioactive element X with a half-life of 20 years. Suppose a 96 g sample of element X were found. How many years will have passed when only 3 g of element X remain?

    (A)   4
    (B)   5
    (C)   50
    (D) 100
    (E) 200

$$Zn(s) + Cu^{2+}(aq) \rightarrow Cu(s) + Zn^{2+}(aq)$$

36. Which of the following is true of the reaction represented above?

    (A) Two moles of electrons are transferred for each 1 mole of $Cu(s)$ produced.
    (B) $Cu^{2+}(aq)$ is the reducing agent.
    (C) $Zn(s)$ is the oxidizing agent.
    (D) $Zn(s)$ is being reduced.
    (E) $Cu^{2+}(aq)$ is being oxidized.

$$CaCO_3(s) \rightleftarrows CaO(s) + CO_2(g)$$

37. Which of the following is the correct expression for the equilibrium constant, K_c, for the reaction represented above?

    (A) $\dfrac{[CO_2]\,[CaO]}{[CaCO_3]}$

    (B) $\dfrac{[CO_2] + [CaO]}{[CaCO_3]}$

    (C) $\dfrac{[CaCO_3]}{[CO_2]\,[CaO]}$

    (D) $\dfrac{[CaCO_3]}{[CO_2] + [CaO]}$

    (E) $[CO_2]$

38. Heating of a hydrate allow scientists to calculate the chemical formula of a compound. The water in the hydrate is released as a vapor and the remains are left intact. A sodium sulfate hydrate was heated and the data are shown in the table below. The molar mass of Na_2SO_4 is 142 g/mol.

Item	Mass
Test tube	20.1 g
Test tube and Na_2SO_4 hydrate	181.1 g
Test tube and Na_2SO_4	91.1 g

    Which of the following is the formula of the hydrate?

    (A) $Na_2SO_4 \cdot 4H_2O$

    (B) $Na_2SO_4 \cdot 5H_2O$

    (C) $Na_2SO_4 \cdot 8H_2O$

    (D) $Na_2SO_4 \cdot 10H_2O$

    (E) $Na_2SO_4 \cdot 12H_2O$

39. Which of the following salts, if any, will hydrolyze in water to form acidic solutions?

    I. K_2SO_4
    II. $Na_3(PO_4)$
    III. NaCl

  (A) I only
  (B) II only
  (C) III only
  (D) I and II only
  (E) None of the above

40. Of the following solutions, which has the highest boiling point?

  (A) 3 M glucose, $C_6H_{12}O_6$
  (B) 3 M KCl
  (C) 3 M $MgBr_2$
  (D) 3 M BCl_3
  (E) 3 M acetic acid, $HC_2H_3O_2$

$$H_2, O_2, CO_2, Ar$$

41. Each of the four different rigid 2.0 L containers contains a 2.0 g sample of one of the gases listed above at 25°C. The pressure is highest in the container containing which gas?

  (A) H_2
  (B) O_2
  (C) CO_2
  (D) Ar
  (E) The pressure is the same in all four containers

$$2\,H_2(g) + O_2(g) \rightarrow 2\,H_2O(g) + 480\text{ kJ}$$

42. How much heat energy is released when 16 grams of hydrogen gas are burned in the above thermal equation?

  (A)   120 kJ
  (B)   240 kJ
  (C)   480 kJ
  (D)   960 kJ
  (E) 1,920 kJ

43. Hydrogen bonding must be accounted for as a vital component of the interaction of all of the following pairs of molecules EXCEPT

  (A) H_2O and HCl
  (B) H_2O and H_2O
  (C) H_2O and CH_3OH
  (D) HCl and H_2S
  (E) $HC_2H_3O_2$ and HF

44. How many grams of $CsNO_3$ (molar mass 195 g/mol) are present in 2.00 L of a 1.00 M $CsNO_3$ solution?

  (A) 48.75 g
  (B) 97.5 g
  (C) 195 g
  (D) 212 g
  (E) 390 g

$$H_2(g) + 2\,AgCl(s) \rightarrow 2\,HCl(aq) + 2\,Ag(s)$$

45. Consider the single-replacement reaction above. If it can be determined, would this reaction be considered spontaneous or nonspontaneous?

  (A) Spontaneous, because hydrogen is more reactive than silver.
  (B) Spontaneous, because hydrogen is less reactive than silver.
  (C) Nonspontaneous, because hydrogen is more reactive than silver.
  (D) Nonspontaneous, because hydrogen is less reactive than silver.
  (E) Cannot be determined from the given information

46. Which of the following chemical formulas is the correct representation for sodium bicarbonate?

  (A) $NaCO_2$
  (B) $NaHCO_2$
  (C) Na_2CO_3
  (D) $NaHCO_3$
  (E) Na_2HCO_3

47. How many liters of oxygen gas at STP can be pre-pared from the decomposition of 123 grams of potassium chlorate (molar mass 123 g/mol)?

    (A) 11.2 L
    (B) 22.4 L
    (C) 33.6 L
    (D) 44.8 L
    (E) 67.2 L

48. Which of the following best describes the type of bonding between bromine atoms in a molecule of Br_2?

    (A) Ionic bonding
    (B) Metallic bonding
    (C) Covalent bonding
    (D) Hydrogen bonding
    (E) London force interactions

49. The amount of charge that reduces 1.0 mol of Zn^{2+} to Zn metal would also reduce how many moles of Al^{3+} to Al metal?

    (A) 0.25 mol
    (B) 0.50 mol
    (C) 0.67 mol
    (D) 1.0 mol
    (E) 1.5 mol

50. A saturated solution of copper (II) sulfide, CuS, contains 4.0×10^{-6} mole per liter of Cu^{2+} ions. What is the K_{sp} value of copper (II) sulfide?

    (A) 4.0×10^{-6}
    (B) 8.0×10^{-6}
    (C) 1.6×10^{-11}
    (D) 1.6×10^{-12}
    (E) 4.0×10^{-12}

51. In which of the following groups of the periodic table of elements is the most electronegative element found?

    (A) Alkali metals
    (B) Alkaline earth metals
    (C) Chalcogens
    (D) Halogens
    (E) Noble Gases

52. The Cu^{3+} ion contains how many electrons?

    (A) 26
    (B) 28
    (C) 29
    (D) 30
    (E) 32

53. Which of the following statements best describes the sp orbital hybridization of the electrons for carbon in carbon dioxide, CO_2?

    (A) The sp orbital is formed by the joining of one s orbital and one p orbital.
    (B) The s orbital electrons are promoted to the p orbital.
    (C) The s orbital decomposes and reforms into a new p orbital.
    (D) The p orbital loses energy and the electrons it contains fall back to the s orbital.
    (E) The sp orbital is a completely new orbital containing electrons from both the original s and p orbitals.

54. What is the pH of a solution that contains 1×10^{-4} moles of OH^- ions for every 1 liter of solution?

    (A) 1
    (B) 4
    (C) 7
    (D) 10
    (E) 13

55. Which of the following pairs of formulas could represent the empirical formula and the molecular formula of a given compound?

    (A) O_2 and O_3
    (B) NaCl and NaBr
    (C) CO and CO_2
    (D) CH_4O and $C_3H_{12}O_3$
    (E) CHO and $C_2H_3O_2$

56. Suppose 2 moles of aluminum sulfate, $Al_2(SO_4)_3$, were placed in an empty container. Approxi-mately how many atoms of oxygen are present in the container?

    (A) 6.02×10^{23}
    (B) 6.02×10^{24}
    (C) 7.22×10^{24}
    (D) 7.22×10^{24}
    (E) 1.44×10^{25}

$$Mg(s) + 2\,HCl(aq) \rightarrow H_2(g) + MgCl_2(aq)$$

57. Consider the reaction above between magnesium solid and dilute hydrochloric acid. Which of the following parameter adjustments would increase the rate of reaction?

   I. Decreasing the temperature of the reaction chamber
   II. Increasing the surface area of magnesium solid exposed to dilute hydrochloric acid
   III. Increasing the concentration of the hydrochloric acid solution

   (A) I only
   (B) II only
   (C) I and II only
   (D) II and III only
   (E) I, II, and III

58. Which of the following compounds does NOT react with a dilute solution of nitric acid?

   (A) NaOH
   (B) $NaNO_3$
   (C) Na_2O
   (D) Na_2CO_3
   (E) Na_3PO_4

59. Consider the amount of energy required to melt 2.0 grams of water at 0°C. This quantity of energy would also heat 4.0 grams of water at 25°C to what final temperature?
   (Heat of fusion = 80 cal/g)

   (A)   4°C
   (B)   44°C
   (C)   50°C
   (D)   65°C
   (E)   100°C

60. Which of the following statements about a liquid, such as acetone, that readily evaporates at 25°C is correct?

   (A) The liquid should be stored in an open container.
   (B) The liquid is considered to be nonvolatile.
   (C) The liquid would make a container feel cold to the touch.
   (D) The liquid has weak intermolecular forces.
   (E) The liquid has a low vapor pressure.

61. The pressure of 3 L of a gas at 20°C is 700 mm Hg. What is the volume of this gas at standard temperature and pressure?

   (A) $V = 3 \times \dfrac{20}{273} \times \dfrac{700}{760}$

   (B) $V = 3 \times \dfrac{273}{293} \times \dfrac{700}{760}$

   (C) $V = 3 \times \dfrac{293}{273} \times \dfrac{700}{760}$

   (D) $V = 3 \times \dfrac{293}{273} \times \dfrac{760}{700}$

   (E) $V = 3 \times \dfrac{273}{293} \times \dfrac{760}{700}$

62. Which of the formulas above represent isomers of one another?

   (A) None
   (B) I and II only
   (C) I and III only
   (D) II and III only
   (E) I, II, and III

$$^{14}_{6}C + \ldots \rightarrow\ ^{14}_{5}B$$

63. Consider the nuclear reaction shown above. Which of the following, when inserted in the blank placeholder above, would correctly complete the reaction?

   (A) An alpha particle
   (B) A beta particle
   (C) A gamma ray
   (D) A neutron
   (E) A positron

$$\ldots NaCl(s) + \ldots SO_2(g) + \ldots H_2O(l) + \ldots O_2(g) \rightarrow \ldots Na_2SO_4(aq) + \ldots HCl(aq)$$

64. When the equation above is balanced and all coefficients are reduced to lowest whole-number terms, the coefficient for $NaCl(s)$ is

(A) 1
(B) 2
(C) 3
(D) 4
(E) 5

$$N \text{ (Hexazine)} + O_2(g) \rightarrow NO_2(g) \qquad \Delta H = 202 \text{ kJ}$$

$$N \text{ (Octaazacubane)} + O_2(g) \rightarrow NO_2(g) \qquad \Delta H = 498 \text{ kJ}$$

65. On the basis of the information above, what is the change in enthalpy, ΔH, for the following reaction?

$$N \text{ (Octaazacubane)} \rightarrow N \text{ (Hexazine)}$$

(A) -700 kJ
(B) -296 kJ
(C) -2 kJ
(D) $+296$ kJ
(E) $+700$ kJ

66. All of the following are oxidation-reduction reactions EXCEPT

(A) $3 HNO_2(aq) + 5 H^+(aq) + Cr_2O_7^{2-}(aq) \rightarrow 3NO_3^-(aq) + 2 Cr^{3+}(aq) + 4 H_2O(l)$

(B) $3 Cu^+(aq) + Fe(s) \rightarrow Fe^{3+}(aq) + 3 Cu(s)$

(C) $Ag(s) + CN^-(aq) + O_2(g) \rightarrow Ag(CN)_2^-(aq)$

(D) $CH_4(g) + 2 O_2(g) \rightarrow CO_2(g) + 2 H_2(g)$

(E) $AgNO_3(aq) + NaCl(aq) \rightarrow AgCl(s) + NaNO_3(aq)$

67. What is the percent dissociation of oxalic acid, $HO_2C_2O_2H$, in a 1 M solution if the concentration of the hydronium ion is 1×10^{-2} mole per liter?

    (A) 0.01%
    (B) 0.1%
    (C) 1.0%
    (D) 1.1%
    (E) 10.0%

68. Consider a flask containing 1,000 g of pure water at 25°C. How would the boiling point of the water change if 2 moles of NaCl were added to the flask? The boiling point of the water would:

    (A) increase by 0.5°C
    (B) increase by 1°C
    (C) increase by 2°C
    (D) decrease by 1°C
    (E) decrease by 2°C

69. When the following gaseous compounds are present in small quantities, which is MOST toxic to humans?

    (A) Oxygen, O_2
    (B) Ozone, O_3
    (C) Carbon monoxide, CO
    (D) Carbon dioxide, CO_2
    (E) Nitrogen dioxide, NO_2

70. At standard temperature and pressure, which of the following gases has the lowest rate of effusion through a semipermeable barrier?

    (A) H_2
    (B) He
    (C) N_2
    (D) Ne
    (E) Cl_2

STOP

**IF YOU FINISH BEFORE TIME IS CALLED, YOU MAY CHECK YOUR WORK ON THIS TEST ONLY.
DO NOT TURN TO ANY OTHER TEST IN THIS BOOK.**

PERIODIC TABLE OF ELEMENTS

1																	2
H 1.0079																	**He** 4.0026
3 **Li** 6.941	4 **Be** 9.012											5 **B** 10.811	6 **C** 12.011	7 **N** 14.01	8 **O** 16.00	9 **F** 19.00	10 **Ne** 20.179
11 **Na** 22.99	12 **Mg** 24.30											13 **Al** 26.98	14 **Si** 28.09	15 **P** 30.974	16 **S** 32.06	17 **Cl** 35.453	18 **Ar** 39.948
19 **K** 39.10	20 **Ca** 40.08	21 **Sc** 44.96	22 **Ti** 47.90	23 **V** 50.94	24 **Cr** 52.00	25 **Mn** 54.94	26 **Fe** 55.85	27 **Co** 58.93	28 **Ni** 58.69	29 **Cu** 63.55	30 **Zn** 65.39	31 **Ga** 69.72	32 **Ge** 72.59	33 **As** 74.92	34 **Se** 78.96	35 **Br** 79.90	36 **Kr** 83.80
37 **Rb** 85.47	38 **Sr** 87.62	39 **Y** 88.91	40 **Zr** 91.22	41 **Nb** 92.91	42 **Mo** 95.94	43 **Tc** (98)	44 **Ru** 101.1	45 **Rh** 102.91	46 **Pd** 106.42	47 **Ag** 107.87	48 **Cd** 112.41	49 **In** 114.82	50 **Sn** 118.71	51 **Sb** 121.75	52 **Te** 127.60	53 **I** 126.91	54 **Xe** 131.29
55 **Cs** 132.91	56 **Ba** 137.33	57 ***La** 138.91	72 **Hf** 178.49	73 **Ta** 180.95	74 **W** 183.85	75 **Re** 186.21	76 **Os** 190.2	77 **Ir** 192.2	78 **Pt** 195.08	79 **Au** 196.97	80 **Hg** 200.59	81 **Tl** 204.38	82 **Pb** 207.2	83 **Bi** 208.98	84 **Po** (209)	85 **At** (210)	86 **Rn** (222)
87 **Fr** (223)	88 **Ra** 226.02	89 **†Ac** 227.03	104 **Rf** (261)	105 **Db** (262)	106 **Sg** (266)	107 **Bh** (264)	108 **Hs** (277)	109 **Mt** (268)	110 **Ds** (271)	111 **Rg** (272)	112 **§** (277)						

§ Not yet named

*Lanthanide Series

58 **Ce** 140.12	59 **Pr** 140.91	60 **Nd** 144.24	61 **Pm** (145)	62 **Sm** 150.4	63 **Eu** 151.97	64 **Gd** 157.25	65 **Tb** 158.93	66 **Dy** 162.50	67 **Ho** 164.93	68 **Er** 167.26	69 **Tm** 168.93	70 **Yb** 173.04	71 **Lu** 174.97

†Actinide Series

90 **Th** 232.04	91 **Pa** 231.04	92 **U** 238.03	93 **Np** 237.05	94 **Pu** (244)	95 **Am** (243)	96 **Cm** (247)	97 **Bk** (247)	98 **Cf** (251)	99 **Es** (252)	100 **Fm** (257)	101 **Md** (258)	102 **No** (259)	103 **Lr** (252)

## CHAPTER 16

PT2

PRACTICE TEST 2

PRACTICE TEST 2

Note: For all solution questions, the solvent used is water unless noted differently.

Throughout the exam the units below have the listed definitions specified unless noted differently.

H = enthalpy	atm = atmosphere(s)
M = molar	g = gram(s)
n = number of moles	J = joule(s)
P = pressure	kJ = kilojoule(s)
R = molar gas constant	L = liter(s)
S = entropy	mL = milliliter(s)
T = temperature	mm = millimeter(s)
V = volume	mol = mole(s)
	V = volt(s)
	Sw = Stillwell(s)

Part A

Directions: Each set of answer choices below pertains to the numbered statements or questions immediately following it. Select the answer choice that best fits each statement. A choice may be used once, more than once, or not at all in each set.

Li	(A)			F	(B)
(C)	Mg	...	(D)		Ar
K	Ca			(E)	Kr

Questions 1-5 refer to the following abbreviated periodic table.

1. The element with the smallest atomic radius

2. The element with the largest ionic radius

3. The element with the lowest electronegativity value

4. The element with the largest second ionization potential

5. The element with a possible oxidation number of 0

Questions 6-9 refer to the following types of bonds.

(A) Ionic bond
(B) Polar covalent bond
(C) Nonpolar covalent bond
(D) Hydrogen bond
(E) Metallic bond

6. The type of bond between the carbon and oxygen atoms in a carbon dioxide molecule

7. The type of bond between the atoms of magnesium in a crystal of magnesium solid

8. The type of bond between the atoms in a iodine molecule

9. The type of bond between the atoms of calcium and oxygen when forming a crystal of calcium oxide

Questions 10-14 refer to the following equations.

(A) $PV = k$

(B) $P_T = P_1 + P_2 + \cdots$

(C) $\dfrac{P}{T} = k$

(D) $\dfrac{V}{T} = k$

(E) $\dfrac{PV}{T} = k$

10. Boyle's law

11. Charles's law

12. Combined gas law

13. Dalton's law

14. Gay-Lussac's law

Questions 15-17 refer to the following diagram.

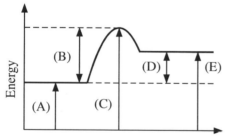

15. Indicates the activation energy of the forward reaction

16. Indicates the heat of reaction

17. Indicates the energy of the products

Questions 18-22 refer to the following terms.

(A) Arrhenius acid
(B) Arrhenius base
(C) Brønsted–Lowry acid
(D) Brønsted–Lowry base
(E) Buffer

18. A substance which donates a proton to a reactant to form its conjugate

19. A substance which receives a proton from a reactant to form its conjugate

20. A substance that resists a rapid change in pH

21. A substance which dissociates into an aqueous solution and yields hydrogen ions

22. A substance which dissociates into an aqueous solution and yields hydroxide ions

Questions 23-25 refer to following orbitals.

(A) $1s$
(B) $3s$
(C) $3p$
(D) $4d$
(E) $5f$

23. Possible valence subshell orbital of transition metals

24. Orbital that describes the probability distribution of the outer most electrons of Uranium-238

25. Subshell that can hold a maximum of 10 electrons

PLEASE USE THE SECTION AT THE LOWER LEFT-HAND CORNER
OF THE ANSWER SHEET AND ANSWER QUESTIONS 101-115
ACCORDING TO THE DIRECTIONS DESCRIBED BELOW.

Part B

Directions: Each question below consists of two statements, I in the left-hand column and II in the right-hand column. For each question, determine whether statement I is true or false <u>and</u> whether statement II is true or false and fill in the corresponding T or F circles on your answer sheet. Fill in circle CE only if statement II is a correct explanation of the true statement I.

	EXAMPLES:		
	I		**II**
EX 1.	Ca(OH)$_2$ is a strong acid	BECAUSE	Ca(OH)$_2$ contains calcium.
EX 2.	In a chemical reaction mass is conserved	BECAUSE	matter is neither created nor destroyed.

SAMPLE ANSWERS

	I	II	CE*
EX 1	Ⓣ ●	● Ⓕ	○
EX 2	● Ⓕ	● Ⓕ	●

<u>I</u>   <u>II</u>

101. A 1 M solution of barium hydroxide has a low pH

BECAUSE   solutions with a high OH$^-$ concentration have a high pH

102. Gases approach ideal behavior at high pressures and low temperatuers

BECAUSE   at high pressures and low temperatures the attractive forces between gas molecules and the actual volume of gas molecules become insignificant.

103. $^3_1$H and $^1_1$H are isotopes of one another

BECAUSE   isotopes of the same element *must* have the same number of electrons but a different number of neutrons.

104. Metals in Group 2 (alkaline earth metals) react more easily as their atomic number increases

BECAUSE   within a group on the periodic table, as atomic number increases electronegativity increases.

105. The oxidation state of oxygen is always −1

BECAUSE   oxygen is located in Group 16 and has 6 valence electrons.

106. Gold in the solid phase is a good electrical conductor

BECAUSE   the atoms in a sample of solid gold are bonded metallically.

<u>I</u>   <u>II</u>

107. The structure of the carbonate ion, CO_3^{2-}, is shown by using more than one structural formula   BECAUSE CO_3^{2-} shows resonance between possible chemical structures.

108. The atoms of Carbon-12 and Carbon-14 have a different number of neutrons but an equal number of protons   BECAUSE   allotropes exist in multiple physical forms.

109. There are 6 atoms in 1 mole of hydrogen sulfate (bisulfate)   BECAUSE   hydrogen sulfate contains 2 hydrogen atoms, 1 sulfur atom, and 4 oxygen atoms.

110. If the reverse reaction of an equilibrium is exothermic, adding heat to the system favors the forward reaction   BECAUSE   adding heat causes a disturbance on the system, which responds by restoring a new equilibrium state.

111. The cycloalkanes are considered a homologous series   BECAUSE   simple cycloalkanes are a collection of compounds that have similar structures.

112. The first ionization energy of Be is greater than that of Mg   BECAUSE   the Be atom has a smaller atomic radius than the Mg atom.

113. The boiling point of liquid water, $H_2O(l)$, is lower than that of a 0.5 M solution of sodium chloride, NaCl,   BECAUSE   the boiling point of water increases proportionally to the number of dissolved ions.

114. At 25°C, the average kinetic energy of $N_2(g)$ molecules is greater than the average kinetic energy of $O_2(g)$ molecules   BECAUSE   the average kinetic energy of gas particles is directly proportional to the temperature.

115. In the laboratory, concentrated hydrochloric acid should never be added to liquid water   BECAUSE   when acid is added to water the energy produced may cause the mixture to splatter.

Part C

Directions: Each of the questions below is followed by five answer choices or completions. Select the one that is best in each case and then bubble in the corresponding circle on the answer sheet.

26. What is the gram formula mass of magnesium sulfate, $Mg(SO_4)$?

(A) 80
(B) 100
(C) 120
(D) 140
(E) 160

$$2\,C_2H_6(g) + 7\,O_2(g) \rightarrow 4\,CO_2(g) + 6\ldots\ldots$$

27. Consider the above combustion reaction of ethane gas $C_2H_6(g)$. The missing product of this reaction is

(A) water
(B) carbon dioxide
(C) oxygen
(D) a hydrocarbon
(E) an alkene

28. In the metric system the unit prefix *nano* that precedes a basic unit of measure indicates a multiplication of

(A) 10^{-9}
(B) 10^{-6}
(C) 10^{-3}
(D) 10^3
(E) 10^9

29. Consider 3.0 moles of each hydrogen gas, H_2, nitrogen gas, N_2, oxygen gas, O_2, and neon gas, Ne, at standard temperature and pressure. Which of the listed gases, if any, would occupy the most volume?

(A) H_2
(B) N_2
(C) O_2
(D) Ne
(E) All of the listed gases would occupy the same volume

30. Of the following listed, which are considered to be a mixture?

   I. $NaCl(g)$
  II. $NaCl(l)$
 III. $NaCl(aq)$

(A) I only
(B) II only
(C) III only
(D) II and II only
(E) I, II, and III

31. Consider the element potassium, K, in its ground state. Potassium will most readily react with another element having which of the following electron configurations?

(A) $1s^2 2s^2 2p^6 3s^1$
(B) $1s^2 2s^2 2p^6 3s^2$
(C) $1s^2 2s^2 2p^6 3s^2 3p^3$
(D) $1s^2 2s^2 2p^6 3s^2 3p^4$
(E) $1s^2 2s^2 2p^6 3s^2 3p^5$

32. Suppose 1.0 mol of carbon dioxide gas, CO_2 (molar mass 44 g/mol), was placed in a container. The density of the carbon dioxide gas in the container at standard temperature and pressure would be approximately

(A) 1 g/L
(B) 2 g/L
(C) 11 g/L
(D) 22 g/L
(E) 44 g/L

33. Which of the following molecules is nonpolar?

(A) BF_3
(B) H_2O
(C) NH_3
(D) SO_2
(E) NaCl

34. Which of the following contains the greatest number of atoms?

    (A) 0.5 g of Cu
    (B) 0.5 g of Ag
    (C) 0.5 g of Au
    (D) 0.5 g of I
    (E) 0.5 g of U

35. Of the following, the conditions under which the molar volume of gaseous neon is greatest are

    (A) 1 atm and 273 K
    (B) 1 atm and 298 K
    (C) 1 atm and 300 K
    (D) 2 atm and 273 K
    (E) 2 atm and 298 K

36. Which of the following is the complete Lewis electron-dot diagram for formaldehyde?

    (A) 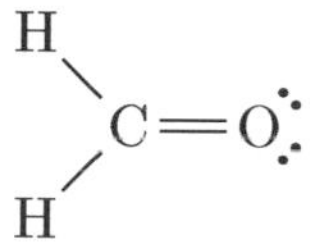 $\overset{\displaystyle H}{\underset{\displaystyle H}{>}}C=\ddot{O}{:}$

    (B) $\overset{\displaystyle H}{\underset{\displaystyle H}{>}}C-\ddot{O}{:}$

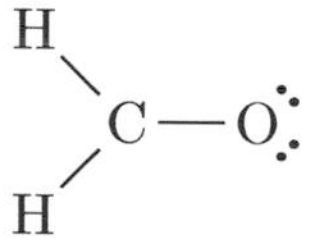

    (C) $\overset{\displaystyle H}{\underset{\displaystyle H}{>}}C=\ddot{O}{:}$

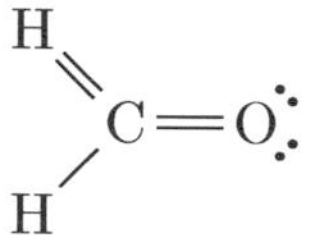

    (D) 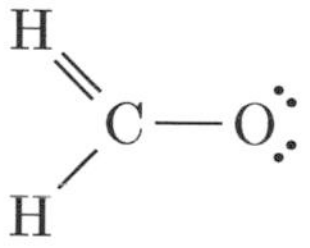 $\overset{\displaystyle H}{\underset{\displaystyle H}{>}}C-\ddot{O}{:}$

    (E) 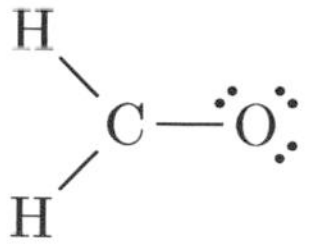 $\overset{\displaystyle H}{\underset{\displaystyle H}{>}}C-\ddot{\ddot{O}}{:}$

37. Which of the following pairs of compounds could be used to illustrate the law of multiple proportions?

    (A) C_2H_4 and C_2H_6
    (B) H_2O and H_3O^+
    (C) $NaCl$ and Na_2O
    (D) NH_3 and NH_4^+
    (E) H_2 and O_2

38. The oxidation number of nitrogen in a molecule of hydrogen nitrite, HNO_2, is

    (A) +1
    (B) +2
    (C) +3
    (D) +4
    (E) +5

$$Fe(s) + O_2(g) \rightarrow Fe_2O_3(g)$$

39. Consider the reduction-oxidation reaction shown above. Which of the following substances is being oxidized?

    (A) Fe(s) only
    (B) O_2(g) only
    (C) Fe_2O_3(g) only
    (D) Fe(s) and O_2(g)
    (E) Fe(s) and Fe_2O_3(g)

40. Which of the following methods is best for separating and recovering non-volatile mixtures and monitoring chemical reactions?

    (A) Distillation
    (B) Filtration
    (C) Reduction
    (D) Crystallization
    (E) Thin-layer chromatography

$$C_9H_{20}(l) + 14\,O_2(g) \rightarrow 9\,CO_2(g) + 10\,H_2O(l) + \text{energy}$$

41. Correct statements about the equation for the reaction represented above include which of the following?

   I. The volume of $O_2(g)$ consumed is greater than the volume of $CO_2(g)$ produced if both are measured at standard temperature and pressure.
   II. For 2 mol of $C_9H_{20}(l)$ consumed, 10×18 g of $H_2O(l)$ is produced.
   III. At standard temperature and pressure, the number of moles of carbon dioxide produced is 9 times the number of moles of $C_9H_{20}(l)$ consumed.

   (A) I only
   (B) I and II
   (C) I and III
   (D) II and III
   (E) I, II, and III

$$2\,C(s) + 2\,O_2(g) \rightarrow 2\,CO_2(g) \qquad \Delta H = -786 \text{ kJ}$$
$$2\,CO(g) + O_2(g) \rightarrow 2\,CO_2(g) \qquad \Delta H = -566 \text{ kJ}$$

42. On the basis of the information above, what is the change in enthalpy, ΔH, for the following reaction?

   $$2\,C(s) + O_2(g) \rightarrow 2\,CO(g)$$

   (A) −220 kJ
   (B) −20 kJ
   (C) −2 kJ
   (D) +20 kJ
   (E) +220 kJ

43. Suppose the molar concentration of Na^+ ions in a 1 L saturated water solution of sodium nitrate was measured to be 1.20×10^{-2}. What is the value of K_{sp} for sodium nitrate?

    (A) 1.20×10^{-2}
    (B) 1.44×10^{-2}
    (C) 2.40×10^{-2}
    (D) 1.44×10^{-4}
    (E) 2.40×10^{-4}

44. How many grams of iron will be oxidized if 4 moles of iron (III) oxide are formed at standard temperature and pressure?

    (A) 56
    (B) 84
    (C) 112
    (D) 224
    (E) 448

45. Suppose 2 mol of NaCl are dissolved in 1,000 g of H_2O at standard temperature and pressure. The resulting boiling point increase is greater than if 2 mol of which other substance was added instead of NaCl?

    (A) $MgCl_2$
    (B) $CaCl_2$
    (C) $Al(NO_3)_3$
    (D) H_2SO_4
    (E) C_3H_7OH

46. How many grams of copper (II) would result from the electrolysis of copper (II) sulfate utilizing $2 \times 6.02 \times 10^{23}$ molecules of electrons?

    (A) 16
    (B) 32
    (C) 48
    (D) 64
    (E) 128

47. When iron metal reacts with dilute HNO_3, bubbles of N_2O gas are formed. When iron metal reacts with highly concentrated HNO_3, no reaction occurs. From these observations alone, it can be concluded that

    (A) $Fe(NO_3)_2$ can be oxidized

    (B) $Fe(NO_3)_2$ can be reduced

    (C) HNO_3 is reduced to form ammonium ions

    (D) 1 M HNO_3 reacts differently with iron than 20 M HNO_3

    (E) 5 mol Fe reacts differently with HNO_3 than does 17 mol Fe

48. What is the maximum number of grams of H_2O that can be produced by combustion of 20 g of hydrogen gas, H_2?

    (A) 18
    (B) 36
    (C) 72
    (D) 90
    (E) 180

49. The formula for the fluoride of cesium is

    (A) CsF
    (B) Cs_2F
    (C) Cs_3F
    (D) CsF_2
    (E) Cs_2F_3

50. When $Mg(NO_3)_2$ dissolves in water, which of the following species has the greatest concentration in the solution?

    (A) $Mg(NO_3)_2(aq)$
    (B) $Mg^{2+}(aq)$
    (C) $(NO_3)^-(aq)$
    (D) $O^{2-}(aq)$
    (E) $N^+(aq)$

51. Which of the following will always be true of a reducing agent? The reducing agent

    (A) contains carbon and hydrogen
    (B) is insoluble in H_2O
    (C) contains a halogen
    (D) can be reduced
    (E) can be oxidized

52. Suppose the empirical formula of a substance is CH and its molecular mass is 52 g. Which of the following represents the molecular formula of the substance?

    (A) CH
    (B) C_2H_2
    (C) C_3H_3
    (D) C_4H_4
    (E) C_5H_5

53. How many milliliters of H_2O must be added to 500 mL of a 4 M HCl to make a 2 M HCl solution?

    (A)   100
    (B)   250
    (C)   500
    (D) 1,000
    (E) 2,000

54. How many liters of oxygen gas can be prepared from the decomposition of 246 g potassium chlorate $KClO_3$ (molar mass 123 g/mol) at standard temperature and pressure?

   (A) 5.6
   (B) 11.2
   (C) 22.4
   (D) 44.8
   (E) 67.2

Questions 55-56 refer to the chemical equation below.

$$N_2(g) + 3 H_2(g) \rightarrow 2 NH_3(g)$$

55. The chemical equation shown above is known as the

   (A) Arrenhius equation
   (B) Butler-Volmer equation
   (C) Henderson-Hasselbalch equation
   (D) Schrodinger equation
   (E) Haber-Bosch process

56. The equilibrium constant, K_{eq}, for the above reaction is

   (A) $K_{eq} = \dfrac{[NH_3]^2}{[N_2][H_2]^3}$

   (B) $K_{eq} = \dfrac{[N_2][H_2]^3}{[NH_3]^2}$

   (C) $K_{eq} = \dfrac{[NH_3]}{[N_2][H_2]}$

   (D) $K_{eq} = \dfrac{[N_2][H_2]}{[NH_3]}$

   (E) $K_{eq} = [NH_3]^2$

57. Isotopes of a given element always have an equal number of

   (A) protons
   (B) neutrons
   (C) orbitals
   (D) ionization numbers
   (E) subatomic particles

58. Which of the following chemical structures represents a carboxylic acid?

(A)
$$H-\overset{\overset{\displaystyle H}{|}}{\underset{\underset{\displaystyle H}{|}}{C}}-\overset{\overset{\displaystyle H}{|}}{\underset{\underset{\displaystyle H}{|}}{C}}-C\overset{\displaystyle O}{\underset{\displaystyle O-H}{}}$$

(B)
$$H-\overset{\overset{\displaystyle H}{|}}{\underset{\underset{\displaystyle H}{|}}{C}}-\overset{\overset{\displaystyle H}{|}}{\underset{\underset{\displaystyle H}{|}}{C}}-C\overset{\displaystyle O}{\underset{\displaystyle H}{}}$$

(C)
$$H-\overset{\overset{\displaystyle H}{|}}{\underset{\underset{\displaystyle H}{|}}{C}}-\overset{\overset{\displaystyle O}{||}}{C}-\overset{\overset{\displaystyle H}{|}}{\underset{\underset{\displaystyle H}{|}}{C}}-H$$

(D)
$$H-\overset{\overset{\displaystyle H}{|}}{\underset{\underset{\displaystyle H}{|}}{C}}-\overset{\overset{\displaystyle O}{||}}{C}-\overset{\overset{\displaystyle H}{|}}{\underset{\underset{\displaystyle H}{|}}{C}}-OH$$

(E)
$$H-\overset{\overset{\displaystyle H}{|}}{\underset{\underset{\displaystyle H}{|}}{C}}-O-\overset{\overset{\displaystyle H}{|}}{\underset{\underset{\displaystyle H}{|}}{C}}-OH$$

59. Bubbling gaseous hydrogen fluoride into distilled water results in a

   (A) precipitate forming
   (B) solution with pH > 7
   (C) solution with pH < 7
   (D) solution that turns litmus paper blue
   (E) solution that turns pink when phenolphthalein is added

60. What piece of equipment can be used to extract and add very tiny amounts of liquid?

   (A) Buret
   (B) Graduated cylinder
   (C) Condenser
   (D) Pipette
   (E) Stopcoch

61. A few drops of lead nitrate, $Pb(NO_3)_2$, were added to a water solution containing certain ions. If a precipitate forms, this could indicate the presence of which ion in the water solution?

    (A) NH_4^+
    (B) Mg^{2+}
    (C) HCO_3^-
    (D) ClO_3^-
    (E) SO_4^{2-}

$$2\,C_2H_6(g) + 7\,O_2(g) \rightarrow 4\,CO_2(g) + 6\,H_2O(l)$$

62. Consider the chemical reaction of C_2H_6 and O_2 above. This reaction can be classified as which of the following?

    I. Synthesis
    II. Single-replacement
    III. Combustion

    (A) II only
    (B) III only
    (C) I and III
    (D) II and III
    (E) I, II, and III

63. Which of the following scenarios would *always* cause the volume of a gas, initially at standard temperature and pressure, to increase?

    I. Increasing the pressure only
    II. Increasing the temperature, but decreasing the pressure
    III. Increasing both the temperature and pressure

    (A) I only
    (B) II only
    (C) III only
    (D) I and II
    (E) I and III

64. At 1 atm, what will be the freezing point of a solution of 1 mol propyl alcohol in 1,000 grams of water?

    (A) $1.86°C$
    (B) $0.93°C$
    (C) $-0.93°C$
    (D) $-1.86°C$
    (E) $-3.72°C$

65. Consider the following showing the differences in boiling points between substances containing hydrogen and group 16 elements.

Substance	Boiling point (°C)
H_2O	100
H_2S	-60
H_2Se	-41

    Which of the following explains the significant difference of the boiling point of H_2O?

    (A) As hydrogen bonds with group 16 elements with less protons, the boiling point of the substance increases.
    (B) As hydrogen bonds with group 16 elements with more protons, the boiling point of the substance increases.
    (C) The fewer the amount of total electrons in a substance, the higher the boiling point
    (D) The greater the amount of total electrons in a substance, the higher the boiling point
    (E) The strong intermolecular force of hydrogen bonding increases the boiling point of H_2O

66. Consider a sample of gas measured at standard temperature and pressure occupying 11.2 L of volume. The number of molecules the sample of gas contains is

    (A) $\dfrac{0.5}{6.02 \times 10^{23}}$ molecules

    (B) $\dfrac{2}{6.02 \times 10^{23}}$ molecules

    (C) $0.5\,(6.02 \times 10^{23})$ molecules

    (D) $1\,(6.02 \times 10^{23})$ molecules

    (E) $2\,(6.02 \times 10^{23})$ molecules

67. How much energy is required to heat 20 g of H_2O from $25.0°C$ to $75.0°C$? (The specific heat of $H_2O(l)$ is 1 calorie/(g·°C))

    (A)   0.4 calories
    (B)   20 calories
    (C)   100 calories
    (D)   500 calories
    (E) 1,000 calories

68. What is the percent dissociation of sulfurous acid, H_2SO_3, in a 0.1 M solution if the hydronium ion, H_3O^+, concentration is 1×10^{-2}?

    (A) 0.001%
    (B) 0.01%
    (C) 0.1%
    (D) 1.0%
    (E) 10%

69. An isotope of element Z forms a chloride that is 70 percent chlorine by mass. If the formula of the chloride is ZCl_2, what is the atomic mass of Z?

    (A) 15 amu
    (B) 30 amu
    (C) 45 amu
    (D) 60 amu
    (E) 70 amu

70. Which of the following shows the release of a positron?

    (A) $^{15}_{7}N + ^{1}_{1}H \rightarrow ^{1}_{1}H + ^{14}_{7}N + ^{1}_{0}n$

    (B) $^{14}_{7}N + ^{1}_{1}H \rightarrow ^{15}_{8}O + ^{0}_{0}\gamma$

    (C) $^{13}_{7}Ne \rightarrow ^{13}_{6}C + ^{0}_{+1}e$

    (D) $^{232}_{90}Th \rightarrow ^{228}_{88}Ra + ^{4}_{2}He$

    (E) $^{3}_{1}H \rightarrow ^{3}_{2}He + ^{0}_{-1}e$

STOP

IF YOU FINISH BEFORE TIME IS CALLED, YOU MAY CHECK YOUR WORK ON THIS TEST ONLY. DO NOT TURN TO ANY OTHER TEST IN THIS BOOK.

CHEMISTRY TEST

PERIODIC TABLE OF ELEMENTS

1	2	3	4	5	6	7	8	9	10	11	12	13	14	15	16	17	18
1 **H** 1.0079																	2 **He** 4.0026
3 **Li** 6.941	4 **Be** 9.012											5 **B** 10.811	6 **C** 12.011	7 **N** 14.01	8 **O** 16.00	9 **F** 19.00	10 **Ne** 20.179
11 **Na** 22.99	12 **Mg** 24.30											13 **Al** 26.98	14 **Si** 28.09	15 **P** 30.974	16 **S** 32.06	17 **Cl** 35.453	18 **Ar** 39.948
19 **K** 39.10	20 **Ca** 40.08	21 **Sc** 44.96	22 **Ti** 47.90	23 **V** 50.94	24 **Cr** 52.00	25 **Mn** 54.94	26 **Fe** 55.85	27 **Co** 58.93	28 **Ni** 58.69	29 **Cu** 63.55	30 **Zn** 65.39	31 **Ga** 69.72	32 **Ge** 72.59	33 **As** 74.92	34 **Se** 78.96	35 **Br** 79.90	36 **Kr** 83.80
37 **Rb** 85.47	38 **Sr** 87.62	39 **Y** 88.91	40 **Zr** 91.22	41 **Nb** 92.91	42 **Mo** 95.94	43 **Tc** (98)	44 **Ru** 101.1	45 **Rh** 102.91	46 **Pd** 106.42	47 **Ag** 107.87	48 **Cd** 112.41	49 **In** 114.82	50 **Sn** 118.71	51 **Sb** 121.75	52 **Te** 127.60	53 **I** 126.91	54 **Xe** 131.29
55 **Cs** 132.91	56 **Ba** 137.33	57 ***La** 138.91	72 **Hf** 178.49	73 **Ta** 180.95	74 **W** 183.85	75 **Re** 186.21	76 **Os** 190.2	77 **Ir** 192.2	78 **Pt** 195.08	79 **Au** 196.97	80 **Hg** 200.59	81 **Tl** 204.38	82 **Pb** 207.2	83 **Bi** 208.98	84 **Po** (209)	85 **At** (210)	86 **Rn** (222)
87 **Fr** (223)	88 **Ra** 226.02	89 **†Ac** 227.03	104 **Rf** (261)	105 **Db** (262)	106 **Sg** (266)	107 **Bh** (264)	108 **Hs** (277)	109 **Mt** (268)	110 **Ds** (271)	111 **Rg** (272)	112 § (277)						

§ Not yet named

*Lanthanide Series

58 **Ce** 140.12	59 **Pr** 140.91	60 **Nd** 144.24	61 **Pm** (145)	62 **Sm** 150.4	63 **Eu** 151.97	64 **Gd** 157.25	65 **Tb** 158.93	66 **Dy** 162.50	67 **Ho** 164.93	68 **Er** 167.26	69 **Tm** 168.93	70 **Yb** 173.04	71 **Lu** 174.97

†Actinide Series

90 **Th** 232.04	91 **Pa** 231.04	92 **U** 238.03	93 **Np** 237.05	94 **Pu** (244)	95 **Am** (243)	96 **Cm** (247)	97 **Bk** (247)	98 **Cf** (251)	99 **Es** (252)	100 **Fm** (257)	101 **Md** (258)	102 **No** (259)	103 **Lr** (262)

PT3

PRACTICE TEST 3

PRACTICE TEST 3

Note: For all solution questions, the solvent used is water unless noted differently.

Throughout the exam the units below have the listed definitions specified unless noted differently.

H = enthalpy		atm = atmosphere(s)	
M = molar		g = gram(s)	
n = number of moles		J = joule(s)	
P = pressure		kJ = kilojoule(s)	
R = molar gas constant		L = liter(s)	
S = entropy		mL = milliliter(s)	
T = temperature		mm = millimeter(s)	
V = volume		mol = mole(s)	
		V = volt(s)	
		Sw = Stillwell(s)	

Part A

Directions: Each set of answer choices below pertains to the numbered statements or questions immediately following it. Select the answer choice that best fits each statement. A choice may be used once, more than once, or not at all in each set.

Questions 1-4 refer to the following terms.

(A) First ionization energy
(B) Second ionization energy
(C) Electronegativity
(D) Activation energy
(E) Standard heat of formation

1. The energy required to remove an electron from an atom with a charge of +1

2. The change of enthalpy when forming 1 mole of a substance from its constituent elements

3. The tendency of an atom to attract a pair of electrons

4. The energy required to remove an electron from an atom in its ground state

5. The element Fluorine holds a value of 3.98 on the Pauling scale for this term

$$KI(aq) + Pb(NO_3)_2(aq) \rightarrow KNO_3(aq) + PbI_2(s)$$

Questions 6-9 refer to the above unbalanced chemical reaction.

(A) 0
(B) 1
(C) 2
(D) 3
(E) 4

6. When the above chemical reaction is balanced using integer coefficients, the coefficient of $PbI_2(s)$

7. The reactant that contains nitrate dissociates into this many moles of ions

8. The oxidation number of the metal in the precipitate

9. The quantity of electrons transferred from potassium to iodine in $KI(aq)$

Questions 10-14 refer to the following pH values.

    (A) Greater than 11
    (B) Equal to 9
    (C) Less than 9 but greater than 7
    (D) Equal to 7
    (E) Equal to 3

10. pH of 1.0 L of $1 \times 10^{-5} M$ NaOH

11. pH of 2.0 L of $1 \times 10^{-3} M$ HCl

12. pH of a solution where $[OH^-] = 1.0 \times 10^{-11} M$

13. pH of a solution prepared by dissolving 1.0×10^{-4} mol of solid NaCl in enough water to yield 3.2 L of solution

14. pH of a sample of normal human blood

Questions 15-19 refer to the following terms.

    (A) Oxidation
    (B) Reduction
    (C) Fission
    (D) Fusion
    (E) Natural transmutation

15. $_1^2H + _1^3H \rightarrow _2^4He + _0^1n$

16. $_{98}^{249}Cf \rightarrow _{98}^{247}Cf + 2_0^1n$

17. $V^{2+} \rightarrow V^{3+} + e^-$

18. $I_2 + 2e^- \rightarrow 2I^-$

19. $_{92}^{235}U + _0^1n \rightarrow _{36}^{92}Kr + _{56}^{141}Ba + 3_0^1n$

Questions 20-23 refer to the following terms.

    (A) Amphoteric
    (B) Deionization
    (C) Dehydration
    (D) Deliquescence
    (E) Dissolution

20. The interaction of a solvent with molecules in a solute

21. Substances that absorb relatively large quantities of water to form aqueous solutions

22. The removal of ions

23. A molecule or ion capable of reacting as both a base and an acid

Questions 24-25 refer to the following substances.

    (A) N_2
    (B) O_2
    (C) O_3
    (D) CO_2
    (E) SO_2

24. An inorganic molecule which helps to prevent damaging ultraviolet light from reaching the Earth's surface

25. A substance which, when rises high into the atmosphere, can lead to the production of acid rain

**PLEASE USE THE SECTION AT THE LOWER LEFT-HAND CORNER
OF THE ANSWER SHEET AND ANSWER QUESTIONS 101-115
ACCORDING TO THE DIRECTIONS DESCRIBED BELOW.**

Part B

Directions: Each question below consists of two statements, I in the left-hand column and II in the right-hand column. For each question, determine whether statement I is true or false and whether statement II is true or false and fill in the corresponding T or F circles on your answer sheet. Fill in circle CE only if statement II is a correct explanation of the true statement I.

EXAMPLES:

<u>I</u>   <u>II</u>

EX 1. Ca(OH)$_2$ is a strong acid BECAUSE Ca(OH)$_2$ contains calcium.

EX 2. **In a chemical reaction** BECAUSE **matter is neither created**
       mass is conserved   **nor destroyed.**

SAMPLE ANSWERS

	I		II		CE*
EX 1	Ⓣ	●	●	Ⓕ	○
EX 2	●	Ⓕ	●	Ⓕ	●

<u>I</u>   <u>II</u>

101. If the change in Gibbs energy, ΔG, of a reaction at a given temperature and pressure is negative, the reaction occurs spontaneously   BECAUSE   the Gibbs energy will then equal the change in entropy, ΔS.

102. Ammonia, NH$_3(aq)$, can be commonly used to neutralize acids   BECAUSE   NH$_3$ reacts to water to form NH$_4^+$ and OH$^-$.

$$ClNO_2(g) + NO(g) \rightleftarrows NO_2(g) + ClNO(g)$$

103. In the equilibrium reaction above, when additional ClNO$_2(g)$ is added, the concentration of NO(g) decreases   BECAUSE   the frequency of effective collisons between ClNO$_2(g)$ and NO(g) increases as the concentration of ClNO$_2(g)$ increases.

104. One mole of N$_2$ contains fewer molecules than one mole of O$_2$ BECAUSE   the molecular mass of N$_2$ is less than the molecular mass of O$_2$.

105. Metallic silver is NOT an electrical conductor   BECAUSE   in metallic silver, the atoms of silver are ionically bonded.

106. According to the kinetic theory of gases, ideal gas particles constantly experience elastic collisions among themselves   BECAUSE   the absolute temperature of the system depends only on the average kinetic energy of the gas particles.

	I		II

107. A reaction between $AgNO_3$ and $NaCl$ will run to completion — BECAUSE — one of the products formed is a precipitate.

108. The pOH of a 5×10^{-4} M solution of $Ca(OH)_2$ is 3 — BECAUSE — the pOH of a solution is calculated by $-\log[OH^-]$.

109. The volume of a gas initially at 273 K and 800 mmHg will decrease when at standard temperature and pressure — BECAUSE — decreasing both the temperature and pressure results in an increase in volume according to: $V_2 = V_1 \times \dfrac{P_1}{P_2} \times \dfrac{T_1}{T_2}$.

110. Of all intermolecular forces, the weakest bond type are London dispersion forces — BECAUSE — the dissociation energy, on average, of London dispersion forces is lower than other intermolecular forces.

$$N_2(g) + 3\,H_2(g) \rightleftarrows 2\,NH_3(g)$$

111. As the above chemical reaction occurs, there is a decrease in the entropy ($\Delta S < 0$) — BECAUSE — gases are more disordered than liquids.

112. The freezing point of a dilute solution of $NaCl(aq)$ is higher than the freezing point of $H_2O(l)$ — BECAUSE — the boiling point of $NaCl(s)$ is higher than the boiling point of $H_2O(l)$.

113. To prepare a 2 M solution of fluoride ions from MgF_2 (molar mass 62 g/mol), 31 g of MgF_2 should be dissolved in 1 L of solution — BECAUSE — each mole of MgF_2 dissolves to produce 2 mol of fluoride ions.

114. After a system has reached chemical equilibrium, there is no change in the concentrations of reactants and products — BECAUSE — reactions at equilibrium are irreversible.

115. The combustion of organic compounds containing sulfur lead to the production of acid rain — BECAUSE — sulfur trioxide has enhanced stability due to resonance.

Part C

Directions: Each of the questions below is followed by five answer choices or completions. Select the one that is best in each case and then bubble in the corresponding circle on the answer sheet.

26. What is the gram formula mass of magnesium sulfate, $Mg(SO_4)$?

(A) 80
(B) 100
(C) 120
(D) 140
(E) 160

27. How many pi bonds are there in the molecule 2-butyne, $CH_3C \equiv CCH_3$?

(A) 1
(B) 2
(C) 4
(D) 6
(E) 8

28. In the ionic solid NH_4NO_3, the ions present are

(A) H^+, N^{3+}, and O^{2-}
(B) NH_4^+, N^{3+}, O^{2-}
(C) NH_3, H^+, and NO_3^-
(D) NH_4^+ and NO_3^-
(E) H^+, N^{3+}, O^{2-}, and NH_4^+

29. Consider a 2 L sample of O_2, initially at standard temperature and pressure. A rise in temperature would cause an increase in all of the following EXCEPT the

(A) mass of the O_2 in the sample
(B) average kinetic energy of the O_2 molecules in the sample
(C) average velocity of the O_2 molecules in the sample
(D) vapor pressure of the O_2 in the sample
(E) volume of the O_2 sample

30. Which substance below experiences resonance stability with both sigma and pi electrons?

(A) Methane
(B) Benzene
(C) Butane
(D) Hydrochloric acid
(E) Sodium iodide

$$\ldots Ag^+ + \ldots S^{2-} \rightarrow$$

31. When the equation for the reaction represented above is balanced by use of lowest integer coefficients, the integer coefficient for Ag^+ is

(A) 1
(B) 2
(C) 3
(D) 4
(E) 5

$$H_2, He, N_2, Ne, NO_2$$

32. Each of five distinct rigid 2.0 L containers contains a 7.0 g sample of one of the gases listed above at 25°C. The pressure is highest in the container containing which of the following gases?

(A) H_2
(B) He
(C) N_2
(D) Ne
(E) NO_2

33. Which of the following about catalysts is true? Catalysts

(A) decrease the value of equilibrium
(B) decrease the amount of product present at equilibrium
(C) decrease the concentration of the reactants
(D) are permanently altered during the chemical reaction
(E) reduce the activation energy of the chemical reaction

34. The conversion of $Cr_2O_7^{2-}$ to Cr^{3+} through a chemical reaction is an example of

(A) neutralization
(B) hydrolysis
(C) oxidation
(D) reduction
(E) displacement

35. A monoprotic weak acid would most likely have which of the following H_3O^+ concentrations?

(A) 1.0×10^{-1}
(B) 1.0×10^{-4}
(C) 1.0×10^{-7}
(D) 1.0×10^{-8}
(E) 1.0×10^{-10}

36. How many milliliters of 0.20 M HCl are required to exactly neutralize 40 mL of 0.10 M NaOH?

(A) 5 mL
(B) 10 mL
(C) 20 mL
(D) 40 mL
(E) 50 mL

37. All of the following substances can act as Bronsted-Lowry bases in aqueous solutions EXCEPT

(A) S^{2-}

(B) H_2O

(C) CH_4

(D) SO_4^{2-}

(E) CO_3^{2-}

38. Which of the following is closest to the percent composition by mass of oxygen in glycerone, $C_3H_6O_3$?

(A) 25%
(B) 33%
(C) 50%
(D) 53%
(E) 75%

39. A certain mass of carbon required 32 grams of oxygen to be converted into carbon monoxide, CO. If this same mass of carbon were to be converted into carbon dioxide, CO_2, the mass of oxygen required would be

(A) 4.0 g
(B) 8.0 g
(C) 12 g
(D) 32 g
(E) 64 g

40. An example of a network solid is

(A) dry ice, CO_2
(B) iodine, I_2
(C) baking soda, $NaHCO_3$
(D) bleach (solid), $NaBO_3$
(E) diamond, C

41. Which of the following ions does NOT have a noble gas electron configuration?

(A) N^{5+}
(B) F^-
(C) Ca^{2+}
(D) Ag^+
(E) Ba^{2+}

42. Consider element X that produces a compound with an empirical formula X_2O_5. Element X is most likely which of the following?

(A) C
(B) N
(C) S
(D) Cl
(E) Ar

43. Liquid water without any noticeable ions does not dissolve limestone, $CaCO_3$, with much efficacy. However, water containing carbonates dissolves limestone very well. This occurs because the water containing carbonates

(A) reacts with the limestone in a double-replacement reaction
(B) is slightly acidic, which helps to dissolve the limestone
(C) is slightly basic, which helps to dissolve the limestone
(D) react to produce a gaseous solution, which helps to dissolve the limestone
(E) is of neutral pH, which is better for dissolving limestone

44. Suppose the molar concentration of Ca^{2+} ions in a 1 L saturated water solution of calcium sulfate at 298 K was measured to be 3.0×10^{-3}. What is the value of K_{sp} for calcium sulfate?

(A) 3.0×10^{-3}
(B) 6.0×10^{-3}
(C) 9.0×10^{-3}
(D) 3.0×10^{-6}
(E) 9.0×10^{-6}

45. How many joules of energy are required to heat 54 g of aluminum from 20°C to 40°C? (The specific heat capacity of aluminum is 0.9 J / mol-K)

(A) 9 J
(B) 18 J
(C) 36 J
(D) 45 J
(E) 72 J

$$2\,\mathrm{Ag}(s) + \mathrm{Zn}^{2+}(aq) + 2\mathrm{OH}^-(aq) \rightarrow \mathrm{Zn}(s) + \mathrm{Ag_2O}(aq) + \mathrm{H_2O}(l)$$

46. Consider the balanced reduction-oxidation chemical reaction shown above. Which of the following is the change of the oxidation number of silver?

    (A) 0 to 1+
    (B) 0 to 2+
    (C) 0 to 2−
    (D) 2+ to 0
    (E) 2− to 0

$$\dots \mathrm{C}(s) + \dots \mathrm{H_2SO_4}(l) \rightarrow \dots \mathrm{SO_2}(g) + \dots \mathrm{CO_2}(g) + \dots \mathrm{H_2O}(l)$$

47. When the equation for the reaction represented above is balanced and the coefficients are reduced to the lowest integer values, the coefficient for sulfur dioxide, $\mathrm{SO_2}(g)$ is

    (A) 1
    (B) 2
    (C) 3
    (D) 4
    (E) 5

Dissociation reaction	K_a
$\mathrm{HCN} \rightleftharpoons \mathrm{H^+} + \mathrm{CN^-}$	4.0×10^{-9}
$\mathrm{H_2CO_3} \rightleftharpoons \mathrm{H^+} + \mathrm{HCO_3^-}$	4.4×10^{-7}
$\mathrm{HC_2H_3O_2} \rightleftharpoons \mathrm{H^+} + \mathrm{C_2H_3O_2^-}$	1.9×10^{-5}
$\mathrm{HF} \rightleftharpoons \mathrm{H^+} + \mathrm{F^-}$	6.6×10^{-4}
$\mathrm{H_3PO_4} \rightleftharpoons \mathrm{H^+} + \mathrm{H_2PO_4^-}$	7.1×10^{-3}

48. Consider the table above, which shows the acid dissociation constants, K_a, of 5 acids. According to this data, which of the following species can be considered the weakest acid?

    (A) HCN
    (B) $\mathrm{H_2CO_3}$
    (C) $\mathrm{HC_2H_3O_2}$
    (D) HF
    (E) $\mathrm{H_3PO_4}$

$$H_2(g) + S(g) \leftrightarrows H_2S(g)$$

49. The equilibrium constant, K_{eq}, for the above reaction is

(A) $K_{eq} = \dfrac{[H_2S]}{[H_2][S]}$

(B) $K_{eq} = \dfrac{[H_2S]^2}{[H_2][S]^2}$

(C) $K_{eq} = \dfrac{[H_2S]^2}{[H_2]^2[S]^2}$

(D) $K_{eq} = [H_2S]^2$

(E) $K_{eq} = [H_2][S]$

50. Consider the product when hydrogen gas, H_2, reacts with nitrogen, N_2. The chemical structure of this product can best be described as

(A) linear
(B) bent
(C) trigonal planar
(D) trigonal pyramidal
(E) tetrahedral

51. The percent by mass composition of a certain compound is 41% boron and 59% nitrogen. What is the empirical formula of this compound?

(A) BN
(B) B_2N
(C) BN_2
(D) B_3N
(E) B_3N_2

52. Proper laboratory procedure is to swirl a test tube containing a liquid while being heated. The purpose of this is to

(A) increase the rate of evaporation of the liquid
(B) decrease the time it takes for the liquid to boil
(C) decrease the heat of vaporization
(D) prevent the forming vapor from ejecting the liquid
(E) ensure the test tube does not expand and break

53.
Mass of empty flask	20.0 grams
Mass of flask + KClO$_3$	32.2 grams
Mass of flask + residue after ignition	29.0 grams

The data above were taken from the decomposition of $KClO_3$ by ignition, which produces oxygen gas and a solid residue. Which of the following represents the amount of moles of oxygen gas that were liberated by ignition?

(A) 0.10
(B) 0.20
(C) 1.0
(D) 1.2
(E) 2.0

54. Which of the following statements is *inconsistent* with the kinetic molecular theory of gases?

(A) The volume that each gas molecule occupies is negligible compared to the volume of the container they occupy
(B) No energy is gained or lost when molecules collide
(C) The molecules are in constant, linear motion
(D) Collisions between molecules are perfectly inelastic
(E) The average kinetic energy of gas molecules is directly proportional to temperature

55. Consider a container initially holding V_i L of O_2 at standard temperature and pressure. If the pressure of the container is doubled which of the following expressions, in terms of V_i, represents the resulting volume at constant temperature?

(A) $\dfrac{V_i}{4}$

(B) $\dfrac{V_i}{2}$

(C) V_i

(D) $2V_i$

(E) $4V_i$

56. The Lewis dot structure of the hydronium ion is which of the following?

   (A) :H:

   (B) $[\text{H} : \ddot{\text{O}} :]^+$

   (C) $\left[\begin{array}{c} \text{H} : \text{O} : \text{H} \\ \text{H} \end{array} \right]$

   (D) $\left[\begin{array}{c} \text{H} : \ddot{\text{O}} : \text{H} \\ \text{H} \end{array} \right]^+$

   (E) $\left[\begin{array}{c} \text{H} \\ \text{H} : \ddot{\text{O}} : \text{H} \\ \text{H} \end{array} \right]^+$

57. Which of the following oxides dissolves in water to form an acidic solution?

   (A) Na_2O
   (B) MgO
   (C) SO_3
   (D) K_2O
   (E) CaO

58. To calculate the concentration of a base solution by titration with an acidic solution, which of the following represents the minimum amount of data needed, assuming the neutralization equation is known?

   I. Concentration of the acid
   II. Volume of the acid
   III. Volume of the base

   (A) II only
   (B) III only
   (C) I and II only
   (D) II and III only
   (E) I, II, and III

59. Which of the following chemical structures represents an ester?

(A) A structure: $H-C(H)(H)-C(H)(H)-C(=O)-O-H$

(B) A structure: $H-C(H)(H)-C(H)(H)-C(=O)-O-CH_3$

(C) A structure: $H-C(H)(H)-C(=O)-C(H)(H)-H$

(D) A structure: $H-C(H)(H)-C(=O)-C(H)(H)-OH$

(E) A structure: $H-C(H)(H)-O-C(H)(H)-OH$

60. Which of the following molecules is considered a saturated hydrocarbon?

   (A) CH_4
   (B) C_2H_2
   (C) C_2H_4
   (D) C_3H_4
   (E) C_3H_6

61. Consider an atom of Uranium-238. If the atom undergoes one alpha decay, then two beta decays, the resulting atom would be

    (A) Th-234
    (B) Po-234
    (C) U-234
    (D) Th-230
    (E) Ra-226

62. Hydrogen sulfide, H_2S, has a boiling point of $-60°C$, whereas water, H_2O, has a boiling point of $100°C$. The large difference in the boiling point of these two species is due to the fact that

    (A) hydrogen sulfide experiences hydrogen bonding, whereas water does not
    (B) hydrogen sulfide does NOT experience hydrogen bonding, whereas water does
    (C) hydrogen sulfide is non polar, whereas water is polar
    (D) hydrogen sulfide is polar, whereas water is non polar
    (E) hydrogen sulfide has a greater molecular mass than water

$$...C_3H_8 + ...O_2 \rightarrow ...CO_2 + ...H_2O$$

63. The unbalanced chemical combustion of propane is shown above. When the chemical equation is balanced using the lowest integer coefficients, the coefficient of O_2 will be

    (A) 1
    (B) 2.5
    (C) 5
    (D) 10
    (E) 12

64. The heat of formation of ozone, O_3, is $\Delta H = 142.7$ kJ/mol. The fact that the heat of formation of O_3 is positive indicates that

    (A) 142.7 kJ must be added to reduce one mole of O_2
    (B) the reaction of O_2 to form O_3 occurs rapidly at standard temperature and pressure
    (C) heat is liberated when O_2 is oxidized
    (D) O_3 is formed from O_2 by an endothermic reaction
    (E) the decomposition of O_3 is non-spontaneous

65. Consider a 0.1 M solution of sulfurous acid, H_2SO_3. What is the concentration of H^+ ions if the solution of H_2SO_3 is 10 percent ionized?

    (A) 0.01 M
    (B) 0.02 M
    (C) 0.1 M
    (D) 0.2 M
    (E) 1.0 M

66. Which of the following chemical structures below violates the octet rule?

    (A) $HC \equiv CH$

    (B) $HN \equiv NH$

    (C)
$$\begin{array}{ccccc} & Br & H & O & H \\ & | & | & \| & | \\ H- & C- & C- & C- & C-O-H \\ & | & | & & | \\ & H & Br & & H \end{array}$$

    (D)
$$\begin{array}{c} O \\ \| \\ H-O-N-O \end{array}$$

    (E)
$$\begin{array}{c} Cl \\ Cl \diagdown \diagup \\ P-Cl \\ Cl \diagup \diagdown \\ Cl \end{array}$$

67. A chemical species is classified as an Arrhenius base if it

    (A) can accept a H^+ ion
    (B) can receive a OH^- ion
    (C) contains the H^+ ion
    (D) contains the H^- ion
    (E) contains the OH^- ion

68. A molecule of which of the following organic compounds contains a triple bond?

    (A) C_3H_4
    (B) C_3H_6
    (C) C_4H_8
    (D) C_4H_{10}
    (E) C_5H_{10}

Electron removed	1st	2nd	3rd	4th
Ionization energy (kilojoules per mole)	900	1,800	14,900	21,000

69. The ionization energies for the removal of different electrons from an atom of element X are shown above. Element X is most likely which of the following?

(A) Helium
(B) Lithium
(C) Beryllium
(D) Boron
(E) Carbon

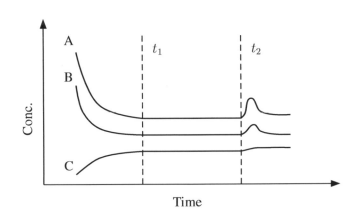

$$A(g) + B(g) \rightleftharpoons C(g)$$

70. The figure above shows that the reaction between A and B to form C reached equilibrium at time t_1. The disturbance of equilibrium that occurred at time t_2 was most likely caused by which of the following?

(A) Adding only more A to the mixture at time t_2
(B) Adding only more B to the mixture at time t_2
(C) Adding more A and B to the mixture at time t_2
(D) Increasing the pressure of the surroundings of the mixture
(E) Increasing the temperature of the surroundings of the mixture

STOP

**IF YOU FINISH BEFORE TIME IS CALLED, YOU MAY CHECK YOUR WORK ON THIS TEST ONLY.
DO NOT TURN TO ANY OTHER TEST IN THIS BOOK.**

PERIODIC TABLE OF ELEMENTS

1	2	3	4	5	6	7	8	9	10	11	12	13	14	15	16	17	18
1 **H** 1.0079																	2 **He** 4.0026
3 **Li** 6.941	4 **Be** 9.012											5 **B** 10.811	6 **C** 12.011	7 **N** 14.01	8 **O** 16.00	9 **F** 19.00	10 **Ne** 20.179
11 **Na** 22.99	12 **Mg** 24.30											13 **Al** 26.98	14 **Si** 28.09	15 **P** 30.974	16 **S** 32.06	17 **Cl** 35.453	18 **Ar** 39.948
19 **K** 39.10	20 **Ca** 40.08	21 **Sc** 44.96	22 **Ti** 47.90	23 **V** 50.94	24 **Cr** 52.00	25 **Mn** 54.94	26 **Fe** 55.85	27 **Co** 58.93	28 **Ni** 58.69	29 **Cu** 63.55	30 **Zn** 65.39	31 **Ga** 69.72	32 **Ge** 72.59	33 **As** 74.92	34 **Se** 78.96	35 **Br** 79.90	36 **Kr** 83.80
37 **Rb** 85.47	38 **Sr** 87.62	39 **Y** 88.91	40 **Zr** 91.22	41 **Nb** 92.91	42 **Mo** 95.94	43 **Tc** (98)	44 **Ru** 101.1	45 **Rh** 102.91	46 **Pd** 106.42	47 **Ag** 107.87	48 **Cd** 112.41	49 **In** 114.82	50 **Sn** 118.71	51 **Sb** 121.75	52 **Te** 127.60	53 **I** 126.91	54 **Xe** 131.29
55 **Cs** 132.91	56 **Ba** 137.33	57 ***La** 138.91	72 **Hf** 178.49	73 **Ta** 180.95	74 **W** 183.85	75 **Re** 186.21	76 **Os** 190.2	77 **Ir** 192.2	78 **Pt** 195.08	79 **Au** 196.97	80 **Hg** 200.59	81 **Tl** 204.38	82 **Pb** 207.2	83 **Bi** 208.98	84 **Po** (209)	85 **At** (210)	86 **Rn** (222)
87 **Fr** (223)	88 **Ra** 226.02	89 **†Ac** 227.03	104 **Rf** (261)	105 **Db** (262)	106 **Sg** (266)	107 **Bh** (264)	108 **Hs** (277)	109 **Mt** (268)	110 **Ds** (271)	111 **Rg** (272)	112 **§** (277)						

§ Not yet named

*Lanthanide Series

58	59	60	61	62	63	64	65	66	67	68	69	70	71
Ce 140.12	**Pr** 140.91	**Nd** 144.24	**Pm** (145)	**Sm** 150.4	**Eu** 151.97	**Gd** 157.25	**Tb** 158.93	**Dy** 162.50	**Ho** 164.93	**Er** 167.26	**Tm** 168.93	**Yb** 173.04	**Lu** 174.97

†Actinide Series

90	91	92	93	94	95	96	97	98	99	100	101	102	103
Th 232.04	**Pa** 231.04	**U** 238.03	**Np** 237.05	**Pu** (244)	**Am** (243)	**Cm** (247)	**Bk** (247)	**Cf** (251)	**Es** (252)	**Fm** (257)	**Md** (258)	**No** (259)	**Lr** (262)

CHAPTER

PT4

PRACTICE TEST 4

PRACTICE TEST 4

Note: For all solution questions, the solvent used is water unless noted differently.

Throughout the exam the units below have the listed definitions specified unless noted differently.

H = enthalpy	atm = atmosphere(s)
M = molar	g = gram(s)
n = number of moles	J = joule(s)
P = pressure	kJ = kilojoule(s)
R = molar gas constant	L = liter(s)
S = entropy	mL = milliliter(s)
T = temperature	mm = millimeter(s)
V = volume	mol = mole(s)
	V = volt(s)
	Sw = Stillwell(s)

Part A

Directions: Each set of answer choices below pertains to the numbered statements or questions immediately following it. Select the answer choice that best fits each statement. A choice may be used once, more than once, or not at all in each set.

Questions 1-5 refer to the following compounds.

(A) HCl
(B) KCl
(C) NH_3
(D) $HC_2H_3O_2$
(E) $NaC_2H_3O_2$

1. Is a carboxylic acid

2. Has a trigonal pyramidal molecular structure

3. Is a strong acid

4. Is a salt that when hydrolyzed forms a basic solution

5. Capable of forming a coordinate covalent bond with H_3O^+

Questions 6-9 refer to the following laboratory items.

(A) Burette
(B) Thermometer
(C) Volumetric flask
(D) Separatory funnel
(E) Mass spectrometer

6. Used to help atoms or molecules in an unknown sample by correlating known masses to identified masses

7. Used to prepare solutions of predetermined concentrations when utilizing a solid solute

8. Used for accurate volume measurements during titration

9. Commonly used to measure the average kinetic energy of ambient air

Questions 10-14 refer to the following chemical reactions.

    (A) $H^+(aq) + OH^-(aq) \rightarrow H_2O(l)$
    (B) $K^+(g) + e^- \rightarrow K(g)$
    (C) $Zn(s) \rightarrow Zn^{2+}(g) + 2e^-$
    (D) $N_2(g) + 3 H_2(g) \rightarrow 2 NH_3(g)$
    (E) $CH_4(g) + 2 O_2(g) \rightarrow CO_2(g) + 2 H_2O(l)$

10. A net neutralization reaction

11. A combustion reaction

12. A synthesis reaction

13. An oxidation half-reaction

14. A reduction half-reaction

Questions 15-18 refer to the following.

    (A) $\Delta S < 0$
    (B) $\Delta S > 0$
    (C) $\Delta G > 0$
    (D) $K_{eq} > 1$
    (E) $K_a \gg 1$

15. Indicates an increase in disorder and chaos in the chemical system

16. Indicates the presence of strong ion dissociation

17. Indicates the favoring of products in a reversible reaction

18. Indicates the chemical process is theoretically non-spontaneous

Questions 19-20 refer to the following terms.

    (A) Ionic substance
    (B) Metallic substance
    (C) Polar covalent molecule
    (D) Nonpolar covalent molecule
    (E) Network solid

19. Francium, Fr

20. Sulfur trioxide, SO_3

Questions 21-25 refer to the following graphs.

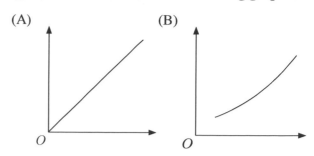

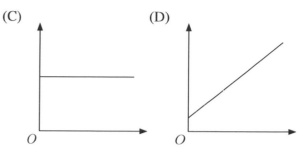

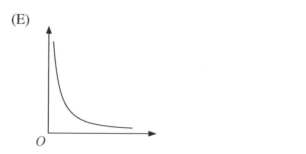

21. Which graph could represent the concentration of one reactant *versus* time as a reaction approaches equilibrium?

22. Which graph could represent the pressure of 1 L of an isochoric ideal gas *versus* its absolute temperature?

23. Which graph could represent the pH of a 0.2 M solution of H_2SO_4 *versus* the volume of a 0.2 M solution of $Ca(OH)_2$ that is added to it?

24. Which graph could represent VP, the product of volume and pressure, for an isothermal ideal gas *versus* its pressure?

25. Which graph could represent the approximate molecular mass of an atom *versus* atomic number?

PLEASE USE THE SECTION AT THE LOWER LEFT-HAND CORNER
OF THE ANSWER SHEET AND ANSWER QUESTIONS 101-115
ACCORDING TO THE DIRECTIONS DESCRIBED BELOW.

Part B

Directions: Each question below consists of two statements, I in the left-hand column and II in the right-hand column. For each question, determine whether statement I is true or false <u>and</u> whether statement II is true or false and fill in the corresponding T or F circles on your answer sheet. Fill in circle CE only if statement II is a correct explanation of the true statement I.

EXAMPLES:

I **II**

EX 1. $Ca(OH)_2$ is a strong acid BECAUSE $Ca(OH)_2$ contains calcium.

EX 2. In a chemical reaction BECAUSE matter is neither created
mass is conserved nor destroyed.

SAMPLE ANSWERS

	I		II		CE*
EX 1	Ⓣ	●	●	Ⓕ	○
EX 2	●	Ⓕ	●	Ⓕ	●

I **II**

101. Carbon-12, $^{12}_{6}C$, is an isotope of BECAUSE atoms between isotopes have the same number of protons but a different number of electrons.

Carbon-14, $^{14}_{6}C$

102. The molecule of carbon dioxide, CO_2, has a net dipole moment of zero BECAUSE the arrangement of atoms in the CO_2 molecule are such that bond polarities within the molecule cancel out.

103. For an equilibrium reaction involving only ideal gases, the volumetric ratio between substances is equivalent to the mole ratio of those substances at standard temperature and pressure BECAUSE each mole of any ideal gas at standard temperature and pressure occupies 22.4 L of volume.

104. The empirical formula of C_2H_6 is CH_2 BECAUSE the empirical formula of a molecule shows the lowest ratio of the elements present in the molecular formula.

105. The half-life of a radioisotope varies with mass of a given sample BECAUSE the radioactive half-life for a given radioisotope is the amount of time for half of the radioactive nuclei in a given sample to undergo radioactive decay.

106. An element that has an electron configuration of $1s^22s^22p^63s^23d^{10}4s^2$ is a transition element BECAUSE transition elements have completely filled $1s$, $2s$, $2p$, $3s$, and $3p$ orbitals in their ground state.

<u>I</u>   <u>II</u>

107. The N^{3-} ion and the Ne atom have similar   BECAUSE   the N^{3-} ion and the neon atom have the
      chemical properties   same number of electrons.

$$NH_4{}^+ + OH^- \leftrightharpoons NH_3 + H_2O$$

108. In the above equilibrium reaction, ammonia,   BECAUSE   a conjugate base is identified as receiving a
      NH_3, is considered the conjugate base to the   proton from its respective acid.
      acid of ammonium, $NH_4{}^+$

109. The combustion of fuels containing sulfur   BECAUSE   the following reaction may be possible
      can lead to the production of acid rain $2SO_2 + 2H_2O + O_2 \rightarrow 2H_2SO_4$, producing
                                                                                         an acid.

110. To prepare a 1 M solution of chloride ions   BECAUSE   each mole of $MgCl_2$ dissolves to produce 2
      from $MgCl_2$ (molar mass 95 g/mol), 95 g of   mol of chloride ions.
      $MgCl_2$ should be dissolved in 1 L of solution

111. When a pure gas at its condensation point is   BECAUSE   when a phase change occurs there is a
      converted from a gas to a liquid at constant   change in potential energy, while kinetic
      pressure, its temperature remains constant   energy remains constant.
      until the phase change is complete

112. When a catalyst is introduced into the system   BECAUSE   the activation energy for the forward
      of a chemical reaction, the rate of both the   reaction is equivalent to the activation
      forward and reverse reactions are increased   energy of the reverse reaction.

$$2\,NO_2(g) \leftrightharpoons N_2O_4(g)$$

113. In the above equilibrium reaction, an   BECAUSE   gas molecules experience more effective
      increase in the pressure of the container at a   collisions at greater pressures and lower
      constant temperature results in an increase in   volumes.
      the number of moles of $N_2O_4(g)$

114. Nearly all alpha particles shot at a thin metal   BECAUSE   according to Rutherford's gold foil
      foil are not disturbed   experiment, the gold atoms tested mostly
                                                                                         contain empty space.

115. A solution with a pH of 5 has a 10^3 times   BECAUSE   the pH scale is a logarithmic scale, with each
      greater concentration of H_3O^+ than one with   increase in pH representing an increase in
      a pH of 2   order of magnitude of $[OH^-]$.

PRACTICE TEST 4

Part C

Directions: Each of the questions below is followed by five answer choices or completions. Select the one that is best in each case and then bubble in the corresponding circle on the answer sheet.

26. What is the gram formula mass of calcium carbonate, $Ca(CO_3)$?

    (A) 80
    (B) 100
    (C) 120
    (D) 140
    (E) 160

27. Consider a 120 g sample of $MgSO_4$ (molar mass 120 g/mol). If the sample of $MgSO_4$ were dissolved in water to form a 2 L solution, the molarity of the solution would be

    (A) 0.5 M
    (B) 1.0 M
    (C) 2.0 M
    (D) 2.5 M
    (E) 4.0 M

28. In the ionic solid NH_4OH, the ions present are

    (A) N^{5+}, H^+, and O^{2-}
    (B) N^{5+}, H^-, and O^{2-}
    (C) NH_4^+ and OH^-
    (D) NH_4^+, N^{5+}, and O^{2-}
    (E) NH_4^+, NH_3, and H^+

29. How many grams of oxygen gas, O_2, are required to completely react with 1 mol of methane, CH_4, to form carbon dioxide, CO_2?

    (A) 4 g
    (B) 8 g
    (C) 16 g
    (D) 32 g
    (E) 64 g

30. Which of the following pairs of products would result from a reaction containing reactants KNO_3 and $Mg(MnO_4)_2$?

    (A) Potassium nitrate and magnesium permanganate
    (B) Potassium permanganate and magnesium nitrate
    (C) Potassium nitrite and magnesium permanganate
    (D) Potassium permanganate and magnesium nitrite
    (E) Phosphorous permanganate and magnesium nitrate

31. Which of the following is the chemical formula for sulfurous acid?

    (A) H_2SO_4
    (B) HSO_4^-
    (C) H_2SO_3
    (D) HSO_3^-
    (E) HSO_2^+

$$2\,N_2O_5(g) \rightleftarrows O_2(g) + 4\,NO_2(g)$$

32. Which of the following is the correct expression for the equilibrium constant, K_c, for the reaction represented above?

    (A) $\dfrac{[NO_2]^4\,[O_2]}{[N_2O_5]^2}$

    (B) $\dfrac{[NO_2]\,[O_2]}{[N_2O_5]}$

    (C) $\dfrac{[N_2O_5]}{[NO_2]\,[O_2]}$

    (D) $\dfrac{[N_2O_5]^2}{[NO_2]^4\,[O_2]}$

    (E) $[O_2]\,[NO_2]^4$

33. Of the following, which are NOT good laboratory practices?

    I. Placing a hot glass beaker on a cool surface
    II. Pouring water slowly into an acid for dilution
    III. Rinse a burette with the solution that will be used to eventually fill the burette in the experiment

    (A) I only
    (B) III only
    (C) I and II only
    (D) I and III only
    (E) None of the above

34. Consider a titration experiment where 2. M HCl was used to complete titrate 100 mL of a 1. M Ca(OH)$_2$ solution. How many milliliters of HCl were used?

    (A) 50 mL
    (B) 100 mL
    (C) 150 mL
    (D) 200 mL
    (E) 400 mL

$$^{40}_{19}K \rightarrow\ ^{0}_{-1}e + ?$$

35. The missing product in the equation above is

    (A) $^{40}_{18}$Ar

    (B) $^{40}_{19}$K

    (C) $^{40}_{20}$Ca

    (D) $^{39}_{18}$Ar

    (E) $^{39}_{20}$Ca

36. Which of the following is the complete Lewis electron-dot diagram for oxygen gas, O$_2$?

    (A) $\cdot$O$\vdots\vdots$O$\cdot$

    (B) $\vdots$O$\vdots\vdots$O$\vdots$

    (C) $\vdots$O$::$O$\vdots$

    (D) $\vdots$O$::$O$\vdots$

    (E) $\vdots$O$\cdot\cdot$O$\vdots$

37. Which of the following K_a values is that of an acid that is the weakest electrolyte?

    (A) 1.2×10^{-2}
    (B) 3.1×10^{-2}
    (C) 2.7×10^{-3}
    (D) 9.9×10^{-3}
    (E) 1.0×10^{-4}

38. Complete combustion of hydrocarbons produces

    (A) $CH_4 + H_2O$
    (B) $CO_2 + H_2O$
    (C) C_3H_7OH
    (D) $HC_2H_3O_2$
    (E) $CH_3CH_2CH_2CH_3 + H_2O$

39. When 1 L of K$_2$CO$_3$(aq) and 2 L of Cu(NO$_3$)$_2$(aq) are mixed to form a 3 L solution, and the reaction observed, which of the following statements is NOT a result of direct observations?

    (A) A solution of K$_2$CO$_3$(aq) is colorless and odorless
    (B) A solution of Cu(NO$_3$)$_2$(aq) is colorless and odorless
    (C) The NO$_3^-$ ions in solutions are surrounded by water molecules with positive poles directed inward
    (D) A solution of KNO$_3$(aq) is colorless and odorless
    (E) A green precipitate forms

40. Which of the following is the best explanation as to why complex ions of transition metals can become colored? Transition metals

    (A) are soluble in water
    (B) have unfilled d orbitals
    (C) reflect light at various ultraviolet wavelengths
    (D) absorb light at various visible wavelengths
    (E) have large energy formation constants

$$2\,X(aq) \leftrightharpoons\ Y(aq) + Z(aq)$$

41. Which of the following is most likely to have the greatest effect on the equilibrium constant, K, in the chemical reaction represented above?

    (A) Adding a large amount of a catalyst to the system
    (B) Increasing the temperature of the system by 1 K
    (C) Adding 1 mol of 2 X(aq) to the system
    (D) Adding 1 mol of Y(aq) to the system
    (E) Removing 1 mol of Z(aq) from the system

42. Of the following, which apparatus or procedure is best to use when separating miscible liquids?

    (A) Mass spectrometer
    (B) Infrared spectrometer
    (C) Distillation
    (D) Ion-exchange chromatography
    (E) Thin-layer chromatography

$$CH_3CH_2COOH + CH_3OH \rightarrow CH_3CH_2COOCH_3 + H_2O$$

43. Consider the organic chemical reaction shown above. The reaction is best classified as which of the following?

(A) An addition reaction
(B) A substitution reaction
(C) A fermentation reaction
(D) A dehydration synthesis reaction
(E) An esterification reaction

$$\begin{array}{ccccccccc} I & & II & & III & & IV & & V \\ 2s & \rightarrow & 3s & \rightarrow & 2p & \rightarrow & 3p & \rightarrow & 3s & \rightarrow & 2s \end{array}$$

44. The electronic transitions shown above are observed when sodium atoms are sprayed into a hot flame. The transitions are numbered for tracking purposes. Which of these transitions would result in *emission* of electromagnetic radiation?

(A) I and II only
(B) I and III only
(C) II and V only
(D) II and IV only
(E) II, IV, and V only

$$\ldots Fe_2O_3(s) + \ldots H_2SO_4(aq) \rightarrow \ldots Fe_2(SO_4)_3(aq) + \ldots H_2O(l)$$

45. When the equation above is balanced and all coefficients are reduced to lowest whole-number terms, the coefficient for $H_2O(l)$ is

(A) 1
(B) 2
(C) 3
(D) 4
(E) 5

46. Consider a reaction where the potential energies of the reactants, products, and activated complex are 75 kJ/mol, 40 kJ/mol, and 80 kJ/mol. Which of the following statements, if any, are true?

    I. The activation energy of the forward reaction is greater than the activation energy of the reverse reaction.
    II. The activation energy of the reverse reaction is greater than the activation energy of the forward reaction.
    III. The reaction is endothermic.

    (A) I only
    (B) II only
    (C) I and III
    (D) II and III
    (E) None of the statements are true

47. What is the percent composition of magnesium in magnesium chloride, $MgCl_2$?

    (A) 20%
    (B) 25%
    (C) 33%
    (D) 71%
    (E) 95%

48. The oxidation number of sulfur is 0 in which of the following compounds?

    (A) S_8
    (B) MgS
    (C) Na_2SO_3
    (D) H_2SO_4
    (E) $K_2S_2O_7$

49. Which of the following statements best describes the bonding found in methane, CH_4?

    (A) The carbon atom is sp hybridized
    (B) The carbon atom is sp^2 hybridized
    (C) The carbon atom is sp^3 hybridized
    (D) There are three sigma bonds and one pi bond around the carbon atom
    (E) There are four sigma bonds and one pi bond around the carbon atom

50. The rate at which $C_6H_{12}O_6$ dissolves in water is increased by which of the following?

    I. Using a magnet stirrer in the water
    II. Increasing the surface area of $C_6H_{12}O_6$
    III. Increasing the temperature of the water

    (A) I only
    (B) I and II only
    (C) I and III only
    (D) II and III only
    (E) I, II, and III

$$Zn(s) + Cu^{2+}(aq) \rightarrow$$

51. When the equation for the reaction represented above is completed and balanced by the use of lowest whole-number coefficients, the coefficient for $Zn(s)$ is

    (A) 0
    (B) 1
    (C) 2
    (D) 3
    (E) 4

52. The formula for the fluoride of barium is

    (A) BaF
    (B) BaF_2
    (C) BaF_3
    (D) Ba_2F
    (E) Ba_2F_3

53. Which of the following trends is observed as the atomic number decreases in the series of alkaline earth metals Be, Mg, Ca, and Sr?

    (A) The ionic radius increases
    (B) The electronegativity increases
    (C) The first ionization energy decreases
    (D) The number of valence shell electrons decreases
    (E) The primary oxidation number increases

54. Which of the following chemical structures contains at least one pi bond?

    I. H_2C-CH_2

    II. $HN\equiv NH$ III.

    (A) I only
    (B) III only
    (C) I and II only
    (D) II and III only
    (E) I, II, and III

55. Consider a 1 L container of each of the following gases at standard temperature and pressure: He, Ne, Ar, Kr, and Xe. Which gas listed is expected to have the least rate of effusion?

    (A) He
    (B) Ne
    (C) Ar
    (D) Kr
    (E) Xe

Element	Electronegativity
Na	0.9
H	2.2
S	2.6
O	3.4

56. On the basis of electronegativity values given above, in which of the following are the bonds strongest?

(A) H_2
(B) H_2O
(C) SO_3
(D) Na_2S
(E) Na_2O

57. Which of the following chemical structures represents a ketone?

(A)
$$H-\underset{\underset{H}{|}}{\overset{\overset{H}{|}}{C}}-\underset{\underset{H}{|}}{\overset{\overset{H}{|}}{C}}-C\underset{O-H}{\overset{O}{\diagup\diagdown}}$$

(B)
$$H-\underset{\underset{H}{|}}{\overset{\overset{H}{|}}{C}}-\underset{\underset{H}{|}}{\overset{\overset{H}{|}}{C}}-C\underset{H}{\overset{O}{\diagup\diagdown}}$$

(C)
$$H-\underset{\underset{H}{|}}{\overset{\overset{H}{|}}{C}}-\overset{\overset{O}{\|}}{C}-\underset{\underset{H}{|}}{\overset{\overset{H}{|}}{C}}-H$$

(D)
$$H-\underset{\underset{H}{|}}{\overset{\overset{H}{|}}{C}}-O-\underset{\underset{H}{|}}{\overset{\overset{H}{|}}{C}}-OH$$

(E)
$$H-\overset{\overset{O}{\|}}{C}-\underset{\underset{H}{|}}{\overset{\overset{H}{|}}{C}}-OH$$

58. How many negatively charged subatomic particles are present in one atom of $^{42}_{20}Ca^+$?

(A) 18
(B) 19
(C) 20
(D) 21
(E) 22

59. Two samples, A and B, were weighed using different instruments and the following data obtained

Sample A = 0.51 gram
Sample B = 1.991 grams

The total mass of the samples should be published as

(A) 2.5 grams
(B) 2.50 grams
(C) 2.501 grams
(D) 2.5010 grams
(E) 3.0 grams

60. Which of the following does NOT increase the entropy of a system?

(A) Evaporating $H_2O(l)$
(B) Melting $Cu(s)$
(C) Decomposing $H_2CO_3(aq)$
(D) Dissolving $C_4H_9OH(l)$ in $H_2O(l)$
(E) Condensing $H_2O(g)$

$$Ag^+(aq) + e^- \rightarrow Ag(s)$$
$$Cu^{2+}(aq) + 2e^- \rightarrow Cu(s)$$

61. Consider the two half-reactions shown above. If a certain quantity of electric charge formed 2 moles of silver solid, $Ag(s)$, from a solution containing $Ag^+(aq)$ ions, that same quantity of electric charge would yield how many moles of copper metal, $Cu(s)$, from a solution containing Cu^{2+} ions?

(A) 0.5 moles
(B) 1.0 moles
(C) 1.5 moles
(D) 2.0 moles
(E) 2.5 moles

62. How many moles of sodium dichromate, $Na_2Cr_2O_7$, are present in 26.2 grams of this compound?

    (A) 0.01 mole
    (B) 0.05 mole
    (C) 0.1 mole
    (D) 0.5 mole
    (E) 1.0 mole

63. What is the concentration of H^+ ions in a 0.1 M HCl solution that is 15% ionized?

    (A) 0.015 M
    (B) 0.01 M
    (C) 0.10 M
    (D) 0.15 M
    (E) 1.5 M

64. How much energy is required to heat 10. g of copper solid, $Cu(s)$, from 50°C to 60°C? (The specific heat of $Cu(s)$ is 39 J/(g·°C))

    (A)   39 J
    (B)   195 J
    (C)   390 J
    (D) 1,950 J
    (E) 3,900 J

$$2\,NO_2(g) \rightleftarrows N_2O_4(g)$$

65. For the system represented above, which of the following actions will shift the position of equilibrium to the right?

    (A) Increasing the pressure of the reaction container
    (B) Increasing the volume of the reaction container
    (C) Adding additional $N_2O_4(g)$ to the reaction container
    (D) Removing some $NO_2(g)$ from the reaction container
    (E) Using a more malleable reaction container material

66. An isotope of element A forms an oxide that is 80 percent oxygen by mass. If the chemical formula of the oxide is A_2O, what is the atomic mass of element A?

    (A) 2 amu
    (B) 8 amu
    (C) 16 amu
    (D) 32 amu
    (E) 40 amu

$$NH_3(g) + HCl(g) \rightarrow NH_4Cl(s)$$

67. If 2.0 moles of $HCl(g)$ and 3.0 moles of $NH_3(g)$, each measured at 25°C and 1. atm, are allowed to react to completion according to the above equation, the final system will contain

    (A) 1 mole of $HCl(g)$ only
    (B) 1 mole of $NH_3(g)$ only
    (C) 1 mole of $HCl(g)$ and 2 moles of $NH_4Cl(s)$
    (D) 1 mole of $NH_3(g)$ and 2 moles of $NH_4Cl(s)$
    (E) 1 mole of $HCl(g)$, 1 mole of $NH_3(g)$, and 2 moles of 2 moles of $NH_4Cl(s)$

68. A student recorded observations from an experiment involving 3 indicators in a basic solution

Trial	Indicator	Color
1	Litmus	Blue
2	Phenolphthalein	Pink
3	Bromothymol blue	Yellow

    Which of the following trials did the student make an error in her observation?

    (A) Trial 2 only
    (B) Trial 3 only
    (C) Trials 1 and 2 only
    (D) Trials 2 and 3 only
    (E) Trials 1, 2, and 3

69. Which of the following aqueous solutions has the highest boiling point?

  (A) 0.10 M NaCl
  (B) 0.10 M MgCl$_2$
  (C) 0.20 M KBr
  (D) 0.20 M Na$_2$SO$_4$
  (E) 0.20 M HC$_2$H$_3$O$_2$

70. The half-life for the radioactive decay of rhenium-186(m), $^{186m}_{75}$Re, is 20,000 years. If 100. g of $^{186m}_{75}$Re are present initially, how many grams of $^{186m}_{75}$Re will remain after 60,000 years?

  (A) 50.00 g
  (B) 25.00 g
  (C) 12.50 g
  (D) 6.25 g
  (E) 0.00 g

S T O P

**IF YOU FINISH BEFORE TIME IS CALLED, YOU MAY CHECK YOUR WORK ON THIS TEST ONLY.
DO NOT TURN TO ANY OTHER TEST IN THIS BOOK.**

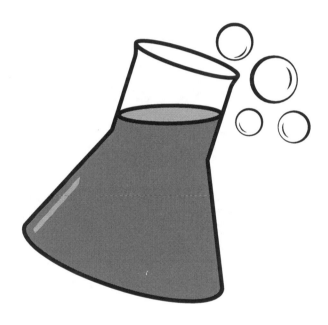

CHAPTER +19

ak

ANSWER KEY

Sec.	Name	Answers
1.1	The Atom and Periodic Table	1. (A) 2. (A) 3. (B) 4. (C) 5. (C) 6. (B) 7. (A) 8. (C)
1.2	Nuclear Chemistry	1. (E) 2. (B) 3. (B) 4. (A) 5. (C) 6. (C) 7. (E) 8. (D)
1.3	Orbital configuration	1. (D) 2. (E) 3. (C) 4. (B) 5. (E) 6. (C) 7. (C) 8. (B) 9. (E) 10. (D)
1.4	Quantum energy	1. (C) 2. (A) 3. (D) 4. (E) 5. (B)
1.5	Periodic Trends	1. (E) 2. (E) 3. (A) 4. (E) 5. (E) 6. (A) 7. (D) 8. (B) 9. (A) 10. (C)

Chapter 1 Quiz

#	Ans.	Explanation
1	D	Silver, Ag, is in group 11, which makes it a transition metal.
2	C	Potassium, K, is in group 1, which makes it an alkali metal.
3	B	Helium, He, is in group 18, which makes it a noble gas.
4	E	Strontium, Sr, is in group 2, which makes it an alkaline earth metal.
5	A	Bromine, Br, is in group 17 which makes it a halogen.
6	D	$_0^0\gamma$ is used to indicate gamma emission.
7	A	$_2^4$He is used to indicate an alpha particle, which is a product of alpha decay.
8	E	$_0^1$n is used to indicate a neutron.
9	B	$_{-1}^{0}\beta$ is used to indicate a beta particle, which is a product of beta decay.
10	C	$_{+1}^{0}\beta$ is used to indicate a positron, which is a product in positron emission.
101	T, T, CE	The atomic mass of C can be found by looking at the bottom number of the cell for carbon on the periodic table. This value is, in fact, 12.011; statement 1 is correct. Elements with the same number of protons but a differing number of neutrons are known as isotopes, but some isotopes are more common than others. The number on a periodic table that indicates the atomic mass of an element is the weighted verage of all naturally occurring isotopes; the second statement is correct, and it correct explains the first statement.

#	Ans.	Explanation
102	F, T	During beta decay, a neutron emits a beta particle transforming it into a proton; there is a net gain of one proton and a net loss of of neutron during beta decay. Statement 1 is false. A beta particle, which is emitted during beta decay, is denoted with the $_{-1}^{\ 0}\beta$ symbol; statement 2 is true.
103	F, T	Gamma emission does not result in the transmutation of an element; therefore, statement 1 is false. Radioactive isotopes are, in fact, radioactive because they are unstable; statement 2 is true.
104	T, F	A grounded helium, He, has an electron configuration of $1s^2$, which indicates that it has 2 electrons. An elements with an electron configuration of $1s^2 2s^1$ has 3 electrons; therefore, statement 1 is correct. A grounded helium, He, has an electron configuration of $1s^2$, which indicates that it has 2 electrons; statement 2 is false.
105	T, T	An atom is ionized when an electron is removed from it through the excitation if an electron. The electron is excited through the addition of energy; therefore, statement 1 is true. Electrons that drop into lower energy levels do release energy; statement 2 is correct, but it does not correctly explain statement 1.
106	T, T	The s orbital holds, 2 electrons. The p orbital holds 6 electrons. The d orbital holds 10 electrons, and the f orbital holds 14 electrons. Statement 1 is correct. Cu is in group 11, which makes it a transition metal. Statement 2 is correct, but it does not explain statement 1.
107	F, F	The reaction presented is a nuclear fusion reaction, because in nuclear fusion two isotopes come together to form a larger isotope.
11	C	C-14 indicates a carbon atom with an atomic mass of 14. A carbon always contains 6 protons. The number of neutron in an atom can be determined by subtracting the known number of protons from the atomic mass. $14 - 6 = 8$. There must be 8 neutrons in C-14.
12	B	Magnesium, Mg, is in group 2 which makes it an alkaline earth metal.
13	D	$_2^4$He is on the products side of the reaction and is the way to denote an alpha particle. This suggests that the reactans side should be a heavier element that has the atomic mass that is the sum of the atomic masses of $_{28}^{61}$Ni and $_2^4$He. Our elements must also increase in atomic number by 2 from our $_{28}^{61}$Ni. Our new element should have an atomic mass of $61 + 4 = 65$ and an atomic number of $28 + 2 = 30$. $_{30}^{65}$Zn must be the answer.
14	B	Given that our reaction shows a change from $_{17}^{32}$Cl to $_{18}^{31}$Ar, we can observe that we need a product that would suggest a reaction that results in the increase of protons while maintaining atomic mass. Beta decay results in a $_{-1}^{\ 0}\beta$ and an isotope that has an atomic number 1 greater than our reactant side. $_{-1}^{\ 0}$e is another way of writing a beta particle in addition to $_{-1}^{\ 0}\beta$. $_{-1}^{\ 0}$e must be the answer.
15	B	Li has an electron configuration of $1s^2 1s^1$. The notation Li$^+$ indicates a Li with one fewer electron, which would leave Li$^+$ with an electron configuration of $1s^2$.

#	Ans.	Explanation
16	C	An electron in an excited state can be denoted by having one fewer electron than it is supposed to have in a lower energy level written to be in a higher energy level. $1s^2 2s^1 2p^6 3s^1$ shows an electron missing from the $2s$ orbital that should be filled and an electron in the $3s$ orbital.
17	D	A change that would result in the increase in a principle quantum number would need to be a positive change from a state of lower energy to a state of higher energy. Transitions 1 and 2 indicate a positive change.
18	D	A change that would result in the release of energy would need to be the drop of an electron from a higher energy state to a lower energy state. This would be indicated through a negative change in electron energy. transitions 3 and 4 indicate a negative change.
19	E	The highest energy electron is the electron that leaves when an atom undergoes first ionization. Li^+ indicates an Li atom that has undergone the ionization of its outermost electron. The $2s^1$ electron is the electron that leaves, due to that fact that it is the outermost electron. Thus, there is no significant change in the energy level of the $1s^1$ electron. Leaving us with 0 as our best answer.

19.2- Chapter 2 - Bonding and intermolecular forces

Sec.	Name	Answers
2.1	Octet Rule / Covalent & Ionic Bonding	1. (B) 2. (B) 3. (B) 4. (D) 5. (A) 6. (C) 101. (T, T, CE) 102. (F, F) 103. (F, T) 104. (F, F) 105. (T, T)
2.2	Single, Double, and Triple Bonds	1. (B) 2. (D) 3. (C) 4. (C) 5. (C) 6. (A) 7. (E) 8. (B) 9. (C) 10. (C)
2.3	Polar & Nonpolar Bonds	1. (C) 2. (C) 3. (B) 4. (D) 5. (C) 6. (B) 7. (D) 101. (T, T, CE) 102. (T, F) 103. (T, T, CE) 104. (F, F) 105. (T, T)
2.4	Orbital Hybridization	1. (C) 2. (B) 3. (A) 4. (C) 5. (A) 6. (C) 7. (C) 8. (B) 9. (C) 10. (C) 11. (E) 12. (B) 13. (B) 14. (B) 15. (B) 16. (E) 17. (D) 18. (E) 19. (C) 20. (E) 21. (C) 22. (B)
2.5	Intermolecular Forces	1. (A) 2. (C) 3. (E) 4. (A) 5. (E) 101. (T, T, CE) 102. (T, T, CE) 6. (C) 7. (C)

Chapter 2 Quiz

#	Ans.	Explanation
1	D	The electronegativity difference between hydrogen, H, and nitrogen, N, is 0.9 which makes the bond between N and H polar. The molecular geometry of NH_3 is trigonal pyramidal which creates an unequal distribution of the regions of partial negative charge in the NH_3 molecule.
2	C	The electronegativity difference between carbon, C, and oxygen, O, is 1.4, which makes the bonds between the two atoms polar. A molecule of CO2, however, is linear, which leads to an equal distribution of partial negative charges around the molecule. This means that, although a molecule of CO_2 contains polar covalent bonds, the molecule exhibits the character of a nonpolar molecule.
3	C	Carbon, C, has 4 valence electrons, which means that the carbon in this compound needs 4 more electrons to satisfy its octet. Each oxygen, O, in the compound has 6 valence electrons, which means that each oxygen needs an additional 2 electrons to satisfy its octet. A DOUBLE bond is formed between the carbon and each of the oxygens. This satisfies the octet for all of the atoms in the compound.

#	Ans.	Explanation
4	E	The electronegativity of Mg is 1.2, and the electronegativity of O is 3.5. The difference between the electronegativities is, therefore, 2.3. We did not necessarily need to calculate the exact Δ EN; by seeing that an alkaline earth metal, Mg, is being bonded to a non metal in the upper right corner of the periodic table, O, we can know the bond between them is ionic. Ionic bonds result from an electronegativity difference that is greater that 2.0.
5	D	The OH at the end of CH_3CH_2OH is capable of producing hydrogen bonds with water molecules in aqueous solution.
6	C	Sodium Sulfate, Na_2SO_4, breaks up into Na^+ ions and SO_4^- ions. These ions are then able to attract to the positive and negative regions of an H_2O molecule. This behavior is known as Ion-Dipole bonding.
7	D	H-N bond is polar. This allows for a region of partial positive charge on the hydrogen atoms and a region of partial negative charge on the nitrogen atoms. This results in is a polar substance that can then create hydrogen bonds with itself. Hydrogen bonds are a very strong intermolecular force. When solutions boil the intermolecular forces of that substance must be broken quite rapidly. The presence of such a strong intermolecular force corresponds to the need for a relatively high temperature for NH_3 to boil.
8	A	The C-H bond is nonpolar. This results in a molecule that doesn't have any regions of significantly higher electron density than any others, so the molecule is nonpolar. Nonpolar molecules can only take advantage of London dispersion forces.
9	B	Triple bonds require the sharing of 6 electrons. To share this many electrons, the nuclei must get relatively close to one another. This results in triple bonds being quite short.
10	E	When sodium a sodium ion, Na^+, is bonded to a chloride ion, Cl^-, the positive ion is refereed to as the cation.
11	C	An INTRAmolecular force is the force between two atoms WITHIN a molecule. If both of the electrons that form a bond between two atoms come from the same atom then it is known as a coordinate covalent bond.
12	D	A negatively charged ion is known as an anion.
13	A	An INTRAmolecular force is the force between two atoms WITHIN a molecule. For a double covalent bond to occur, 4 electrons must be shared between two atoms.
14	A	HETEROatomic means DIFFERENT atoms. To determine how polar a molecule is that is composed of different atoms, we use the electronegativity values of each atom involved.
15	B	When the Lewis dot structure of a molecule is drawn and multiple structures are equally possible, there is no reason a molecule must choose between the two in the real world. In fact, molecules will tend to split the difference between multiple structures that are just as energetically favorable. Resonance is the term used to indicate this process of splitting the difference.

#	Ans.	Explanation
101	T, F	H_2O has a boiling point of 100 degrees Celsius at standard atmospheric pressure. H_2F has a boiling point of -60 degrees Celsius at standard atmospheric pressure. The first statement is true. Hydrogen bonds are much stronger than London dispersion forces. Statement 2 is false.
102	T, T	NH_4^+ contains both polar covalent bonds and coordinate covalent bonds. The first statement is true. Nonpolar covalent bonds occur when electrons are shared equally between two atoms. Coordinate covalent bonds occur when one atom must donate both electrons to a covalent bond between a pair of atoms. The second statement is true. The two bonds in our first statement are POLAR covalent and coordinate covalent, and the second statement describes NONPOLAR covalent bonds; therefore, the second statement is not sufficient to explain the first statement.
103	F, F	The electronegativity of sulfur, S, is 2.5, and the electronegativity of oxygen, O, is 3.5; therefore, their Δ EN is 1.0, making the bond between them polar covalent. The first and second statement are both false.
104	T, T	The electronegativity of Cs is 0.8. The electronegativity of Cl is 3.0. The electronegativity difference between Cs and Cl is 2.2 making the bond between them ionic. Ionic substances dissolve readily in water. The first statement is true. The 2 lone pairs of electrons on the oxygen of the water molecule cause the molecule to bend slightly, and the electronegativity difference between oxygen and hydrogen is 1.4. The second statement is true. The second statement would need to explicitly state that water, as a substance, is polar, and, therefore, readily ionizes CsCl for it to be a complete explanation of the first statement.
16	D	NH_4^+ contains covalent bonds between nitrogen and hydrogen. Then NH_4^+, as an ion, creates an ionic bond with the Cl^- ion.
17	E	Hydrogen bonds can only occur in substances that have an N-H, O-H, and/or F-H bonds.
18	A	Fluorine, F, is in period 17 and, therefore, has 7 valence electrons.
19	A	If we choose a number for the number of carbon (let's say 2), we can see that our formula for this compound will be C_2H_6. When we draw the Lewis dot structure for this compound we only produce single bonds. Any number for the number of carbon would have worked to test this.
20	E	Answer choice D and E are the only two that have atoms in them that differ enough in electronegativity to potentially be polar molecules. D, however, is completely symmetrical all around which means that the dipoles cancel out and the molecule as a whole becomes nonpolar. PCl_3 is a polar molecule because its bonds are polar and it is asymmetrical.
21	C	Benzene has the molecular formula of C_6H_6 and is arranged in a hexagonal ring. Once the ring is created and the hydrogen are each attached to their own carbon, however, each carbon still needs an extra electron. 3 double bonds can then be drawn within the ring, however, there is more than one possibility for the different ways the double bonds can be arranged. This results in resonance. The words stability and resonance should stay very closely related to you in your mind. When you see one, the other will likely be in the correct answer.

#	Ans.	Explanation
22	E	All of these species have 18 electrons, the electron configuration of Ar, except Ne, which has 10 electrons.
23	D	All of these substances, except for H_2, are either polar molecules or ionic compounds. H_2 is not soluble in water because it is neither polar nor ionic.
24	E	CF_2Cl_2 does not have resonance, so E must be the answer.

Sec.	Name	Answers
3.1	Stoichiometry	1. (A) 2. (E) 3. (D) 4. (E) 5. (C) 6. (A) 7. (A) 8. (E) 9. (D) 10. (C) 11. (A) 12. (A) 13. (E) 14. (E) 15. (E) 16. (C) 17. (D) 18. (E) 19. (C)
3.2	Balancing reactions	1. (B) 2. (B) 3. (B) 4. (A) 5. (B) 6. (A) 7. (D) 8. (C) 9. (B)

Chapter 3 Quiz

#	Ans.	Explanation
1	A	Hydrogen has a gram formula mass of 1 g/mol. H_2 has two hydrogen atoms, so $1 + 1 = 2$.
2	C	Carbon has a gram formula mass of 12 g/mol, while hydrogen has a gram-formula mass of 1 g/mol. CH_4 has one carbon atom and four hydrogen atoms, so $12 + 1(4) = 16$.
3	D	If 1 mol = 22.4 L for a gas at STP, then the highest gram formula mass will lead to the smallest quantity of moles, which will give the smallest volume. CO_2 has the largest gram-formula mass of any option at 44 g/mol.
4	A	See explanation for the question above, but the opposite trend occurs here. The smallest gram formula mass of any option is H_2 at 2 g/mol.
5	A	CO_2 has a gram formula mass of 44 g/mol. Hence, 44 grams would equal exactly 1 mole.
6	A	H_2 has a gram formula mass of 2 g/mol. Hence, 2 grams would equal exactly 1 mole.
7	B	CH_4 has a gram formula mass of 16 g/mol. Hence, 32 grams would equal exactly 2 moles.
8	B	O_2 has a gram formula mass of 32 g/mol. Hence, 64 grams would equal exactly 2 moles.

#	Ans.	Explanation
101	F, F	1 mol of any gas occupies 22.4 L. 20 g of Xe is 0.15 moles, while 20 g of He is 10 moles. Hence, there are more moles of He so it would occupy a larger volume.
102	T, T, CE	Divide each subscript of a molecular formula by the greatest common factor to arrive at the empirical formula.
103	F, T	Because 1 mole = 22.4 L, 89.6 L would mean that there are 4 moles of gas present.
9	E	The gram formula mass of NH_3 is 17 g/mol. For 5 moles, $5 \times 17 = 85$ g.
10	A	Assume 100 g. If 75 g of C, this results in 6.25 moles. If 25 g of H, this results in 25 moles. The greatest common factor of 6.25 and 25 is 6.25. Dividing each by 6.25 yields 1 for C and 4 for H.
11	E	The gram formula mass of KCl is 74.5 g/mol. For 2 moles, $2 \times 74.5 = 149$ g.
12	D	The gram formula mass of $CaCl_2$ is 111 g/mol. For 3 moles, $3 \times 111 = 333$ g.
13	C	The largest volume will come from the gas with the lowest gram formula mass. Ne has a gram formula mass of 20 g/mol, lower than any other choice.
14	A	Assume 100 g. If 42 g of C, this results in 3.5 moles. If 58 g of O, this results in 3.625 moles. Both quantities are essentially equal, hence there are equal atom quantities of C and O.
15	D	The gram formula mass of H_2SO_4 is 98 g/mol. For 1 mole, $1 \times 98 = 98$ g.
16	A	The gram formula mass of Li_3PO_4 is 116 g/mol. For 1 mole, $1 \times 116 = 116$ g.
17	C	The gram formula mass of AlI_3 is 408 g/mol. For 2 moles, $2 \times 408 = 816$ g.
18	D	Assume 100 g. If 4 g of H, this results in 4 moles. If 96 g of O, this results in 6 moles. H_4O_6 reduces to empirical formula H_2O_3.
19	A	HNO_3 and NO_2 must have the same coefficient since they both have the only nitrogen atom. Hence, let's begin by changing the H_2O coefficient to 2. This will allow us to have an even number of oxygen atoms on both sides of the equation. There are now 8 oxygens on the product side, and 3 oxygens on the reactant side. If we put a 6 in front of HNO_3 we now have 18 oxygens on the reactant side. We can then put a 6 in front of NO_2 to keep the nitrogens balanced and also have 18 oxygens on the product side. H_2SO_4 never changes, and hence, there is always 1 sulfur on both the reactant and product side.

Sec.	Name	Answers
4.1	Gases	1. (E) 2. (E) 3. (E) 4. (A) 5. (B) 6. (C) 7. (D) 8. (E) 9. (B)
4.2	Dalton's Law of Partial Pressures	1. (C) 2. (E) 3. (D) 4. (D) 5. (D) 6. (B) 7. (E) 8. (E) 9. (A) 10. (D)

Chapter 4 Quiz

#	Ans.	Explanation
1	A	40% of 5 atm is $0.40 \times 5 = 2$ atm.
2	A	2 mol of H_2 out of 10 mol total is 20%. 20% of 10 atm is $0.20 \times 10 = 2$ atm.
3	A	70 g of Cl_2 is 1 mole (70 g/mol). 80 g of Ar is 2 moles (40 g/mol). Since there is a 1:2 mole ratio, and 6 total atm, that means there is a 2:4 atm ratio. Hence, Cl_2 occupies 2 atm.
4	E	14 g of N_2 is 0.50 moles (14 g/mol). 20 g of Ne is 1 mole (20 g/mol). There are 1.5 moles total, and Ne is 1 mole, so 1/1.5 simplifies to 2/3 Ne. If there are 9 atm, then two-thirds of 9 atm is 6 atm.
5	B	Room temperature is 298 K or about 25°C, and standard pressure is 1 atm or 760 mm Hg.
6	A	1 mole of gas occupies 22.4 L at standard temperature and pressure. Standard temperature is 273 K or 0°C.
7	C	Gases exhibit most ideal behavior at high temperatures and low pressures.
8	D	Gases exhibit least ideal behavior at low temperatures and high pressures.

#	Ans.	Explanation
101	T, T, CE	For gases, the volume ratios are equivalent to the partial pressure ratios. Since there is an equivalent quantity of liters for both oxygen and nitrogen, they have the same partial pressures. Each must be 0.5 atm to total 1 atm.
102	F, F	Graham's Law states that molecular mass of a gas and the rate of effusion are *inversely* proportional, not directly proportional.
103	T, F	Boyle's Law states that the *product* of the pressure and volume of a gas is constant, not the ratio.
104	T, F	Gay-Lussac's Law states that the *ratio* of the pressure and temperature is constant, not the product.
105	F, T	As temperature increases volume increases, since Charles' Law states that temperature and volume of a gas are directly related.
9	D	There are equal quantities of O_2 and F_2, so they both must be 1.5 atm to add to 3.0 atm.
10	A	The highest rate of effusion will come from the lightest gas. Helium is the lighest option of the choices.
11	D	Gases exhibit most ideal behavior at high temperatures and low pressures.
12	E	Begin by changing 25°C to 298 K. Using the combined gas law, we begin with $\frac{PV}{T} = \frac{PV}{T}$, hence, $\frac{(2)(1.5)}{298} = \frac{(1)V}{(273)}$. To isolate V, multiply 273 K to the other side. This means 273 K will be a numerator. This leaves (C) and (E) as possible answers. Because the 2 atm is already a numerator, we know the correct answer is (E).

Sec.	Name	Answers
5.1	Entropy and Heating/Cooling Curve	1. (D) 2. (B) 3. (E) 4. (C) 5. (A) 6. (B) 7. (D) 8. (E) 9. (C) 10. (A) 11. (E) 12. (B) 13. (A) 14. (E) 15. (A) 16. (D)
5.2	Vapor Pressure and Boiling Point	1. (B) 2. (C) 3. (E) 4. (C) 5. (B) 6. (B)
5.3	Types of Solids	1. (C) 2. (E) 3. (E) 4. (A) 5. (E) 6. (D)

Chapter 5 Quiz

#	Ans.	Explanation
1	D	Freezing is the word used to describe the process of a liquid substance turning into a solid.
2	A	Boiling is the word used to describe the process of a liquid substance turning into a gas.
3	E	Entropy is the word used to describe the amount of disorder in a system. High entropy values indicate a large amount of disorder. Low entropy values indicate a small amount of disorder.
4	A	When a system boils it is changing from liquid to gas. The change from liquid to gas as a change from a state of being more highly ordered to a state of being more highly disordered.
5	B	Since caesium, Cs, is an alkali METAL, when it produces bonds with with itself it makes METALLIC bonds, resulting in a METALLIC substance.
6	D	The S-O bond is a polar covalent bond; however, due to the symmetric trigonal planar geometry of the SO_3 molecule, the molecule is then NONPOLAR covalent, which makes the substance NONPOLAR covalent.
7	E	Diamonds are made up of a large network of carbon atoms that are linked together through uninterrupted covalent bonds. Making it a covalent network solid.
8	A	$NaHCO_3$ is made from Na^+ and HCO_3^- IONS. This will result in an overall IONIC substance.
9	B	Gold, Au, is in group 11, making it a transition METAL. Au is, therefore a METALLIC substance.

#	Ans.	Explanation
101	T, T, CE	As temperature increases, the amount of disorder in a system increases as well. Entropy is the word used to describe disorder. Therefore, statement 1 and 2 are true, and statement 2 correctly explains why statement 1 is correct.
102	F, F	As temperature increases the amount of movement of each molecule, on average, increases. This increase in movement makes it more difficult for intermolecular forces to take hold between molecules; therefore, statement 1 in false. The strength of intermolecular forces decreases as the average kinetic energy of the particles in a system increases. This is an indirect or inverse relationship. Statement 2 is false.
103	F, T	Boiling point is the point at which the pressure produced by the vapor escaping a system in its liquid phase, vapor pressure, becomes equal to the pressure of the atmosphere pressing down on the system, atmospheric pressure. If the atmospheric pressure is higher than the vapor pressure, the system will not be boiling. The first statement is, therefore, false. For a molecule to enter the vapor phase, it must escape the intermolecular forces holding it into the liquid phase; statement 2 is true.
104	F, T	Network solids are formed when a network of covalent bonds hold together a series of atoms; statement 1 is false. London dispersion forces are present in substances composed of individual and separate molecules in the solid phase; therefore, statement 2 is true.
10	E	Diamonds are made up of a large network of carbon atoms that are linked together through uninterrupted covalent bonds. Making it a covalent network solid.
11	B	As substances move from the gas to the solid phase, the strength of their intermolecular forces goes up; therefore $H_2O(s)$ must have the strongest intermolecular forces of attraction.
12	C	Condensing the the term used to describe the process through which molecules of a gaseous substance come together into the liquid phase. When going from the gas to liquid phase there is an increase in order, which is the same as a decrease in disorder(entropy).
13	B	When the vapor pressure of a liquid substance is equal to the atmospheric pressure the system will boil.
14	E	Intermolecular forces are the forces that hold the molecules of a system together in their liquid phase. If a liquid easily evaporates at room temperature, $25°C$, then the intermolecular forces that hold the molecules together are relatively weak.
15	A	The amount of energy in a system does not affect the mass of the molecules that make up the system.

Sec.	Name	Answers
6.1	Solution definitions	1. (C) 2. (A) 3. (E) 4. (E) 5. (A) 6. (C) 7. (A)
6.2	Solubility & B.P. elevation and F.P. depression	1. (A) 2. (B) 3. (E) 4. (B) 5. (C) 6. (D) 7. (A) 8. (E) 9. (B)

Chapter 6 Quiz

#	Ans.	Explanation
1	D	Saturation is the point at which the rate of a solute dissolving into a solvent is equal the the rate at which it is coming out. This is known as a dynamic equilibrium. At this point the solution is holding the exact amount of solute that the specific amount of solvent can hold.
2	E	Supersaturation occurs when a given amount of solvent has been tricked into holding more solute than it typically can hold. This is done by heating up the solution to a point of higher solubility, adding more solute, then bringing the solution back down in temperature.
3	C	A solution is unsaturated when the rate of the forward reaction of the solute dissolving into the solvent is slower than the reverse reaction. Under this condition, the solution can dissolve more solute than it currently has in it.
4	B	A solution is considered concentrated when there is a relatively high quantity of solute compared to solvent. This is a qualitative term not a quantitative term; it cannot be precisely measured.
5	A	A solution is considered dilute when there is a relatively low quantity of solute compared to solvent. This is a qualitative term not a quantitative term; it cannot be precisely measured.
6	A	As the concentration of a solute or solvent goes up the boiling point goes up. This is known as a direct relationship. Note that both molality and molarity are ways of expressing concentration.
7	B	As the concentration of a solute or solvent goes up the freezing point goes down. This is known as an inverse or indirect relationship. Note that both molality and molarity are ways of expression concentration.
8	C	The ability for a solute to dissolve into a solvent is expressed as solubility.

#	Ans.	Explanation
101	F, F	Saturation and dilute are completely unrelated terms, so one cannot be described in terms of the other or have an effect on the other; the first statement is false. Saturation is defined as the point at which the rate of a solute dissolving into a solvent is equal to the rate coming out if the solution. The second statement is, therefore, also false.
102	F, T	Supersaturation and concentrated are completely unrelated terms, so one cannot be described in terms of the other; the first statement is false. The definition of concentrated is the condition such that the ratio of the solute to solvent is relatively high; the second statement is true.
103	F, F	Freezing point is lowered, or depressed, when solute is added to a liquid solution; the first statement is false. The freezing point of pure sugar is high than the freezing point of water. Consider pure sugar at room temperature. It is commonly known to be a solid. Consider the pure water at room temperature. It is commonly known to be liquid; therefore, the freezing point of pure sure is lower than that of pure water. The second statement must be false.
104	T, T, CE	When solute is dissolved into solvent the boiling point is raised. Therefore, the boiling point of pure water is lower than the boiling point of a 0.2 M solution of potassium sulfate, K_2SO_4. Therefore, the first and second statements are true, and the second statement correctly explains the first statement.
9	A	The solution with the lowest concentration of ions will have the highest freezing point. Given that $C_6H_{12}O_6$ does not ionize at all, a $C_6H_{12}O_6$ m solution will have a higher freezing point than any of the other solutions listed.
10	C	The solution with the highest concentration of ions will have the highest boiling point. The molarity of each substance dissolved is the same, so we can simply look at the number of ions that each substance will produce to determine our answer. $C_6H_{12}O_6$ does not ionize. NaCl produces 2 ions. $MgCl_2$ produces 3 ions. BF_3 is not ionic, so it does not ionize. $HC_2H_3O_2$ produces 2 ions. The substance that produces the most ions is $MgCl_2$.
11	D	The solution with the highest concentration of ions will have the highest boiling point. C, D, and E all have higher molarities than A or B, and they have the same concentration, so we should determine which substance out of the ones in C, D, and E produces the most ions. NaBr produces 2 ions. K_2SO_4 produces 3 ions. $HC_2H_3O_2$ produces 2 ions. The substance that produces the most ions is K_2SO_4.
12	A	The solution with the lowest concentration of ions will have the highest freezing point. A and B have the same molalities and both have lower molalities than C, D, or E, so we should determine which substance from the ones given in A and B produces the fewest number of ions. KCl produces 2 ions. $CaCl_2$ produces 3 ions. The substance that produces the fewest number of ions is KCl.
13	A	The substance that produces the same number of ions as NaCl, 2 ions, will give the same increase in boiling point. $HC_2H_3O_2$ produces 2 ions.
14	C	The substance that produces fewer moles of ions than NaCl, 2 ions, will give a smaller increase in boiling point that the addition of NaCl will. C_2H_5OH does not ionize.

#	Ans.	Explanation
15	E	The substance that produces 3 moles of ions will produce an increase in boiling point that is 3 times the increase that the addition of $C_6H_{12}O_6$ will produce. Na_2SO_4 produces 3 ions.
16	E	Recall the formula $\Delta T = iK_f m$. i = 2. $K_f = 1.86$ kg°C mol^{-1}. $m = 1$ mol kg^{-1}. Therefore, $\Delta T = 3.72$ K. The freezing point is lowered by 3.72 K because the addition of solute results in a freezing point depression.
17	B	Recall the formula $\Delta T = iK_b m$. i = 2. $K_b = 0.5$ kg°C mol^{-1}. $m = 1$ mol kg^{-1}. Therefore $\Delta T = 1$ K. The boiling point is raised by 1 K because the addition of solute results in a boiling point elevation.

Sec.	Name	Answers
7.1	Factors that affect Reaction Rate	1. (A) 2. (A) 3. (B) 4. (E) 5. (C) 6. (E)
7.2	Activation Energy and Catalysts	1. (A) 2. (E) 3. (C) 4. (B) 5. (D)
7.3	Reaction rate laws	1. (D) 2. (D) 3. (A) 4. (B) 5. (E) 6. (C)

Chapter 7 Quiz

#	Ans.	Explanation
1	E	Reaction rate is measured in concentration per time.
2	B	Catalysts increase the rate that a reaction occurs by reducing the activation energy of the reaction. Catalysts are not used up through the course of a reaction.
3	A	The area on the surface of a substance is what can be exposed to other substances and thus the region that dictates whether or not an effective collision has occurred.
4	C	Potential energy can take many forms. Chemical bonds are one form of potential energy.
5	D	The activation energy is the energy required to cause a reaction to proceed.
6	A	The energy of the reactants is the energy that the reactants sit at before the reaction has proceeded forward.
7	E	The energy of the products is the energy that the products sit at after the reaction has finished.
8	D	The heat of formation is the same as the difference in energy between the energy of the products and the reactants.
9	B	The activation energy is the additional amount of energy it takes for a reaction to get started.
10	C	The activated complex is the theoretical intermediate between the products and the reactants. It is the highest point of energy that a reaction reaches.

#	Ans.	Explanation
101	F, F	By decreasing the surface area of the reactants, there are essentially fewer places for an effective collision to occur. This means that a decrease in the surface area of the reactants actually decreases the reaction rate; the first statement is false. Surface area is measured in spacial units squared; the second statement is false.
102	T, T	Introducing a catalyst into the system reduces the activation energy of the reaction, therefore, increasing the rate of the reaction. This makes the first statement true. Catalysts are not chemically altered during the course of reaction; the second statement is true. The second statement does not, however, fully explain that the first statement is correct.
103	F, T	The activation energy of a reaction is the difference between the energy of the reactants and the activated complex; therefore, the first statement is false. The potential energy of a compound is sum of all of the bond energies within a compound; therefore the second statement is true.
104	F, T	The potential energy of the products is not dependent on the potential energy of the reactants or the activation energy; therefore, the first statement is false. In an exothermic reaction energy is released to the environment. This is why exothermic reactions tend to feel hot or warm; the second statement is true.
105	T, T, CE	Increasing the temperature of a reaction will increase the rate of a reaction because the number of collisions will increase, therefore, increasing the probability of an effective collision. The first and second statements are both correct, and the second statement correctly explains the first statement.
106	T, T, CE	When the magnesium solid is crushed, it increases the surface area of the reactants, which allows for a greater opportunity for effective collisions. The first and second statements are both correct, and the second statement correctly explains the first statement.
11	E	Decreasing the temperature of the system will decrease the average kinetic energy of the system. Decreasing the average kinetic energy of the system will decrease the likelihood of effective collisions.
12	E	Catalysts, by definition, are not altered during the process of a reaction.
13	A	The slowest reaction rate will occur when the least amount of kinetic energy is in the system. A decrease in temperature is a way of expressing a decrease in average kinetic energy. Reaction rate slows down at lower temperatures because there is a decrease in the probability of an effective collision occurring.
14	A	In exothermic reactions the ΔH value is negative. In exothermic reactions the energy of the reactants is greater than the energy of the products due to the release of energy that occurs.
15	C	The activation energy is the additional energy that must be added into the system for the reaction to proceed forward.
16	E	Catalysts increase the rate of reactions by reducing the activation energy required for the reaction to proceed forward.

Sec.	Name	Answers
8.1	Equilibrium	1. (B) 2. (B) 3. (D) 4. (A) 5. (B) 6. (B) 7. (D) 8. (C)
8.2	LeChatlier's Principle	1. (A) 2. (D) 3. (B) 4. (C) 5. (B) 6. (B)

Chapter 8 Quiz

#	Ans.	Explanation
1	E	Exothermic reactions release heat as a product
2	C	mol L^{-1} s^{-1} can be translated to $\frac{mol}{L\,s}$. Since time (in seconds) is a denominator, this indicates the measure of a rate.
3	B	Solubility product represents the quantity of dissociation of a solid into a solvent.
4	D	Endothermic reactions absorb heat as a reactant
5	A	Equilibrium constants, K, are calculated by the concentration of the products over reactants
6	D	As volume increases, pressure decreases. With a lower pressure, less effective collisions happen on the side with more moles of gas.
7	C	See question 6 explanation. With a higher pressure, more effective collisions happen on the side with more moles of gas.
8	B	When a gas evolves in a reaction this typically indicates a reaction that will go to completion.
9	A	This is the definition of LeChatlier's principle

#	Ans.	Explanation
101	F, T	Adding heat to an exothermic reaction would favor more effective collisions on the product side, thus favoring the reverse reaction.
102	T, T, CE	Adding heat to an endothermic reaction would favor more effective collisions on the reactant side, thus favoring the forward reaction.
103	F, T	More pressure would cause more effective collisions on the side with more moles of gas, thus favoring the side with less moles of gas.
104	T, T	When writing K ratios, only gas (g) and aqueous (aq) are accounted for. Because of their high temperatures, gases have high kinetic energies, but this is independent of equilibrium ratio notations.
105	T, T, CE	As temperature increases, the particles move faster with more energy. Because they move faster, they will collide more frequently.
106	T, T, CE	Solids that have high dissociations, such as strong acids and bases, essentially completely dissociate into solution.
10	E	The solubility product of KCl is $K_{sp} = [K^+][Cl^-] = [2.0 \times 10^{-2}][2.0 \times 10^{-2}] = 4.0 \times 10^{-4}$
11	C	The solubility product of $CaSO_4$ is $K_{sp} = [Ca^{2+}][SO_4^{2-}] = [2.0 \times 10^{-2}][2.0 \times 10^{-2}] = 4.0 \times 10^{-4}$
12	C	An equilibrium constant is concentration of products over reactants, each raised to its respective coefficient.
13	A	Solid substances do not appear in equilibrium ratios.
14	B	Because the equilibrium constant is a *constant*, adding or removing substances does NOT change the value of the equilibrium constant. However, adding a catalyst or changing the temperature of the reaction chamber will. Adding a catalyst only increases the rate of the reaction, but will not alter the equilibrium constant. However, changing the temperature of the reaction chamber will change the equilibrum constant. This leads us to (B).
15	A	More pressure would cause more effective collisions on the side with more moles of gas, thus favoring the side with less moles of gas.

Sec.	Name	Answers
9.1	Enthalpy - endothermic and exothermic	1. (A) 2. (A) 3. (D) 4. (D)
9.2	Hess' Law	1. (B) 2. (A) 3. (B) 4. (A)
9.3	Synthesis and Decomposition	1. (A) 2. (C) 3. (B) 4. (D) 5. (E) 6. (C)
9.4	Single and Double replacement	1. (A) 2. (B) 3. (E) 4. (C) 5. (B) 6. (A)
9.5	Gibbs Free Energy	1. (A) 2. (E) 3. (D) 4. (A) 5. (A) 6. (C) 7. (E)

Chapter 9 Quiz

#	Ans.	Explanation
1	B	The total energy of the products of an exothermic reaction are less than the total energy of the reactants.
2	A	The total energy of the products of an endothermic reaction are more than the total energy of the reactants.
3	E	Follow solubility rules in chapter 13 and any compound that is insoluble can also be labeled as a precipitate.
4	B	See explanation to question 1.
5	C	Isolated elements are located in single-replacement reactions.
6	A	$Na + Cl \rightarrow NaCl$
7	D	$3\ NaOH(aq) + Fe(NO_3)_3(aq) \rightarrow 3\ NaNO_3 + Fe(OH)_3(aq)$
8	C	$Br_2(l) + 2\ KI(aq) \rightarrow 2\ KBr(aq) + I_2(s)$
9	E	$H_2SO_4(aq) + 2\ NaOH(aq) \rightarrow Na_2SO_4(aq) + 2\ H_2O(l)$
10	B	$Zn(s) + 2\ HCl(aq) \rightarrow ZnCl_2(aq) + H_2(g)$

#	Ans.	Explanation
101	T, T, CE	Irreversible reactions occur if insoluble precipitates are formed. Typically, a reversible reaction has all gaseous or all aqueous substances.
102	T, T, CE	Substances naturally converge towards lower energy states.
103	T, T, CE	A state function is said to be a function that only depends on its starting point and ending point. The intermediate steps do not change the overall change, rather, they can be used to calculate the overall change.
104	T, F	More active elements will replace less active elements. For a single replacement reaction to occur, the isolated element must be more active. If not, the reaction is said to be non-spontaneous.
105	T, T, CE	$CuSO_4(aq) + NaOH(aq) \rightarrow Na_2SO_4(aq) + Cu(OH)_2(s)$. A solid precipitate, $Cu(OH)_2(s)$, is formed.
11	B	There are no isolated elements, so the reaction shown cannot be considered a synthesis nor a single-replacement reaction.
12	A	Because there is one isolated element being combined with a compound, this is classified as a single-replacement reaction.
13	B	Choice (A) is false because the ΔH value is negative, which means heat is released. Choice (C) is false because energy is not required for reduction. Choice (D) is false because an endothermic reaction would have a positive ΔH value. Choice (E) is false because reactions can occur at many temperatures and pressures. This leaves choice (B).
14	E	See the explanation from the previous question for similar answer choices. A positive ΔH means that energy must be absorbed for the reaction to occur. This does NOT allow the reaction to occur spontaneously.
15	D	First, we must flip the first equation to have CO and H_2O as reactants. This will change the sign of ΔH to +1,200 kJ. Next, we multiply the second equation by 4 so that the number of moles of H_2O equal that in the first reaction. This will change the ΔH of the second reaction to −200 kJ. Adding down we achieve +1,000 kJ, answer choice (D).

Chapter 9 - Types of Reactions

Sec.	Name	Answers
10.1	Acids & Bases Definitions	1. (C) 2. (A) 3. (B) 4. (B) 5. (A) 6. (D) 7. (E) 8. (C) 9. (A)
10.2	Conjugates	1. (C) 2. (D) 3. (D) 4. (C) 5. (D) 6. (C) 7. (D) 8. (B)
10.3	pH Scale	1. (E) 2. (B) 3. (D) 4. (A) 5. (E) 6. (B) 7. (A) 8. (D) 9. (C) 10. (E) 11. (E) 12. (B) 13. (C) 14. (E) 15. (E) 16. (A) 17. (B) 18. (C) 19. (B) 20. (A) 21. (A)
10.4	Ka	1. (D) 2. (D) 3. (E) 4. (A) 5. (C) 6. (C)

Chapter 10 Quiz

#	Ans.	Explanation
1	A	Acids have a pH lower than 7 and bases have a pH higher than 7
2	C	The higher the K_a value, the stronger the acid
3	E	Buffers hold salts and conjugates, which help to resist a change in pH
4	B	Sodium hydroxide is known as a common strong base
5	A	Sulfuric acid is known as a common strong acid
6	E	The analyte is the unknown acid during a titration experiment. See chapter 13 for a more detailed titration apparatus.
7	B	The Bronsted-Lowry descriptions of an acid and a base deal with proton donors and proton acceptors.
8	D	An example would be NH_3 becoming NH_4^+. NH_4^+ accepted a proton, and now has 1 more hydrogen atom than the original NH_3.
9	A	The Arrenhius descriptions of an acid and a base deal with whether a compound has a H^+ ion or OH^- ion.
10	C	The Lewis descriptions of an acid and a base deal with whether the compound accepts or donates electrons.

#	Ans.	Explanation
101	T, T	Since HSO_4^- is 1 hydrogen less than H_2SO_4, it is indeed the conjugate base. The second statement is true because H_2SO_4 is a strong acid, but does not explain conjugate pairing.
102	T, T, CE	The second statement is the textbook definition as to how a buffer behaves. Human blood is a common example.
103	F, T	Larger K_a values indicate stronger acids. However, *smaller* pK_a values indicate stronger acids.
104	F, T	Acids have lower pH values. Adding an acid would decrease the pH of a solution.
105	T, T	Strong acids pair with weak conjugate bases, and strong bases pair with weak conjugate acids. Acids typically behave as proton donors since they tend to have H^+ ions in their compound.
106	F, F	The numbers on a pH scale are calculated by taking the negative log of the hydrogen ion concentration. The numbers on a pOH scale are calculated by taking the negative log of the hydroxide ion concentration.
11	A	$KClO + H_2O \rightarrow HClO + KOH$. $HClO$ is a weak acid and KOH is a strong base.
12	D	$NH_4I \rightarrow HI + NH_3$. HI is a strong acid and NH_3 is a weak base.
13	B	$Ca(NO_3)_2 + H_2O \rightarrow 2\,HNO_3 + Ca(OH)_2$. HNO_3 is a strong acid and $Ca(OH)_2$ is a strong base.
14	C	Sulfuric acid donates one proton (losing 1 hydrogen) to form HSO_4^-.
15	B	A base would accept a proton and gain a hydrogen atom. NH_3 turns into NH_4^+ by doing this.
16	B	Choice (A) is false because we know ammonium is the conjugate acid of ammonia, so it must have a higher K_a. Choice B is false because it does not react with hydroxide, it reacts with water. Choice D is false because it would only completely dissociate if it were a strong acid, which it is not. And choice (E) is false because ammonium is not a solid at room temperature. This leaves (B), which accurately describes ammonium as a weak acid.
17	C	Water should not appear in the correct answer, which eliminates (B) and (D). The K_a ratio is products over reactants, which leaves (C) as the correct answer.

Sec.	Name	Answers
11.1	Finding oxidation numbers	1. (A) 2. (D) 3. (C) 4. (E) 5. (D) 6. (B) 7. (C) 8. (D) 9. (D) 10. (E) 11. (C) 12. (D)
11.2	Voltaic Cell	1. (C) 2. (B) 3. (C) 4. (B) 5. (A) 6. (E) 7. (A) 8. (B)
11.3	Cell potential	1. (B) 2. (D) 3. (E) 4. (D) 5. (E)

Chapter 11 Quiz

#	Ans.	Explanation
1	D	The oxidation number of O is -2, which leads to a sum of -6. The oxidation number of H is $+1$, which leads to a sum of $+2$. This total is -4, so the carbon must be $+4$ since the molecule is neutral.
2	E	The oxidation number of O is -2, which leads to a sum of -8. The oxidation number of Na is $+1$, which leads to a sum of $+3$. This total is -5, so the phosphorous atom must be $+5$ since the molecule is neutral.
3	D	The oxidation number of O is -2, which leads to a sum of -8. The oxidation number of each Na and H is $+1$, which leads to a sum of $+2$. This total is -6. So, the phosphorous oxidation should be $+4$ to leave a -2 remaining since the oxidation charge of the whole molecule is $2-$.
4	A	The oxidation number of O is -2, except when in perioxides it is -1.
5	C	The oxidation number of K is $+1$ since it is an alkali metal.
6	C	The salt bridge connects the two charged groups of the voltaic (electrochemical) cell.
7	A	At the anode, oxidation occurs and releases electrons
8	E	Reduction is denoted by a decrease in the oxidation state of an element in a reaction
9	B	At the cathode, reduction occurs and electrons are absorbed
10	D	Oxidation is denoted by an increase in the oxidation state of an element in a reaction

#	Ans.	Explanation
101	F, T	Remember A to C or oxidation to reduction. The electrons start at the anode and flow towards the cathode, which is the positively charged electrode in the voltaic cell.
102	T, T, CE	If electrons are transferred then the oxidation state will change of an element. This is the sign of a reduction-oxidation reaction.
103	T, T, CE	Noble gases, or group 18 elements, have perfect octets and are inert (do not react).
104	F, T	An *electrolytic* cell requires a power source, NOT a voltaic cell. The anode is the negative electrode, while the cathode is the positive electrode. Electrons flow from negative to positive.
105	F, T	Alkali metals are group 1 metals, NOT alkaline earth metals.
106	F, F	The positive electrode in a voltaic cell is the cathode, which gains mass over time due to undergoing reduction.
11	D	The oxidation number of O is -2, which leads to a sum of -6. Because the molecule has a charge of -1, the N must have an oxidation number of $+5$.
12	E	The sulfate ion, SO_4^{2-}, has an oxidation charge of $2-$. Since there are 3 SO_4 molecules in this compound, that leads to a sum of $6-$. There are 2 Al atoms, so each must be $+3$ to have a neutral molecule.
13	E	HCO_3 has an oxidation charge of $1-$. Since O has an oxidation charge of -2, this leads to a sum of -6. Since H has a charge of $+1$, C must have a charge of $+4$.
14	A	The anode is the electrode that undergoes oxidation, NOT reduction
15	C	Look for reactions with isolated elements. These tend to be oxidation-reduction reactions because the oxidation state of the isolated element changes from 0 to a different integer. This eliminates choices (A), (B), (D), and (E).
16	E	CN^- has an oxidation charge of -1. Since there are 6 cyanide ions in this molecule, that is a sum of -6. Potassium, K, has an oxidation charge of $+1$, which leads to a sum of $+3$. This yields a remaining $+3$ for Fe for the molecule to be neutral.
17	C	NH_4^+ has an oxidation charge of $+1$. This is due to the fact that H has a charge of $+1$ in the ammonium ion.
18	D	The $Cr_2O_7^{-2}$ ion has a charge of -2. Since O has a charge of -2 and there are 7 oxygen atoms, this leads to a sum of -14. Cr must have an oxidation number of $+6$, since there are 2 Cr atoms, for the ion to have an overall charge of -2.
19	C	To spot what is being oxidized, look for the element to be a solid as a reactant and an ion as a product.
20	A	Isolated elements tend to change oxidation state. The H in $H_2(g)$ has an oxidation state of 0, but the H in $H_2O(l)$ has an oxidation state of $+1$.

Sec.	Name	Answers
12.1	Properties of organic compounds	1. (A) 2. (A) 3. (D) 4. (B) 5. (A) 6. (A)
12.2	Functional groups	1. (E) 2. (C) 3. (B) 4. (B) 5. (D) 6. (C) 7. (E) 8. (A) 9. (B) 10. (B) 11. (E) 12. (E) 13. (D) 14. (B) 15. (C) 16. (B) 17. (A) 18. (A) 19. (D) 20. (D) 21. (E) 22. (C)

Chapter 12 Quiz

#	Ans.	Explanation
1	E	Chains of carbon and hydrogen can be referred to generally as hydrocarbons.
2	A	The -ANE in methANE tells us that it is an alkANE.
3	C	Alkynes are hydrocarbons that have at least one triple bond.
4	D	An isomer is a compound that is made from the same number and type of atoms but is in a different structural arrangement.
5	C	The -YNE in butYNE tells us that it is an alkYNE.
6	C	The -ONE in acteONE tells us that it is a ketONE.
7	D	Ethanal is the common name for acetALDEHYDE; therefore, ethanal is an aldehyde.
8	C	The -ONE in propanONE tells us that it is a ketONE. The more common name for propanone is acetone.
9	B	Methoxy methane is another name for dimethyl ether. This is an ether.
10	E	The ACID at the end of pentanoic ACID tells us that this is a carboxylic ACID.

#	Ans.	Explanation
101	F, T	Generally, organic compounds are insoluble in water; however, some organic compounds, like ethanol, are miscible in water; therefore, not all organic compounds are insoluble in water; statement 1 is false. Organic acids are typically not very strong relative to some of the stronger inorganic acids. This comes from the low degree to which organic acids deprotonate. Statement 2 is true.
102	F, T	A hydrocarbon must have at least one C-H bond, but it doesn't not need to have double or triple bonds. Alkanes are hydrocarbons that have only single bonds. Statement 1 is false, and statement 2 is true.
103	T, T, CE	There are 4 valence electrons around a carbon atom; this gives carbon the opportunity to bond with up to at least 4 other atoms covalently. Statement 1 and 2 are both correct, and statement 2 correctly explains statement 1.
104	T, F	Alcohols have an -OH, hydroxy, group which allows for hydrogen bonds. Statement 1 is, therefore, correct. Hydrogen bonding occurs when a partially positively charged hydrogen is allowed to bond with a partially negatively charged adjacent nitrogen, oxygen, or fluorine. In hydrogen bonding the hydrogen does not ionize; therefore, statement 2 is false.
105	T, F	Carboxylic acids are substances that are capable and willing to donate H^+ ions to a solution. This will lead to a general increase in H^+ ion concentration of a solution with a carboxylic acid, lowering the pH. Statement 1 is correct. Carboxylic acids do not, however, donate hydroxide ions to a solution. Statement 2 is false.
106	T, F	$C_6H_{12}O_6$ contains C-H bonds, which make it an organic compound; therefore, statement 1 is true. Organic compounds must have a C-H bond, they do not need to contain oxygen; therefore, statement 2 is false.
11	D	Organic compounds must contain a C-H bond. C_5H_{12} is the only substance in the answer choices that contain both hydrogen and oxygen.
12	C	A carboxylic acid is a chain of hydrocarbons that contains a carbonyl group attached to a hydroxy group.
13	E	Answer choice E does not contain a C-H bond.
14	B	An amine group contains at least one carbon atom covalently bonded to a nitrogen atom.
15	C	An amine group refers to the nitrogenous part of a compound. It does not have any other requirements.
16	D	Dimethyl ether is an ether; therefore it has both C-H and C-O bonds, but it does not have C=O bonds.

Chapter 12 - Organic Chemistry

19.13- CHAPTER 14 - 101 TRUE/FALSE QUESTIONS

#	Ans.	#	Ans.	#	Ans.	#	Ans.
101	F, T	126	F, F	151	T, T	176	F, T
102	T, T	127	T, T, CE	152	F, T	177	T, T
103	T, T	128	T, T, CE	153	T, T, CE	178	F, F
104	F, F	129	T, F	154	T, T, CE	179	T, T, CE
105	F, F	130	F, F	155	T, F	180	T, T, CE
106	T, T, CE	131	T, T, CE	156	T, T	181	T, T, CE
107	F, F	132	F, T	157	F, T	182	F, T
108	T, F	133	T, T, CE	158	F, T	183	T, F
109	T, T	134	T, T, CE	159	F, T	184	F, F
110	T, T, CE	135	T, T, CE	160	T, T, CE	185	F, T
111	F, F	136	T, T, CE	161	F, T	186	T, T, CE
112	T, T, CE	137	T, T	162	T, T, CE	187	T, F
113	T, T, CE	138	T, F	163	T, T, CE	188	F, T
114	T, F	139	T, T, CE	164	T, T, CE	189	T, T, CE
115	T, F	140	F, T	165	T, T, CE	190	T, T, CE
116	F, T	141	T, T, CE	166	F, T	191	T, T, CE
117	F, F	142	F, T	167	F, T	192	T, T, CE
118	F, F	143	F, T	168	F, T	193	F, F
119	F, T	144	F, F	169	T, T	194	T, T, CE
120	T, T	145	T, F	170	T, T, CE	195	T, T
121	T, T, CE	146	T, T, CE	171	T, T	196	T, T
122	T, T, CE	147	F, F	172	F, F	197	T, F
123	F, T	148	F, T	173	T, F	198	T, F
124	T, T, CE	149	F, T	174	T, T, CE	199	T, F
125	F, F	150	T, T	175	F, T	200	F, T
						201	T, T, CE

#	Ans.	Chapter	Explanation
1	D	6	Molarity, also referred to as molar concentration, is a concentration measure of the amount of solute in the solution. Molarity is measured in moles of solute per liters of solution; M = mol of solute/ L of solution.
2	A	6	Density is a measurement of the mass to volume ratio of a substance; D = mass (kg or g) / volume(mL or L)
3	C	1	The atomic mass represents the weighted average of all the naturally occurring isotopes of the element.
4	B	3	According to Avogadro's number, one mole of any substance is 6.02×10^{23} units, meaning that one mole of any element is 6.02×10^{23} particles; it is the amount of a chemical substance that contains as many particles as there are atoms in 12 grams of carbon-12.
5	C	13	According to VSEPR theory, the central atom of $H_2O(l)$ has four electron pairs at the vertices of a tetrahedron. Specifically, the central atom oxygen is bonded to two hydrogen atoms and two lone pairs of electrons. Thus, the molecular shape of $H_2O(l)$ is bent.
6	D	13	The chemical compound silicon dioxide, SiO_2, could be extremely toxic as a solid when finely divided and inhaled. Specifically, exposure to crystalline silica can cause disabling illnesses and even fatalities.
7	B	2	A nonpolar molecule has equivalent bonds, no lone pair of electrons on the central atom, and a symmetrical shape, which cancels out the dipole bonds and forms a net dipole of zero. Choice (A) and (C) are eliminated because NO_2 and H_2O are both polar molecules due to the lone pair of electrons on the central atoms. To determine the type of covalent bond, the electronegativity difference between atoms is examined. The atoms in a nonpolar covalent bond have an electronegativity difference less than 0.5, which sustains an equal sharing of electrons. Choice (E) is eliminated because the oxygen molecule is one of the diatomic elements (Br_2, I_2, N_2, Cl_2, H_2, O_2, F_2), which means that the molecule is made up of two oxygen atoms and has nonpolar covalent bonds. The atoms in a polar covalent bond have an electronegativity difference between 0.5 and 1.6, which creates an unequal sharing of electrons. The more electronegative atom has a stronger pull on the shared electrons, which forms a partially negative charge. The less electronegative atom forms a partially positive charge. Thus, Choice (B) is the only molecule that has all of these requirements. CO_2 consists of polar covalent bonds because the oxygen atom is more electronegative than the carbon atom, which indicates that the oxygen atom has a stronger pull on the shared electrons. But, the dipoles cancel out because O=C=O is symmetrical and has no lone pairs on the carbon atom. Thus, $CO_2(g)$ has a nonpolar structure and polar covalent bonds.
8	E	2	A nonpolar molecule has equivalent bonds, no lone pair of electrons on the central atom, and a symmetrical shape, which cancels out the dipole bonds and forms a net dipole of zero. Choice (A) and (C) are eliminated because NO_2 and H_2O are both polar molecules due to the lone pair of electrons on the central atoms. Choice (B) is eliminated because the oxygen atom is more electronegative than the carbon atom, which indicates that the oxygen atom has a stronger pull on the shared electrons. The atoms in a nonpolar covalent bond have an electronegativity difference less than 0.5, which sustains an equal sharing of electrons. Choice (E) is correct because the oxygen molecule is one of the diatomic elements (Br_2, I_2, N_2, Cl_2, H_2, O_2, F_2), which means that the molecule is made up of two oxygen atoms of same electronegativity. Additionally, $O_2(g)$ is nonpolar structure because O = O has equivalent bonds, symmetry, and shares electrons equally because each O atom has the same electronegativity.
9	E	1	The ground state is the lowest energy state available to electrons, and the most stable state of an atom. When an electron absorbs an exact amount of energy, then the electron becomes "excited" and moves to any higher principal energy level (compared to ground state). The electron configuration $1s^2 2s^2 2p^2 3p^1$ (Choice E) represents an excited state configuration because an electron that originally occupied the 2p subshell moved to the 3p subshell.

#	Ans.	Chapter	Explanation
10	D	1	Compared to the electron configuration of the neutral nitrogen atom, the electron configuration for N^{2-} expresses the addition of two valence electrons. So, if the ground state configuration of N is $1s^2 2s^2 2p^3$, then the N^{2-} electron configuration is $1s^2 2s^2 2p^5$
11	D	1	The oxidation number of an element can be determined by location on the periodic table; the group/column number can help assign oxidation number to an element. Specifically, elements in group 17, which are also referred to as the halogens, have seven valence electrons and only need one more valence electron to have a complete octet. As a result, an element in group 17 tends to gain one valence electron, which results in an oxidation number of -1. Thus, Choice (D) is correct because the ground state configuration of the halogen fluorine is represented by $1s^2 2s^2 2p^5$.
12	A	1	Ionization energy is the amount of energy per mole required to remove an electron from the valence shell of an atom. As one of the major trends on the periodic table, ionization energy increases while moving from left to right (across a period) and from bottom to top (up a group) on the periodic table. So, the electron configuration of the element with the lowest first-ionization energy is $1s^2 2s^2$ because it is the farthest to the left and the farthest to the bottom of the periodic table.
13	C	1, 12	Organic compounds are chemical compounds that contain the two elements carbon and hydrogen. The electron configuration $1s^2 2s^2 2p^2$ represents the element carbon.
14	E	9, 12	The balanced equation $2\,C_2H_6(g) + 7\,O_2(g) \rightarrow 4\,CO_2(g) + 6\,H_2O(l)$ is a combustion reaction, also referred to as "burning." Combustion is an exothermic redox-reaction where a hydrocarbon reacts with oxygen and produces carbon dioxide, water, and a lot of energy in the form of light and heat.
15	B	11	The balanced equation $Zn(s) \rightarrow Zn^{2+}(aq) + 2e^-$ is an oxidation reaction. In these reactions, the oxidized substance loses electrons and increases in oxidation number. Zinc has an oxidation number of 0 in $Zn(s)$ and +2 in $Zn^{2+}(aq)$, which indicates an increase in oxidation state. Thus, $Zn(s)$ is being oxidized.
16	D	9	The balanced equation $3\,H_2(g) + N_2(g) \rightarrow 2\,NH_3(g)$ is a synthesis reaction, which is also referred to as a combination reaction. This type of reaction combines multiple reactants to produce one product.
17	C	9	The balanced equation $2\,MgO(s) \rightarrow 2\,Mg(s) + O_2(g)$ is a decomposition reaction, also known as a analysis reaction. Decomposition is a reaction that breaks down one reactant to produce multiple different compounds or individual elements.
18	A	2	Hydrogen Bonding is the strongest type of intermolecular force. The hydrogen bond is a special type of dipole-dipole attraction that involves a hydrogen atom bonding with fluorine (F), oxygen (O), or nitrogen (N). One molecule will contain a partially positive charge on the hydrogen atom, while the other molecule contains a partially negative charge on the fluorine, oxygen, or nitrogen atom. Hydrogen bonding is a very strong intermolecular force and is responsible for the high boiling point of water.
19	C	2	London dispersion forces are the weakest type of intermolecular force and can be found in both polar and nonpolar molecules.
20	D	5	Metallic bonding is the attraction between metal cations and valence electrons. The metal atoms have a very free relationship with their valence bonds, which allows for a sea of delocalized electrons. The freedom of movement the electrons have is what makes metallic solids so good at conducting electricity. A metallic bond is formed by the electrostatic attractive forces between delocalized electrons and positively charged metal ions.
21	E	2	Network covalent bonding occurs when covalent bonds forms in a continuous network of atoms together. Common examples of network covalent bonding include diamond, graphite, silicon dioxide, or quartz. Extremely high temperatures and pressures are required to form these substances.

#	Ans.	Chapter	Explanation
22	A	13	O_3, also referred to as ozone, makes up the protective layer in the stratosphere. The three oxygen atoms bonded together form the solar radiation protection layer by absorbing ultraviolet (UV) rays. The chemical equation of ozone formation is $$O(g) + O_2(g) \rightarrow O_3(g)$$
23	D	13	Acid rain is formed when sulfur dioxide and nitrogen oxides react with rainwater. Choice (D) is correct because the chemical equations involved in the formation of acid rain are $2\,SO_2(g) + O_2(g) \rightarrow 2\,SO_3(g)$ and $SO_3(g) + H_2O(l) \rightarrow H_2SO_4(aq)$.
24	B	13	The ozone layer is the protective layer in the stratosphere that absorbs ultraviolet rays from the sun. Chlorofluorocarbons are chemicals that attack and destroy the ozone layer, which allow more ultraviolet rays to reach Earth's surface. Therefore, trichlorofluoromethane (CCl_3F) is harmful against the solar radiation protection layer in the atmosphere.
25	C	13	The main constituent of natural gases is methane (CH_4).
101	T, F	2	The water molecule is made up of polar covalent bonds because the electronegativity difference between oxygen and hydrogen is between 0.5 and 1.6, which creates an unequal sharing of electrons. The oxygen atom is more electronegative than the hydrogen atom, so the oxygen atom has a stronger pull on the shared electrons. As a result, the oxygen atom forms a partially negative charge while the hydrogen atom forms a partially positive charge. The central atom of $H_2O(l)$ has four electron pairs at the vertices of a tetrahedron. Specifically, the central atom oxygen is bonded to two hydrogen atoms and two lone pairs of electrons. Thus, the molecular shape of $H_2O(l)$ is bent. As a result, the bond dipoles are not canceled due to the molecular geometry, and the molecule is a polar substance, which exhibits an asymmetrical molecular structure at all temperatures.
102	T, F	12, 3	C_8H_{18} is a hydrocarbon, so it will easily undergo combustion when exposed to oxygen. Additionally, hydrofluoric acid is a highly corrosive molecule, which does not mean it is flammable. To find the mass percent of an element hydrogen within a given molecule, the four following steps are used: 1) find the mass of all the hydrogen atoms in the molecule, 2) find the total gram formula mass of the entire molecule, 3) divide mass of the hydrogen atoms in the molecule by the total gram formula mass of the molecule, and 4) multiply the answer by 100 to get the percent by mass of hydrogen. Thus, the percent composition of hydrogen in HF is $1/20 \times 100 = 5\%$ and the percent composition of hydrogen in C_8H_{18} is $18/114 \times 100 \approx 4/20 \approx$ is 20%; the mass percent of hydrogen is smaller in HF than it is in C_8H_{18}.
103	F, T	6	Molarity, also referred to as molar concentration, is measured in moles of solute per liters of solution. The balanced dissociation reaction is $MgF_2 \rightarrow Mg^+(aq) + 2\,F^-(aq)$. To determine whether or not 62 grams of MgF_2 would prepare 1 M solution of fluoride ions, the following steps must be followed: 1) molar mass is used to convert from grams of MgF_2 to moles of MgF_2 2) balanced equation is used to convert moles of MgF_2 to moles of F^- ions, and 3) divide moles of F^- ions by the L of solution. So, the following calculation is used: 62 g MgF_2 × (1 mol MgF_2 / 62 g MgF_2) × (2 mol F^- / 1 mol MgF_2) = 2 mol F^- / 1 L of solution. Thus, the molar concentration of the solution of fluoride ions is 2 M.
104	F, T	1	The amount of electrons in an atom's outer shell, also referred to as the atom's valence electrons, are found using the group/column number in the periodic table. The ground state of a sodium atom has 1 valence electron because it is in group 1, while a calcium atom has 2 valence electrons because it is in group 2. Additionally, the number of electrons a in neutral atom is equivalent to the atomic number (# of protons). So, sodium (Na) has 11 electrons and calcium (Ca) has 20 electrons.
105	T, T, CE	4	Charles's Law is the gas law that states the direct relationship between volume and temperature at a constant pressure. V/T = constant; $V_1/T_1 = V_2/T_2$. Thus, at constant pressure, an ideal gas heated from 25 degrees Celsius to 30 degrees Celsius will expand proportionally in volume. So, both statements are true, and the second statement is a correct explanation for the first statement.

#	Ans.	Chapter	Explanation

106   T, T, CE   10   Water undergoes the process called autoionization; $H_2O(aq)$ spontaneously dissociates into H_3O^+ and OH^- ions. The K_w, also referred to as the equilibrium constant or autoionization constant, is 10^{-14} M at 25 degrees Celsius for pure water. Since $K_w = [H_3O^+][OH^-] = 10^{-14} M$ at 25 degrees Celsius for pure water, the concentration of H_3O^+ is $10^{-7} M$ and the concentration for OH^- is 10^{-7} at 25 degrees Celsius. So, both statements are true, and the second statement is a correct explanation for the first statement.

107   F, T   10   Strong acids react completely with bases and form weak conjugate bases; weak acids react partially or have reversible dissociation with bases and form strong conjugate bases. The following list includes 6 strong acids that must be memorized: 1) hydrochloric acid (HCl), 2) hydrobromic acid (HBr), 3) hydroiodic acid (HI), 4) nitric acid (HNO_3), 5) sulfuric acid (H_2SO_4), and perchloric acid ($HClO_4$). If an acid is not on that list, it is considered to be weak. So, the first statement is false because HF is a weak acid and H_2SO_4 is a strong acid. HF has two atoms (1 Hydrogen and 1 Fluoride) and $HClO_3$ has 5 atoms (1 Hydrogen, 1 Chlorine, and 3 Oxygen). As a result, the second statement is true.

108   T, T, CE   5   Calorie is a unit used to measure heat; a calorie is the amount of heat required to raise the temperature of one gram of water by one degree Celsius. Also, the specific heat capacity of water 1 calorie/gram $°C$ or 4.186 joule/gram $°C$. So, both statements are true, and the second statement is a correct explanation for the first statement.

109   T, F   10   Nonmetallic oxides react with water to form acidic solutions, while metallic oxides react with water to form basic solutions. When a nonmetallic oxide reacts with water, it will most likely form an acid called an oxyacid. As a result, this oxyacid will donate hydronium ions (H^+) to the solution, which allows this reaction to form an acidic solution.

110   F, T   9   The thermodynamic state function, G, is also referred to as Gibbs Free energy. Gibbs free-energy equation, $\Delta G = \Delta H - T\Delta S$, is used to predict the spontaneity of a reaction; a negative ΔG value represents a spontaneous reaction, and a positive ΔG value represents a nonspontaneous reaction. The calculation requires values for entropy, enthalpy, and temperature. Thus, a negative value for heat of reaction (exothermic reaction) would most likely result in a negative ΔG value. If ΔH is negative and ΔS is positive, the reaction is spontaneous at all temperatures. However, if ΔH is negative and ΔS is negative, the reaction is only spontaneous at low temperatures. Additionally, all reactions require some amount of initial absorption of energy to activate.

111   T, T, CE   9   Entropy is the degree of disorder in a system and is used to measure randomness. Solids are rigid and have a fixed position, so this phase has the lowest amount of entropy. Gases have the greatest amount of entropy because their particles freely move and have the most disorder. As the strength of IMF in a system goes up, the amount of order increases. In the given combustion reaction, entropy decreases as the products form because there are six gaseous reactants and only three gaseous products. Additionally, in the given combustion reaction, the reactants only consist of gaseous substances while there is at least one product that is a non-gaseous substance, specifically 4 liquid products of H_2O.

112   F, T   13   Rather than Rutherford's gold foil experiment, J.J. Thomson's cathode ray tube experiment led to the discovery of the electron. However, Rutherford's gold foil experiment was tremendously impactful because the results provided significant information about the atomic structure. Alpha particles, which are identical to a helium nuclei, were shot through the foil. The results of experiment portrayed that there were only a few deflections of the alpha particles, which expressed that an atom is mostly empty space between the nucleus and electrons.

113   F, F   6   The four main colligative properties of solutions are freezing point, boiling point, vapor pressure, and osmotic pressure; colligative properties of solutions depend on the concentration of solute particles and not the identity/nature of the solute particles. When the concentration of particles in a solution increases, then the following effects on the solvent take place: 1) the freezing point decreases, 2) the boiling point increases, 3) vapor pressure decreases, and 4) the osmotic pressure increases. Thus, a dilute solution of sugar in water has a higher solute concentration than pure water, so the freezing point of a dilute solution of sugar in water will be lower. At room temperature, pure sugar is a solid and pure water is a liquid. As a result, the freezing point of pure sugar is higher than the freezing point of water.

#	Ans.	Chapter	Explanation
114	F, F	8	According to Le Châtelier's principle, a reaction will proceed to counteract any disturbance on the system. Thus, after a reaction has reached equilibrium, the addition of one of the reactants will lead favor the forward reaction and form more products, not less. Additionally, increasing the concentration of reactants will increase the reaction rate because the reaction rate is proportional to the concentration of reactants; if there are more molecules, there is a higher likelihood of effective collisions.
115	T, F	1	Ionization energy is the amount of energy per mole required to remove an electron from the valence shell of an atom. When you remove a valence electron from an atom, the atomic radius will decrease. The second ionization potential is the amount of energy needed to remove the second electron from a neutral atom. The second ionization potential is always higher than the first ionization potential because removing the first valence electron from an atom decreases the atomic radius, decreases the shielding effect, and creates a cation (positively charged ion). Thus, the first ionization energy of K is less than the second ionization energy of K because the positively nucleus has a tighter pull on the remaining electrons, making it more difficult to remove the second electron from the valence shell. Additionally, there are 19 electrons within the neutral K atom, while there are 18 electrons within the K^+ cation.
26	A	13	A chemical change, also referred to as a chemical reaction, alters the chemical composition of the matter, while a physical change alters the physical state of the matter. A common physical change is phase change, while decomposition reactions, oxidation reactions, burning, and combustion are all chemical changes.
27	D	1	Ground state is the lowest energy state of electrons. Valence electrons are the electrons in the outermost shell of an atom. The group with the most valence electrons are the Noble gases because the electronic configuration fulfills the octet rule.
28	A	3	The balanced equation of the combustion reaction is $CH_4(g) + 2 O_2(g) \rightarrow CO_2(g) + 2 H_2O(l)$ Combustion is an exothermic reaction where a hydrocarbon reacts with oxygen and produces carbon dioxide, water, and a lot of energy in the form of energy or light. To find the number of moles of CO_2 produced if 8.0 grams of methane were completely consumed, the calculations are as follows: 8.0 g $CH_4(g) \times$ (1 mol of $CH_4(g)$ / 16 g $CH_4(g)$) $\times$ (1 mol $CO_2(g)$ / 1 mol of $CH_4(g)$) = 0.5 mol of $CO_2(g)$.
29	A	3	The balanced equation for the given reaction is as follows: $$2\ NH_3(g) + 3 F_2(g) \rightarrow 1\ N_2(g) + 6HF$$ The coefficient for $N_2(g)$ in the balanced equation is 1.
30	A	13	According to the Pauli Exclusion Principle, an orbital holds a maximum of two electrons with opposite spins.
31	A	7	The activation energy is the minimum amount of energy needed to undergo a chemical reaction. The activation energy of the forward is calculated by subtracting the the initial amount of energy held within the reactants from the amount of energy at the transition state (highest energy point/least stable).
32	B	12	An aromatic compound has a very stable structure. Aromatic compounds are cyclic, planar and consists of a structure where all carbons in the ring are sp^2 hybridized. Compound III is cyclic, planar, and obtains alternating double and single bonds in its ring.
33	C	13	Distillation is a separation method used to separate a pure liquid from a mixture of liquids. This method involves evaporation and condensation; distillation separates the liquids based on boiling point.
34	C	10	A neutralization reaction is defined as Acid + Base $\rightarrow$ Salt + Water. The chemical reaction CH_3COOH (weak acid) + NaOH (strong base) $\rightarrow$ Na^+ CH_3COO^- (salt) + H_2O (water) forms a basic solution. The strength of the conjugate base in acid-base reactions depends on the strength of the acid. A strong acid forms a weaker conjugate base, while a weak acid forms a stronger conjugate base. However, although CH_3COO^- is a stronger conjugate base, it is not considered a strong base. A strong base is a group I or group II metal linked to a hydroxide ion.

#	Ans.	Chapter	Explanation

35   D   13   The half-life of a radioactive element is the amount of time needed for half of the radioactive atoms to decay. The original 96 g of element X had to undergo 5 half-lives to have only 3 g of element X remain. The calculations are as follows:

$$96 \text{ g} \rightarrow 48 \text{ g} \rightarrow 24 \text{ g} \rightarrow 12 \text{ g} \rightarrow 6 \text{ g} \rightarrow 3 \text{ g}$$

Since radioactive element X has a half-life of 20 years, 100 years must have passed because 5 half-lives × 20 years / half-life = 100 years.

36   A   11   The given equation $Zn(s) + Cu^{2+}(aq) \rightarrow Cu(s) + Zn^{2+}(aq)$ represents a redox-reaction. The two half-reactions of the redox-reaction are the following two equations: $Zn(s) \rightarrow Zn^{2+}(aq) + 2e^-$ and $Cu^{2+}(aq) + 2e^- \rightarrow Cu(s)$. The zinc half-reaction illustrates oxidation (lose electrons), while the copper half-reaction illustrations reduction (gain electrons). Thus, $Zn(s)$ is being oxidized and is referred to as the reducing agent. $Cu^{2+}(aq)$ is being reduced and is referred to as the oxidizing agent. Additionally, two moles of electrons are transferred for each 1 mol of $Cu(s)$ produced and 1 mol of $Zn(s)$ consumed.

37   E   8 K_c, also referred to as the equilibrium constant, is calculated by dividing the total product of all gaseous products of a balanced chemical reaction by the total product of all gaseous reactants of a balanced chemical reaction. Additionally, the coefficients of the reactants and products in the balanced chemical reaction are equivalent to the power the respective reactants and products are raised to when calculating the K_c value. For example, the reaction $aA(g) + bB(g) \rightarrow cC(g) + dD(g)$ will have a K_c value of $[C]^c[D]^d/[A]^a[B]^b$. Thus, $[CO_2]$ is the equilibrium constant because we only include gaseous products and reactants in this calculation.

38   D   3   To find the formula of the hydrate, the moles of Na_2SO_4 and the moles of water in the hydrate released must be calculated. Using the chart provided in the question stem, the following calculations must be performed:

$$\text{Test tube and } Na_2SO_4 \text{ hydrate} - \text{test tube} = Na_2SO_4 \text{ hydrate}$$
$$181.1 \text{ g} - 20.1 \text{ g} = 161 \text{ g } Na_2SO_4 \text{ hydrate}$$

$$\text{Test tube and } Na_2SO_4 - \text{test tube} = Na_2SO_4$$
$$91.1 \text{ g} - 20.1 \text{ g} = 71 \text{ g } Na_2SO_4$$

$$Na_2SO_4 \text{ hydrate} - Na_2SO_4 = \text{hydrate}$$
$$161 \text{ g} - 71 \text{ g} = 90 \text{ g hydrate}$$

To find the formula of the hydrate, grams of Na_2SO_4 and grams of hydrate have to be converted into moles. So, 71 g Na_2SO_4 × (1 mol/ 142 g Na_2SO_4)= 0.5 moles of Na_2SO_4; 90 g H_2O × (1 mol/ 18 g H_2O) = 5 moles of H_2O. The ratio of moles of Na_2SO_4 to moles of hydrate driven off is 0.5 moles: 5 moles. Thus, the formula of the hydrate has the same ratio in the compound $Na_2SO_4 \times 10H_2O$.

39   E   10   When a salt, also known as an ionic compound, is added to water, it will dissociate into a cation and anion. The identity of the ions determine whether the solution is acidic, basic, or neutral. The salt's cation will be categorized based on if it came from a strong or weak base while the salt's anion will be categorized based on if it came from a strong or weak acid. To form an acidic solution, the cation of the salt must be the conjugate acid of a weak base and the anion of the salt must be the conjugate base of a strong acid. This is because the conjugate acid of a weak base will act as an acid in water while the conjugate base of a strong acid will not react. K_2SO_4 is eliminated because the ionic compound is made up of K^+ and SO_4^{2-}; K^+ is the conjugate acid of KOH (strong base) and SO_4^{2-} is the conjugate base of HSO_4^- (weak acid), so the solution would be basic. $Na_3(PO_4)_2$ is also eliminated because a basic solution forms when the salt is hydrolyzed in water. Na^+ is the conjugate acid of a NaOH (strong base) and PO_4^{3-} is the conjugate base of HPO_4^{2-} (weak acid). Thus, the conjugate base will act a proton from the water and form HPO_4^{2-}(aq) and OH^-(aq). Lastly, a neutral solution pH = 7 forms when the ionic salt NaCl dissociates in water because Na^+ and Cl^- both remain unreactive in solution. Na^+ is a conjugate acid of the strong base NaOH, and Cl^- is the conjugate base of strong acid HCl.

#	Ans.	Chapter	Explanation
40	D	6	The four main colligative properties of solutions are freezing point, boiling point, vapor pressure, and osmotic pressure; colligative properties of solutions depend on the concentration of solute particles and not the identity/nature of the solute particles. When the concentration of particles in a solution increases, the boiling point of the solvent is elevated. 3 M of BCl_3 has the highest boiling point because the degree of ionization for the ionic substance is 4 because BCl_3 dissociates into 1 mol of B^{+3} and 3 moles of Cl^-.
41	A	4	The ideal gas law is PV = nRT or V = (nRT) / P. The volume and temperature are equal for all four containers and the R is a constant. So, the number of moles of gas is directly proportional to the amount of pressure in the container. Each container has the 2 grams of gas, so divide 2 grams by the gram formula mass of each gas to calculate the amount of moles in each container. Thus, the lighter the molecule of gas in grams, the greater the amount of moles of gas in the container, and the higher the pressure. Thus, H_2 has the lowest molecular mass and the highest pressure in the container of gas.
42	E	3	To find the amount of heat energy released, a dimensional analysis problem must be set up. Given the balanced equation 2 $H_2(g)$ + $O_2(g)$ → 2 $H_2O(g)$ + 480 kJ, the calculation are as follows: 16 g H_2 × (1 mol H_2 / 2 g H_2) × (480 kJ / 2 mol H_2) = 1,920 kJ. Thus, 1,920 kJ of heat energy is released.
43	D	2	The hydrogen bond is a special type of dipole-dipole attraction that involves a hydrogen atom bonding with fluorine (F), oxygen (O), or nitrogen (N). There must be a hydrogen donor and a hydrogen acceptor. A hydrogen donor has a polar covalent bond between a hydrogen atom and a highly electronegative atom (usually F, O or N), and a hydrogen acceptor is a neighboring electronegative atom that has lone pairs. Thus, HCl and H_2S are unable to hydrogen bond.
44	E	3, 6	Since Molarity (moles of solute per liters of solution) and the molar mass are given , the calculation is as follows: 2.00 L × (1 mol $CsNO_3$ / 1 L of solution) × (195 g $CsNO_3$ / 1 mol $CsNO_3$) = 390 g $CsNO_3$.
45	E	9	Gibbs free-energy equation is used to predict the spontaneity of a reaction. Gibbs Equation is $\Delta G = \Delta H - T\Delta S$; a negative ΔG value represents a spontaneous reaction and a positive ΔG value represents a nonspontaneous reaction. The calculation requires values for entropy, enthalpy, and temperature. Thus, spontaneity cannot be determined given just a balanced chemical reaction.
46	D	13	The chemical formula of sodium bicarbonate is determined by following the nomenclature rules for polyatomic ionic compounds. Sodium is the name of the cation Na^+ and bicarbonate is the name of the polyatomic anion HCO_3^{-1}. Thus, the combined chemical formula is $NaHCO_3$.
47	C	3	The balanced equation for the decomposition reaction is $2KClO_3$ → $3O_2$ + $2KCl$. To convert grams of potassium chlorate to liters of oxygen gas at STP, the following steps must be followed: 1) the molar mass is used to convert from grams of $KClO_3$ to moles of $KClO_3$, 2) balance equation is used to convert from moles of $KClO_3$ to moles of O_2, and 3) Avogadro's principle, which states that one mole of any gas at STP has a volume of 22.4 L, is used to convert moles of O_2 to liters of O_2. So, the following calculation is used: 123 g $KClO_3$ × (1 mol $KClO_3$ / 123 g $KClO_3$) × (3 mol O_2 / 2 mol $KClO_3$) × (22.4 L of O_2 / 1 mol O_2) = 33. 6 L of O_2.
48	C	2	Ionic bond (A) and metallic bond (B) are eliminated because bromine atoms are nonmetals. Hydrogen bonding (D) and London force interactions (E) are also eliminated because the bond between a bromine atom and a bromine atom in one diatomic molecule is intramolecular (not intermolecular). Covalent bonding best describes the type of bonding between bromine atoms because Br is a nonmetal and this is an intramolecular force.
49	C	11	The two reduction reactions in the question stem are: $$Zn^{2+}(aq) + 2e^- \rightarrow Zn(s)$$ $$Al^{3+}(aq) + 3e^- \rightarrow Al(s)$$ The amount of charge that reduces 1.0 mol of $Zn^{2+}(aq)$ to 1.0 mol of $Zn(s)$ is 2 electrons. So, the following is calculated to determine how many moles of $Al^{3+}(aq)$ this amount of charge would reduce to $Al(s)$: 2 moles of electrons × (1 mol $Al^{3+}(aq)$ / 3 moles of electrons) = 0.67 mol $Al^{3+}(aq)$

#	Ans.	Chapter	Explanation
50	C	8	The formula CuS displays a 1:1 ratio of copper ions to sulfur ions. Thus, if the molar concentration of Cu^{2+} ions is 4.0×10^{-6} g/mol, then the molar concentration of S^{2-} ions is also 4.0×10^{-6} mol/L. Thus, the solubility constant of copper (II) sulfide is $K_{sp} = [Cu^{2+}][S^{2-}] = (4.0 \times 10^{-6})(4.0 \times 10^{-6}) = 1.6 \times 10^{-11}$.
51	D	1	Electronegativity is the tendency of an atom to attract a bonding pair of electrons to itself or "how badly an atom wants to add an electron." As one of the major trends on the periodic table, electronegativity increases while moving from left to right (across a period) and from bottom to top (up a group) on the periodic table. So, the halogens (group 17 elements) are located on the upper right side of the periodic table and have the greatest electronegativity because they have seven valence electrons and only need one more electron to have an octet.
52	A	1	The total number of electrons in neutral atom of copper (Cu) is the same as the atomic number of the element Cu, so a neutral Cu atom has 29 electrons. Cu^{3+} is a cation, which lost three electrons. Thus, 29 electrons $-$ 3 electrons = 26 electrons.
53	E	2	CO_2 is a molecule with a double bond between each oxygen atom and the central carbon atom. This produces two regions of electron density, which means that the hybridization is sp.
54	D	10	To calculate the pH of a solution with OH^- ions, the following two equations are used: pOH $= -\log [OH^-]$ and pH + pOH = 14. Molarity, also known as molar concentration, is measured in moles of solute per liters of solution; M = mol of solute/ L of solution. The molarity of OH^- ions is calculated as $(1 \times 10^{-4}$ moles of OH^- ions)/ 1 L of solution. Thus, the pOH $= -\log [1 \times 10^{-4}\ M] = 4$, which means the pH of the solution is = 14 $-$ 4 = 10.
55	D	3	The empirical formula of a substance provides the simplest whole-number ratio of atoms in the compound, while the molecular formula provides the actual number of atoms in the compound. The empirical formula (simplest form) and the molecular formula (actual form) of the same compound will always have the same ratio. Thus, CH_4O and $C_3H_{12}O_3$ have a 1:4:1 mole ratio of carbon atoms to hydrogen atoms to oxygen atoms, which indicates the pair of formulas represent the empirical and molecular.
56	E	3	To convert from mol of aluminum sulfate, $Al_2(SO_4)_3$, to atoms of O, the following steps must be followed: 1) Avogadro's number is used to convert moles of gas to molecules of gas and 2) convert molecules of $Al_2(SO_4)_3$ to atoms of O. Thus, the calculation is: 2 moles $Al_2(SO_4)_3 \times$ $(6.02 \times 10^{23}$ molecule of $Al_2(SO_4)_3$ / 1 mole of $Al_2(SO_4)_3) \times$ (12 atoms of O / 1 molecule of $Al_2(SO_4)_3) = 1.44 \times 10^{25}$ atoms of O.
57	D	7	Factors that impact the reaction rate between magnesium solid and dilute hydrochloric acid do so by affecting the rate of molecular collisions and/or the energy of the collisions. (I) is eliminated because as you decrease the temperature, the average kinetic energy of the particles decreases. Subsequently, both the frequency of molecular collisions and the energy of the collision are lowered. (II) is correct because increasing the surface area of Mg (s) will increase the number of collisions, which increases the reaction rate. Lastly, (III) is also correct because the reaction rate is proportional to the concentration of reactants; thus, if there are more molecules, there is a higher likelihood of effective collisions.
58	B	10	$NaNO_3$ does NOT react with a dilute solution of nitrate acid, HNO_3, because the products would be the same as the reactants. In a dilute solution, HNO_3 dissociates into $H^+(aq)$ + $NO_3^-(aq)$ while $NaNO_3$ dissociates into $Na^+(aq)$ + $NO_3^-(aq)$.
59	D	5	The equation used to calculate the amount of energy released/ absorbed during a phase change is $q = m\Delta H$ and the equation used to calculate the amount of energy released/absorbed during temperature change is $q = mC\Delta T$. The calculation $q = (2.0$ g $H_2O)(80$ cal/g) determines that the amount of energy required to melt 2.0 grams of water at 0 degrees Celsius is 160 calories. Now, plug in 160 calories in the second question to solve for the final temperature: 160 calories = (4 grams H_2O)(1 calorie/gram °C)(T_f $-$ 25°C).
60	D	2, 5	A liquid that "readily evaporates" is also referred to as volatile. Liquid molecules are more likely to escape into the gas phase at a high vapor pressure and low boiling point. Lastly, the boiling point of a substance is closely related to its intermolecular force strength. The stronger the IMF, the more energy required to break bonds, and the higher the boiling point. Thus, a volatile liquid has a high vapor pressure, low boiling point, and weak intermolecular forces.

#	Ans.	Chapter	Explanation
61	B	4	The Combined Gas Law states the relationship between pressure, volume, and temperature. $P_1V_1/T_1 = P_2V_2/T_2$. Based on the question stem, all of the values are given besides V_2. Standard temperature is 273 K and standard pressure is 760 mmHg. Thus, the calculation is as follows: $$P_1V_1/T_1 = P_2V_2/T_2$$ $$(P_1/P_2)(V_1)(T_2/T_1) = V_2$$ $$(700 \text{ mmHg}/760 \text{ mmHg})(3L)(273 \text{ K }/(273+20 \text{ K})) = V_2$$
62	A	12	An isomer is a molecule with the same molecular formula, but a different chemical structure. The three molecular formulas for the given structures are $C_2Br_2H_2$, C_2Br_3H, and C_2Br_4. As a result, none of the above are isomers.
63	B	1	Considering the nuclear reaction, there must be a balanced atomic number and atomic mass. The reactant side and product side of the given reaction have an equal number for atomic mass, but an unequal number for atomic number. The reactants have 6 protons and the products have 5 protons. A beta particle is inserted in the placeholder because it will emit an electron on the reactant side without changing the atomic mass. Thus, it will even out the charges; $6 + (-1) = 5$.
64	D	3	The balanced equation for the given reaction is as follows: $$4 \text{ NaCl}(s) + 2 \text{ SO}_2(g) + 2 \text{ H}_2\text{O}(l) + 1 \text{ O}_2(g) \rightarrow 2 \text{ Na}_2\text{SO}_4(g) + 4\text{HCl}$$ The coefficient for $\text{NaCl}(s)$ in the balanced equation is 4.
65	D	9	Based on Hess's Law of Heat Summation, the two equations listed below are algebraically manipulated to yield the net reaction N (Octaazacubane) $\rightarrow$ N (Hexazine) and to find to its change in enthalpy (ΔH). $$\text{Equation (1) N (Hexazine)} + \text{O}_2(g) \rightarrow \text{NO}_2(g) \ \Delta H = 202 \text{ kJ.}$$ $$\text{Equation (2) N (Octaazacubane)} + \text{O}_2(g) \rightarrow \text{NO}_2(g) \ \Delta H = 498 \text{ kJ.}$$ So, to form N(Hexazine) monoxide as a product in the net reaction, the first equation is reversed, which also changes the sign of the enthalpy of formation for equation (1). Lastly, the ΔH of equation one and two must be summed in order to find the change in enthalpy for the net reaction: N (Octaazacubane) $\rightarrow$ N (Hexazine). Thus, ΔH is 296 kJ because that is the sum of -202 kJ and 498 kJ.
66	E	11	An oxidation-reduction reaction (redox reaction) is a chemical reaction that involves the transfer of electrons, which causes the oxidation number of elements to change. The chemical reaction $\text{AgNO}_3(aq) + \text{NaCl}(aq) \rightarrow \text{AgCl}(s) + \text{NaNO}_3(aq)$ is not a redox reaction because all of the elements involved keep the same oxidation number on both sides of the reaction. Whether the element is a reactant or product, the following oxidation states remain constant: Ag is +1, N is +5, O is -2, Na is +1, and Cl is -1.
67	C	6, 10	The percent dissociation of the oxalic acid is expressed as (the molar concentration of the hydronium ion / the original molar concentration of the oxalic acid) $\times$ 100. So, the percent dissociation of oxalic acid is calculated using the following equation: $$[\text{H}^+]/[\text{HO}_2\text{C}_2\text{O}_2\text{H}] \times 100 = (1 \times 10^{-2} \ M \ / \ 1 \ M) \times 100 = 1\%.$$

#	Ans.	Chapter	Explanation
68	C	6	

Boiling point is one of the four main colligative properties of solutions, which means that it depends on the concentration of solute particles and not the identity/nature of the solute particles. When the concentration of particles in a solution increases, then the boiling point of the solvent elevates. The following equation is used to calculate the boiling point of water when 2 moles of NaCl were added to the flask: $\Delta T_b = imK_b$. Since the K_b value of pure water is a known constant $(0.51°C$ kg/mol), the van 't Hoff factor (i) and the molality (moles of solute/ kg of solvent) must be found to calculate the ΔT_b.

The molality of the NaCl solution is 2 moles of NaCl / 1 kg of H_2O and the degree of ionization for NaCl (ionic substance) is 2 because NaCl dissociates into 1 mol of Na^+ and 1 mol of Cl^-. The following calculation is used to find the change in boiling point when 2 moles of NaCl were added to water:

$$\Delta T_b = imK_b = (2)(2 \text{ moles of } NaCl(s) \text{ / 1 kg of } H_2O(l))(0.51°C \text{ kg/mol}) = 2°C.$$

Thus, the boiling point of the water would increase by 2 degrees Celsius.

| 69 | C | 13 | The chemical compound carbon monoxide, CO, is the most toxic to humans of the answer choices. |

| 70 | E | 4 | Effusion is when a gas moves through a pinhole into a vacuum, while diffusion is when a gas moves from one container into another container that is already occupied by some amount of gas. According to Graham's Law of Effusion/Diffusion, the rate of effusion/diffusion for a gas is inversely proportional to the square root of the gases molar mass; the smaller the molar mass the higher the rate of effusion/diffusion and the lower the amount of time required. Thus, the gas with the largest molar mass (Cl_2) has the lowest rate of effusion through a semipermeable barrier. |

#	Ans.	Chapter	Explanation
1	B	1	Atomic radius measures the size of an atom. More specifically, it is the distance from the center of the nucleus to the furthest electron in the atoms boundary. Atomic radius is calculated by dividing the distance between the center of two atoms by 2. As one of the major trends on the periodic table, atomic radius increases while moving from right to left (across a period) and from top to bottom (down a group) on the periodic table. Therefore, element B has the smallest atomic radius because it is located on the upper right side of the periodic table.
2	E	1	Ionic radius measures the size of an ion (atom with an unequal amount of electrons and protons). If an atom loses an electron (forming a cation), the ionic radius is smaller than the neutral atom. If an atom gains an electron (forming a anion), the ionic radius is bigger than the neutral atom. Similar to the atomic radius trend on the periodic table, ionic radius increases while moving from top to bottom (down a group) on the periodic table because it has more shells. Therefore, element E has the largest ionic radius because it has the most electron shells.
3	C	1	Electronegativity is the tendency of an atom to attract a bonding pair of electrons to itself or "how badly an atom wants to add an electron." As one of the major trends on the periodic table, electronegativity increases while moving from left to right (across a period) and from bottom to top (up a group) on the periodic table. So, element C has the lowest electronegativity because it is located on the lower left side of the periodic table.
4	C	1	The second ionization potential is the amount of energy needed to remove the second electron from a neutral atom. The second ionization potential is always higher than the first ionization potential. As one of the major trends on the periodic table, ionization potential increases while moving from left to right (across a period) and from bottom to top (up a group) on the periodic table. The second ionization potential is the largest for the element that is the most stable or "happiest" after removing the first electron from its valence shell. So, element C has the largest second ionization energy because it is a group I metal, adopting the electron configuration of a noble gas (stable and inert) after removing one electron from the valence shell.
5	B	1, 11	A positive number is assigned to an element when the atom loses electrons and vice versa for a negative number. An element with a possible oxidation number of 0 is an element that does not readily react with other elements. Element B would have an oxidation number of 0 because it is located in group 18, which indicates that the element is a noble gas. Noble gases, also known as inert gases, have a complete octet which makes them very stable and unreactive. As a result, element B would not transfer electrons.
6	B	2	Ionic bond (A) and metallic bond (E) are eliminated because carbon and oxygen are both non-metals, while hydrogen bond (D) is also eliminated because the bond between carbon and oxygen atoms in a carbon dioxide molecule is intramolecular (not intermolecular). To determine the type of covalent bond, the electronegativity difference between carbon and oxygen is examined. The atoms in a polar covalent bond have an electronegativity difference between 0.5 and 1.6, which creates an unequal sharing of electrons. The more electronegative atom has a stronger pull on the shared electrons, which forms a partial negative charge. The less electronegative atom forms a partial positive charge. The atoms in a nonpolar covalent bond have an electronegativity difference less than 0.5, which sustains an equal sharing of electrons. CO_2 consists of polar covalent bonds (B) because the oxygen atom is more electronegative than the carbon atom, which indicates that the oxygen atom has a stronger pull on the shared electrons.
7	E	2	Polar covalent bond (B) and nonpolar covalent bond (C) are eliminated because magnesium is a metal, while hydrogen bond (D) is also eliminated because the bond between magnesium atoms in a crystal of magnesium solid is intramolecular (not intermolecular). Ionic bond (A) is eliminated because a magnesium atom (metal) is not bonding with a nonmetal atom. A metallic bond (E) is the correct choice because this bond is formed between metals. Within a metallic solid, there is a sea of valence electrons, also referred to as delocalized electrons, that has an electrostatic attraction with the positively charged metal ions. Thus, the crystal of magnesium solid has metallic bonds between the atoms of magnesium.

#	Ans.	Chapter	Explanation
8	C	2	Molecular iodine is diatomic, which means that the molecule is made up of two iodine atoms. Ionic bond (A) and metallic bond (E) are eliminated because an iodine molecule bonds two nonmetal iodine atoms, while hydrogen bond (D) is also eliminated because the bond between two iodine atoms in one iodine molecule is intramolecular (not intermolecular). Additionally, the iodine atoms have the same electronegativity, which means there is an equal sharing of electrons. Thus, polar covalent bond (B) is eliminated and nonpolar covalent bond (C) is correct.
9	A	2	A crystal of calcium oxide (CaO) is made up of calcium atoms (metal) and oxygen atoms (non-metal), which is why an Ionic bond (A) is formed between them. The metal transfers electrons to the nonmetal in order to create the bond. Polar covalent bond (B), nonpolar covalent bond (C) and metallic bond (E) are eliminated because a crystal of calcium oxide has a bond between one metal (calcium) and one non metal (oxygen), while hydrogen bond (D) is also eliminated because the bond between a calcium atom and a oxygen atom in a crystal of calcium oxide is intramolecular (not intermolecular).
10	A	4	Boyle's Law is the gas law that states the inverse relationship between pressure and volume at a constant temperature. PV = constant; $P_1 V_1 = P_2 V_2$.
11	D	4	Charles's Law is the gas law that states the direct relationship between volume and temperature at a constant pressure. V/T = constant; $V_1/T_1 = V_2/T_2$
12	E	4	Combined Gas Law integrates the following three gas laws: Boyle's Law, Charles's Law, and Gay-Lussac's Law. The Combined Gas Law states the relationship between pressure, volume, and temperature. PV/T = constant; $P_1 V_1/T_1 = P_2 V_2/T_2$.
13	B	4	Dalton's Law, also referred to as Dalton's Law of Partial Pressure, states that gases mixed within the same closed system are assumed to behave independently. As a result, Dalton's Law of Partial Pressure indicates that the total pressure of a mixture of gases is equal to the sum of the pressures of each gas. $P_{total} = P_1 + P_2 + P_3 + ... + P_n$
14	C	4	Gay-Lussac's Law is the gas law that states the direct relationship between pressure and temperature at a constant volume. P_1/T_2 = constant; $P_1/T_1 = P_2/T_2$.
15	B	7	The activation energy of the forward reaction is calculated by subtracting the initial amount of energy held within the reactants (A) from the amount of energy at the activated complex/transition state (highest energy point/least stable) (C). So, the activation energy of the forward reaction is expressed as $C - A = B$.
16	D	7	The heat of reaction (ΔH), also referred to as the enthalpy of the reaction, is calculated by subtracting the energy of the reactants from the energy of the products; $\Delta H = H_f - H_i$. So, the energy of the products (E) − the energy of the reactants (A) = the change in enthalpy (D).
17	E	7	The energy of the products is found by following the reaction. In a forward reaction, the products are represented by the last horizontal line (E), which is after the activated complex/transition state (C).
18	C	10	The Brønsted-Lowry acid is the reactant that donates protons (H^+) to a different reactant in the chemical equation.
19	D	10	The Brønsted-Lowry base is the reactant that accepts protons (H^+) from a different reactant in the chemical equation.
20	E	10	A buffer is a solution that has the ability to resist rapid pH change when an acid or base is added. A buffer solution is composed of either a weak acid and its conjugate base or a weak base and its conjugate acid.
21	A	10	The Arrhenius acid dissociates into an aqueous solution and yields hydrogen ions (H^+)
22	B	10	The Arrhenius base dissociates into an aqueous solution and yields hydroxide ions (OH^-).
23	D	1	Transition metals are found on the periodic table between groups three and twelve. The 4d sublevel is found in the fourth period (4 = n) and the d sublevel contains 5 orbitals, which cover groups 3 through 12.

#	Ans.	Chapter	Explanation
24	E	1	Orbitals represent the most probable location of electrons. Uranium-238 has an atomic number of 92 and an electron configuration of $[Rn]5f^{3}6d^{1}7s^{2}$.
25	D	1	Subshell d contains five (5) orbitals and each orbital can hold a maximum of two electrons. Thus, subshell d can hold a maximum of 10 electrons.

101   F, T   10   Barium Hydroxide consists of a group II metal and a hydroxide ion, indicating that $Ba(OH)_2$ is a strong base. A pH scale is used measure the acid/base concentration of a substance. These are a few of the following equations used:

$$pH = -\log [H^+], pOH = -\log [OH^-], \text{and } pH + pOH = 14.$$

The pH scale ranges from 0 to 14 and is categorized into the three following groups:

acidic $(0 < x < 7)$, neutral (7), and basic $(7 < x < 14)$.

As a strong base, $Ba(OH)_2(aq)$ has a high molar concentration of OH- ions in the solution. Thus, $Ba(OH)_2$ has a high pH and a low pOH.

102   F, F   4   The ideal gas law is used to predict the behavior of hypothetical ideal gases. This ideal gas law is expressed as $PV = nRT$ or $V = (nRT) / P$, predicting the relationship between pressure, volume, temperature and moles of gas. Based on assumptions from the kinetic molecular theory, ideal gases exhibit no intermolecular attractions or repulsions and have no volume compared to the volume of its container. Real gases deviate from these ideal gas behaviors, especially at high pressures and low temperatures; the actual volume of gas molecules and the attractive forces between gas molecules become more significant when gas molecules are closer in proximity with one another and move more slowly. Thus, real gases approach ideal behavior at low pressures and high temperatures because under these conditions the real gases are further apart from one another and move around more quickly, which increases volume and reduces IMF.

103   T, F   1   Isotopes of an element have the same number of protons (atomic number) but a different number of neutrons. So, since protons + neutrons = atomic mass, isotopes of the same element will also vary in atomic mass. Hydrogen-3 has a neutral charge, an atomic number of 1 and an atomic mass of 3, while Hydrogen-1 has a neutral charge, an atomic number of 1 and an atomic mass of 1. As a result, H-3 has 1 proton, 1 electron, and 2 neutrons and H-1 has 1 proton, 1 electron and 0 neutrons. Thus, H-3 and H-1 are isotopes because they have the same number of protons and a different number of neutrons.

104   T, F   1   Reactivity of metals measures how violent a reaction is when an metal is placed in water. In reference to the periodic table, the reactivity of alkali metals (group I) and alkaline earth metals (group 2) increases while moving from the top to bottom (down a group). Thus, within group 2, as the atomic number increases the reactivity increases. Electronegativity is the tendency of an atom to attract a bonding pair of electrons to itself or "how badly an atom wants to add an electron." As one of the major trends on the periodic table, electronegativity increases while moving from the left to right (across a period) and from bottom to top (up a group) on the periodic table. Thus, within a group, as the atomic number increases the electronegativity decreases.

105   F, T   11   Oxidation numbers, also known as oxidation states, are positive and negative integers that are assigned to atoms and are used to indicate if a specific atom has been reduced (gained electrons) or oxidized (lost electrons) in a chemical reaction. One of the oxidation rules is that the oxidation state of oxygen in MOST compounds is -2. However, in peroxide compounds (ex: H_2O_2, Na_2O_2, BaO_2), the oxidation state of oxygen is -1. Peroxides have two oxygen atoms linked together by a single covalent bond. Also, the oxidation number of an element can be determined by location on the periodic table; the group/column number can help assign oxidation number to an element. Thus, Group 16 elements have 6 valence electrons.

#	Ans.	Chapter	Explanation
106	T, T, CE	5	Solid gold is a metallic solid and the main metallic properties include, but are not limited to, the following: luster, malleable, ductile, conduct heat and electricity, large atomic radii, high density, high melting point, solid at room temp (besides Mg). Metallic solids have metals atoms linked together by metallic bonds. The metal atoms have a very free relationship with their valence bonds, which allows for a sea of delocalized electrons. The freedom of movement the electrons have is what makes metallic solids so good at conducting electricity. Both statements are true, and the second statement is a correct explanation for the first statement.
107	F, T	2	The carbonate ion, CO_3^{2-}, can be drawn in three resonance forms. The three resonance structures have the same arrangement of atoms and are made up of two C-O bonds and one C=O bond. The main difference between these resonance structures is the way the electrons are distributed across the molecule, not the structural formula. The actual CO_3^{2-} molecule is a hybrid of these three different resonance structures.
108	T, T	1	Carbon-12 and carbon-14 are different versions of the same element, also referred to as isotopes. Isotopes of an element have the same number of protons (atomic number), but a different number of neutrons. To calculate number of protons and neutrons, the following equation is used: protons + neutrons = atomic mass. Carbon-12 has an atomic number of 6 and an atomic mass of 12, while carbon-14 has an atomic number of 6 and an atomic mass of 14. As a result, C-12 has 6 protons and 6 neutrons, while C-14 has 6 protons and 8 neutrons. Thus, the atoms of carbon-12 and carbon-14 are isotopes because they have the same number of protons, but a different number of neutrons. Allotropes are different forms of the same element, in the same physical state (solid, liquid, gas), but have different physical properties due to the different bonding arrangement of atoms. Allotropes exist in multiple physical forms. Allotropes of carbon are diamond and graphite; both allotropes are in the solid state, but diamond and graphite differ in bond arrangement.
109	F, F	3	There are not 6 atoms in 1 mol of hydrogen sulfate (bisulfate). The following calculation is used to find number of atoms in 1 mole of hydrogen sulfate: $$(1 \text{ mol of } HSO_4^-) \times (6.02 \times 10^{23} \text{ molecules of } HSO_4^- \text{ / 1 mol of } HSO_4^-) \times$$ $$(6 \text{ atoms of } HSO_4^- \text{ / 1 molecule of } HSO_4^-) = 3.6 \times 10^{24} \text{ atoms of hydrogen sulfate.}$$ The chemical formula of hydrogen sulfate is HSO_4^-; this molecule contains 1 hydrogen atom, 1 sulfur atom, and 4 oxygen atoms.
110	T, T, CE	8	A chemical forward reaction is when one or more substances, known as reactants, transform into one or more different substances, known as products ($A + B \rightarrow C + D$). A reverse reaction is when the products are converted back to the reactants ($C + D \rightarrow A + B$). While the substances undergo changes in composition and/or structure, the chemical reaction is also accompanied by changes in energy. When the reactants absorb less energy (when breaking bonds) than the products release (when forming bonds), this is an exothermic reaction. An endothermic reaction is when the reactants absorb more energy (when breaking bonds) than the amount of energy the products release (when forming bonds). If the reverse reaction of an equilibrium is exothermic, it is expressed as $C + D \rightarrow A + B + \text{energy}$. According to Le Châtelier's principle, the reaction will proceed to counteract any disturbance on the system. Thus, since heat/energy is on the reactant side of the forward reaction, the reaction will favor the forward reaction if the temperature of equilibrium reverse reaction increases. Both statements are true, and the second statement is a correct explanation for the first statement.
111	T, T, CE	12	The cycloalkanes are hydrocarbons that form single-bonded ring compounds with their carbon atoms and may be expressed as C_nH_{2n}. Cycloalkanes are considered a homologous series because they are a series of compounds with the same general formula. Thus, all basic cycloalkanes must have a similar chemical structure. Both statements are true, and the second statement is a correct explanation for the first statement.

#	Ans.	Chapter	Explanation
112	T, T, CE	1	The first ionization energy is the amount of energy needed to remove a valence electron from a neutral atom. As one of the major trends on the periodic table, ionization potential increases while moving from left to right (across a period) and from bottom to top (up a group) on the periodic table. Atomic radius measures the size of an atom. As one of the major trends on the periodic table, atomic radius increases while moving from right to left (across a period) and from top to bottom (down a group) on the periodic table. Thus, since Be is a period higher than Mg in the same group on the periodic table, Be has both a greater first ionization energy and a smaller atomic radius than Mg. Both statements are true, and the second statement is a correct explanation for the first statement.
113	T, T, CE	6	Boiling point is one of the four main colligative properties of solutions, which means that it depends on the concentration of solute particles and not the identity/nature of the solute particles. When the concentration of particles in a solution increases, then the boiling point of the solvent elevates. The following equation is used to calculate the change in boiling point of liquid water when NaCl is added: $\Delta T_b = imK_b$. The van't Hoff factor (i) represents the number of particles formed from a compound in a solution. Thus, since the degree of ionization for the ionic substance NaCl is 2, the boiling point of a 0.5 M solution of sodium chloride is higher than the boiling point of pure water. Both statements are true, and the second statement is a correct explanation for the first statement.
114	F, T	4	Based on assumptions of the kinetic molecular theory of gases, the average kinetic energy of gas particles is proportional to the absolute temperature of the gas. So, at 25 degrees Celsius, the average kinetic energy of $N_2(g)$ molecules is not greater than the average kinetic energy of $O_2(g)$ molecules. Instead, the average kinetic energy would be the same since both gas molecules are at the same temperature.
115	F, T	13	According to the lab safety rules, liquid water should never be added to concentrated acid because the heat produced will cause the mixture to splatter. Instead, the better/safer option would be to add concentrated acid to water. The heat produced in the latter reaction would be absorbed by the excess water, which significantly reduces the likelihood of a splattered mixture. However, although acid added to water is the safer option, it still may cause the mixture to splatter.
26	C	3	Gram formula mass, also referred to as molar mass, is the sum of the atomic weights of all of the atoms in one mole of a molecule. Gram formula mass is measured in grams/mol; molar mass = g/mol. Thus, to solve for the molecular weight of $Mg(SO_4)$, the calculations are as follows: 1 atom of Mg $\times$ (24 g of Mg / mol) = 24 g/mol. 1 atom of S $\times$ (32 g of S / mol) = 32 g/mol. 4 atoms of O $\times$ (16 g of O / mol) = 64 g/mol. Since 24 g/mol + 32 g/mol + 64 g/mol is 120 g/mol; the gram formula mass of $Mg(SO_4)$ is 120 g/mol.
27	A	12	Combustion, also referred to as "burning", is a type of redox-reaction that produces a lot of energy in the form of light and heat. Combustion is an exothermic reaction where a hydrocarbon reacts with oxygen and produces carbon dioxide and water. Thus, the missing product must be H_2O; the balanced equation for the combustion reaction is $$2\,C_2H_6(g) + 7\,O_2(g) \rightarrow 4\,CO_2(g) + 6\,H_2O(l)$$
28	A	13	The metric system, also referred to as the Système Internationale (International System) "SI", is a system of measurement across many countries. This system contains multiple unit prefixes that precede a basic unit of measure. Some of the main unit prefixes are the following: pico, nano, micro, milli, centi, deci, kilo, and mega. The unit prefix nano indicates a multiplication of 10^{-9}.
29	E	3	Avogadro's Principle states that at the same temperature and pressure, ideal gases of equal volume have the same number of molecules. Additionally, the molar volume states that one mole of any gas at STP (standard temperature and pressure) has a volume of 22.4 L. Therefore, at standard temperature and pressure, 3.0 moles of $H_2(g)$, $N_2(g)$, $O_2(g)$, and Ne(g) would all occupy the same volume (22.4 L $\times$ 3).
30	C	13	The two subdivisions of matter are pure substances and mixtures. A mixture, either heterogeneous or homogeneous, is defined as combination of two or more components that can be separated by physical means. NaCl(g) and NaCl(l) are both pure substances, but NaCl(aq) is a mixture. NaCl(aq) is formed by the dissolution of sodium chloride (solid solute) in water (liquid solvent). Thus, NaCl(aq) is mixture (homogeneous) because it is a combination of two different substances and can be separated by physical means.

#	Ans.	Chapter	Explanation
31	E	1	In order to gain stability, elements often join together with other elements to form bonds by sharing or transferring electrons. Elements tend to be most stable when they have eight valence electrons, also referred to as a full octet. The ground state of potassium has an electron configuration of $1s^2 2s^2 2p^6 3s^2 3p^6 4s^1$, which indicates that the element has only has one valence electron. So, instead of gaining 7 valence electrons, potassium will have an easier time achieving an octet by giving up its valence electron and adopting the electron configuration of [Ar]. Therefore, potassium will most readily react with a halogen, which is a nonmetal that has seven valence electrons and only needs one more valence electron to complete its octet. In other words, the potassium will transfer an electron to a halogen and produce an ionic bond. Thus, K will transfer its valence electron to an element with the electron configuration of $1s^2 2s^2 2p^6 3s^2 3p^5$ (the ground state of element chlorine).
32	B	3	Density is a measurement of the mass to volume ratio of a substance; D = mass / volume. The mass of $CO_2(g)$ is found by multiplying the amount of $CO_2(g)$ moles by the gram formula mass of $CO_2(g)$, while the volume of $CO_2(g)$ is found by applying Avogadro's Principle. Avogadro's Principle states that 1) at the same temperature and pressure, all gases have an equal volume and the same number of molecules and 2) one mole of any gas at STP has a volume of 22.4 L. Therefore, since the mass of 1.0 mole of $CO_2(g)$ is 44 g and the molar volume of 1.0 mol of $CO_2(g)$ at STP is 22.4 L, the density is 2 g/L.
33	A	2	A nonpolar molecule has equivalent bonds, no lone pair of electrons on the central atom, and a symmetrical shape, which cancels out the dipole bonds and forms a net dipole of zero. The BF_3 molecule is a nonpolar because the dipoles formed from the three polar covalent bonds between the boron atom and 3 fluoride atoms are canceled due to the molecules symmetrical trigonal planar shape. The molecules H_2O, NH_3, and SO_2 are polar because the atoms do not lie on the same plane and because of the lone pair of electrons on each of the central atoms, making the molecules asymmetrical. NaCl is polar because one end of the molecule is positive and the other end of the molecule is negative.
34	A	3	Avogadro's number states that one mole of any substance is 6.02×10^{23} units, meaning that one mole of any element is 6.02×10^{23} atoms of that element. Given the amount of grams of each element, the following calculation is used to find the number of atoms of each element: 5.0 grams of element A × (1 mol of A / grams of A) × (6.02×10^{23} atoms of A / 1 mol of A) = the number of atoms of element A. So, the molar mass of each element has an inverse relationship with the number of atoms of each element. Thus, Cu has the greatest number of atoms because it has the lowest molar mass.
35	C	4	Molar volume is the measurement of volume that one mole of a substance occupies at a given temperature and temperature. Avogadro's Principle states that one mole of any gas at STP (standard temperature and pressure) has a volume of 22.4 L. However, under non-STP conditions, the ideal gas law is used to find the molar volume of a gas. According to Boyle's law (inverse relationship between pressure and molar volume at constant temperature) and Charles's Law (direct relationship between molar volume and temperature at constant pressure), since R is a constant and n is the same for the gaseous neon, the lowest pressure and the highest temperature will have the greatest molar volume.
36	A	12	A complete Lewis electron-dot diagram of formaldehyde has the correct sum of valence electrons and a complete octet around each atom (disregarding the exceptions to the octet rule). Choice (A) is the only structure that follows the above requirements. Choice (B) and (E) have an incomplete octet around the central carbon atom, choice (C) has more than 8 valence electrons on the central carbon atom (which is not in the third period or greater), and choice (D) has an incomplete octet around the oxygen atom. Summarily, Choice (A) is correct because the structure of formaldehyde has the correct sum of valence electrons (12) and a complete octet around the carbon and oxygen atoms. Hydrogen is an exception to the octet rule because it follows the duet rule and only needs 2 valence electrons to be stable.

#	Ans.	Chapter	Explanation

37   **A**   **3**

The Law of Multiple Proportions states that when two elements combine to form more than one compound and the mass of one of the elements is constant in all versions of compounds, then the mass of the other element (with no constant mass) that combines with the element with the fixed mass will always be a small-whole-number ratio. C_2H_6 and C_2H_4 illustrate the law of multiple proportions and the calculation is shown below:

C_2H_6	C_2H_4
24 g of C and 6 g of H	24 g of C and 4 g of H
24/6 carbon/hydrogen	24/4 carbon/hydrogen
4:1	6:1

Thus, C_2H_6 and C_2H_4 illustrate the law of multiple proportions because the same elements (carbon and hydrogen) can combine in different ratios of mass. Specifically, C_2H_6 has a 4:1 ratio of mass while C_2H_4 has a 6:1 ratio of mass.

38   **C**   **11**

Oxidation numbers, also known as oxidation states, are positive and negative integers that are assigned to atoms and used to indicate if a specific atom has been reduced (gained electrons) or oxidized (lost electrons) in a redox reaction. To find the oxidation number of nitrogen in hydrogen nitrite (HNO_2), the following oxidation rules are used: (1) the sum of the oxidation numbers of all the atoms in a neutral compound is zero (2) the oxidation number of oxygen in most compounds is -2 and (3) the oxidation number of hydrogen is assigned +1 when combined with a non-metal and -1 when combined with a metal. So, the oxidation states of hydrogen and oxygen are first assigned in HNO_2: H $= +1 \times$ (1 atom) $= 1$. O $= -2 \times$ (2 atoms) $= -4$. Lastly, since the sum of all the oxidation numbers in the neutral compound HNO_2 is 0, solve for x to find the oxidation state of nitrogen; $0 = +1 + -4 + x$. Therefore, the oxidation number of nitrogen (x) in HNO_2 is 3+.

39   **A**   **11**

The balanced redox (reduction-oxidation) reaction is $Fe(s) + O_2(g) \rightarrow Fe_2O_3(g)$. This type of chemical reaction involves the transfer of electrons, which causes the oxidation number of elements to change; the oxidized substance loses electrons and increases in oxidation number, while the reduced substance gains electrons and decreases in oxidation number. Iron has an oxidation number of 0 in $Fe(s)$ and +3 in $Fe_2O_3(g)$, while oxygen has an oxidation number of 0 in $O_2(g)$ and -2 in $Fe_2O_3(g)$. Thus, $Fe(s)$ is oxidized and $O_2(g)$ is reduced.

40   **E**   **13**

The best method for separating and recovering non volatile mixtures and monitoring chemical reactions is thin-layer chromatography. TLC is a separation method that separates the components of a mixture based on the difference in degree to which compounds are absorbed onto the plates surface. This method allows students to identify the identity of compounds, the number of components in a mixture, and the purity of compounds.

41   **C**   **3**

The balanced equation of the exothermic chemical reaction is:

$$C_9H_2O(l) + 14\,O_2(g) \rightarrow 9\,CO_2(g) + 10\,H_2O(l)$$

Statement (I) is correct according to Avogadro's Principle; if one mole of any gas at STP has a molar volume of 22.4 L, then the number of moles of any gas at STP is directly proportional to the molar volume. Thus, 14 moles of O2 (g) will have a greater molar volume compared to 9 moles of $O_2(g)$. Statement (II) is eliminated based on the balanced equation; the ratio of moles of $C_9H_2O(l)$ consumed to moles of H2O (l) produced is 1:10, so 2 mol of $C_9H_2O(l)$ consumed would produce 20×18 g of $H_2O(l)$. Lastly, according to the balanced equation, statement (III) is correct because the ratio of moles of $O_2(g)$ produced to moles of $C_9H_2O(l)$ consumed is 9:1. Thus, the moles of carbon dioxide produced is 9 times greater than the moles of $C_9H_2O(l)$ consumed. Summarily, statement (I) and (III) are correct.

#	Ans.	Chapter	Explanation

42 A 9

Based on Hess's Law of Heat Summation, the two equations listed below are algebraically manipulated to yield the net reaction $2\,C(s) + O_2(g) \rightarrow 2\,CO(g)$ and to find its change in enthalpy (ΔH).

$$\text{Equation (1) } 2\,C(s) + 2\,O_2(g) \rightarrow 2\,CO_2(g) \quad \Delta H = -786 \text{ kJ}$$
$$\text{Equation (2) } 2\,CO(g) + O_2(g) \rightarrow 2\,CO_2(g) \quad \Delta H = -566\text{kJ}$$

So, to form carbon monoxide as a product in the net reaction, the second equation is reversed, which also changes the sign of the enthalpy of formation for equation (2). Lastly, the ΔH of equation one and two must be summed in order to find the change in enthalpy for the net reaction: $2\,C(s) + O_2(g) \rightarrow 2\,CO(g)$. Thus, ΔH is 220 kJ because that is the sum of -786 kJ and 566 kJ.

43 D 8

Molarity, also referred to as molar concentration, is measured in moles of solute per liters of solution. The formula $NaNO_3$ displays a 1:1 ratio of sodium ions to nitrate ions. Thus, if the molar concentration of Na+ ions in a 1L saturated water solution of sodium nitrate is 1.20×10^{-2}, then the molar concentration of NO^{3-} ions is also 1.20×10^{-2} M. Lastly, the solubility constant for sodium nitrate is calculated as:

$$K_{sp} = [Na^+][NO_3^-] = (1.20 \times 10^{-2})(1.20 \times 10^{-2}) = 1.44 \times 10^{-4}$$

44 E 3

The balanced equation for the chemical reaction in the question stem is $4\,Fe(s) + 3\,O_2(g) \rightarrow 2\,Fe_2O_3(s)$. The chemical reaction expresses that 4 mol of $Fe(s)$ are used for every 2 mol of $Fe_2O_3(s)$ formed, which displays a 2:1 ratio of iron oxidized to iron (III) oxide formed. Thus, 8 mol of $Fe(s)$ will be oxidized to form 4 moles of $Fe_2O_3(s)$. Next, the gram formula mass of Fe (55.85 g/mol) is used to solve for grams of iron oxidized if 4 moles of $Fe_2O_3(s)$ formed. Summarily, the grams of iron is about 446 grams of Fe = (4 moles of $Fe_2O_3(s)$) $\times$ (4 mol of Fe / 2 mol of $Fe_2O_3(s)$) $\times$ (56 grams of Fe / 1 mol of Fe).

45 E 6

Boiling point is one of the four main colligative properties of solutions, which means that it depends on the concentration of solute particles and not the identity/nature of the solute particles. When the concentration of particles in a solution increases, then the boiling point of the solvent elevates. The following equation is used to calculate the boiling point increase when each substance is dissolved in water : $\Delta T_b = imK_b$. Since the molality (2 moles/1kg) and K_b are the same for each substance, the only difference is the type of substance added to the solvent. The substance with the higher van 't Hoff factor (i) has the greater resulting boiling point increase. The degree of ionization for the ionic substance NaCl is 2, so the substance added needs to have a lower degree of ionization. C_3H_7OH is correct because it is an nonelectrolyte, which means the degree of ionization is 1. The other substances are eliminated because of their degree of ionization was higher than 2 ($MgCl_2 = 3$, $CaCl_2 = 3$, $Al(NO_3)_3 = 4$, $H_2SO_4 = 3$).

46 D 3

The balanced half-reaction equation for copper in the electrolysis of copper (II) sulfate reaction is $Cu^{+2} + 2e^- \rightarrow Cu(s)$. If $2 \times 6.02 \times 10^{23}$ molecules of electron are utilized during electrolysis, then the following steps must be followed to find the amount of grams of copper (II) deposited on the electrode surface: 1) Avogadro's number is used to convert molecules of electrons to moles of electrons, 2) balanced equation is used to convert moles of electrons to moles of copper metal and 3) the GFM is used to convert moles of $Cu(s)$ to grams of $Cu(s)$. So, $(2 \times 6.02 \times 10^{23}$ molecules of electrons) $\times$ (1 mole of electron / 6.02×10^{23} molecules of electrons)x (1 mol of $Cu(s)$ / 2 moles of electrons) is 1 mol of $Cu(s)$. Thus, 64 grams of $Cu(s)$ are produced from the electrolysis because 1 mol of $Cu(s)$ is multiplied by the molar mass, which is 63.55 g of Cu per mole.

47 D 11

The balanced equation for the first reaction is $Fe(s) + HNO_3(aq) \rightarrow N_2O(g)$ and the balanced equation for the second reaction is $Fe(s) + HNO_3(aq) \rightarrow$ no reaction. Although both reactions had the same reactants, the molarity of the reactant HNO3 differed, which could potentially explain the different results. The $HNO_3(aq)$ was dilute in the first equation, but highly concentrated in the second equation. So, using just these observations, Choice (D) is the best answer choice.

#	Ans.	Chapter	Explanation
48	E	3,12	The balanced combustion reaction is $2 H_2(g) + O_2(g) \rightarrow 2 H_2O(l)$. To convert from grams of H_2 used to grams of H_2O produced, the following steps must be followed:

1. the GFM is used to convert grams of $H_2(g)$ to moles of $H_2(g)$

2. balanced equation is used to convert moles of H_2 to moles of H_2O

3. the GFM of H_2O is used to convert moles of $H_2O(l)$ to grams of $H_2O(l)$

So, (20 grams H_2) × (1 mol of H_2 / 2 grams of H_2) × (2 mole of H_2O / 2 moles of H_2) × (18 grams of H_2O / 1 mole of H_2O) calculates the production of 180 grams of H_2O.

#	Ans.	Chapter	Explanation
49	A	3	The oxidation number of cesium (group I element) is +1 and the oxidation number of fluorine (group 17 element) is -1. So, the formula for cesium fluoride is CsF.
50	C	6	The following dissociation equation occurs when the ionic compound $Mg(NO_3)_2$ dissolves in water: $Mg(NO_3)_2(s) + H_2O(l) \rightleftarrows Mg^+(aq) + 2 NO_3^-(aq)$. So, the chemical reaction of 1 mole of $Mg(NO_3)_2$ in water produces 1 mol of $Mg^+(aq)$ and 2 moles of NO_3^-. The solubility constant for magnesium nitrate is calculated as $K_{sp} = [Mg^{2+}][2NO_3^-]^2 = (x)(2x)2$. Thus, the species with the great concentration in the solution is $NO_3^-(aq)$.
51	E	11	A redox (reduction-oxidation) reaction involves the transfer of electrons, which causes the oxidation number of elements to change; the oxidized substance loses electrons and increases in oxidation number, while the reduced substance gains electrons and decreases in oxidation number. In these reactions, the chemical substance being oxidized is also referred to as the reducing agent because the electrons it "loses" is simultaneously being "donated" to another chemical substance, thus acting as an electron donor. So, the chemical substance being reduced is also referred to as the oxidizing agent because it is acting as the electron acceptor for the oxidized substance.
52	D	3	The empirical formula of a substance provides the simplest whole-number ratio of atoms in the compound, while the molecular formula provides the actual number of atoms in the compound. Given the molecular mass of a substance and its empirical formula, the following steps must be followed to calculate the molecular formula: 1)find the gram formula mass of the given empirical formula, 2) divide the molecular mass of the molecular formula by the gram formula mass of the empirical formula, and 3) multiply the empirical formula by the answer from step 2. Subsequently, the gram formula mass of CH is 13 g/mol, so 52 grams per mol/13 grams per mol = 4. Thus, the molecular formula of the substance is C_4H_4 because (CH × 4).
53	C	6	Molarity is measured in moles of solute per liters of solution. According to the question stem, adding a certain amount of milliliters of water will convert $4 M$ HCl solution to $2 M$ HCl solution. To find the amount of milliliters of H_2O that will dilute 500 mL of the $4 M$ HCl solution to the molar concentration of 2, first find the moles of HCl in $4 M$ HCl solution because the amount of moles of HCl remain the same in both solutions (only difference is addition of water). Thus, the calculation 500 mL × (4 mol HCl / 1000 mL of solution) finds 2 moles of HCl in the 500 mL of a $4 M$ HCl solution. Now, to dilute the solution to $2 M$ HCl, there must be 2 moles of HCl per 1 L of solution. Given the 2 moles of HCl, we can assume that 500 mL of H_2O is added to the existing solution of 500 mL to form 1,000 mL of solution (1 L of solution). Thus, 500 mL of H_2O is added to 500 mL of $4 M$ HCl to make 2 moles of HCl / 1 L of solution.
54	E	3	The balanced equation for the decomposition reaction is $2KClO_3 \rightarrow 3O_2 + 2KCl$. To convert grams of potassium chlorate to liters of oxygen gas at STP, the following steps must be followed:

1. the molar mass is used to convert from grams of $KClO_3$ to moles of $KClO_3$

2. balance equation is used to convert from moles of $KClO_3$ to moles of O_2

3. Avogadro's principle, which states that one mole of any gas at STP has a volume of 22.4 L, is used to convert moles of O_2 to liters of O_2

Thus,

(246 g $KClO_3$) × (1 mol $KClO_3$ / 123 g $KClO_3$) is 2 moles of $KClO_3$ and (2 moles of $KClO_3$) × (3 mol O_2 / 2 mol $KClO_3$) × (22.4 L of O_2 / 1 mol O_2) is 67.2 L of O_2 gas.

#	Ans.	Chapter	Explanation
55	E	13	The chemical equation $N_2(g) + 3 H_2(g) \rightarrow 2 NH_3(g)$ is also referred to as the Haber-Bosch process. This process is a common industrial procedure for the production of ammonia today.
56	A	8	K_{eq}, also referred to as the equilibrium constant, is calculated by dividing the total concentration product of all products of a balanced chemical reaction by the total concentration product of all reactants of a balanced chemical reaction. Additionally, the coefficients of the reactants and products in the balanced chemical reaction are equivalent to the power the respective reactants and products are raised to when calculating the K_{eq}. Pure solids and pure liquids are excluded in equilibrium constant. Thus, since the balanced equation of the Haber-Bosch process is $N_2(g) + 3 H_2(g) \rightleftarrows 2 NH_3(g)$, the K_{eq} is $[NH_3]^2 / [N_2][H_2]^3$
57	A	1	Isotopes of an element have the same number of protons (atomic number), but a different number of neutrons.
58	A	12	Carboxylic acid is an organic compound that contains a carboxyl group. The general formula is R-COOH. The carboxyl group consists of a carbonyl group (O=C) and a hydroxyl group (R-OH). Thus, choice A is the only structure that fulfills these requirements.
59	C	10	The balanced equation of the chemical reaction is $HF(g) + H_2O(l) \rightleftarrows H_3O^+(aq) + F^-(aq)$. Although hydrogen fluoride is not one of the 6 strong acids, HF is a weak acid because it dissociates H+ ions in water. Strong acids react completely with bases and form weak conjugate bases, while weak acids react partially or have reversible dissociation with bases and form stronger conjugate bases. Thus, strong acids ionize completely in water and form a very acidic solution (pH of ≈ 2) because the conjugate base remains inert in solution. Weak acids (HF) only ionize partially in water, but the concentration of H^+ ions is large enough to form an acidic solution (pH < 7). Thus, bubbling gaseous HF in distilled water results in a solution with a pH less than 7. Choice (A) is eliminated because no solid forms, and Choice (B) is eliminated because HF is not a base. Choice (D) and (E) are eliminated because the color change of the acid-base indicators (which are used to test pH of solution) represented a basic solution instead of a acidic solution. Litmus paper turns blue in basic solutions and pink in acidic solutions, while phenolphthalein turns pink in basic solutions and colorless in acidic solutions.
60	D	13	Choice (A) is eliminated because burets are used to precisely add small measured volumes of liquid into a solution, NOT extract tiny amounts of liquid. Thus, this piece of equipment is often used in titrations. Choice (B) is eliminated because although graduated cylinders are used to precisely add volume, this piece of equipment is less accurate than burettes and is used to add large volumes. Choice (C) is eliminated because condensers are used to help separate a pure liquid from a mixture of liquids, not to add/extract small liquids. This equipment is used during distillation and involves evaporation and condensation. Choice (E) is eliminated because stopcocks have an entirely different function; stopcocks are attached to specific pieces of laboratory equipment and act as valves to regulate flow of liquid or gas. Thus, although burette and pipettes both are used to add very tiny amounts of liquid, Choice (D) is the correct because it is also used to extract tiny amounts of liquid.
61	E	9	Since the nitrate anion is always soluble, the only way for a precipitate to form after adding a few drops of $Pb(NO_3)_2$ to a water solution (which already contained certain ions) is if the Pb^{2+} cation from lead nitrate combined with an anion to form an insoluble compound (precipitate). Thus, SO_4^{2-} must be an anion in the water solution because $PbSO_4$ is a precipitate. Choice (A) and (B) are eliminated because NH_4^+ and Mg^{2+} are both cations and nitrate is always soluble, while choice (C) and (D) are eliminated because HCO_3^- and ClO_3^- are both soluble anions.

#	Ans.	Chapter	Explanation
62	B	9	The chemical equation $2\,C_2H_6(g) + 7\,O_2(g) \rightarrow 4\,CO_2(g) + 6\,H_2O(l)$ is only classified as a combustion reaction. (I) is eliminated because synthesis, also referred to as combination, is a reaction that combines multiple reactants to produce one product. Thus, since the given chemical equation has 2 products, synthesis is eliminated. (II) is also eliminated because a single-replacement reaction, also referred to as a single displacement reaction, is when one element displaces another element in a compound. The chemical equation for a single-replacement reaction is $A + BC \rightarrow B + AC$; the reactants consist of one element and one compound, while the products consist of a different element and a different compound. Therefore, the given chemical reaction $2\,C_2H_6(g) + 7\,O_2(g) \rightarrow 4\,CO_2(g) + 6\,H_2O(l)$ is not a single-replacement reaction because the both reactants are compounds. (III) is correct because combustion, also referred to as "burning" is an exothermic reaction where a hydrocarbon reacts with oxygen and produces carbon dioxide, water, and a lot of energy in the form of light and heat. Thus, the reaction can only be classified as a combustion reaction.
63	B	4	To determine the scenarios that cause the volume of gas to increase, the Gas Laws must be analyzed. Specifically, Boyle's law states the inverse relationship between pressure and volume at a constant temperature and Charles's Law states the direct relationship between volume and temperature at a constant pressure. (I) is eliminated because of Boyle's Law; if you increase the pressure of a gas ONLY at a constant temperature, the volume of a gas decreases. (II) is correct because of both laws cited above; increasing the temperature and decreasing the pressure would both cause the volume to increase. Lastly, (III) is eliminated because the effect on the volume of gas is ambiguous.
64	D	6	Freezing point is one of the four main colligative properties of solutions, which means that it depends on the concentration of solute particles and not the identity/nature of the solute particles. When the concentration of particles in a solution increases, then the freezing point of the solvent decreases. The freezing point depression expression is $\Delta T_f = -imK_f$. The degree of ionization is 1 because propyl alcohol is a nonelectrolyte and the K_f constant for water is 1.86 °C kg/mol. Since 1000 grams of water is 1 kg of water, the molality (mol of solute/ kg of solvent) is 1 mol of propyl alcohol / 1 kg of water. Thus, the change in freezing point is -1.86 °C because $(-1)(1$ mol of propyl alcohol/ kg of water) $(1.86$ °C kg/mol)
65	E	2	The boiling point of a substance is closely related to the intermolecular force strength of a substance. The stronger the IMF, the more energy required to break bonds, and the higher the boiling point. Hydrogen bonding is the strongest intermolecular force and is responsible for the exceptionally high boiling point of water. The hydrogen bond is a special type of dipole-dipole attraction between a hydrogen atom and one of the following highly electronegative atoms: fluorine (F), oxygen (O), or nitrogen (N). One molecule will contain a partially positive charge on the hydrogen, while the other molecule contains a partially negative charge on the fluorine, oxygen, or nitrogen.
66	C	3	Avogadro's Principle is used to find the number of moles the sample of gas contains and Avogadro's number is used to convert moles of gas to molecules of gas. According to Avogadro's Principle, one mole of any gas at STP has a molar volume of 22.4 L. Thus, the following calculation $11.2\,L \times (1\,mol\,/\,22.4\,L)$ finds that the sample of gas contains 0.5 moles of gas. Avogadro's number states that one mole of any substance is 6.02×10^{23} units, meaning that one mole contains 6.02×10^{23} molecules. As a result, the number of molecules the samples of gas contains is $0.5(6.02 \times 10^{23})$ molecules.
67	E	5	The following equation is used to measure the heat released or absorbed by an object as a result of a change in temperature: $q = mC\Delta T$. Based on the question stem, multiply $(20\,g)\,(1\,cal/gram$ °C) $(75°C - 25°C)$ to get 1000 calories.
68	E	3,6	The percent dissociation of the sulfurous acid is expressed as (the molar concentration of the hydronium ion / the original molar concentration of the H_2SO_3 acid) $\times$ 100. So, the percent dissociation of sulfurous acid is calculated using the following equation: $$[H^+]/[H_2SO_3] \times 100 = (1 \times 10^{-2}\,M\,/\,0.1\,M) \times 100 = 10\%$$

#	Ans.	Chapter	Explanation
69	B	3	Based on the question stem, the percent chlorine by mass is 70%. To find the atomic mass of Z in ZCl_2, the first step is to find the molar mass of Cl in ZCl_2; 2×35.45 is about 70. The mass percent of an element Cl within the given molecule is found by dividing the mass of element Cl by the total mass of the molecule and then multiplying that number by 100. So, 70% of Cl = (mass of chlorine / total mass of molecule) $\times$ 100. The molar mass of Cl in ZCl_2 is 70 g/mol (2×35.45). To find the total mass of the molecule, we solve for x (total mass of molecule): $0.70 = (70 \text{ g/mol}) / x$. The total mass of molecule ZCl_2 is 100 g/mol, which means that the atomic mass of Z is 30 amu (100 g/mol $-$ 70 g/mol).
70	C	1	Positron emission is a common decay type in nuclear chemistry. A positron ($_{+1}^{0}e$ or $_{+1}^{0}\beta$) is a positively charged beta particle. In this type of nuclear reaction, the positron as a product; $A \rightarrow B + {}_{+1}^{0}e$. The mass of A and B remain the same, but the atomic number of B goes down by 1.

#	Ans.	Chapter	Explanation
1	B	1	Ionization energy is the amount of energy per mole required to remove an electron from the valence shell of an atom. When you remove a valence electron from an atom, the atomic radius will decrease. The second ionization potential is the amount of energy needed to remove the second electron from a neutral atom or the amount of energy needed to remove an electron from an atom with a charge of +1.
2	E	1	Standard heat of formation is the change in enthalpy (ΔH_f) when one mole of a substance is formed from its pure constituent elements at STP. For example, the balanced equation for the chemical equation of the standard heat of formation, ΔH_f, per mole of liquid water is $$H_2(g) + \tfrac{1}{2} O_2(g) \rightarrow H_2O(l)$$ A positive ΔH indicates an endothermic reaction, while a negative ΔH indicates an exothermic reaction.
3	C	1	Electronegativity is the tendency of an atom to attract a bonding pair of electrons to itself or "how badly an atom wants to add an electron." As one of the major trends on the periodic table, electronegativity increases while moving from the left to right (across a period) and from bottom to top (up a group) on the periodic table.
4	A	1	Ionization energy is the amount of energy per mole required to remove an electron from the valence shell of an atom. The first ionization potential is the amount of energy needed to remove an electron from a neutral atom, NOT the energy needed to remove an electron from an atom with a charge of +1 (second ionization energy).
5	C	1	The Pauling scale, which was created by Linus Pauling, is an numerical scale of electronegativities based on bond-energy calculation.
6	B	3	The balanced equation for the given reaction is as follows: $$2\,KI(aq) + 1\,Pb(NO_3)_2(aq) \rightarrow 2\,KNO_3(aq) + PbI_2(s)$$ Thus, the coefficient of $PbI_2(s)$ in the balanced equation is 1.
7	D	3	The nitrate containing reactant is $Pb(NO_3)_2(aq)$ in following balanced equation: $$2\,KI(aq) + 1\,Pb(NO_3)_2(aq) \rightarrow 2\,KNO_3(aq) + PbI_2(s)$$ The degree of ionization for lead (II) nitrate is 3 because 1 mole of $Pb(NO_3)_2(aq)$ in water dissociates into 1 mol of $Pb^{2+}(aq)$ and 2 moles of $NO_3^-(aq)$.
8	C	11	The precipitate in the balanced equation $2\,KI(aq) + 1\,Pb(NO_3)_2(aq) \rightarrow 2\,KNO_3(aq) + PbI_2(s)$ is lead (II) iodide, since it is an insoluble chemical compound. The oxidation number of the metal in $PbI_2(s)$ is +2, based on the following oxidation rules: (1) the sum of the oxidation numbers of all the atoms in a neutral compound is zero and (2) the oxidation number of halogens in most compounds is -1, unless combined with oxygen or fluorine. So, since the iodine atom (a halogen) is assigned a -1 oxidation number and the sum of the oxidation numbers of all the atoms in the neutral precipitate $PbI_2(s)$ is 0, solve for x in the following equation to find the oxidation state of the metal lead: $0 = x + -1(2\text{ atoms})$. Therefore, the oxidation number of lead (x) in the precipitate $PbI_2(s)$ is +2.
9	A	3	A oxidation-reduction reaction (redox reaction) is a chemical reaction that involves the transfer of electrons, which causes the oxidation number of elements to change. Thus, the quantity of electrons transferred from potassium to iodine in $KI(aq)$ is 0 because the oxidation number for potassium and iodide remain the same on both sides of the reaction. Specifically, whether the element is a reactant or product, the oxidation states remain constant for potassium and iodide; K is +1 and I is -1.

#	Ans.	Chapter	Explanation
10	B	10	To calculate the pH of a solution with OH^- ions, the following two equations are used: $pOH = -\log[OH^-]$ and $pH + pOH = 14$. Molarity (M), also known as molar concentration, is measured in moles of solute per liters of solution. Since sodium hydroxide (strong base) completely dissociates into 1 mol of $Na^+(aq)$ and 1 mol of $OH^-(aq)$, the molar concentration of the ion OH^- is 1×10^{-5} M. Thus, the $pOH = -\log[1 \times 10^{-5}\ M] = 5$, which means the pH of the solution is $= 14 - 5 = 9$.
11	E	10	Since hydrochloric acid (strong acid) completely dissociates into 1 mol of $H^+(aq)$ and 1 mol of $Cl^-(aq)$, the molar concentration of the ion H^+ is 1×10^{-3} M. 2.0 L can be ignored because it does not have an affect on the Molarity value. Lastly, the pH of 2.0 L of 1×10^{-3} HCl is 3 because pH is calculated as $-\log[H^+]$, so $-\log[1 \times 10^{-3}] = 3$.
12	E	10	The following two equations are used to calculate the pH of a solution with OH^- ions: $pOH = -\log[OH^-]$ and $pH + pOH = 14$. So, given the molar concentration of the ion OH^- is 1.0×10^{-11}, the $pOH = -\log[1.0 \times 10^{-11}] = 11$. Thus, the pH must be 3 because $pH + pOH = 14$.
13	D	10	The solid NaCl does not impact the pH of the solution because Cl^- is the conjugate base of a strong acid (HCl) and Na^+ is the conjugate acid of a strong base (NaOH). Thus, the conjugate base and the conjugate acid are extremely weak and remain unreactive in a solution. Thus, the pH is 7 because the solvent is water.
14	C	10	The pH of a sample of normal human blood is around 7.4.
15	D	1	Nuclear fusion is the reaction where two lighter nuclei combine to produce a heavier nucleus. This indicates the release of large amounts of energy; fusion reactions commonly take place in the sun and stars.
16	E	1	The balanced equation is a natural transmutation, which is a nuclear reaction that spontaneously occurs due to an unstable neutron-to-proton ratio. In other words, a single nucleus undergoes decay without being bombarded or struck by other particles. Thus, it is a natural transmutation because there is one reactant that spontaneously decays to form a new element and neutron.
17	A	1	Oxidation takes place when the reactant loses electrons and increases oxidation number. V^{2+} has an oxidation number of +2 and V^{3+} has an oxidation number of +3, which means vanadium has increased in oxidation state. The chemical equation $V^{2+} \rightarrow V^{3+} + e^{-1}$ also shows an electron as a product, indicating the loss of electrons.
18	B	11	Reduction takes place when the reactant gains electrons and decreases oxidation number. I_2 has an oxidation number of 0 and I^{-1} has an oxidation number of -1, which means iodine has decreased in oxidation state. Also, the chemical equation $I_2 + 2e^- \rightarrow 2I^-$ also shows electrons as a reactant, indicating the gain of electrons.
19	C	1	Nuclear fission is the reaction where a heavier nucleus is split to produce a lighter nuclei. Additionally, it is one out of the two nuclear reactions (the other reaction being nuclear fusion) where the total mass of the products is less than the total nuclear mass of the reactants. This indicates the release of large amounts of energy; fission reactions commonly take place nuclear power plants.
20	E	6	Dissolution is when a the chemical solute dissolves in a solvent and forms a solution.
21	D	6	Deliquescence is the process by which a substance absorbs moisture from the atmosphere until it dissolves in the absorbed water and forms a solution.
22	B	6	Deionization is the removal of ions.
23	A	10, 13	An amphoteric compound has the ability to act as both an acid and a base. Common amphoteric molecules are amino acids, water, metal oxides and hydroxides.
24	C	13	$O_3(g)$, also referred to as ozone, is an inorganic molecule (not made up of carbon and hydrogen atoms) that makes up the protective layer in the stratosphere. The three oxygen atoms bonded together form the solar radiation protection layer and absorbs ultraviolet (UV) rays. The chemical reaction for the formation of ozone is $O(g) + O_2(g) \rightarrow O_3(g)$.

#	Ans.	Chapter	Explanation
25	E	13	Acid rain is formed when sulfur dioxide, $SO_2(g)$, and nitrogen oxides react with rainwater. The chemical equations producing acid rain are $2\,SO_2(g) + O_2(g) \rightarrow 2\,SO_3(g)$ and $SO_3(g) + H_2O(l) \rightarrow H_2SO_4(aq)$.
101	T, F	9	The thermodynamic state function, G, is also referred to as Gibbs free energy. Gibbs free energy equation is used to predict the spontaneity of a reaction. Gibbs equation is $\Delta G = \Delta H - T\Delta S$; a negative ΔG value represents a spontaneous reaction and a positive ΔG value represents a nonspontaneous reaction. The calculation requires values for entropy, enthalpy, and temperature. Gibbs energy is not equal to solely the change in entropy (ΔS) because it also depends on the change in enthalpy (ΔH) and the temperature in Kelvins.
102	T, T	10	The balanced equation of the neutralization reaction is as follows $$NH_3(aq) + H_2O(l) \rightarrow NH^+(aq) + OH^-(aq)$$ Since ammonia (weak base) accepts protons, $NH_3(aq)$ is used to neutralize $H_2O(l)$ (acid) and form $NH^+(aq)$ and $OH^-(aq)$.
103	T, T	8	According to Le Châtelier's principle, a chemical reaction will proceed to counteract any disturbance on the system in equilibrium. Thus, in the equilibrium reaction $ClNO_2(g) + NO(g) \rightleftarrows NO_2(g) + ClNO(g)$, when additional reactant is added to a system in equilibrium, the equilibrium will shift right and restore the relative concentrations by producing more products and consuming more reactants. So, adding more of reactant $ClNO_2$ will increase the concentration of product $ClNO$ and decrease the concentration of the other reactant NO. Additionally, considering kinematics, the main factors that affect the reaction rate include, but are not limited to: bond type, surface area, concentration, temperature, and presence of a catalyst. These factors impact the rate of the chemical reaction by affecting the rate of molecular collisions and/or the energy of the collisions. Specifically, the concentration of reactants is directly proportional to the reaction rate because the more molecules of $ClNO_2(g)$, the higher the likelihood of effective collisions between reactant $ClNO_2(g)$ and reactant $NO(g)$.
104	F, T	13	Avogadro's number states that one mole of any substance is 6.02×10^{23} units, meaning that one mole of N_2 and one mole of O_2 are both 6.02×10^{23} molecules. Thus, one mole of N_2 contains the same amount of molecules as one mole of O_2. In addition, the molecular mass, also referred to as gram formula mass, is the sum of the atomic weights of all of the atoms in one mole of a molecule. So, the molecular mass of N_2 is 28 (2 atom of N $\times$ 14 g of N / 1 mol of N) and the molecular mass of O_2 is 32 (2 atoms of O $\times$ 16 g of O / 1 mol of O). Thus, N_2 molecular mass is greater than O_2.
105	F, F	5	Metallic silver is a metallic solid, which indicates that the chemical substance is an electrical conductor. The properties of a metallic compounds include, but are not limited to: luster, malleable, ductile, conduct heat and electricity, large atomic radii, high density, high melting point, solid at room temp (besides Mg). In addition, metallic solids have metals atoms linked together by metallic bonds, not ionic bonds. The metal atoms have a very free relationship with their valence bonds, which allows for a sea of delocalized electrons; since the outermost electrons are so loosely bound to the atom, the electrons in metals can be referred to as "free electrons." Subsequently, the mobility of the outermost electrons is what makes metallic solids good at conducting electricity.
106	T, T	4	The ideal gas law is used to describe the behavior of hypothetical ideal gases and is expressed as $PV = nRT$; thus, the law predicts how moles of gas would behave under certain changes in pressure, volume, and temperature. The Kinetic Molecular Theory of Gases is used to explain the gas laws and to help us understand the behavior of ideal gases. The following assumptions of the kinetic molecular theory are: (1) ideal gases have no volume compared to the volume of their container (2) ideal gases exhibit no intermolecular attractions or repulsions (3) gas particles move in a random straight line motion (4) collisions of ideal gas particles are elastic, which indicates no energy is lost, and (5) the average kinetic energy of a gas particles is proportional to the absolute temperature of the gases, which indicates all gases at a given temperature have the same average kinetic energy. Based on the fourth and fifth assumption cited above, ideal gas particles experience elastic collisions and the absolute temperature of the system depends on the average kinetic energy of the gas particles.

#	Ans.	Chapter	Explanation
107	T, T	9	The chemical reaction $AgNO_3(aq)$ + $NaCl(aq)$ → $AgCl(s)$ + $NaNO_3(aq)$ is a double replacement precipitation reaction, which means it will run to completion. When $AgNO_3$ and $NaCl$ are added to a water solvent, the ionic compounds dissociate into cations and anions. Specifically, in a dilute solution, $AgNO_3$ dissociates into 1 mol of $Ag^+(aq)$ and 1 mol of $NO_3^-(aq)$ while $NaCl$ dissociates into 1 mol of $Na^+(aq)$ and 1 mol of $Cl^-(aq)$. In the water solution, the silver cation Ag^+ and chlorine anion Cl^- will combine to form the insoluble compound/precipitate of solid silver chloride.
108	T, T	10	The equation $pOH = -\log[OH^-]$ is used to calculate the pOH of a 5×10^{-4} M solution of $Ca(OH)_2$. Molarity, also known as molar concentration, is measured as moles of solute per liters of solution. Since $Ca(OH)_2$ (strong base) completely dissociates into 1 mol of $Ca^{2+}(aq)$ and 2 moles of $OH^-(aq)$, the molar concentration of the ion OH- is $2(5 \times 10^{-4}$ $M) = 10 \times 10^{-4}$ M or 1×10^{-3} M. Thus, the $pOH = -\log[1 \times 10^{-3}$ $M]$ is 3.
109	F, F	4	The Combined Gas Law states the relationship between pressure, volume, and temperature and is expressed as $P_1V_1/T_1 = P_2V_2/T_2$. Based on the initial conditions of the gas in the question (273 K, 800 mmHg), the following calculation is used to evaluate how the volume of the gas changes after decreasing the pressure to STP (273K and 760 mmHg): $$P_1V_1/T_1 = P_2V_2/T_2. \ (P_1/P_2)(T_2/T_1) = (V_2/V_1)$$ $$(800 \text{ mmHg} / 760 \text{ mmHg}) \ (273 \text{ K} / 273 \text{ K}) = V_2/V_1$$ $$1.05 = V_2/V_1$$ The ratio of V_2:V_1 is greater than 1, which indicates that V_2 is larger than V_1. Thus, the volume of a gas increases when the pressure decreased.
110	T, T, CE	2	London dispersion forces are the weakest type of intermolecular forces and can be found in both polar and nonpolar molecules. The bond dissociation energy (BDE) is the amount of energy (change of standard enthalpy) required to break a chemical covalent bond. So, since stronger intermolecular forces are more difficult to break than weaker intermolecular forces, the strength of an intermolecular force is directly proportional to its dissociation energy. Thus, the intermolecular forces with the the lowest dissociation energy are the London dispersion forces.
111	T, T	5	The balanced equation of the chemical reaction is as follows: $N_2(g)$ + 3 $H_2(g)$ ⇌ 2 $NH_3(g)$ To determine the change in entropy of the chemical reaction, the ratio of moles of gaseous reactants to moles of gaseous products is significant. Entropy is the degree of disorder in a system and is used to measure randomness. Solids are rigid and have a fixed position, so this phase has the lowest amount of entropy. The gas phase has the highest amount of entropy because gases particles move around freely, which creates disorder. So, there is a decrease in entropy in the given chemical reaction because the ratio of moles of gaseous reactants to moles of gaseous products is 4:2, which indicates a decrease in disorder. In addition, gases are more disordered than liquids because they have weaker intermolecular forces; thus, the strength of the intermolecular force is inversely proportional to entropy.
112	F, T	6	Freezing point is one of the four main colligative properties of solution, which means that it depends on the concentration of solute particles and not the identity/nature of the solute particles. When the concentration of particles in a solution increases, the freezing point of the solvent decreases. The following equation is used to calculate the change in freezing point of liquid water when NaCl is added: $\Delta T_f = imK_f$. The van't Hoff factor (i) represents the number of particles formed from a compound in a solution. Thus, since the degree of ionization for the ionic substance NaCl is 2, the freezing point of a dilute solution of sodium chloride is lower than the freezing point of pure water. In addition, at room temperature, pure sugar is a solid and pure water is a liquid, indicating that the boiling point of pure sugar is higher than the boiling point of water.

#	Ans.	Chapter	Explanation
113	F, T	6	Molarity, also referred to as molar concentration, is measured as moles of solute per liters of solution. The balanced dissociation reaction is $MgF_2 \rightarrow Mg^+(aq) + 2\,F^-(aq)$. To determine whether or not 31 grams of MgF_2 would prepare 1 M solution of fluoride ions, the following steps must be followed: 1. use molar mass to convert from grams of MgF_2 to moles of MgF_2 2. use the balanced equation to convert moles of MgF_2 to moles of F^- ions 3. divide moles of F^- ions by the L of solution So, the following calculation is used: $(31\text{ g }MgF_2) \times (1\text{ mol }MgF_2 / 62\text{ g }MgF_2) \times (2\text{ mol }F^- / 1\text{ mol }MgF_2) = 62\text{ mol }F^- / 62$ L of solution. Thus, the molar concentration of the solution of fluoride ions is 1 M, not 2 M.
114	T, F	8	A chemical equilibrium is often represented as $A + B \rightleftarrows C + D$. The reversible reaction reaches equilibrium when the rate of the forward reaction equals the rate of the reverse reaction. Thus, if the rate to form products equals the rate to form reactants, the concentration of the reactants and products should not change over time.
115	T, T	13	When fossil fuels are burned during combustion, products are formed and often released into the atmosphere. Specifically, two compounds that are released into the atmosphere are sulfur dioxide and nitrogen oxide. Acid rain is formed when sulfur dioxide (SO_2) and nitrogen oxides react with rainwater in the atmosphere. The chemical equations producing acid rain are $2\,SO_2(g) + O_2(g) \rightarrow 2\,SO_3(g)$ and $SO_3(g) + H_2O(l) \rightarrow H_2SO_4(aq)$. Thus, combustion of organic compounds can lead to the production of acid rain. In addition, the molecule sulfur trioxide has multiple resonance forms, which enhances the compounds stability due to resonance.
26	C	3	Gram formula mass, also referred to as molecular mass, is the sum of the atomic weights of all of the atoms in one mole of a molecule. Gram formula mass is measured in grams per mol. Thus, to solve for the molecular weight of $Mg(SO_4)$, the calculations are as follows: 1 atom of Mg $\times$ (24 g of Mg / mol) = 24 g/mol. 1 atom of S $\times$ (32 g of S/ mol) = 32 g/mol. 4 atoms of O $\times$ (16 g of O / mol) = 64 g/mol. Since 24 g/mol + 32 g/mol + 64 g/mol is 120 g/mol, the gram formula mass is $Mg(SO_4)$ is 120 g/mol.
27	B	2	The molecule 2-butyne consists of a triple bond, which indicates there are 2 pi bonds present. A sigma (σ) bond is formed between the bond axis of an s orbital and an s orbital or the bond axis of an s orbital and another orbital, which creates direct head-on overlap of atomic orbitals. A pi (π) bond is formed between two unhybridized p orbitals. The pi (π) bond is a weaker covalent bond than the sigma (σ) bond because the parallel orientation of the unhybridized p orbitals allows for less overlap of pi electrons. All types of bonds (single, double, triple) consist of a sigma bonds, but only certain bonds consist of a pi bonds; a single bond consists of one sigma bond and zero pi bonds, a double bond consists of one sigma bond and one pi bond, and a triple bond consists of one sigma bond and two pi bonds. Subsequently, based on the molecular structure shown in the question stem, the triple bond indicates that 2 π bonds are present.
28	D	2	An ionic solid, also referred to as a salt, is a network of ions being held together by ionic bonds. The ionic solid dissociates into ions when added to water because the ionic bonds break apart. Thus, the ionic solid NH_4NO_3 dissociates into the polyatomic cation NH_4^+ and the polyatomic anion NO_3^-.
29	A	4	Choice (A) is correct because mass of the O_2 in the sample is the only answer that is not correlated with temperature change. Choices (B) and (C) are eliminated based on the following assumption from the kinetic molecular theory: the average kinetic energy of gas particles is proportional to the absolute temperature of the gases. The kinetic energy equation $KE = \frac{1}{2}mv^2$ indicates a direct relationship between the average kinetic energy of a gas particle and the average velocity of a gas particle. So, an increase in temperature would increase the average kinetic energy of the gas, which increases the average velocity of the gas. Choice (D) is eliminated because of the relationship between average kinetic energy of a gas and vapor pressure. An increase in average kinetic energy of a sample indicates that the sample has more energy to escape into the gas phase. Thus, an increase in temperature increases the KE of the O_2 sample, which makes it more volatile and increases the vapor pressure. Choice (E) is eliminated based Charles's Law. The gas states the direct relationship between volume and temperature at a constant pressure. V/T = constant; $V_1/T_1 = V_2/T_2$. So, an increase in temperature would increase the volume.

#	Ans.	Chapter	Explanation
30	B	2	Based on its molecular structure, benzene is the only chemical substance that experiences resonance stability with both sigma and pi electrons. A sigma (σ) bond is formed between the bond axis of an s orbital and an s orbital or the bond axis of an s orbital and another orbital, which creates direct head-on overlap of atomic orbitals. A pi (π) bond is formed between two unhybridized p orbitals. The pi (π) bond is a weaker covalent bond than the sigma (σ) bond because the parallel orientation of the unhybridized p orbitals allows for less overlap of pi electrons. All types of bonds (single, double, triple) consist of a sigma bonds, but only certain bonds consist of a pi bonds; a single bond consists of one sigma bond and zero pi bonds, a double bond consists of one sigma bond and one pi bond, and a triple bond consists of one sigma bond and two pi bonds. Thus, in order to experience resonance stability with both sigma and pi electrons, the structure must have either a double bond or a triple bond. Choice (B) is correct because benzene is a hydrocarbon ring and is made up of three double bonds, while Choices (A), (C), (D) and (E) are eliminated because each structure consists of only single bonds.

| 31 | B | 3 | The balanced equation for the given reaction is as follows: $2Ag^+ + S^{2-} \rightarrow Ag_2S$. The coefficient of Ag^+ in the balanced equation is 2. |

| 32 | A | 3, 4 | The ideal gas law is PV = nRT or V = (nRT) / P. Given the question stem, the volume and temperature are equal for all five containers (2L, 273 K) and the R is a constant. So, the number of moles of gas is directly proportional to the amount of pressure in the container. Since each container has a 7 gram sample gas, divide 7 grams by the gram formula mass of each gas to calculate the amount of moles of gas. Thus, the lower the molecular mass of the gas, the greater amount of moles of gas in the container, and the higher the pressure. Subsequently, the container with a 7.0 g sample of $H_2(g)$ has the highest pressure. |

| 33 | E | 7 | The activation energy is the minimum amount of energy needed to undergo a chemical reaction. In other words, in order for a reaction to take place, a certain amount of energy is required. Thus, the larger the activation energy required, the longer it takes to complete the reaction. Catalysts speed up the rate of chemical reactions by lowering the activation energy needed for a reaction. These substances remain unaltered and are not consumed in reactions. Additionally, the amount of products produced or reactants consumed is not affected. Instead, catalysts only alter the kinetics of the chemical reaction. |

| 34 | D | 11 | The balanced equation of the reduction reaction is as follows: |

$$Cr_2O_7^{2-} + 14H^+ + 6e^- \rightarrow 2Cr^{3+} + 7H_2O$$

In a reduction reaction, the reduced substance gains electrons and decreases in oxidation number. Based on the balanced reaction, six electrons are reactants in the conversion of $Cr_2O_7^{2-}$ to Cr^{3+}, indicating the gain of electrons. So, to determine if this the oxidation number of Cr also decreases, the following oxidation rules must be followed:

1. the sum of the oxidation numbers of all the atoms in a polyatomic ion is equal to the charge on the ion

2. the oxidation number of a monatomic ion is equal to the charge of the ion

3. the oxidation number of oxygen in most compounds is usually -2

So, since the oxidation number of oxygen is usually -2 and the sum of the oxidation numbers of all the atoms in the polyatomic ion $Cr_2O_7^{2-}$ is -2, solve for x in the following equation to find the oxidation state of the chromium in $Cr_2O_7^{2-}$: $-2 = 2$ atoms of Cr (x) + 7 atoms of O (-2). Therefore, the oxidation number of chromium (x) in the polyatomic ion PbI_2 is +6. Lastly, in reference to the second oxidation rule cited above, the oxidation state of chromium in the monatomic ion is equal to +3. Summarily, $Cr_2O_7^{2-}$ is converted to Cr^{3+} through a reduction reaction because chromium decreases in oxidation number (+6 in $Cr_2O_7^{2-}$ to +3 in Cr^{3+}) and gains electrons.

#	Ans.	Chapter	Explanation

35   B   10

K_a, also referred to as the acid dissociation constant, measures the degree to which an acid dissociates and releases protons into a solution. Based on the chemical equation of an acid in aqueous solution: $HA(aq) + H_2O(l) \rightleftarrows H_3O^+(aq) + A^-(aq)$, the K_a is:

$$[H_3O^+(aq)][A^-(aq)]/[HA] \text{ or } [H^+][A^-]/[HA]$$

Since weak acids do not completely dissociate, a small K_a value indicates a weak acid (small numerator, large denominator). However, based on the question stem, the pH cannot be found using K_a because the initial concentration of the monoprotic weak acid is unknown. So, since pH = $-\log [H_3O^+]$, the next best way to estimate the H_3O^+ concentration is using the pH scale. The pH scale ranges from 0 to 14 and is categorized into the three following groups: acidic (0 < x < 7), neutral (7), and basic (7 < x < 14). Thus, Choices (C), (D) and (E) are eliminated because the pH is too high and Choice (A) is eliminated because the pH is too low. Thus, Choice (B) is the best answer because a monoprotic weak acid has a pH of about 4.

36   C   6, 10

The balanced reaction $HCl + NaOH \rightarrow NaCl + H_2O$ is a neutralization reaction, which is defined as Acid + Base $\rightarrow$ Salt + Water. In a dilute solution, HCl dissociates into 1 mol of $H^+(aq)$ and 1 mol of $Cl^-(aq)$ while NaOH dissociates into 1 mole of $Na^+(aq)$ and 1 mole of $OH^-(aq)$. So, the ratio of moles of $H^+(aq)$ to moles of $OH^-(aq)$ is 1:1, which means the neutralization reaction is calculated using $M_1V_1 = M_2V_2$. So, 20 mL of HCl is required to exactly neutralize 40 mL of 0.10 M NaOH. Because the moles of H^+ would equal the moles of OH^- in solution; (0.1 M NaOH) (40 mL) is 0.004 mol of OH^- and (0.2 M HCl) (20 mL) is 0.004 mole of H^+.

37   C   10

The Brønsted-Lowry base is any substance that accepts protons (H^+) in the chemical equation and should not be confused with the Arrhenius base (any substance that dissociates in an aqueous solution and yields the hydroxide ion). CH_4 is not a Brønsted-Lowry base because it is NOT a proton-acceptor.

38   D   3

To find the mass percent of oxygen within the molecule glycerone ($C_3H_6O_3$), the four following steps are used:

1. find the mass of oxygen in the molecule

2. find the gram formula mass of the glycerone molecule

3. divide mass of oxygen atoms in glycerone by the gram formula mass of glycerone

4. multiply the answer by 100 to get the percent by mass of oxygen

Thus, the percent composition by mass of oxygen in $C_3H_6O_3$ is (48/90) × 100, which is a little above 50% since 45/90 is 1/2.

39   E   3

To find the solution, the two following chemical reactions are analyzed:

1. $2C + O_2 \rightarrow 2CO$

2. $C + O_2 \rightarrow CO_2$

Given that the same mass of carbon is used to form carbon monoxide and carbon dioxide, the amount of carbon required to convert 32 grams of oxygen into carbon monoxide in the first reaction is pivotal to determine the mass of oxygen required to produce carbon dioxide in the second reaction. So, first convert the initial grams of O_2 for reaction 1 to moles of O_2 (use gram formula mass), then convert moles of O_2 to moles of C (use balanced equation), and lastly, convert moles of C to grams of C (use gram formula mass) to find the amount of carbon required to form carbon monoxide; 32 g O_2 × (1 mol O_2 / 32 g O_2) × (2 mol C / 1 mol O_2) × (12 g C / 1 mol C) = 24 g C. So, since the question stem indicates that the mass of carbon is the same in both chemical reactions, 24 g of carbon is used to determine the mass of oxygen required to produce carbon dioxide. Thus, the following calculation is used: 24 g C × (1 mol C / 12 g C) × (1 mol O_2 / 1 mol C) × (32 g O_2 / 1 mol O_2) = 64 g O_2.

40   E   5

Network covalent bonding occurs when covalent bonds forms in a continuous network of atoms together. Common examples of covalent network solids include diamond, graphite, silicon dioxide, or quartz.

#	Ans.	Chapter	Explanation
41	D	1	The noble gases, also known as inert gases, are non-reactive, stable, and are located in group 18 on the periodic table. The following elements are the noble gases: He, Ne, Ar, Kr, Xe, and Rb. The electron configuration for each noble gas is represented as a full valence shell, which is a complete octet. In order to gain stability, elements often join together with other elements to form bonds by sharing or transferring electrons. An ion is an atom with an unequal amount of electrons and protons; a positively charged ion (cation) forms when an atom loses an electron, while a negatively charged ion (anion) forms when an atom gains an electron. Thus, if an atom loses or gains the right amount of valence electrons, it can achieve an octet by adopting the electron configuration of a noble gas. Ag^+ is correct because its electron configuration is $1s^2 2s^2 2p^6 3s^2 3p^6 4s^2 3d^{10} 4p^6 5s^2 4d^8$, which does not represent a noble gas. The other ions are eliminated because their electron configurations represent noble gases; N^{5+} is [Ne], F^- is [Ne], Ca^{2+} is [Ar], and Ba^{2+} is [Xe].
42	B	3	Nitrogen can be element X in the compound X_2O_5. Based on prior knowledge of how compounds are formed, it can be inferred that the elements combined were X^{+5} and O^{-2}. The oxidation number of an element can be determined by location on the periodic table; the group/column number can help assign oxidation number to an element. Oxygen is an element in group 16, which indicates an oxidation number of -2. As a result, element X must be from group 15 because this group tends to lose/gain 5 electrons, which results in an oxidation number of $+5$ or -5.
43	B	10, 13	The balanced equation of the dissolution of limestone is $CaCO_3(s) \rightleftarrows Ca^{2+}(aq) + CO_3^{2-}(aq)$. The solid compound $CaCO_3$ (limestone) in liquid water has a low solubility, which means there are only some Ca^{2+} ions and CO_3^{2-} ions dissolved in the solvent water. However, the addition of carbonates in the water would increase the dissolution of limestone because $CO_3^{2-}(aq) + H_2O(l) \rightleftarrows H_2CO_3^-(aq)$. According to Le Châtelier's principle, a reaction will proceed to counteract any disturbance on the following system in equilibrium: $CaCO_3(s) \rightleftarrows Ca^{2+}(aq) + CO_3^{2-}(aq) + H_2O(l) \rightleftarrows H_2CO_3^-(aq)$. Based on the balanced chemical reaction, the addition of carbonates in the water would form carbonic acid and decrease the concentration of $CO_3^{2-}(aq)$, causing the equilibrium of the dissolution of limestone to shift to the right. Thus, water containing carbonates is slightly acidic because it forms carbonic acid, which pushes the equilibrium to the right and increases the solubility of the solid limestone.
44	E	8	The molecular formula of calcium sulfate $CaSO_4$ displays a 1:1 ratio of calcium ions to sulfate ions. Thus, if the molar concentration of Ca^{2+} ions is measured to be 3.0×10^{-3} mol/L, then the molar concentration of SO_4^{2-} ions is also 3.0×10^{-3} mol/L. So, the solubility constant for calcium sulfate is $K_{sp} = [Ca^{2+}][SO_4^{2-}] = (3.0 \times 10^{-3})(3.0 \times 10^{-3}) = 9.0 \times 10^{-6}$.
45	C	5	The following equation is used to measure the heat released or absorbed by an object as a result of a change in temperature: $q = mC\Delta T$. Given the specific heat capacity of aluminum (0.9 J/mol°K) and the temperature change (20 degrees Celsius to 40 degrees Celsius), the grams of Al must be converted to moles of Al using molar mass to measure change in heat. So, 54g Al × (1 mol / 27 g Al) determines 2 moles of Al. Now, multiply (2 mol Al) (0.9 J/mol °K) (40°C−20°C) to get $(40 \times 9)/(10)$ and simplify to 4×9, which is 36 Joules.

#	Ans.	Chapter	Explanation

46   A   11   The following balanced chemical reaction

$$2\,Ag(s) \;+\; Zn^{2+}(aq) \;+\; 2\,OH^-(aq) \;\rightarrow\; Zn(s) \;+\; Ag_2O(aq) \;+\; H_2O(l)$$

is a reduction-oxidation (redox) reaction, which indicates that the oxidation numbers of elements actually change. Oxidation numbers, also known as oxidation states, are positive and negative integers that are assigned to atoms and used to indicate if a specific atom has been reduced (gained electrons) or oxidized (lost electrons) in a chemical reaction. To determine the change of the oxidation number of Ag in the redox reaction, the following oxidation rules must be followed:

1. the sum of the oxidation numbers of all the atoms in a neutral compound is zero

2. the oxidation number of oxygen in most compounds is -2.

Thus, in reference to these oxidation rules cited above, silver has an oxidation number of 0 in $Ag(s)$ and +1 in $Ag_2O(aq)$. Since $Ag_2O(aq)$ is a neutral compound and oxygen is usually -2, solve for x in the following equation to find the oxidation state of the metal silver: $0 - 2$ atoms of Ag (x) + 1 atom of O (-2). Therefore, the oxidation number of silver (x) in the precipitate Ag_2O is +1.

47   B   3   The balanced equation for the given reaction is as follows:

$$1\,C(s) \;+2\,H_2SO_4(l) \;\rightarrow 2\,SO_2(g) \;+1\,CO_2(g) \;+2\,H_2O(l)$$

The coefficient for sulfur dioxide in the balanced equation is 2.

48   A   10 K_a, also referred to as the acid dissociation constant, is calculated by dividing the total concentration product of all products of a balanced chemical reaction by the total concentration product of all reactants of a balanced chemical reaction. In addition, the coefficients of the reactants and products in the balanced chemical reaction are equivalent to the power the respective reactants and products are raised to when calculating the K_a value. Pure solids and liquids are excluded in equilibrium constant. K_a measures the degree to which an acid dissociates and releases protons into a solution. Based on the chemical equation of an acid in aqueous solution:
$HA(aq) + H_2O(l) \rightleftarrows H_3O^+(aq) + A^-(aq)$, the K_a is $[H_3O^+][A^-]/[HA]$ or $[H^+][A^-]/[HA]$. A large K_a value indicates a strong acid, while a small K_a value indicates a weak acid. Thus, HCN is the weakest acid because it is the acid with the lowest K_a value.

49   A   8 K_{eq}, also referred to as the equilibrium constant, is calculated by dividing the total concentration product of all products of a balanced chemical reaction by the total concentration product of all reactants of a balanced chemical reaction. Additionally, the coefficients of the reactants and products in the balanced chemical reaction are equivalent to the power the respective reactants and products are raised to when calculating the K_{eq} value. Pure solids and liquids are excluded in equilibrium constant. Based on chemical equation in the question stem:
$H_2(g) + S(g) \rightleftarrows H_2S(g)$, the K_{eq} is $[H_2S]/[H_2][S]$.

50   D   13   The balanced equation of the chemical reaction is as follows: $3\,H_2(g) + N_2(g) \rightarrow 2\,NH_3(g)$ According to VSEPR theory, the central atom of ammonia gas has four electron pairs at the vertices of a tetrahedron. Specifically, the central atom nitrogen is bonded to three hydrogen atoms and one lone pair of electrons. Thus, the molecular shape of $NH_3(g)$ is trigonal pyramidal.

#	Ans.	Chapter	Explanation
51	A	3	

The empirical formula of a substance provides the simplest whole-number ratio of atoms in the compound, while the molecular formula provides the actual number of atoms in the compound. To calculate the empirical formula given only the percent by mass composition of a certain compound, the following steps must be followed:

1. consider the percent by mass of each element as its weight in grams

2. divide the weight in grams of element by its molecular mass to calculate moles of each element

3. identify the element with the smallest quotient from step 2 (lowest number of moles) and divide this into the moles of each element

Thus, if the percent by mass composition of a certain compound is 41% boron and 59% nitrogen, then the compound is made up of 41 grams of boron and 59 grams of nitrogen.
Boron 41 g / 11 g/mol $\approx$ (40 g / 10g/mol) $\approx$ 4 moles $\rightarrow$ 4 moles/4 moles = 1
Nitrogen 59 g/ 14 g/mol $\approx$ (60 g/ 15g/mol) $\approx$ 4 moles N $\rightarrow$ 4 moles/ 4 moles = 1 mole
Thus, since the ratio of boron atoms to nitrogen atoms is about 1:1, the empirical formula is B_1N_1.

52 D 13

Proper laboratory procedure is to swirl a test tube containing a liquid while being heated to avoid bumping. Bumping is the fast formation of bubbles, which is a serious potential hazard because these bubbles could eject at high speeds. So, as a precaution, swirling is performed to lessen the frequency of vapor bubble formation.

53 A 3

The balanced equation for the decomposition reaction in the question stem is:
$2KClO_3 \rightarrow 3\ O_2(g)\ + 2\ KCl(s)$. Based on the information given, to calculate the amount of moles of oxygen gas that were liberated by ignition, the following calculation is used to first find the mass of oxygen gas liberated: (mass of flask + $KClO_3$) − (mass of flask + residue after ignition) = 32.2 grams - 29 grams = 3.2 grams oxygen gas liberated. Then, convert from grams to moles using the the molar mass of O_2, such as which (3.2 g of O_2) × (1 mol of O_2 / 32 g of O_2) = 0.1 moles of $O_2(g)$.

54 D 4

The ideal gas law is used to describe the behavior of hypothetical ideal gases and is expressed as PV = nRT; thus, the law predicts how moles of gas would behave under certain changes in pressure, volume, and temperature. The Kinetic Molecular Theory of Gases is used to explain the gas laws and to help us understand the behavior of ideal gases. The following assumptions of the kinetic molecular theory are: (1) ideal gases have no volume compared to the volume of their container (2) ideal gases exhibit no intermolecular attractions or repulsions (3) gas particles move in a random straight line motion (4) collisions of ideal gas particles are elastic, which indicates no energy is lost, and (5) the average kinetic energy of a gas particles is proportional to the absolute temperature of the gases, which indicates all gases at a given temperature have the same average kinetic energy. Based on the fourth assumption cited above, collisions between molecules are NOT perfectly inelastic.

55 B 4

Boyle's Law describes the inverse relationship between pressure and volume at a constant temperature. PV = constant; $P_1V_1 = P_2V_2$. If the pressure of the container is doubled, then the volume of O_2 would be halved. Thus, $V_2 = V_i/2$.

56 D 2

A complete Lewis-dot diagram has the correct number of the compounds sum of valence electrons and a complete octet around each atom (disregarding the exceptions to the octet rule). Hydrogen is an exception to the octet rule because it follows the duet rule and only needs 2 valence electrons to be stable. A complete Lewis-dot structure of the hydronium ion, H_3O^+, has the correct number of the compounds sum of valence electrons and a complete octet around each atom (disregarding the exceptions to the octet rule). Choice (D) is the only structure that follows these requirements; Choice (A) has more than 2 valence electrons on the hydrogen atom, (B) and (E) have the incorrect atoms in the chemical structure, and choice (C) has an incomplete octet of electrons around the oxygen atom. Choice (D) is correct because there are 8 valence electrons, the central oxygen atom follows the octet rule, and the hydrogen atoms follow the duet rule.

57 C 10

Nonmetallic oxides react with water to form acidic solutions. When a nonmetallic oxide reacts with water, the oxyacid will donate hydronium ions (H^+) to the solution, which allows this reaction to form an acidic solution. Thus, SO_3 is correct because it is a nonmetallic oxide, which forms an acidic solution when dissolved in water.

#	Ans.	Chapter	Explanation
58	E	13	A neutralization reaction is defined as Acid + Base $\rightarrow$ Salt + Water, where the number of H+ ions = number of OH^- ions. If there is 1 mole of H^+ in the acid and 1 mole of OH^- in the base, then there is a 1:1 mole ratio of the acid and base in the neutralization reaction, so the $M_1V_1 = M_2V_2$ equation is used. Thus, to calculate the concentration of base solution (M_1), the following data is needed: volume of base (V_1), concentration of the acid (M_2), and the volume of the acid (V_2).
59	B	12	Esters are chemical compounds formed from an acid, usually carboxylic acids, and an alcohol. This organic compound contains a ketone and an ether. The general formula is $R\text{-}COOR_1$, where R_1 is a carbon chain. The ester consists of a carbonyl group (O=C) and a ether group (R-O-R), when R = hydrocarbon chain. Thus, choice B is the only structure that fulfills these requirements.
60	A	12	A saturated hydrocarbon, also referred to as an alkane, has the general formula of C_nH_{2n+2}. Thus, CH_4 is a saturated hydrocarbon because it adheres to the formula. If n=1, then 2n+2 is 2(1)+2 = 4.
61	C	1	An alpha particle/helium nucleus (^4_2He or $^4_2\alpha$) and two negatively charged beta particles/electrons ($^{\ 0}_{-1}e$ or $^{\ 0}_{-1}\beta$) are respectively emitted from a radioactive substance in alpha decay and two beta decays. Being "emitted" indicates that these particles are products in their respective chemical reactions. The three balanced equations for an Uranium-238 atom undergoing one alpha decay and then two beta decays are as follows: 1. $^{238}_{92}U \rightarrow {}^4_2He + {}^{234}_{90}Th$ 2. $^{234}_{90}Th \rightarrow {}^{\ 0}_{-1}e + {}^{234}_{91}Pa$ 3. $^{234}_{91}Pa \rightarrow {}^{\ 0}_{-1}e + {}^{234}_{92}U$ Thus, the resulting atom is $^{234}_{92}U$, which can also be represented as U-234.
62	B	2, 6	The boiling point of a substance is closely related to its intermolecular force strength. The stronger the IMF, the more energy required to break bonds, and the higher the boiling point. Hydrogen bonding is the strongest intermolecular force and is responsible for the high boiling point of water. The hydrogen bond is a special type of dipole-dipole attraction that involves a hydrogen bonding with fluorine (F), oxygen (O), or nitrogen (N). One molecule will contain a partial positive charge on the hydrogen, while the other molecule contains a partial negative charge on the F, O, or N. Thus, H_2O (hydrogen bonding) has a higher boiling point than H_2S (dipole-dipole).
63	C	3	The balanced equation for the given reaction is as follows: $$1C_3H_8 + 5O_2 \rightarrow 3CO_2 + 4H_2O$$ The coefficient of $O_2(g)$ in the balanced equation is 5.
64	D	9	The standard heat of formation is the change in enthalpy (ΔH) when one mole of a substance is formed from its pure constituent elements at STP. Thus, change in enthalpy is $\Delta H = +142.7$ kJ/mol for the balanced reaction $3/2\ O_2(g) \rightarrow 1\ O_3(g)$. A positive change in enthalpy (ΔH) indicates an endothermic reaction, which is when the reactants absorb more energy than the amount of energy the products release in the equation.
65	A	3, 10	The percent dissociation of the sulfurous acid is expressed as (the molar concentration of the hydronium ion / the original molar concentration of the "X" acid) $\times$ 100. So, the concentration of H^+ ions of the sulfurous acid is calculated using the equation ($[H^+]/[H_2SO_3]) \times 100 = \%$, which can be rearranged as $[H^+] = (\% \times [H_2SO_3])/100)$. So, $(10 \times 0.1)/100$ calculates a 0.01 M of H^+ ions.

#	Ans.	Chapter	Explanation
66	E	2	Most elements are stable when they have eight valence electrons, also referred to as a full octet. Noble gases, also known as inert gases, have a complete octet which makes them very stable and unreactive. Choice (E) is the only structure that violates the octet rule, while choices (A), (B), (C), and (D) are structures that have a complete octet around each atom. So, Choice (E) is correct because there are more than 8 valence electrons on the central phosphorus atom.
67	E	10	The Arrhenius base dissociates into an aqueous solution and yields hydroxide ions (OH^-). Therefore, an Arrhenius base must contain an OH^- ion.
68	A	2, 12	An organic compound that contains a triple bond is an alkyne compound. An alkyne is an unsaturated hydrocarbon and has the general formula of C_nH_{2n-2}. Thus, C_3H_4 has a triple bond because it adheres to the formula. If n=3, then $2n-2$ is $2(3)-2 = 4$.
69	C	1	Ionization energy is the amount of energy per mole required to remove an electron from the valence shell of an atom. When you remove a valence electron from an atom, the atomic radius will decrease, which decreases the shielding effect and creates a cation (positively charged ion). As a result, the nucleus of the cation has a tighter pull on the remaining electrons, making it more difficult to remove the next electron from the valence shell. Element X is most likely Beryllium because the biggest jump in ionization energy is between the second ionization potential and the third ionization potential. The ion Be^{2+} has the electron configuration of [He], which is a noble gas. Thus, removing the 3rd electron from Beryllium is similar to removing an electron from a noble gas, which requires a huge amount of energy. So, Choice (C) is the best answer because it makes sense that the biggest jump in ionization energy is between an Be^{2+} (stable noble gas) and Be^{+3} (1 valence electron away from stability).
70	C	8	According to Le Châtelier's principle, a reaction will proceed to counteract any disturbance on the system in equilibrium. A disturbance is caused when there is a change of conditions on a equilibrium, specifically change of volume, pressure, concentration, and/or temperature. The given figure displays the relationship between time and concentration of the reactants and products in $A+B \rightarrow C$. The horizontal line for each compound at time t_1 demonstrates a constant concentration, indicating the reaction has reached equilibrium. Thus, the change of slope for each line at time t_2 depicts disturbance of equilibrium. Based on the figure, the disturbance of equilibrium at time t_2 causes the following to occur:

70 (continued):

1. the concentrations of reactant A and reactant B to immediately increase, and then drop down to concentrations that are a little above their original concentration

2. the concentration of product C to increase

Thus, the correct change of condition that caused the disturbance has to match the concentration fluctuations on the figure. In a system of equilibrium, the addition of reactant(s) will favor the forward reaction to restore equilibrium; increasing the rate of the forward reaction will consume more reactants and produce more products. Choice A and Choice B are eliminated because adding more of only ONE reactant to the mixture would display an immediate increase of only one reactant, not both. Thus, Choice C is the disturbance because adding more of reactant A and reactant B to the mixture is the only change of condition that immediately increases the concentration of both A and B.

#	Ans.	Chapter	Explanation
1	D	10	A carboxylic acid is an organic compound that contains a carboxyl group. The general formula is R-COOH. The carboxyl group consists of a carbonyl group (O=C) and a hydroxyl group (R-OH). Thus, Choice (D) is the only structure that fulfills this requirement; $HC_2H_3O_2$ is equivalent to CH_3COOH, which is acetic acid.
2	C	13	The trigonal pyramidal molecular structure has four electron pairs at the vertices of a tetrahedron and a sp^3 hybridization; according to VSEPR theory, the central atom is bonded to three atoms and has one lone pair of electrons. Thus, the molecular shape of $NH_3(g)$ is trigonal pyramidal. The central atom nitrogen is bonded to three hydrogen atoms and also has one lone pair of electrons.
3	A	10	Strong acids dissociate completely into H^+ ions and its conjugate base. The following list are the six strong acids: hydrochloric acid (HCl), hydrobromic acid (HBr), hydroiodic acid (HI), nitric acid (HNO_3), sulfuric acid (H_2SO_4), and perchloric acid ($HClO_4$).
4	E	10	When a salt, also known as an ionic compound, is hydrolyzed (added to water), it will dissociate into a cation and anion. The identity of the ions determine whether the solution is acidic, basic, or neutral. The salt's cation will be categorized on if it came from a strong or weak base while the salt's anion will be categorized on if it came from a strong or weak acid. To form a basic solution, the cation of the salt must be the conjugate acid of a strong base and the anion of the salt must be the conjugate base of a weak acid. This is because the conjugate acid of a strong base will not react in water while the conjugate base of a weak acid will react in water. $NaC_2H_3O_2$ is correct because the ionic compound is made up of Na^+ and $C_2H_3O_2^-$; Na^+ is the conjugate acid of NaOH (strong base) and $C_2H_3O_2^-$ is the conjugate base of $HC_2H_3O_2$ (weak acid). So, the conjugate base of the weak acid will react with water in the following equation to form a basic solution: $C_2H_3O_2^-(aq) + H_2O(l) \rightleftarrows HC_2H_3O_2(aq) + OH^-(aq)$.
5	C	2	Coordinate covalent bonds occur when one element has to donate an entire lone pair of electrons to help satisfy the octet around each element in a molecule. Thus, ammonia is the only compound that is able to form a coordinate covalent bond with H_3O^+ due to its lone pair of electrons on the central atom nitrogen.
6	E	13	Mass spectrometer is a separation technique that utilizes electric and magnetic fields to quantify the mass of electrically charged particles. This device is extremely beneficial because it helps identify atoms or molecules in an unknown sample by correlating known masses to identified masses.
7	D	13	Immiscible liquids are liquids that cannot mix together and form separate layer of solvent due to differences in density. The separatory funnel is the laboratory item that is used to separate the immiscible liquids.
8	A	13	The laboratory item used to precisely add small measured volumes of liquid into a solution during titration is a burette.
9	B	13	Based on assumptions of the kinetic molecular theory of gases, the average kinetic energy of gas particles is proportional to the absolute temperature of the gas. Thus, the thermometer can be used to measure the average kinetic energy of ambient air.
10	A	10	A neutralization reaction is defined as $Acid(aq) + Base(aq) \rightarrow Salt(aq) + Water(l)$, while a net ionic reaction only expresses the species participating in the chemical reaction. For example, in the equation $HCl(aq) + NaOH(aq) \rightarrow NaCl(aq) + H_2O(l)$, the aqueous solutions dissolve into ions in water, which can be donated as the following: $$H^+(aq) + Cl^-(aq) + Na^+(aq) + OH^-(aq) \rightarrow Na^+(aq) + Cl^-(aq) + H_2O(l)$$ Thus, after omitting the spectator ions, the net neutralization reaction is $$H^+(aq) + OH^-(aq) \rightarrow H_2O(l)$$

#	Ans.	Chapter	Explanation
11	E	9, 12	Combustion, also referred to as "burning," is a type of redox-reaction that produces a lot of energy in the form of light and heat. Combustion is an exothermic reaction where a hydrocarbon reacts with oxygen and produces carbon dioxide and water. The chemical reaction is $C_xH_y + O_2(g) \rightarrow H_2O(l) + CO_2(g)$. Thus, the balanced equation for a combustion reaction is as follows: $$CH_4(g) + 2\,O_2(g) \rightarrow CO_2(g) + 2\,H_2O(l)$$
12	D	9	Synthesis, also referred to as combination, is a reaction that combines multiple reactants to produce one product. The chemical reaction is A + B → AB. Thus, the balanced equation for a synthesis reaction is as follows: $N_2(g) + 3\,H_2(g) \rightarrow 2\,NH_3(g)$.
13	C	11	Oxidation takes place when the reactant loses electrons and increases oxidation number. $Zn(s)$ has an oxidation number of 0 and Zn^{2+} has an oxidation number of +2, which means zinc has increased in oxidation state. The chemical equation $Zn(s) \rightarrow Zn^{2+} + 2e^-$ also shows an electron as a product, indicating the loss of electrons.
14	B	11	Reduction takes place when the reactant gains electrons and decreases oxidation number. K+ has an oxidation number of +1 and K has an oxidation number of 0, which means potassium has decreased in oxidation state. The chemical equation $K^+ + 1e^- \rightarrow K$ also shows electrons as a reactant, indicating the gain of electrons.
15	B	5	Entropy is also referred to as the degree of disorder in a system. The change in entropy (ΔS) is used to measure the randomness and chaos in the chemical system. A positive ΔS indicates a increase in entropy (disorder), while a negative ΔS indicates a decrease in entropy. Solids are rigid and have a fixed position, so this phase has the lowest amount of entropy. Gases have the greatest amount of entropy because their particles freely move and have the most disorder.
16	E	8	K_a, also referred to as the acid dissociation constant, measures the degree to which an acid dissociates and releases protons into a solution. Based on the chemical equation of an acid in aqueous solution: $HA(aq) + H_2O(l) \rightleftarrows H_3O^+(aq) + A^-(aq)$, the K_a is $[H_3O^+][A^-]/[HA]$ or $[H^+][A^-]/[HA]$. A large K_a value indicates a strong acid, while a small K_a value indicates a weak acid. Subsequently, $K_a >> 1$ indicates a higher concentration of products than reactants, which indicates a strong ion dissociation.
17	D	8	K_{eq}, also referred to as the equilibrium constant, measures the ratio of the concentration of products formed to the concentration of reactants consumed at equilibrium. A large K_{eq} indicates that the concentration of products is greater than concentration of reactants, while a small K_{eq} indicates that the concentration of products is less than concentration of reactants. Thus, if K_{eq} is greater than 1, the rate of the forward reaction is favored (products are favored).
18	C	9	The thermodynamic state function, G, is also referred to as Gibbs free energy. Gibbs free energy equation is used to predict the spontaneity of a reaction. Gibbs equation is $\Delta G = \Delta H - T\Delta S$; a negative ΔG value represents a spontaneous reaction and a positive ΔG value represents a nonspontaneous reaction. Thus, $\Delta G > 0$ indicates the chemical process is theoretically non-spontaneous.
19	B	5	Francium is a metal, which indicates that $Fr(s)$ is a metallic substance. The properties of a metallic compounds include, but are not limited to: luster, malleable, ductile, conduct heat and electricity, large atomic radii, high density, high melting point, solid at room temp (besides Mg). In addition, metallic solids have metals atoms linked together by metallic bonds. The metal atoms have a very free relationship with their valence bonds, which allows for a sea of delocalized electrons. Choice (A) is eliminated because the francium atom (metal) is not bonded to a nonmetal atom, Choices (C) and (D) are eliminated because no nonmetals are involved in francium, and Choice (E) is eliminated because no covalent bonds exist in within a metal atom, so no continuous network of atoms form.

#	Ans.	Chapter	Explanation
20	D	2, 13	The molecule sulfur trioxide consists of a central sulfur atom attached to three oxygen atoms. Thus, Choices (A) and (B) are eliminated because sulfur and oxygen are both nonmetals, and Choice (E) is eliminated because sulfur trioxide is not one of the common network solids (diamond, graphite, silicon dioxide, quartz, etc) that form a continuous network of atoms together. To determine the type of covalent bond of SO_3, the electronegativity difference between atoms is examined. The atoms in a nonpolar covalent bond have an electronegativity difference less than 0.5 (which sustains an equal sharing of electrons), while the atoms in a polar covalent bond have an electronegativity difference between 0.5 and 1.6 (which creates an unequal sharing of electrons). Thus, SO_3 contains polar covalent bonds because the oxygen atom is more electronegative than the sulfur atom. But, the dipoles cancel out in sulfur trioxide because the molecular geometry is trigonal planar; thus, SO_3 is symmetrical and has no lone pairs on the sulfur atom. Thus, Choice (E) is eliminated and Choice (D) is correct because $SO_3(g)$ is nonpolar covalent compound and consists of polar covalent bonds.
21	E	8	Considering kinematics, the main factors that affect the reaction rate include, but are not limited to: bond type, surface area, concentration, temperature, and catalysts. Specifically, the concentration of reactants is directly proportional to the reaction rate. If there are more molecules of reactants, there is a higher likelihood of effective collisions, which INCREASES the reaction RATE and DECREASES the TIME of the reaction. So, Choices (A), (B) and (D) are eliminated because there is not a direct relationship between concentration of reactants and time of reaction, while Choice (C) is eliminated because there is a relationship between concentration of reactants and time of reaction. Choice (E) is the only graph that displays this inverse relationship between the concentration of reactants and the time of reaction.
22	A	4	Gay-Lussac's Law is the gas law that states the direct relationship between pressure and absolute temperature at a constant volume. P_1/T_2 = constant; $P_1/T_1 = P_2/T_2$. So, Choice (C) and (E) are eliminated because if an isochoric (constant volume) ideal gas increases in pressure, its absolute temperature will also increase. Choice (B) is eliminated because the absolute temperature of a gas could be 0, while Choice (D) is eliminated because there is a DIRECT relationship (upward CONSTANT slope) between pressure and temperature. Choice (A) is the only graph that displays this direct relationship between pressure and absolute temperature at a constant volume.
23	D	4	The pH scale measures the acid/base concentration of a substance using the following equations: pH = $-\log$ [H^+], pOH = $-\log$ [OH^-], and pH + pOH = 14. The pH scale ranges from 0 to 14 and is categorized into the three following groups: acidic ($0 < x < 7$), neutral (7), and basic ($7 < x < 14$). As a strong base, $Ca(OH)_2(aq)$ has a high molar concentration of OH^- ions in the solution. Thus, adding more 0.2 M $Ca(OH)_2$ will increase the amount of OH^- ions in the solution, which decreases the pOH and increases the pH. So, Choice (E) is eliminated because there is not an inverse relationship between volume of $Ca(OH)_2$ in solution and pH and Choice (C) is eliminated because there is a relationship between these two factors. Choices (A) and (B) are eliminated because when a volume of 0 L of $Ca(OH)_2$ is added the starting pH of H_2SO_4 should be measurable and not 0.
24	C	4	Boyle's Law is the gas law that states the inverse relationship between pressure and volume at a constant temperature. PV = constant; $P_1V_1 = P_2V_2$. Thus, if you increase the pressure of an isothermal (constant temperature) ideal gas, the volume will decrease proportionally to counteract the disturbance on the system and maintain the constant temperature. Subsequently, PV will remain constant when you increase the pressure of an isothermal ideal gas, which is displayed in Choice (C). Choices (A), (B), (D), and (E) are all eliminated because there is no direct or inverse relationship between PV and pressure.
25	B	1, 3	The atomic number of an atom is the number of protons that make up the atom, while the atomic mass of an atom is the combination of the number of protons and neutrons that make up the atom. Thus, increasing the atomic number (# of protons) of an atom will immediately increase the atomic mass (# of protons + # of neutrons) of the atom. So, Choice (E) is eliminated because there is not an inverse relationship between atomic number and atomic mass, while choice (C) is eliminated because there is a relationship between atomic number and atomic mass. Choices (A) and (D) are eliminated because an atom will never have a value of 0 for both atomic mass and atomic number. Thus, choice (B) is the only graph that displays a direct relationship between atomic mass and atomic number and also does not start atomic mass or atomic number at 0.

#	Ans.	Chapter	Explanation
101	T, F	1	Carbon-12 and Carbon-14 are different versions of the same element, also referred to as isotopes. Isotopes of an element have the same number of protons (atomic number), but a different number of neutrons. So, since protons + neutrons = atomic mass, isotopes of the same element will also vary in atomic mass. Additionally, isotopes differ from ions because isotopes are electrically neutral (# of protons = # of electrons). Carbon-12 has a neutral charge, an atomic number of 6 and an atomic mass of 12, while Carbon-14 has a neutral charge, an atomic number of 6 and an atomic mass of 14. As a result, C-12 has 6 protons, 6 electrons, and 6 neutrons, while C-14 has 6 protons, 6 electrons, and 8 neutrons. Thus, Carbon-12 is an isotope of Carbon-14 because they have same # of protons (and electrons), but different # of neutrons
102	T, T, CE	2	A polar covalent bond is formed between two nonmetals that have an electronegativity difference between 0.5 and 1.6. The atoms share the electrons unequally and the more electronegative atom has a stronger pull on the electrons. Thus, since the oxygen atom (nonmetal) is more electronegative than the carbon atom (non metal), a partial negative charge forms on the oxygen and a partial positive charge forms on the central carbon. But, the dipoles cancel out because O=C=O is symmetrical and has no lone pairs on the carbon atom. So, $CO_2(g)$ has a nonpolar structure and polar covalent bonds.
103	T, T, CE	3, 4, 8	The ideal gas law is $PV = nRT$ or $V = (nRT)/P$. Since each ideal gas in the equilibrium reaction is at STP (standard temperature and temperature) and R is a constant, the volumetric ratio between substances is equivalent to the mole ratio of those substances because the number of moles of each gas is directly proportional to its volume. Additionally, Avogadro's Principle, a principle that explains Gay-Lussac's Law, states that at the same temperature and pressure, all gases have an equal volume and the same number of molecules. Additionally, the molar volume states that one mole of any gas at STP (standard temperature and pressure) has a volume of 22.4 L, which indicates that comparing volume of two substances at STP is equivalent to comparing number of moles.
104	F, T	3	The empirical formula of a substance provides the simplest whole-number ratio of atoms in the compound, while the molecular formula provides the actual number of atoms in the compound. The empirical formula (simplest form) and the molecular formula (actual form) of the same compound will always have the same ratio. The empirical formula of C_2H_6 is CH_3, which has the same 1:3 ratio of carbon to hydrogen.
105	F, T	13	The half-life of a radioactive element is the amount of time needed for half of the radioactive atoms to decay.
106	F, T	1	Transition metals are found on the periodic table between groups three and twelve. The 4d orbital is found in the fourth period (4=n) and the d subshell covers groups 3 through 12. The electron configuration $1s^22s^22p^63s^23p^64s^23d^{10}$ represents the ground state configuration of a copper atom, which is a transition metal.
107	F, T	1	The N^{3-} ion and the Ne atom do not have the similar chemical properties, but they do have the same electron configuration ($1s^22s^22p^6$). The ground state configuration of nitrogen atom is $1s^22s^22p^3$, but the addition of three valence electrons fills the remaining orbitals in the p-sublevel. Although the nitrogen anion and the neon atom have the same number of valence electrons, the chemical properties differ since Ne is a noble gas. Despite gaining an octet, the N^{3-} anion is not nearly as stable as the Ne atom.
108	T, F	8	The balanced equation of the equilibrium reaction is as follows: $NH_4^+(aq) + OH^-(aq) \rightarrow NH_3(aq) + H_2O(l)$. In the chemical reaction, ammonium (weak acid) donates a proton to the hydroxide ion (base), which forms ammonia (conjugate base) and the byproduct H_2O (conjugate acid).
109	T, T, CE	13	When fossil fuels are burned during combustion, products are formed and often released into the atmosphere. Specifically, two compounds that are released into the atmosphere are sulfur dioxide and nitrogen oxide. Acid rain is formed when sulfur dioxide (SO_2) and nitrogen oxides react with rainwater in the atmosphere. The chemical equations producing acid rain are $$2\,SO_2(g) + O_2(g) \rightarrow 2\,SO_3(g) \text{ and } SO_3(g) + H_2O(l) \rightarrow H_2SO_4(aq)$$

#	Ans.	Chapter	Explanation
110	F, T	6	Molarity, also referred to as molar concentration, is measured in moles of solute per liters of solution. To prepare a 1 M solution of chloride ions from $MgCl_2$, 47.5 g of $MgCl_2$ is dissolved in 1 L of solution (not 95 grams). The balanced dissociation reaction is $MgCl_2 \rightarrow Mg^+(aq) + 2\ Cl^-(aq)$. To determine whether or not 95 grams of $MgCl_2$ would prepare 1 M solution of chloride ions, the following steps must be followed:

1. use molar mass to convert from grams of $MgCl_2$ to moles of $MgCl_2$

2. use the balanced equation to convert moles of $MgCl_2$ to moles of Cl^- ions

3. divide moles of Cl^- ions by the L of solution

So, the following calculation is used:
(95 g $MgCl_2$ / 1 L of solution) $\times$ (1 mol $MgCl_2$ / 95 g $MgCl_2$) $\times$ (2 mol Cl^- / 1 mol $MgCl_2$) = 2 mol Cl^- / 1 L of solution. Thus, the molar concentration of the solution of chloride ions is 2 M, not 1 M.

#	Ans.	Chapter	Explanation
111	T, T	5	The equation used to calculate the amount of energy released / absorbed during a phase change is $q = m\Delta H$ and the equation used to calculate the amount of energy released/absorbed during temperature change is $q = mC\Delta T$. The latter equation involves change in temperature because the absorbed/released heat energy is being used to increase/decrease the temperature. Based on assumptions of the kinetic molecular theory of gases, the average kinetic energy of gas particles is proportional to the absolute temperature of the gas. However, during phase changes, the absorbed/released heat energy is being used to break bonds/form bonds, which changes the potential energy. Thus, during condensation, the amount of energy released is changing gas to liquid, not temperature. Specifically, the energy released is forming bonds between the gas molecules.
112	F, F	7	Considering kinematics, the main factors that affect the reaction rate include, but are not limited to: bond type, surface area, concentration, temperature, and presence of a catalyst. These factors impact the rate of the chemical reaction by affecting the rate of molecular collisions and/or the energy of the collisions. Specifically, catalysts speed up the rate of chemical reactions by lowering the activation energy needed for a reaction. The activation energy is the minimum amount of energy needed to undergo a chemical reaction. In other words, in order for a reaction to take place, a certain amount of energy is required. Thus, the larger the activation energy required, the longer it takes to complete the reaction. The activation energy of the forward reaction is calculated by subtracting the the initial amount of energy held within the reactants from the amount of energy at the transition state/activated complex (highest energy point/least stable), while the activation energy of the reverse reaction is calculated by subtracting the the amount of energy held within the products from the amount of energy at the activated complex. Since the amount of energy of the reactants and products can differ, the activation energy of the forward and reverse reaction do not have to be the same. Thus, the introduction of a catalyst into the system of a chemical reaction will speed up the reaction by lowering the activation energy of both the forward and reverse reactions.
113	T, T	8	According to Le Châtelier's principle, a chemical reaction will proceed to counteract any disturbance on the system in equilibrium. Thus, in the equilibrium reaction $2\ NO_2(g) \rightleftarrows N_2O_4(g)$, when the pressure of the container at constant temperature increases, the system will counteract the increase in partial pressure of the gases by shifting the equilibrium to the side with fewer moles of gas. So, the balanced equation will favor the forward reaction because there are two gaseous reactants and one gaseous product. Additionally, considering kinematics, the main factors that affect the reaction rate do so by affecting the rate of molecular collisions and/or the energy of the collisions. Specifically, pressure is directly proportional to the reaction rate because the greater the pressure of the container, the higher the likelihood of effective collisions between the reactant gaseous reactants.
114	T, T, CE	1, 13	Rutherford's gold foil experiment was tremendously impactful because the results provided significant information about the atomic structure. Alpha particles, which consist of two protons and two neutrons, were shot through the foil. The results of experiment portrayed that there were only a few deflections of the alpha particles, which expressed that an atom is mostly empty space between the nucleus and electrons. These positively charged particles only deflected when it hit the positively charged nucleus, which means that almost all alpha particles were not disturbed.

#	Ans.	Chapter	Explanation
115	F, T	10	The pH scale measures the acid/base concentration of a substance using the following equations: $pH = -\log[H^+]$, $pOH = -\log[OH^-]$, and $pH + pOH = 14$. The scale ranges from 0 to 14 and is categorized into the three following groups: acidic ($0 < x < 7$), neutral (7), and basic ($7 < x < 14$). Based on the equation $pH = -\log[H^+]$, a solution with a pH of 5 has $1.0 \times 10^{-5}\ M$ of H^+ ions, while a solution with a pH of 2 has a $1.0 \times 10^{-2}\ M$ of H^+ ions. Thus, a solution with a pH of 2 has a 10^3 times greater concentration of H_3O^+ than a solution with a pH of 5.
26	B	3	Gram formula mass, also referred to as molar mass, is the sum of the atomic weights of all of the atoms in one mole of a molecule. Gram formula mass is measured in grams per mol. Thus, to solve for the molecular weight of $Ca(CO_3)$, the calculations are as follows: 1 atom of Ca $\times$ (40 g of Ca / mol) = 40 g/mol. 1 atom of C $\times$ (12 g of C / mol) = 12 g/mol. 3 atoms of O $\times$ (16 g of O / mol) = 48 g/mol. Since 40 g/mol + 12 g/mol + 48 g/mol is 100 g/mol, the gram formula mass is $Ca(CO_3)$ is 100 g/mol.
27	A	3	Molarity, also referred to as molar concentration, is measured in moles of solute per liters of solution. Thus, the molarity of $MgSO_4$ is found by converting grams of $MgSO_4$ to moles of $MgSO_4$ using the molar mass (120 g/mol) and then dividing moles of $MgSO_4$ by the L of solution. So, 120 g of $MgSO_4$ $\times$ (1 mol of $MgSO_4$ / 120 g of $MgSO_4$) = 1 mol of $MgSO_4$ and (1 mol of $MgSO_4$ / 2 L of solution) = 0.5 M of $MgSO_4$.
28	C	2, 6	An ionic solid, also referred to as a salt, is a network of ions being held together by ionic bonds. The ionic solid dissociates into ions when added to water because the ionic bonds break apart. Thus, the ionic solid NH_4OH dissociates into the polyatomic cation NH_4^+ and the anion OH^-.
29	E	3	This is a combustion reaction, which is an exothermic reaction where a hydrocarbon reacts with oxygen and produces carbon dioxide, water, and a lot of energy in the form of light and heat. According to the question stem, the combustion reaction is as follows: $$CH_4(s) + 2\,O_2(g) \rightarrow CO_2(g) + 2\,H_2O(l)$$ There is a 1:2 ratio of moles of methane consumed to moles of oxygen consumed and a 1:1 ratio of moles of methane consumed to moles of carbon dioxide produced. Thus, the calculations are as follows: 1 mol $CH_4(s)$ $\times$ (2 mol of $O_2(g)$ / 1 mol $CH_4(s)$) $\times$ (32 mol $CO_2(g)$ / 1 mol of $O_2(g)$) = 64 grams of $O_2(g)$
30	B	9	The balanced equation for the given reaction is as follows: $$2KNO_3 + Mg(MnO_4)_2 \rightarrow Mg(NO_3)_2 + 2KMnO_4$$ KNO_3 and $Mg(MnO_4)_2$ are both ionic compounds, which means the substances dissolve in water to form ions; 1 mol of KNO_3 dissolves into 1 mol of $K^+(aq)$ and 1 mol of NO_3^-, while 1 mole of $Mg(MnO_4)_2$ dissolves into 1 mol of Mg^{+2} and 2 moles of MnO_4^-. Thus, potassium permanganate, $KMnO_4$, and magnesium nitrate, $Mg(NO_3)_2$, form.
31	C	13	The chemical formula of sulfurous acid is determined by following the nomenclature rules for polyatomic compounds. To determine the chemical formula, the following nomenclature rules are applied: (1) an acid formed from an anion that ends with -ite will use the suffix -ous, (2) an acid formed from an anion that ends with -ate will use the suffix -ic, (3) an oxyanion that ends in -ate has one more oxygen than an oxyanion that ends in -ite. Thus, sulfuric acid (H_2SO_4), one of the 6 strong acids, has one more oxygen than sulfurous acid (H_2SO_3).
32	A	8	K_c, also referred to as the equilibrium constant, is calculated by dividing the total concentration product of all products of a balanced chemical reaction by the total concentration product of all reactants of a balanced chemical reaction. Pure solids and liquids are excluded in equilibrium constant. Based on chemical equation in the question stem: $$2\,N_2O_5(g) \rightleftarrows O_2(g) + 4\,NO_2(g)\text{, the }K_c\text{ is }[O_2][NO_2]^4/[N_2O_5]^2$$

#	Ans.	Chapter	Explanation
33	C	13	(I) is correct because placing a hot glass beaker on a cool surface will cause the glass beaker to potentially crack. (II) is also correct because the better/safer option would be to add concentrated acid to water. Liquid water should never be added to concentrated acid because the heat produced will cause the mixture to splatter. Lastly, (III) is eliminated because it is a good laboratory practice to rinse a burette with the solution that will be used to eventually fill the burette in the experiment.
34	B	13	The balanced reaction $2HCl + Ca(OH)_2 \rightarrow CaCl_2 + 2H_2O$ is a neutralization reaction, which is defined as Acid + Base $\rightarrow$ Salt + Water. In a titration experiment, the number of OH^- moles must equal the number of H^+ moles. Since there is 1 mole of H^+ in 1 mol of HCl and 2 moles of OH^- in 1 mol of OH^-, there is a 2:1 mole ratio of HCl and NaOH in the neutralization. In other words, 2 moles of HCl is used to titrate 1 mol of $Ca(OH)_2$. So, the number of OH^- moles is calculated to determine the number of H^+ moles needed, which allows us to find milliliters of HCl used. Thus, (0.1 L) $\times$ (1 mol $Ca(OH)_2$ / 1 L of solution) $\times$ (2 moles of OH^- / 1 mol $Ca(OH)_2$) is 0.2 moles of OH^-, which means there must be 0.2 moles of H^+. Subsequently, 100 mL of 2 M HCl is required because (0.1 L of HCl) $\times$ (2 moles of HCl / 1 L) $\times$ (1 moles of H^+ / 1 mol HCl) is 0.2 mol of H^+.
35	C	1	The unbalanced equation of the nuclear reaction is as follows: $^{40}_{19}K \rightarrow {}^{0}_{-1}e + ?$. As a complete nuclear reaction, there must be a balanced atomic number and atomic mass on both sides of the equation. However, the sole reactant has an atomic number of 19 and atomic mass of 40, while the given product has an atomic number of -1 and an atomic mass of 0. Thus, the missing product is Ca-40 because the product side needs to gain an element with 20 protons and 20 neutrons in order to balance both sides of the equation.
36	D	2	A complete Lewis dot diagram typically follows two rules: (1) the correct number of valence electrons for each atom of each compound and (2) a complete octet around each atom. Choice (D) is the only structure that follows these requirements; Choices (A), (C), and (E) have an incomplete octet of electrons around the each oxygen atom, while choice (B) has an the incorrect sum of valence electrons of the compound. Choice (D) is correct because there are 12 valence electrons and each oxygen atom has a complete octet.
37	E	10	An electrolyte is a substance that dissociates into ions when dissolved in water and conducts an electric current in solution. Strong electrolytes (strong acids, strong bases or ionic salts) completely ionize in water, while weak electrolytes (weak acids, weak bases) only partially ionize in water. Nonelectrolytes (molecular compounds) do not conduct electric current in solution because these compounds do not dissociate in water. K_a, also referred to as the acid dissociation constant, a measures the degree to which an acid dissociates and releases protons into a solution. Based on the chemical equation of an acid in aqueous solution: $HA(aq) + H_2O(l) \rightleftarrows H_3O^+ (aq) + A^-(aq)$, the K_a is $[H_3O^+][A^-]/[HA]$. A large K_a value indicates a strong electrolyte because there are more products than reactants, while a small K_a value indicates a weak electrolyte because there are more reactants than products. Thus, the smallest K_a value (choice E) is the weakest electrolyte because the smaller acid dissociation constant indicates less ionization.
38	B	12	Combustion, also referred to as "burning," is a type of redox-reaction that produces a lot of energy in the form of light and heat. The chemical reaction is $C_xH_y + O_2(g) \rightarrow H_2O(l) + CO_2(g)$. Combustion is an exothermic reaction where a hydrocarbon reacts with oxygen and produces carbon dioxide and water.
39	C	13	The balanced equation for the precipitation reaction is as follows: $$K_2CO_3(aq) + Cu(NO_3)_2(aq) \rightarrow KNO_3(aq) + CuCO_3(s)$$ The aqueous solutions K_2CO_3, $Cu(NO_3)_2$, and KNO_3 are colorless and odorless, while the precipitate copper carbonate is green. As an ionic compound, $KNO_3(aq)$ will dissociate into the water solvent as $K^+(aq)$ and $NO_3^-(aq)$. Due to their charges, the nitrate anions (NO_3^-) in solution are surrounded by partial positive hydrogens on water, while the potassium cations (K^+) are surrounded by partial negative oxygen atoms. However, although the ion-dipole intermolecular force exists, Choice (C) is the correct answer because it cannot be directly observed, unlike color and/or odor.

#	Ans.	Chapter	Explanation
40	C	1	Transition metals are found on the periodic table between groups three and twelve. The 4d orbital is found in the fourth period (4=n) and the d subshell covers groups 3 through 12. Although it is true transition metals have unfilled d orbitals, the best explanation as to why complex ions of transition metals become colored is that transition metals reflect light at various wavelengths. A substance can both absorb and reflect light at certain wavelengths, but the reflected wavelengths are important because that is the color of the substance. For example, if a plant reflects green wavelengths and absorbs red, yellow, orange, blue and violet wavelengths, the plant is the color green.

K_{eq}, also referred to as the equilibrium constant, measures the ratio of the concentration of products formed to the concentration of reactants consumed at equilibrium. K_{eq} is calculated by dividing the total concentration product of all gaseous or aqueous products of a balanced chemical reaction by the total concentration product of all gaseous or aqueous reactants of a balanced chemical reaction. Additionally, the coefficients of the reactants and products in the balanced chemical reaction are equivalent to the power the respective reactants and products are raised to when calculating the K_{eq}. A large K_{eq} indicates that, at equilibrium, the concentration of products is greater than concentration of reactants, while a small K_{eq} indicates that, at equilibrium, the concentration of products is less than concentration of reactants. The only factor that could affect the equilibrium constant is temperature, which is choice (B). Choices (A), (C), (D), and (E) are eliminated because even though these factors will shift the equilibrium based on the Le Châtelier's principle, the K_{eq} ratio will remain the same.

41 B 8

42 C 13 — Miscible liquids are liquids that mix together and form one single layer of mixed liquid. Distillation separates miscible liquids based on boiling point. This method involves evaporation and condensation.

43 E 12 — An esterification reaction combines a carboxylic acid with a alcohol to form an ester and water. Carboxylic acids are organic compounds that contain a carboxyl group and have the general formula of R-COOH, while alcohols are organic compounds that contain a hydroxyl group bound to a carbon. Esters are organic compound that contain a ketone and an ether and have the general formula of $R-COOR_1$ (but R_1 is not a hydrogen). Thus, the balanced equation

$$CH_3CH_2COOH \text{ (carboxylic acid)} + CH_3OH \text{ (alcohol)} \rightarrow CH_3CH_2COOCH_3 + H_2O$$

is an esterification reaction.

44 E 1 — The ground state is the lowest energy state available to electrons, and the most stable state of an atom. Based on the Bohr Model, when an electron absorbs an exact amount of energy, then the electron becomes "excited" and moves to any higher principal energy level (compared to ground state). In addition, when an electron releases/emits an exact amount of energy, then the electron moves from an excited state to a lower state. Thus, the transitions (II), (IV), and (V) would result in emission of electromagnetic radiation because an electron moves from a higher principal energy level to a lower principal energy level or from a higher energy state to a lower energy state. Transition (I) and (III) are eliminated because these transitions require an absorption of energy.

45 C 3 — The balanced equation for the given reaction is as follows:

$$1\,Fe_2O_3(s) + 3\,H_2SO_4(aq) \rightarrow 1\,Fe_2(SO_4)_3(aq) + 3\,H_2O(l)$$

The coefficient for $H_2O(l)$ in the balanced equation is 3.

#	Ans.	Chapter	Explanation
46	B	7	A chemical forward reaction is when one or more substances, known as reactants, transforms into one or more different substances, known as products (A + B → C + D). A reverse reaction is when the products are converted back to the reactants (C + D → A + B). The activation energy is the minimum amount of energy needed to undergo a chemical reaction. In other words, in order for a reaction to take place, a certain amount of energy is required. The activation energy of the forward reaction is calculated by subtracting the the initial amount of energy held within the reactants from the amount of energy at the transition state/activated complex (highest energy point/least stable), while the activation energy of the reverse reaction is calculated by subtracting the the amount of energy held within the products from the amount of energy at the activated complex. Thus, the activation energy of the forward reaction is 5 kJ/mol (80 kJ/mol − 75kJ/mol) and the activation energy of the reverse reaction is 40 kJ/mol (80 kJ/mol − 40kJ/mol). Additionally, while the substances undergo changes in composition and/or structure, the chemical reaction is accompanied by changes in energy. The heat of reaction (ΔH), also referred to as the enthalpy of the reaction, is calculated by subtracting the energy of the reactants from the energy of the products; $\Delta H = H_f − H_i$. When the reactants absorb less energy than the products release, this is an exothermic reaction (negative ΔH). An endothermic reaction (positive ΔH) is when the reactants absorb more energy than the amount of energy the products release. So, the change in enthalpy (ΔH) of the forward reaction is −35 kJ/mol (40 kJ/mol − 75 kJ/mol), which indicates the reaction is exothermic.

47 B 3 To find the percent composition of magnesium in magnesium chloride ($MgCl_2$), the four following steps are used:

1. find the mass of magnesium in the molecule

2. find the total gram formula mass of the entire molecule

3. divide mass of magnesium in the molecule by the total gram formula mass of $MgCl_2$

4. multiply the answer by 100 to get the percent by mass of magnesium

Thus, the percent composition of magnesium in $MgCl_2$ is (24/94) × 100, which is about 25%.

48 A 11 Oxidation numbers, also known as oxidation states, are positive and negative integers that are assigned to atoms and used to indicate if a specific atom has been reduced (gained electrons) or oxidized (lost electrons) in a chemical reaction. The oxidation number of sulfur is 0 in S_8 because the sum of the oxidation numbers of all the atoms in a neutral compound is zero.

49 C 2 The compound methane has four electron pairs at the vertices of a tetrahedron with a bond angle of 109.5 degrees between any two vertices, indicating an sp^3 hybridization. According to VSEPR theory, the molecular shape is tetrahedral because the central carbon atom forms four single bonds to four hydrogen atoms.

50 E 7 Factors that impact the rate at which glucose dissolves in water do so by affecting the rate of molecular collisions and/or the energy of the collisions. Using a magnet stirrer in the water would increase the rate of dissolution because stirring glucose increases the surface area of the solute to the solvent (water), which leads to faster dissolution. Increasing the surface area of $C_6H_{12}O_6(s)$ increases the reaction rate because there would be a greater number of collisions. Additionally, increasing the temperature of the solvent (water) would also increase the rate of dissolution because as you increase the temperature, the average kinetic energy of the particles increase. So, both the frequency of molecular collisions and the energy of the collision is increased. Thus, Choice (E) is correct because all of these factors would increase the rate of glucose dissolution.

51 B 3 The balanced equation of the redox-reaction is as follows:
$Zn(s) + Cu^{2+}(aq) \rightarrow Cu(s) + Zn^{2+}(aq)$

The two half-reactions are:
$Zn(s) \rightarrow Zn^{2+}(aq) + 2e^-$ and $Cu^{2+}(aq) + 2e^- \rightarrow Cu(s)$

Thus, the coefficient for $Zn(s)$ is 1.

#	Ans.	Chapter	Explanation
52	B	13	The oxidation number of an element can be determined by location on the periodic table; the group/column number can help assign oxidation number to an element. Group 17, also referred to as the halogens, have 7 valence electrons and only need one more electron to have an octet. As a result, a group 17 element (fluorine) tends to gain a electron, which results in an oxidation number of -1. Group 2, also referred to as the alkaline earth metals, have 2 valence electrons and need to gain 6 more electron or lose 2 electrons to have an octet. As a result, a group 2 element (barium) tends to give up 2 electrons, which results in an oxidation number of $+2$. Thus, the chemical formula for fluoride of barium is BaF_2.
53	B	1	Electronegativity is the tendency of an atom to attract a bonding pair of electrons to itself or "how badly an atom wants to add an electron." As one of the major trends on the periodic table, electronegativity increases while moving from the left to right (across a period) and from bottom to top (up a group) on the periodic table. Thus, within a group, as the atomic number increases the electronegativity decreases and as atomic number decreases the electronegativity increases.
54	E	2	Each of the chemical structures consist of either a double bond or a triple bond, which indicates that pi bonds are present. A sigma (σ) bond is formed between the bond axis of two s orbitals or an s orbital and another orbital, which creates direct head-on overlap of atomic orbitals. A pi (π) bond is formed between two unhybridized p orbitals. The pi (π) bond is a weaker covalent bond than the sigma (σ) bond because the parallel orientation of the unhybridized p orbitals allows for less overlap of pi electrons. A single bond consists of one sigma bond, while a double bond consists of one sigma bond and one pi bond and a triple bond consists of one sigma bond and two pi bonds. Subsequently, based on the molecular structure of the three compounds, each compound contains at least one π bond.
55	E	4	Effusion is when a gas moves through a pinhole into a vacuum (diffusion is when a gas moves from one container into another container that is already occupied by some amount of gas). According to Graham's Law of Effusion/Diffusion, the rate of effusion/diffusion for a gas is inversely proportional to the square root of the gases molar mass; the smaller the molar mass the higher the rate of effusion/diffusion. Thus, the gas with the largest molar mass (Xe) has the lowest rate of effusion through a semipermeable barrier.
56	E	2	Electronegativity is the tendency of an atom to attract a bonding pair of electrons to itself or "how badly an atom wants to add an electron." As one of the major trends on the periodic table, electronegativity increases while moving from left to right (across a period) and from bottom to top (up a group) on the periodic table. The Pauling scale is a numerical scale of electronegativities based on bond-energy calculation and can be used to determine the type of intramolecular bond between two atoms. Specifically, the electronegativity difference between two atoms is categorized into the three intramolecular bonds: nonpolar covalent ($0 < x < 0.5$), polar covalent ($0.5 < x < 1.6$), and ionic ($x > 1.6$). Thus, the greater the electronegativity difference between two atoms, the stronger the bond. Choices (A), (B), and (C) are eliminated because all the elements involved in these compounds are nonmetals (covalent bond), and the strongest bond involves the transfer of electrons between a metal and a nonmetal (ionic bond). Although Choice (D) is composed of a metal and a nonmetal (ionic bond), Choice (E) is the better answer because the metal and nonmetal have the greatest difference in electronegativity.
57	C	12	Ketones are organic compounds and consists of a carbonyl functional group (O=C). The general formula of a ketone is R-CO-R_1, where R and R_1 are the same or different alkyl groups, not hydrogen. Thus, Choice (C) is the only structure that fulfills these requirements.
58	B	1	The negatively charged subatomic particle can also be referred to as an electron. The total number of electrons in a neutral atom of calcium (Ca) is the same as the atomic number (number of protons) of a neutral atom calcium (Ca), so a neutral Ca atom has 20 electrons. Ca^+ is a positively charged cation due to the loss of one electron. Thus, 20 electrons $-$ 1 electron = 19 electrons.
59	B	13	Based on the addition/subtraction rule with significant figures, the sum/difference (result) must consist of the same number of figures after the decimal point as the reactant with the fewest number of figures after the decimal point. The amount of places after the decimal place in the mass of Sample A (0.51 grams) is 2, while the amount of places after the decimal place in the mass of Sample B (1.991 grams) is 3. Thus, the sum of Sample A and Sample B is 2.50, which consists of 2 figures after the decimal point.

#	Ans.	Chapter	Explanation
60	E	5	Entropy is the degree of disorder in a system and is used to measure randomness. Solids are rigid and have a fixed position, so this phase has the lowest amount of entropy. The gas phase has the highest amount of entropy because gases particles move around freely, which creates disorder. Thus, the strength of the intermolecular force is inversely proportional to entropy. To determine the change in entropy of the chemical reaction, the phase of the reactants compared to the phase of the products is significant. Choice (E) is correct because condensation converts water vapor to liquid water, which increases the IMF and decreases entropy. Choices (A), (B), (C), and (D) are eliminated because evaporation (liquid → gas), melting (solid → liquid), decomposing (AB → A + B), and dissolving (solid → aqueous solution) all decrease the IMF and increase entropy.
61	B	11	The two half-reactions are as follows: $Ag^+(aq) + e^- \rightarrow Ag(s)$ and $Cu^{2+}(aq) + 2e^- \rightarrow Cu(s)$ Both the silver half-reaction and copper half-reaction illustrate reduction reactions because the chemical equations have electrons as a reactant, indicating the addition of electrons. The amount of charge that reduces 1.0 mol of $Ag^+(aq)$ to 1.0 mol of $Ag(s)$ is 1 electron. Based on stoichiometry, to form 2 moles of silver solid from a solution containing $Ag^+(aq)$, the quantity of electric charge must be 2 electrons. Thus, according the balanced copper half-reaction, 2 moles of electrons would yield 1 mol of copper metal from a solution containing $Cu^{2+}(aq)$.
62	C	3	Given grams of sodium dichromate, convert to moles of sodium dichromate using the molar mass of $Na_2Cr_2O_7$. The gram formula mass is the sum of the atomic weights of all of the atoms in one mole of a molecule, so the molar mass of $Na_2Cr_2O_7$ is 262 g/mol. So, to convert from grams to moles, the following calculation is used: 26.2 g $Na_2Cr_2O_7$ × (1 mol $Na_2Cr_2O_7$ / 262 g $Na_2Cr_2O_7$) = 1/10 = 0.1 moles of $Na_2Cr_2O_7$.
63	A	3, 6	The percent dissociation of the "X" acid is expressed as (the molar concentration of the hydronium ion / the original molar concentration of the "X" acid) × 100. So, the concentration of H^+ ions of the hydrochloric acid is calculated using the equation $([H^+]/[HCl]) \times 100 = \%$, which can be rearranged as $[H^+] = (\% \times [H_2SO_3]) / 100)$. So, $(15 \times 0.1)/100$ calculates a 0.015 M of H^+ ions.
64	E	5	The following equation is used to measure the heat released or absorbed by an object as a result of a change in temperature: $q = mC\Delta T$. Based on the units in the question stem, both the specific heat capacity (J/g°K) and ΔT (°C) can be plugged in directly to the equation because the difference in °C is equivalent to the difference in °K. Based on the question, multiply (10 g) (39 J/gram °C) (60°C−50°C) to get 3900 calories.
65	A	8	According to Le Châtelier's principle, a reaction will proceed to counteract any disturbance on the system. Thus, after the equilibrium reaction $2NO_2(g) \rightleftharpoons N_2O_4(g)$ has reached equilibrium, Choice (A) is the only stress that would shift the position of equilibrium to the right. When the pressure of the reaction container increases, the system will counteract the increase in partial pressure of the gases by shifting the equilibrium to the side with fewer moles of gas. So, the balanced equation will favor the forward reaction because the reactant side has 2 moles of gases while the product side has 1 mole of gas. Choice (B) is eliminated because Boyle's law states the inverse relationship between pressure and volume at a constant temperature. So, increasing the volume of the reaction container will decrease the partial pressures of the gases, which shifts the position of equilibrium to the left to favor the side with more moles of gas. Choice (C) and Choice (D) are eliminated because, after an equilibrium reaction has reached equilibrium, the addition of some product or the removal of some reactant will lead to more reactants formed. Lastly, Choice (E) is irrelevant.
66	A	3	Based on the question stem, the percent oxygen by mass is 80%. To find the atomic mass of element A in the oxide A_2O, one must understand percent by mass. The mass percent of an element O within the given molecule is found by dividing the mass of element O by the total mass of the molecule and then multiplying that number by 100 to be expressed as a percent. Based on the question stem, 80% of O = (mass of oxygen / total mass of oxide) × 100. The molar mass of O in A_2O is 16 g/mol, since there is one O atom in the oxide and 1 mole of O is 16 grams. Thus, the following expression is used to find the total mass of A_2O (x) is 20 g/mol: $(8/10) = (16 \text{ g/mol} / x)$. The oxide molecule A_2O consists of 2 atoms of element A and 1 atom of element O, which means that 4 grams of the oxide is element A (20 g/mol − 16 g of O/mol) and the atomic mass of element A is 2 amu (4 g of element A / 2 atoms of A).

#	Ans.	Chapter	Explanation

67   D   3

The balanced equation for the given reaction is as follows:

$$NH_3(g) + HCl(g) \rightarrow NH_4Cl(s)$$

Based on the question stem, there are different quantities of two reactants reactants, which usually indicates that one of the reactants (limiting reactant) will be used up and one of the reactants (excess reactant) will remain after completion. According the the balanced equation, there is a 1:1 mole ratio of moles of NH_3 to moles of NH_4Cl and moles of HCl to moles of NH_4Cl. Thus, 2 moles HCl produces 2 moles NH_4Cl while 3 moles of NH_3 produces 3 moles of NH_4Cl, indicating that HCl is the limiting reactant because it limits the amount of product formed. Thus, 2 moles of HCl combine with only 2 moles of NH_3 to form 2 moles of NH_4Cl, which means 1 mole of NH_3 remains.

68   B   10, 13

Litmus paper, phenolphthalein, and bromothymol blue are three acid-base indicators that are used to test the pH of a solution. Acid-base indicators are substances that change color with pH, indicating whether or not the solution is acidic or basic. Litmus paper turns blue in a basic solution, and red in a acidic solution. Phenolphthalein turns pink in a basic solution, and remains colorless in an acidic solution. Lastly, bromothymol blue turns blue in a basic solution, and yellow in an acidic solution. Thus, blue litmus paper and pink phenolphthalein both indicate a basic solution, while the bromothymol blue indicator should have been blue.

69   D   6

Boiling point is one of the four main colligative properties of solutions, which means that it depends on the concentration of solute particles and not the identity/nature of the solute particles. When the concentration of particles in a solution increases, then the boiling point of the solvent elevates. The following equation is used to calculate the boiling point of each substance: $\Delta T_b = imK_b$. Since all aqueous solutions have the same K_b (0.51°C kg/mol) value, the van't Hoff factor (i) and the molality (moles of solute/ kg of solvent) determine the difference in boiling point. The molarity is correlated to molality, which indicates a 0.2 M of a solution has a higher boiling point than 0.1 M of solution and eliminates Choice (A) and Choice (B). Lastly, the degree of ionization for the remaining choices are analyzed:

$$KBr \text{ (ionic substance) is 2 } (KBr \rightarrow K^+ + Br^-)$$
$$Na_2SO_4 \text{ (ionic substance) is 3 } (Na_2SO_4 \rightarrow 2Na^+ + SO_4^-)$$
$$HC_2H_3O_2 \text{ (weak acid) is 2}$$

Thus, the boiling point of the 0.2 M of Na_2SO_4 solution is the highest.

70   C   13

The half-life of a radioactive element is the amount of time needed for half of the radioactive atoms to decay. Based on the question, the half-life of rhenium-186(m) is 20,000 years, which means rhenium-186(m) will undergo 3 half-lives over a period of 60,000 years because 60,000 years × (1 half-life/ 20,000) = 3. So, the following calculation is used to find how many grams of element rhenium will remain after 3 half-lives: 100g → 50g→ 25 g→ 12.5 g.

CHAPTER +20

abc

INDEX

INDEX

ABOUT PRIVATE PREP

Private Prep is an education services company that offers individually customized lessons in all K-12 academic subjects, standardized test prep, and college admissions consulting. We believe personal attention is fundamental to academic achievement and lies at the forefront of every student-tutor relationship. Designing curriculum for each student's unique learning style, we focus not only on improving grades and increasing test scores but also on building confidence and developing valuable skills—like work ethic, growth mindset, and anxiety management—that will last a lifetime.

One of the most significant points of differentiation between us and other educational services companies is our team approach. Our directors work in tandem with tutors and support staff to provide comprehensive, collaborative support to families.

We also focus on giving back to the communities in which we work. Through the Private Prep Scholarship Program, we place high-achieving students from low-income or underserved backgrounds with individual tutors, who work with them to navigate the test prep and college application process and ultimately gain admission to best-fit colleges.

At Private Prep, we deliver a superior academic experience—in the U.S., abroad, and online—that is supported by diverse and excellent resources in recruitment, curriculum design, professional training, and custom software development.

Made in the USA
San Bernardino,
CA